The Hughes Court

ABC-CLIO SUPREME COURT HANDBOOKS

The Burger Court, Tinsley E. Yarbrough
The Hughes Court, Michael E. Parrish
The Stone Court, Peter G. Renstrom
The Warren Court, Melvin I. Urofsky

Forthcoming:
The Fuller Court, James W. Ely, Jr.
The Jay-Ellsworth Court, Matthew P. Harrington
The Rehnquist Court, Thomas R. Hensley
The Taft Court, Peter G. Renstrom
The Taney Court, Timothy S. Huebner
The Vinson Court, Michal R. Belknap

Peter G. Renstrom, Series Editor

ABC-CLIO SUPREME COURT HANDBOOKS

The Hughes Court

Justices, Rulings, and Legacy

Michael E. Parrish

ABC CLIO

Santa Barbara, California • Denver, Colorado • Oxford, England

Library of Congress Cataloging-in-Publication Data

Parrish, Michael E.
The Hughes Court : justices, rulings, and legacy / Michael E. Parrish.
p. cm.—(ABC-CLIO Supreme Court handbooks)
Includes bibliographical references and index.
ISBN 1-57607-197-9 (hardcover : alk. paper) 1-57607-737-3 (e-book)
1. United States. Supreme Court—History. 2. Constitutional history—United States. I. Title. II. Series.
KF8742 .P334 2002
347.73'2634'09—dc21
2002006178

06 05 04 03 02 01 10 9 8 7 6 5 4 3 2 1

ABC-CLIO, Inc.
130 Cremona Drive, P.O. Box 1911
Santa Barbara, California 93116-1911

This book is printed on acid-free paper ♾.
Manufactured in the United States of America

For Peggy Strand

Contents

Series Foreword

There is an extensive literature on the U.S. Supreme Court, but it contains discussion familiar largely to the academic community and the legal profession. The ABC-CLIO Supreme Court series is designed to have value to the academic and legal communities also, but each volume is intended as well for the general reader who does not possess an extensive background on the Court or American constitutional law. The series is intended to effectively represent each of fourteen periods in the history of the Supreme Court with each of these fourteen eras defined by the chief justice beginning with John Jay in 1789. Each Court confronted constitutional and statutory questions that were of major importance to and influenced by the historical period. The Court's decisions were also influenced by the values of each of the individual justices sitting at the time. The issues, the historical period, the justices, and the Supreme Court's decisions in the most significant cases will be examined in the volumes of this series.

ABC-CLIO's Supreme Court series provides scholarly examinations of the Court as it functioned in different historical periods and with different justices. Each volume contains information necessary to understand each particular Court and an interpretative analysis by the author of each Court's record and legacy. In addition to representing the major decisions of each Court, institutional linkages are examined as well—the political connections among the Court, Congress, and the president. These relationships are important for several reasons. Although the Court retains some institutional autonomy, all the Court's justices are selected by a process that involves the other two branches. Many of the significant decisions of the Court involve the review of actions of Congress or the president. In addition, the Court frequently depends on the other two branches to secure compliance with its rulings.

The authors of the volumes in the ABC-CLIO series were selected with great care. Each author has worked extensively with the Court, the period, and the personalities about which he or she has written. ABC-CLIO wanted each of the volumes to examine several common themes, and each author agreed to work within certain guidelines. Each author was free, however, to develop the content of each volume, and many of the volumes advance new or distinctive conclusions about the Court under examination.

Each volume contains four substantive chapters. The first chapter will introduce the Court and the historical period in which it served. The second chapter will examine each of the justices who sat on the particular Court. The third chapter will represent the most significant decisions rendered by the particular Court. Among other things, the impact of the historical period and the value orientations of the individual justices will be developed. A fourth and final chapter will address the impact of each particular Court on American constitutional law—its doctrinal legacy.

Each volume contains several features designed to make the volume more valuable to those whose previous exposure to the Supreme Court and American constitutional law is limited. Each volume will have a reference section that will contain brief entries on some of the people, statutes, events, and concepts introduced in the four substantive chapters. Entries in this section are arranged alphabetically. Each volume will also contain a glossary of selected legal terms used in the text. Following each of the four chapters, a list of sources used in the chapter and suggestions for further reading will appear. Each volume will also have a comprehensive annotated bibliography. A listing of Internet sources is presented at the end of the bibliography. Finally, there will be a comprehensive subject index and a list of cases (with citation numbers) discussed in each volume. ABC-CLIO is delighted with the quality of scholarship represented in each volume and is proud to offer this series to the reading public.

Permit me to conclude with a personal note. This project has been an extraordinarily rewarding undertaking for me as series editor. Misgivings about serving in this capacity were plentiful at the outset of the project. After tending to some administrative business pertaining to the series, securing authors for each volume was the first major task. I developed a list of possible authors after reviewing previous work and obtaining valuable counsel from several recognized experts in American constitutional history. In virtually every instance, the first person on my list agreed to participate in the project. The high quality of the series was assured and enhanced as each author signed on. I could not have been more pleased. My interactions with each author have been most pleasant, and the excellence of their work will be immediately apparent to the reader. I sincerely thank each author.

Finally, a word about ABC-CLIO and its staff. ABC-CLIO was enthusiastic about the project from the beginning and has done everything necessary to make this series successful. I am very appreciative of the level of support I have received from ABC-CLIO. Alicia Merritt, senior acquisitions editor, deserves special recognition. She has held my hand throughout the project. She has facilitated making this project a reality in every conceivable way. She has encouraged me from the beginning, provided invaluable counsel, and given me latitude to operate as I wished while keeping me on track at the same time. This project would not have gotten off the ground without Alicia, and I cannot thank her enough.

—Peter G. Renstrom

Preface

In 1930, the year Charles Evans Hughes became chief justice of the United States, more than 1,000 American banks closed their doors, unable to pay their depositors. The first federal census of unemployment reported that 3 million Americans could not find work. The slang term "Hoover blanket," a description of the newspapers that covered those who slept on park benches, entered our vocabulary. The nation's economy, social relations, and political system appeared to be unraveling. But in that same year, a Detroit radio station launched a new program called "The Lone Ranger," which began with the *William Tell* overture and the voice of an announcer who introduced the hero astride "A fiery horse with the speed of light, a cloud of dust, and a hearty 'Hi-yo Silver.'" That year, too, saw the introduction of Twinkies, Snickers, Wonder sliced bread, French's Worcestershire sauce, and the founding of four airlines that would soon knit the nation together in new ways—Braniff, TWA, United, and American.

In 1941, the year Hughes stepped down as chief justice, his Court sustained the New Deal's Fair Labor Standards Act, which mandated uniform national standards for minimum wages, maximum hours, and the abolition of child labor (*United States v. Darby Lumber Co.*), and the justices also upheld the authority of Congress to regulate state primary elections when they were an integral part of the process of choosing candidates for national office (*United States v. Classic*). That fateful year, climaxed by the Japanese attack at Pearl Harbor, saw the introduction of Spam, the first use of shopping carts at American supermarkets, and the first franchising of hotels and restaurants by Howard Johnson.

Hughes's tenure as chief justice, corresponding to the worst economic collapse in American history—the Great Depression—began in a year of acute domestic crisis and ended a decade later in an equally catastrophic international one, with Nazi Germany astride most of Western Europe, her troops slicing through the Soviet Ukraine and the United States on a collision course with Japan in the Pacific. The experience of World War II, lasting four years, would soon make the United States one nation as never before, subjecting her people to a common discipline and sacrifice hardly imaginable in 1930—price controls, forced savings, rationing, and conscription, a process that tended to erode long established boundaries of gender, race, class, and region. Women fired up blow torches in the shipyards of Seattle. African Americans became officers in the Navy and Air Corps. The sons of machinists died at Utah beach beside the sons of Chicago bankers. No one cared at Okinawa whether you hailed from Tucson, Rapid City, Tuscaloosa, or Bangor, Maine. The Servicemen's Readjustment Act of 1944, better known as the G.I. Bill of Rights, provided an unprecedented national floor of economic entitlements to veterans—unemployment insurance, medical care, and educational and housing subsidies.

"America," so the old Pledge of Allegiance went, "one nation, indivisible, with liberty and justice for all." Of course, it was an ideal, not a fact, either in 1930 or in 1941 or 1945, when the war ended. But the Hughes Court and Franklin Roosevelt's New Deal, so often in conflict during the 1930s, collaborated along with the manufacturers of Twinkies, Wonder Bread, Spam, the major radio networks, and leading Hollywood film studios to fashion a United States knit together as never before by a common array of consumer products, popular culture, political entitlements, and legal standards. While American capitalists gave American consumers Birds Eye frozen vegetables, Walgreen drugstores, vitamin pills, Tampax, nylon stockings, and air conditioned automobiles, the New Deal provided federal deposit insurance for bank accounts, standardized real estate appraisal methods, uniform corporate accounting standards, nationwide unemployment insurance and old age pensions for retirees, and a national framework for resolving disputes between labor and management. The Hughes Court ultimately put the stamp of constitutional approval upon these new national entitlements forged by the New Deal and itself imposed new legal norms upon the nation when it required state and local governments to bring their laws into conformity with many of the standards mandated by the federal Bill of Rights, including freedom of the press, the right peaceably to assemble, and to freely exercise one's religion. In addition, the Hughes justices took the first tentative steps toward developing through the Due Process Clause of the Fourteenth Amendment, a more uniform code of criminal justice that applied to New York and Connecticut as well as to Mississippi and Alabama.

In short, the era of the Great Depression and the Hughes Court was both an historical moment when the United States seemed to be on the verge of social disintegration and also a moment when economic, political, and legal institutions came together to forge a stronger, more perfect union envisioned by the founders. This volume tells the story of how and under what circumstance the Supreme Court, led by Hughes, contributed to that salutatory outcome. The Hughes Court is often remembered as a conservative bulwark against the liberal and progressive vision of Roosevelt's New Deal. Some truth resides in that narrative. But it should also be recalled that in the same year Hitler's Germany adopted the Nuremberg laws (1935), stripping German Jews of basic rights, the Hughes Court reversed the conviction and death sentence of an African American in Alabama because persons of his race had been systematically excluded from grand and trial juries in his case. And in 1938, as German troops extinguished freedom in Czechoslovakia and German Jews endured the destruction of their homes and shops during *Kristalnacht*, the Hughes Court ordered the admission of an African American to the all-white law school of the University of Missouri and required the federal government to provide legal counsel to all persons accused of crimes against the United States. This side of the Hughes Court merits more than glancing notice.

I owe a large intellectual debt to the many legal and political historians who have traversed this terrain before me, not a few of whom have forced me to rethink interpretations and conclusions long embedded in my own and the popular imagination. In this regard I thank especially William E. Leuchtenburg, Richard Friedman, Barry Cushman, G. Edward White, Bruce Ackerman, and David A. Pepper, who, although reaching very different conclusions about the relationship of the Hughes Court to the constitutional landscape of the 1930s, have never failed to stimulate critical thinking about this contentious era in our legal history. Four very bright and energetic undergraduates at UCSD provided invaluable research assistance at an early stage of this project—Laura Schroeder, Hilary Johns, Beth Slutsky, and Melissa Hammond. I am very grateful for their help. I also thank Peter Renstrom, who had the persistence to encourage me to undertake this volume for the series and the unbounded energy to read several versions of the manuscript. Alicia Merritt, senior acquisitions editor at ABC-CLIO, kept me on schedule and offered timely advice and Melanie Stafford's superb editorial production efforts spared me numerous gaffes. And, finally, for her friendship, love, and encouragement, I dedicate this effort to my wife, Peggy Strand, who each day practices real law in the real world.

—Michael Parrish

The Hughes Court

PART ONE

Justices, Rulings, and Legacy

1

The Hughes Court and the Period

Beginning with John Jay, every chief justice of the United States and his Supreme Court have redesigned the architecture of our constitutional structure—one intended, as John Marshall expressed it in *McCulloch v. Maryland* (1819), "to endure for ages to come, and consequently, to be adapted to the various crises of human affairs." But some chief justices and their Courts have faced more grave upheavals than others, a circumstance that has required the skills of master builders, not simply those of good journeyman carpenters. The Civil War and Reconstruction, of course, presented such a period of crisis. Another, equally profound, struck the American nation during the decade of the 1930s: the collapse of the nation's economic system, the worldwide Great Depression, and the spread of totalitarian states across much of Europe and Asia. The Court that encountered that era of crisis was led by a gifted architect, Chief Justice Charles Evans Hughes, a former governor of New York, Republican presidential candidate, secretary of state, and associate justice of the Supreme Court from 1910 to 1916.

Hughes became chief justice one year after the Great Crash, the collapse of stock prices on the New York Stock Exchange in October 1929, a selling panic that drove down the value of virtually all equities and provoked a massive liquidity crisis in the heart of the nation's financial structure. Although the market crash did not "cause" the Great Depression that followed, it inflicted major damage upon America's weak, decentralized commercial banking system. This system propelled the larger credit machine that had fueled the market boom by allowing investors to purchase stocks on margin with little regard for the underlying health of particular companies or the economy as a whole.

The Great Crash and the liquidity squeeze of 1929–1932 combined, however, to expose the deep structural flaws in the American economy that, despite the aura of prosperity between 1922 and 1929, could no longer be ignored. Americans had solved the problem of production by the third decade of the twentieth century, as the nation's farms and factories poured forth an abundance of everything from wheat and hogs to automobiles and clothing. But at the same time, Americans had yet to solve the problem of consumption in a land where by 1929 the wealthiest one-tenth of the population received nearly one-third of the national income (McElvaine 1984, 38–39). This distribution of economic rewards left the vast majority of wage earners, farmers, laborers, and the self-employed unable to participate in the new consumer society.

Conventional economic wisdom in 1930 maintained that in a truly free economy, where supply and demand functioned according to immutable laws, everything that was produced generated the income to consume it. Conventional economic wisdom did not take into account, however, the power of corporate oligopolies to manipulate prices; the overinvestment and excess capacity in certain older sectors of the economy; the unequal distribution of bargaining power between employers and employees; and the skewed distribution of income produced by tax laws that favored the rich at the expense of the middle class and the poor. Taken together, these profound structural problems turned the financial disaster of the stock market crash into the longest economic depression in American history. And because credit and investments from the United States had also underwritten the post–World War I economic recovery in Europe, Latin America, and many parts of Asia, the collapse of the American financial markets soon spread its blight across the globe. The Great Depression left few nations unscathed and roiled the political waters in London, Berlin, Tokyo, Mexico City, and Buenos Aires.

In the United States, as elsewhere, the economic crisis fueled a political and social crisis of unprecedented magnitude by 1930–1931 as banks closed their windows, credit dried up, production fell, unemployment reached nearly one-quarter of the labor force, and millions of Americans faced the prospect of destitution in the polity without a safety net of significant public assistance (McElvaine 1984, 75). Americans met the crisis both with direct, spontaneous action and demands for relief from local, state, and national governments. Farmers banded together to stop foreclosures and keep produce from reaching markets. The unemployed in cities organized councils to protest their joblessness and to protect tenants from eviction. Those with work rebelled against wage cuts and demanded recognition for unions and collective bargaining.

Republican president Herbert Hoover, who had predicted after his election in 1928 that the nation would soon be on the verge of eliminating poverty, took what many at the time regarded as unprecedented action to combat the spreading economic misery. Although relying chiefly on voluntary cooperation to reverse the price deflation, shore up the banking system, and minister to the unemployed, Hoover also invoked federal authority in an effort to stabilize markets. The Agricultural Marketing Act encouraged the creation of cooperatives and the Federal Farm Board began open-market purchases of wheat and cotton in an attempt to boost prices without curbing production. A new federal agency, the Reconstruction Finance Corporation (RFC), extended loans to faltering banks, railroads, and corporations. By the end of Hoover's tenure the RFC had made similar loans to state and local governments for the purposes of funding self-liquidating public works projects to aid the unemployed.

Hoover, however, refused to travel further down the road of more intervention by the federal government, a posture shared by most political leaders as late as 1933. Direct aid to the millions of unemployed, he believed, would dry up private charity, sap individual initiative, and undermine the constitutional structure. More coercive controls over production and prices would lead the nation to socialism or other forms of state planning. By 1932, with the federal budget in the red due to falling revenues and rising expenditures for programs like the RFC and the Farm Board, Hoover recommended an increase in taxes in order to balance the federal government's accounts. Congress, controlled by Democrats, endorsed this decision with enthusiasm. The tax increase, of course, further dampened purchasing power and worsened the depression. So, too, did Hoover's decision to sign into law a substantial increase in the tariff on foreign goods, with the result that other nations retaliated, protectionism flourished, American exports withered, and international trade dried up.

Hoover's successor, New York governor Franklin D. Roosevelt, promised the American people a New Deal, one based on more vigorous federal intervention and executive leadership. In his inaugural address, he vowed to ask Congress for "broad Executive power to wage war against the emergency, as great as the power that would be given to me if we were in fact invaded by a foreign foe" (Kennedy 1999, 134). Over the next seven years, twice confirmed by the electorate, FDR and his New Deal transformed the relationship between the federal government and the American people, executing what one scholar has called "the third American revolution" (Degler 1959, 379–416).

Although a fiscal conservative at heart (he, too, pledged to balance the federal budget and actually cut government employment in his first year), Roosevelt became more willing than Hoover to use the coercive power of public law to effect economic and social change. Given the depths of the crisis by 1933 and Hoover's failures, he had little choice. During the so-called Hundred Days of 1933 and again in 1935, a torrent of new statutes, many shaped in the White House by the president's advisers, poured forth from Congress, all designed to stabilize, subsidize, regulate, and redistribute the American economy and its rewards.

The RFC, for example, emerged under the New Deal to become a major stockholder in commercial banks and by 1940 was the largest single source of investment capital in the nation. Federal public works programs, the Public Works Administration (PWA), the Civil Works Administration (CWA), and the Works Progress Administration (WPA) put the unemployed to work building bridges, highways, airports, schools, parks, and irrigation systems, as well as cataloging books and performing Shakespeare's plays and Mozart's symphonies. Roosevelt and Congress took the country off the gold standard and devalued the dollar by 25 percent, a policy that outraged creditors but reduced the debt load on farmers, homeowners, and many corporations. The Agricultural Adjustment Act (AAA) encouraged farmers to curb production in return for government cash subsidies. The National Industrial Recovery Act (NIRA) suspended the antitrust laws and permitted business trade associations to develop "codes of fair competition" that restricted output and curbed price cutting.

Labor unions received the right to organize and to bargain collectively in the National Labor Relations Act of 1935. That same year the Social Security Act initiated old-age pensions, aid to the blind, the disabled, and dependent children, and unemployment insurance. The Fair Labor Standards Act three years later put a ceiling on hours, a floor under wages, and attacked the ancient evil of child labor. To pay for these programs, the New Deal engaged in deficit spending and also raised taxes (very modestly) on the rich. And each new program raised complex constitutional questions and faced a gauntlet of judicial hurdles before federal judges who had been appointed largely by conservative Republican presidents in the 1920s.

While Roosevelt and Congress reshuffled the economic deck in Washington, reformers at the state level launched "little New Deals" across the nation to cope with local dimensions of the economic crisis. They sought to impose moratoriums on farm and home foreclosures, to raise labor standards through minimum wage legislation, to curtail price cutting, and to curb the power of banks, insurance companies, utilities, and chain stores. These efforts, too, faced legal challenge from those who feared the destruction of property rights and freedom of contract.

Roosevelt's New Deal, attacked in the conservative press and the courts as dangerously radical, unconstitutional, and un-American, faced serious challenges from the left of the political spectrum as well. Both the Socialist Party and the American Communist Party experienced rapid growth during the decade, especially as the economy continued to sputter and New Deal programs failed to bring immediate relief. Roosevelt's tax reforms in 1935–1937 responded in part to the political challenge raised by Louisiana's smart, flamboyant United States senator, Huey Long, who launched a "Share Our Wealth Society" dedicated to an even more drastic redistribution of income. In California, gubernatorial candidate Upton Sinclair, the old muckraking journalist, ran on a platform labeled EPIC (End Poverty in California), which proposed to turn idle farmland and factories over to the unemployed. In addition to Sinclair, Roosevelt's own party in Congress contained voices advocating drastic inflation of the money supply, government ownership of the banks, heavier taxes on wealth, and a thirty-hour workweek.

In addition to reinventing the role of government, Roosevelt's New Deal transformed both the political and social landscape of the United States in the 1930s. The Republican Party, which had dominated national politics since 1896 with the exception of the Wilson years (1913–1920), went into electoral eclipse and did not capture the White House again until 1952. Even then, the Democrats would continue to hold sway in Congress well into the decade of the 1970s. Roosevelt built a sturdy political coalition whose tattered and battered remnants still managed to win elections as late as Bill Clinton's second term. Even Republicans in the 1980s and 1990s made appeals to those they called "Roosevelt Democrats," blue-collar union members and white ethnic voters, especially Roman Catholics, in the cities and suburbs of the Northeast and Midwest.

Given a boost by the labor provisions of the National Industrial Recovery Act and later the National Labor Relations Act, industrial workers rejected the staid craft structure of the American Federation of Labor (AFL) and flocked to the new, militant unions organized by the Committee for Industrial Organization (later the Congress of Industrial Organizations, CIO), headed by the charismatic leader of the United Mine Workers, John L. Lewis. By 1938, galvanized by sit-down strikes in the automobile industry, industrial unionism swept through the major sectors of the economy, bringing in its wake a new generation of labor leaders like Walter Roy and Victor Reuther in the United Automobile Workers Union (UAW) and Philip Murray of the United Steelworkers, all of whom wedded their organizations to the Democratic Party and ensured Roosevelt's reelection in both 1940 and 1944.

The New Deal not only raised the status and power of blue-collar industrial workers, it also propelled other outsiders and minorities into the mainstream of American life by expanding the boundaries of the American establishment. Roosevelt brought large numbers of Catholics and Jews into the government as lawyers and administrators, notably Joseph P. Kennedy and Jerome Frank as chairmen of the new Securities and Exchange Commission (SEC). White Southerners, long a part of the old Democratic coalition, reaped a host of benefits from New Deal programs—cheap electricity, flood control, irrigation projects, and price supports for agriculture. In 1935 FDR named a Mormon banker from Utah, Marriner Eccles, who espoused the radical ideas of a British economist, John Maynard Keynes, to be the first chairman of the restructured Federal Reserve Board.

Behind the scenes, Roosevelt met occasionally with African American leaders, notably Walter White of the National Association for the Advancement of Colored People (NAACP). In 1936, for the first time since Reconstruction, a majority of blacks voted for the Democratic ticket. Eleanor Roosevelt did far more than her husband to cement this new alliance between the Democrats and African Americans when she spoke out against segregation, endorsed a federal antilynching law, and organized a public concert by Marian Anderson at the Lincoln Memorial after the Daughters of the American Revolution had turned down a request to use Constitution Hall in the District of Columbia.

The turbulent political, economic, and social changes in the United States during the years of the depression took place against a backdrop of unsettling world events punctuated by the flourishing of right- and left-wing dictatorships and a rising tide of domestic and international violence. In response to the economic crisis, everywhere the power of central governments increased to cope with unemployment and mounting social unrest. The government of Lazaro Cardenas in Mexico nationalized foreign petroleum companies, provoking a brief crisis with the Roosevelt administration over issues of compensation. Conservative regimes were swept from power in Cuba and Spain briefly, but old elites recaptured power by military means and fastened right-wing dictatorships on both countries. Cuba's survived until 1959, Spain's well into the 1970s. In the Soviet Union, Marshal Stalin's five-year plan for modernizing the economy brought starvation and death to peasants who resisted collectivization. The Weimar Republic in Germany, unable to accommodate its contending economic interests, collapsed and ushered in the long nightmare of Adolf Hitler's National Socialist Party, which pulled the country out of the depression with massive doses of spending, first on highways and public buildings, then on tanks and fighter aircraft.

When governments could not contain the domestic consequences of the economic crisis through a combination of reforms and repression, they engaged in expansion and war. The Fascist government of Benito Mussolini in Italy subdued the African nation of Ethiopia with the aid of petroleum from members of the League of Nations and the United States. In the Far East, Japan tightened its grip on Manchuria in 1931, and by 1937 its army, navy, and air force blockaded the Chinese coast and attacked the major cities of Shanghai and Nanking. The empire of the rising sun seemed determined to subdue all of China, to establish a Japanese-dominated "Co-Prosperity Sphere," and to drive the Europeans and Americans out of Asia. By decade's end, Germany had reoccupied the Rhineland, annexed Austria to the greater Reich, extinguished the independence of Czechoslovakia, and by invading Poland in September 1939, brought total war once again to Europe. Preoccupied with their own domestic ills and still disillusioned by the carnage of the First World War, the citizens of the United States and their national leaders responded to these events by occasional rhetorical denunciation and by taking refuge behind a series of neutrality laws that limited American economic support, even for nations brutalized by dictatorships and foreign invaders. Roosevelt, his ear always attuned to the voice of the public, endorsed much of this legislation until the Japanese assault on China in 1937. But after his speech calling for a "quarantine" on aggressor nations roused the powerful forces of isolationism, he retreated quickly.

Against the backdrop of these grim developments in Europe and Asia, the New Deal appeared to many a mild and benign experiment in the uses of state power, but to its opponents, mostly on the right, Roosevelt could be accused of promoting an American version of dictatorship. And the Constitution, long cherished as the palladium of American liberty when enforced by an independent judiciary, could be perceived as the only bulwark against unlimited state power and the extinction of economic and political freedoms. Accustomed to enjoying a wide range of private autonomy from government controls, many citizens rebelled against the incursions of public authority. Still others, facing economic ruin and a decline in their standard of living, clamored for assistance from state and federal authorities. The many notorious examples of religious, ethnic, and class oppression raging abroad in the 1930s gave new meaning and salience to the American constitutional ideal of fundamental civil rights, also enshrined in the Bill of Rights and protected by an independent judiciary. And as international crises and the clouds of war threatened the United States by the mid-1930s, both the judiciary and a majority in Congress appeared more willing to grant President Roosevelt broader latitude in the conduct of foreign relations than in the management of the nation's domestic economy. Such deference to the chief executive's conduct abroad had profound consequences for the traditions of separation of powers and federalism. And although the roots of such deference could be traced back to the turn of the century, it foreshadowed even greater presidential aggrandizement of power during World War II and the Cold War that followed.

Appointments

Chief Justice Hughes stepped down from the Court on July 1, 1941, six months before the Japanese attack on Pearl Harbor decisively ended the isolation of the United States, thrust it into the maelstrom of a new global war, and ended the Great Depression that had so shaped the agenda of his Court since 1930. Hughes, remarked Felix Frankfurter, "is among the very few really sizeable figures in my lifetime. He is three-dimensional and has impact" (Danelski and Tulchin 1973, xxvii–xxix). The chief justice, according to Attorney General and future Justice Robert Jackson, "looks like God and talks like God" (Danelski and Tulchin 1973, xxviii).

Few observers of the Court doubted that the former governor and secretary of state relished and mastered his role as chief, even in the face of sharp differences among the justices and intense political pressures emanating from outside. "Hughes has real energy and intelligence," Justice Louis Brandeis wrote soon after the new chief justice had taken his seat. "In the conference, time is not much wasted . . . in needlessly stating matters and he uses good judgment in selecting writers for opinions" (Urofsky and Levy 1991, 431). Frankfurter, who later served with Hughes from 1939 to 1941, compared him to maestro Arturo Toscanini conducting a symphony orchestra. On the other hand, Justice Harlan Stone would often lay the blame for the Court's confrontation with President Roosevelt and Congress squarely on Hughes's deviousness and lack of leadership in the crucial years of 1935–1936.

The retirement of ailing Chief Justice William Howard Taft in February 1930 and the death a month later of Associate Justice Edward Sanford (only a few hours after Taft himself succumbed on March 8, 1930) gave a beleaguered President Hoover the opportunity to impress his vision of progressive Republicanism upon the nation's highest court at a time when the stock market had collapsed and the country tottered on the brink of a serious economic downturn. That downturn, soon to become the

Great Depression, largely fixed the agenda for Hughes's tenure as chief justice, although the true depths of the crisis could not have been foreseen when the Senate confirmed his nomination by a vote of fifty-two to twenty-six on February 13, 1930.

Hughes had not been Hoover's first choice to occupy the Court's center chair, despite his previous service as an associate justice (1910–1916) and his stature as senior statesman of the Republican Party. The nominee's long and distinguished resume included the governorship of New York, secretary of state, membership on the Permanent Court of International Justice, and a lucrative law practice in New York City. Hoover had hoped to appoint his medicine ball exercise partner, Associate Justice Stone, the former dean of the Columbia Law School and the attorney general of the United States during the Coolidge years, who had cleaned up the Augean stables of the Department of Justice following the assorted scandals of the Harding era. The president's advisers, however, urged him to offer the post to Hughes as a matter of political courtesy and in the belief that he would decline the appointment for two obvious reasons. He would lose substantial income from private practice. His own son, Charles Evans Jr., then solicitor general of the United States, the government's advocate before the Supreme Court, would be forced to abandon that prestigious post if his father became chief justice.

Much to the surprise of both Hoover and his advisers, the elder Hughes did not hesitate to accept the nomination, a decision that led to his son's resignation as solicitor general on February 13, 1930, and which left a residue of bitterness in the younger Hughes's family for many years thereafter. Despite his record as governor of New York and as an associate justice prior to World War I who displayed considerable toleration for government regulation of private markets and contracts, Hughes's nomination encountered heavy rhetorical seas of opposition in the Senate, climaxed by twenty-six dissenting votes. Republican progressives and Democrats denounced his recent list of clients as evidence of the nominee's devotion to monopolists and the rich. "No man in public life so exemplifies the influence of powerful combinations in the political and financial worlds as does Mr. Hughes," declared Nebraska's George W. Norris, a leading advocate of public electric power and the defender of the federal government's continued ownership of dams, steam plants, and nitrate factories built during World War I at Muscle Shoals on the Tennessee River (*Congressional Record* 1930, 3373). Another Hughes opponent, Senator Clarence Dill of Washington, regarded his vote as indicating support only for those judges "who hold economic theories which are fair and just to all, and not in the interest of the privileged few" (*Congressional Record* 1930, 3500). Hughes did not qualify for such distinction.

Unable to block Hughes, although many observers believed he would bring a far more liberal spirit to the Court than the deceased Taft, Senate opponents like Norris turned their wrath successfully on Hoover's nominee to succeed Sanford, Judge John J. Parker of North Carolina, a Republican who had served on the federal circuit court

The Hughes Court from 1930 to 1932 (front row, left to right): James Clark McReynolds, Oliver Wendell Holmes, Jr., Charles Evans Hughes, Willis Van Devanter, Louis Brandeis; (back row, left to right): Harlan Fiske Stone, George Sutherland, Pierce Butler, Owen Roberts (Harris and Ewing, Collection of the Supreme Court of the United States)

of appeals since 1925. On that bench Parker had earned the enmity of labor unions with a decision upholding the validity of a "yellow-dog" contract in the mining industry. Such contracts limited an employee's right to join a union or assist in its organization. Civil rights groups, led by the National Association for the Advancement of Colored People (NAACP), also accused Parker of racism, based on his rulings in cases involving voting rights for African Americans. After a bitter debate, the Senate turned down his nomination, forty-one votes to thirty-nine.

Rebuffed by the Senate, Hoover next offered the Sanford seat to a stolid if colorless Pennsylvania lawyer, Owen J. Roberts, a man soon destined to become one of the most enigmatic and controversial justices in the history of the Court. Born into a prosperous and well-connected Philadelphia family, Roberts had served as district attorney of that city and as a special federal prosecutor in the Teapot Dome oil scandal, where his efforts put Secretary of the Interior Albert B. Fall behind bars. A former law professor at the University of Pennsylvania with a private practice that included some of the state's largest corporations—including the Pennsylvania Railroad—Roberts did not stir the opposition directed at Hughes or Parker. And although Roberts expressed privately some hesitation about his own intellectual fitness for the office, the Senate confirmed him by a voice vote at the end of May 1930.

Early in his tenure, Roberts often aligned himself with Hughes in cases involving the scope of the states' authority to regulate commercial affairs without running afoul of due process, a voting pattern that encouraged many to believe the Court would display like toleration for similar efforts by the Roosevelt administration at the national level. But by mid-decade, when New Deal statutes first came before the justices, Roberts drifted into the camp of the Court's ultraconservative block in important cases that voided significant federal programs aimed at fighting the depression. And his apparent reversal of positions in 1937 subjected him and the entire Court to charges of political expediency and opportunism that continue to haunt their reputation even today.

Two years after Hughes became chief justice, the venerable Oliver Wendell Holmes Jr., age ninety, retired after thirty-one years on the Court, thereby giving Hoover his final and, many claimed, most distinguished appointment: Benjamin N. Cardozo. Serving at the time of his nomination as the chief judge of the New York Court of Appeals, Cardozo then loomed, with the exception of Holmes himself, as the nation's most celebrated and widely quoted jurist. The author of three books on legal philosophy and jurisprudence, Cardozo was renowned among other judges and legal intellectuals for his opinions that had subtly altered the common law of torts and contracts in New York. He easily won Senate approval on a voice vote after Hoover, prodded by leading Republican senators, overcame his hesitation to nominate to the Court a third New Yorker (the others being Hughes and Harlan Stone) and a second Jew (the other being Brandeis).

Over the next six years, until his retirement and sudden death in 1938, Cardozo proved to be a worthy successor to Holmes and the most faithful justice with respect to upholding the programs of Franklin Roosevelt's New Deal. Possessed of a strong conviction in the competence of professional and academic experts, unmoved by conservative shibboleths about the dangers of government meddling in the marketplace, and usually comfortable with the uses of state power, Cardozo dissented often. He also received less than his share of memorable assignments from Hughes, a pattern that led Frankfurter at the time to denounce the chief justice.

Prior to his final illness, Chief Justice Taft had expressed the fear that a few new appointments might tip the balance on his Court away from its stout defense of property rights. "If a number of us die," he told his brother, "Hoover would put in some rather extreme destroyers of the Constitution" (Gunther 1994, 424). Taft's fears were exaggerated because Hughes, although sensitive to the depths of the economic crisis facing the country, inherited the leadership of a tribunal deeply fractured over fundamental questions of governmental power and one dominated by four justices who owed their appointments to Taft, Wilson, and Harding—Justices Willis Van Devanter, James McReynolds, George Sutherland, and Pierce Butler. The new chief justice also loathed the appearance of sudden shifts in the inherited categories of constitutional

The Hughes Court from 1932 to 1937 (front row, left to right): Louis Brandeis, Willis Van Devanter, Charles Evans Hughes, James Clark McReynolds, George Sutherland; (back row, left to right): Owen Roberts, Pierce Butler, Harlan Fiske Stone, Benjamin Cardozo (Harris and Ewing, Collection of the Supreme Court of the United States)

analysis, hesitated to overrule existing precedents unless absolutely necessary, and defended the Court's independence with vigor and cunning.

Mocked by federal judge Learned Hand as "the mastiffs" and by journalists during the 1930s as the "Four Horsemen of the Apocalypse," Van Devanter, McReynolds, Sutherland, and Butler had faithfully manned the ramparts of Taft's Court against those "extreme destroyers of the Constitution" whose toleration of government regulation threatened in their view to produce an American variety of communism.

Formidable in the justices' private conferences, but suffering from writer's block that reduced his output of opinions, Van Devanter owed his appointment to President Taft, who as chief justice put him in charge of drafting the historic Judiciary Act of 1925 that decisively expanded the Court's discretionary jurisdiction to be invoked by writs of certiorari. Like most of his judicial colleagues of the time, Van Devanter believed that the Constitution contained indelible boundaries between the spheres of private autonomy and public authority, as well as clear demarcations separating federal from state responsibilities. This rigid framework of analysis, inherited from the nineteenth century, made him skeptical of governmental powers generally, except in the case of Congress's broad power to spend money and its implied power to conduct investigations. He displayed consistent opposition to governmental intrusions into private contractual relations directed at prices and wages and assertions of federal authority beyond the narrowest interpretation of the Commerce Clause.

While sharing his colleague's antipathy to government meddling with the market, Justice McReynolds also displayed an intolerance toward those who indulged in tobacco as well as those born female or into the Jewish faith. A thorough-going anti-Semite, he defied the Court's ancient tradition by refusing even to shake hands prior to conference with Justices Brandeis and Cardozo. Once a trust-busting attorney general under Wilson, his passion for freedom of contract remained so intense that it occasionally led him to support civil liberties in contexts beyond the usual rough and tumble of the marketplace. He authored Court opinions in the Taft era, for example, that struck down a state law prohibiting the teaching of modern languages other than English (*Meyer v. Nebraska* [1923]), and an Oregon initiative, sponsored by the Ku Klux Klan and tinctured with anti-Catholicism, that required nearly all parents to send their children between the ages of eight and sixteen to a public school (*Pierce v. Society of Sisters* [1925]). McReynolds found little constitutional sanction for federal or state efforts to cope with the economic crisis after 1929. The last of the Four Horsemen to retire, in 1941, he dissented to the bitter end against the governmental innovations sanctioned by other members of the Hughes Court.

Justice Sutherland, appointed by Harding in 1922 after serving the state of Utah in the House of Representatives and the United States Senate for fifteen years, shared much of Van Devanter's antipathy to government meddling in the marketplace, except when it came to issues of taxation and spending. A faithful guardian of the distinction between private and public spheres of ordering, he articulated these views forcefully during the Taft era in *Adkins v. Children's Hospital* (1923), in which the majority struck down federal minimum wage legislation on grounds that it violated freedom of contract. He would find equally unpalatable most of the legislation emanating from the New Deal as well as state efforts to impose debt moratoriums or to put a floor under prices in industries such as dairy farming and milk processing, both hard hit by the depression. At the same time, Sutherland's libertarian streak manifested itself from time to time in cases touching due process and the Bill of the Rights. He would write for the Court in the first Scottsboro case, *Powell v. Alabama* (1932), in which the justices reversed the convictions of young African Americans condemned to death for a sexual assault on the grounds that the defendants, poor and mostly illiterate, had been denied effective legal counsel.

Pierce Butler, a prominent railroad attorney from Minnesota, nominated by Harding following a vigorous campaign on his behalf by Chief Justice Taft and Justice Van Devanter, did not disappoint his conservative sponsors during Hughes's tenure. Labor and progressive groups had attacked his nomination in 1923 on the grounds of Butler's close ties to major railroads and other utilities, two corporate interests toward whom he continued to manifest solicitude in the 1930s whenever they encountered what he called "unreasonable" rate regulations. He died while still on the Court in 1939, hurling dissents against the New Deal. But like Sutherland, Butler's libertarian sympathies often spilled over into noneconomic areas. He condemned wiretapping as a violation of the Fourth Amendment in *Olmstead v. United States* (1928) and was the lone dissenter in the infamous Virginia case *Buck v. Bell* (1927), in which the Taft Court, led by Holmes, upheld coerced sterilization, a vote influenced perhaps by his Roman Catholic faith. During the Hughes years, however, Butler seldom manifested comparable regard for civil liberties.

Until Cardozo took Holmes's seat in 1932, the undoubted leader of the Court's progressive wing remained Justice Louis Brandeis, the famous "people's lawyer" from Boston, whose nomination by President Wilson in 1916 had thrilled reformers and shocked conservatives because of his sympathies for labor and frequent hostility to monopolies. The opposition to Brandeis's appointment had been tinctured as well by anti-Semitism. From 1916 forward, "the people's lawyer" forged a close intellectual and personal bond with Holmes, the two men sharing a deep antipathy to the use of substantive due process against economic legislation and a robust defense of the First Amendment in cases involving political dissenters.

Chief Justice Taft nursed a grudge against Brandeis for the latter's role in the Ballinger-Pinchot controversy, in which the "people's lawyer" had taken up the cause of Chief Forester Gifford Pinchot in his fight with Secretary of the Interior Richard Ballinger over the sale of Alaskan coal lands to private interests. In the course of this battle, Brandeis demonstrated that President Taft and his attorney general had tampered with crucial evidence sent to Congress. The former president regarded Brandeis as the most dangerous figure on the Supreme Court because of the latter's endorsement of far-reaching government regulation of property and contract interests, a toleration that at times exceeded even that of the agnostic Holmes. Brandeis's radicalism, however, had its roots in his conservative temperament, which deplored the rampant commercialism of American life, what he called "the curse of bigness," and the coarsening of public life manifested in raucous advertising, installment debt, conspicuous consumption, and waste. During the New Deal years as well he extended his critique of "bigness" to include the burgeoning federal bureaucracy spawned by the Roosevelt administration's recovery efforts.

Although a lifelong Republican, nominated by President Coolidge to replace Justice McKenna in 1925, and a close friend of the beleaguered Hoover, Harlan Fiske Stone usually voted with Brandeis and Cardozo to sustain many of the controversial programs of the New Deal and the states during the Hughes era. A former dean of the Columbia Law School and attorney general of the United States, Stone shared with Brandeis and Holmes a deep skepticism about judicial activism. He would author one of the depression decade's most pungent dissents in *United States v. Butler* (1936), in which six justices, including Hughes and Roberts, struck down the first Agricultural Adjustment Act. "A tortured construction of the Constitution is not to be justified by recourse to extreme examples of reckless congressional spending," he wrote. "Courts are not the only agency of government that must be assumed to have capacity to govern." In private, he expressed bitter disappointment in Hughes's leadership of the Court during its confrontation with the New Deal in 1935–1937.

Six months before Pearl Harbor, when Hughes retired, President Roosevelt nominated Stone to be the twelfth chief justice of the United States, a position he held until his death in 1946. With war looming, FDR had recruited other Republicans for key posts in his administration, including Henry Stimson, Frank Knox, and Robert Patterson. In choosing Stone to replace Hughes, Roosevelt passed over his own personal choice for chief justice, Attorney General Robert Jackson, who instead filled Stone's seat as an associate justice. With his elevation in 1941, Stone had the unique distinction of becoming the only justice to occupy every seat on the Court during his tenure from the most junior to that of chief justice.

Beginning in 1937 with the retirement of Justice Van Devanter, President Roosevelt gained the opportunity to fill seven vacancies on the Hughes Court during the next four years. He would also nominate a new chief justice (Stone) and add an eighth justice (Wiley Rutledge) in 1943, two years after Hughes stepped down. With the exception of George Washington, no American president saw more of his nominees confirmed or had a greater possibility of reshaping the philosophical orientation of the Court. To a greater or lesser degree, chastened by the experience of the constitutional crisis of the mid-1930s, all of FDR's nominees practiced some version of judicial restraint when it came to general questions of economic policy. Legislatures, they believed, disciplined by the electoral process, had the basic responsibility for managing America's commercial life, which included everything from monetary policy and taxation to labor relations and agriculture. They soon manifested deep disagreement, however, when it came to the judicial role respecting civil liberties and civil rights.

Roosevelt's first nominee, Senator Hugo Black of Alabama, a solid prolabor Democrat, had advocated a thirty-hour week in 1933 and later spearheaded investigations of corporate skullduggery in the airline, marine, and public utilities industries. However, he encountered controversy soon after his confirmation when a Pittsburgh newspaper revealed that he had joined the Ku Klux Klan in Birmingham in 1923 and resigned two years later, shortly before his first campaign for the Senate. Black managed to diffuse these facts that would have destroyed a nominee a few decades later, when he made an impassioned radio address in which he stressed his resignation from the "Invisible Empire" rather than his membership.

Within a few years, Black silenced many skeptics who doubted his commitment to racial justice as he authored opinions in cases coming from Southern state courts

The Hughes Court from 1940 to 1941 (front row, left to right): Owen Roberts, James Clark McReynolds, Charles Evans Hughes, Harlan Fiske Stone, Hugo Black; (back row, left to right): William Orville Douglas, Stanley Foreman Reed, Felix Frankfurter, Frank Murphy (Harris and Ewing, Collection of the Supreme Court of the United States)

involving African American defendants. He wrote for the Court in *Chambers v. Florida* (1940), in which the justices reversed the convictions of four African Americans whose confessions had been obtained under duress. That same year in *Smith v. Texas* (1940) he again wrote the majority opinion holding that a black defendant had not received a fair trial because of the systematic exclusion of African Americans from the jury.

Black stirred more consternation among his brethren during his first term on the Court when he dissented in *Connecticut General Life Insurance Co. v. Johnson* (1938) to argue that the justices should overturn fifty years of precedent holding that corporations were "persons" within the meaning of the Fourteenth Amendment. That venerable doctrine had deep roots in the nineteenth-century decision *Santa Clara County v. Southern Pacific Railroad* (1886). Black's salvo prompted Justice Stone to enlist Felix Frankfurter's aid in an effort to remind the newest justice about the importance of *stare decisis*, the doctrine that judges should follow precedent. "There are enough present day battles of importance to be won," Stone wrote, "without wasting our effort to remake the Constitution *ab initio*, or using the judicial opinion as a political tract" (Parrish 1982, 277)

To fill the vacancy created by the retirement of Justice Sutherland in early January 1938, Roosevelt turned to his solicitor general, Kentuckian Stanley Reed, who quickly won Senate confirmation a month later on a voice vote. Reed had the distinction of serving both Hoover and FDR, first as general counsel to Hoover's Federal Farm Board and Reconstruction Finance Corporation; and later as special assistant to the attorney general and as solicitor general in the New Deal. He also had the distinction of being the only lawyer to argue cases before the Hughes Court and to later become a member of that same tribunal. And finally, he would outlive all his brethren who served with Hughes, surviving until April 1980.

As solicitor general, Reed suffered stinging defeats at the hands of the Hughes Court, especially in the fateful years 1935–1936. He lost the so-called hot oil case, *Panama Refining Co. v. Ryan* (1935) and *Schechter Poultry Corp. v. United States* (1935), both of which dealt fatal blows to Roosevelt's National Industrial Recovery Act. Nor did he prevail in *Humphrey's Executor v. United States* (1935), when the justices curbed the president's power to remove members of independent regulatory commissions such as the Federal Trade Commission without congressional approval. A year later the Hughes majority rejected arguments in the Triple A case, *United States v. Butler* (1936), and in the litigation over the constitutionality of the Bituminous Coal Conservation Act, *Carter v. Carter Coal Co.* (1936).

On the other hand, Reed successfully defended the administration's monetary policy, which included abrogating clauses in private contracts that called for payment in gold (*Norman v. Baltimore and Ohio Railroad Co.* [1935]), and improved his batting average dramatically in 1937 when the justices upheld both the National Labor Relations Act (*National Labor Relations Board v. Jones & Laughlin Steel Corp.* [1937]) and the provisions of the Social Security Act (*Steward Machine Co. v. Davis* [1937] and *Helvering v. Davis* [1937]).

Once on the bench, Reed displayed the core jurisprudential beliefs of a Roosevelt appointee who had been through the constitutional wars of the New Deal and chastened by the activism of the Four Horsemen. He regularly deferred to the policy judgments of Congress, state legislatures, and the expanding federal regulatory apparatus, the only exceptions coming in a few cases touching organized labor. On issues of civil liberties, Reed manifested similar restraint and aligned himself with the more conservative members of the Hughes Court.

His body weakened by several previous heart attacks, a debilitating case of shingles, and strokes, Justice Cardozo died in the summer of 1938 from coronary failure at the home of his close friend Irving Lehman. After some hesitation about nominating another Northerner, but flooded with petitions from leading New Dealers, Roosevelt sent the name of Felix Frankfurter to the Senate to occupy the Holmes-Cardozo seat. Only Frankfurter, argued Attorney General Jackson, had the legal resources "to face Chief Justice Hughes in conference and hold his own in discussion" (Lash 1975, 64).

Building on a relationship that dated back to World War I when both served in the wartime Wilson administration, Frankfurter and Roosevelt established a close partnership, with the Harvard Law School professor serving as FDR's informal legal adviser, recruiter, and unabashed cheerleader. His friendship with Justice Brandeis, also dating from the Wilson years, was equally close, the latter regarding Frankfurter as "half brother, half son" (Urofsky and Levy 1991, 5). Never content merely to teach law, Frankfurter had entered some of the most controversial legal cases arising from the war on the side of civil liberties, notably those of Tom Mooney, a labor radical convicted of a bombing in San Francisco; communist aliens threatened with deportation during the Palmer Raids; and the Italian anarchists, Nicolo Sacco and Bartolomeo Vanzetti, sentenced to death in Massachusetts for an alleged robbery and murder at a shoe factory.

A cofounder of the liberal magazine, *The New Republic*, Frankfurter appeared regularly in its pages during the 1920s and 1930s in unsigned articles that praised Holmes and Brandeis and denounced the judicial activism of the Taft and Hughes Courts, especially the use of substantive due process to strike down state laws. Appearing on behalf of the National Consumers League in *Adkins v. Children's Hospital* (1923), he argued for the constitutionality of a congressionally mandated minimum wage law for women in the District of Columbia, but lost in a five-to-four decision with Justice Sutherland's majority rejecting his voluminous social data and upholding the doctrine of freedom of contract as an essential part of due process. Frankfurter soon argued for the complete judicial abandonment of the Due Process Clause.

As a law professor, he sent many of his brightest students to Washington to serve as secretaries to Holmes and Brandeis, including Dean Acheson, James Landis, Alger and Donald Hiss, Thomas Corcoran, and Paul Freund. And although he turned down Roosevelt's offer of the solicitor generalship in 1933, Frankfurter sent wave upon wave of his acolytes to the nation's capitol to work in the burgeoning agencies of the New Deal, where their idealism, brains, and energy often alienated the old-line politicians and bureaucrats. "A plague of young lawyers settled on Washington," complained one Frankfurter critic. "They floated airily into offices, took desks, asked for papers and found no end of things to be busy about. I never found out why they came, what they did or why they left" (Parrish 1982, 228).

But contrary to such dissenting views, the lawyers Frankfurter recruited for the New Deal, many well seasoned like Jerome Frank and Ben Cohen, played a decisive role in upgrading the administration's resources when it came to drafting complex statutes like the Public Utilities Holding Company Act and defending them before hostile federal judges. The second wave of New Deal reforms in 1935 and after (the National Labor Relations Act, for example) fared much better in the courts due in part to more astute legal craftsmanship than statutes written hastily in 1933–1934.

Despite their longtime collaboration, Roosevelt did not inform Frankfurter beforehand of his controversial proposal to enlarge the Supreme Court in 1937, a decision that flowed no doubt from his fear that the professor's often-expressed reverence for the institution would lead him to criticize the plan. During the bitter fight over what critics called the "court-packing" plan, however, Frankfurter advised FDR in private while maintaining a public silence. He urged the president, in fact, not to emphasize the issues of age or efficiency, but to stress instead the ideological dimensions of the Court's opposition to the New Deal. Hughes and six of his brethren, he believed, had abused their power and, as he told Brandeis in a letter, "the fear of God should be instilled so that they may walk humbly before their Lord" (Parrish 1982, 270). His loyalty to the president, although behind the scenes, chilled his relationship with Brandeis, but furthered his future claim upon Cardozo's seat.

Aside from a few cranky right-wing zealots who accused Frankfurter of being part of a vast communist conspiracy, his confirmation in the Senate came quickly on a voice vote in January 1939. As a disciple of Holmes, Brandeis, and Cardozo; a fervent New Dealer; and a trenchant critic of the Taft and Hughes Courts, Justice Frankfurter became a leading exponent of judicial restraint in both economic matters as well as civil liberties, a position that put him at odds with other of Roosevelt's appointees. He soon warmed to the chief justice, whose performance had drawn his scorn in the past, but whose disciplined management of the weekly conference and generous disposition of assignments won high praise from the newest justice. And in an ironic twist, Frankfurter, the apostle of judicial restraint, struck down a state law in his maiden opinion for the court, a Florida statute that placed a discriminatory tax on concrete cement imported from other states (*Hale v. Bimco Trading, Inc.* [1939]).

To fill the Brandeis seat in 1939, Roosevelt turned to another former law professor and New Deal loyalist, William O. Douglas, who had taught at Columbia and Yale before his appointment to the new Securities and Exchange Commission in 1936. At forty-one, he became the youngest man since Joseph Story to serve on the Court, and at his retirement in 1975, he surpassed Stephen Field as the justice with the longest tenure. At Columbia and Yale, Douglas identified himself with the loose-knit intellectual movement labeled legal realism, which attacked the idea that judges merely "found" the law and advocated more attention to the social consequences of legal rules.

As chairman of the SEC from 1937–1939, Douglas often disappointed Roosevelt's more radical supporters by stressing cooperative forms of regulation with the securities industry and the major power companies, the latter brought under federal control through the Public Utilities Holding Company Act. The commission was prepared, he said at one point, "to meet business on business terms," and its future "will in large part be molded by business" (Parrish 1970, 181). Four senators voted against his confirmation in 1939 on grounds that Douglas had become a tool of Wall Street by promoting excessive self-government by the stock exchanges themselves.

Once on the Court, Douglas aligned himself with the New Deal block in all cases touching the authority of Congress, the states, and independent regulatory commissions to oversee the nation's economic relationships. He wrote for a near-unanimous bench in *Sunshine Anthracite Coal Co. v. Adkins* (1940), for example, which sustained a new federal statute aimed at stabilizing the coal industry by placing a prohibitive tax on all coal sold in interstate commerce when the producers violated price and competition regulations set by the government.

Frank W. Murphy, a former mayor of Detroit, U.S. high commissioner for the Philippines, governor of Michigan, and attorney general of the United States, became Roosevelt's fifth appointment in 1940, when he took the seat opened by the death of the unrepentant conservative, Pierce Butler. Another fervent New Dealer, Murphy had lost his bid for reelection in the 1938 Michigan gubernatorial race largely because of his support for the 135,000 autoworkers who engaged in sit-down strikes against General Motors in 1937. Despite hysterical demands for intervention from the business community and his own belief that the strikes were illegal, Murphy refused to send in the National Guard to drive the union members from the auto plants. He would not go down in history, he remarked at the time, "as Bloody Murphy" (Watkins 1999, 329).

Rescued from political defeat and brought into Roosevelt's cabinet as attorney general in 1939, Murphy proved effective in reshaping the Department of Justice by purging the second-rate lawyers recruited in the early years of the New Deal and by securing the indictment and conviction of corrupt public officials—most notably Martin T. Manton, a federal appeals court judge in New York, and Thomas J. Pendergast, the boss of the Democratic Party machine and Harry Truman's benefactor in Kansas City. He also left a lasting legacy in the department by organizing a Civil Liberties Unit, renamed as the Civil Rights Division in 1941. The Department of Justice, he believed, should be a force for the protection of individual rights.

Under Murphy's leadership, the new Civil Liberties Unit soon became such a force by resurrecting statutes from the Reconstruction era passed pursuant to the Fourteenth and Fifteenth Amendments, including the Ku Klux Klan Acts that prohibited interference with rights guaranteed by the Constitution and laws of the United States. Lawyers in Murphy's new section initiated the suit against New Orleans officials that produced *United States v. Classic* (1941) and later *Screws v. United States* (1945), the federal prosecution of a Georgia sheriff who had beaten to death an African American suspect in his custody.

Murphy quickly added his vote to the emerging liberal wing of the Hughes-Roosevelt Court led by Black and Douglas. He seldom wavered in his support for economic reforms and the right of unions to organize, strike, and picket. Murphy also came to favor "incorporation plus" by arguing that the Bill of Rights should apply to the states in addition to the separate limitation of the Fourteenth Amendment's Due Process Clause, a position that Black rejected as one sanctioning the dis-

Table 1.1 Hughes Court Justices

	Birth Year	App't Year	App't Pres.	App't Age	Replaced by
HOLMES	1841	1902	T. ROOSEVELT	61	CARDOZO
VAN DEVANTER	1859	1910	TAFT	51	BLACK
MCREYNOLDS	1862	1914	WILSON	52	BYRNES
BRANDEIS	1856	1916	WILSON	59	DOUGLAS
SUTHERLAND	1862	1922	HARDING	60	REED
BUTLER	1866	1922	HARDING	56	MURPHY
STONE	1872	1925	COOLIDGE	52	JACKSON
HUGHES	1862	1930	HOOVER	67	STONE
ROBERTS	1875	1930	HOOVER	55	BURTON
CARDOZO	1870	1932	HOOVER	61	FRANKFURTER
BLACK	1886	1937	FDR	51	POWELL
REED	1884	1938	FDR	53	WHITTAKER
FRANKFURTER	1882	1939	FDR	56	GOLDBERG
DOUGLAS	1898	1939	FDR	40	STEVENS
MURPHY	1890	1940	FDR	49	CLARK

credited doctrine of substantive due process and allowing for unchecked judicial discretion. Critics soon labeled his opinions as "justice tempered with Murphy." He wrote 132 opinions for the majority before his death in 1949, most notably *Chaplinsky v. New Hampshire* (1942), which placed "fighting words" outside the protection of the First Amendment. He is most remembered, however, for his outspoken opposition to the forced relocation of Japanese Americans following Pearl Harbor, although throughout the war years he served as an infantry officer at Fort Benning, Georgia, during recess periods and often wore his uniform into the Court building, a practice that dismayed several of his brethren.

Table 1.1 provides a quick snapshot of the Hughes Court, noting the year of each justice's birth, the year each came to the Supreme Court, the president who nominated him, his age at the time of appointment, and the justice who succeeded him.

The Court and Its Record

The years of Hughes's tenure as chief justice remain especially notable for a number of reasons. First, few Courts since the founding era confronted more profound questions touching basic issues of legislative and judicial federalism: the scope of congressional authority under Article I, Section 8 of the Constitution; the relationship of those powers to private rights of contract and property; and the extension of federal judicial authority, via the Fourteenth Amendment, the Commerce Clause, and Section 34 of the original Judiciary Act to matters of state governance in the areas of economic regulation, civil liberties, and criminal justice.

In domestic and foreign affairs the justices also faced complex questions involving the separation of powers as both Congress and the president attempted to cope with an unprecedented economic catastrophe and world events that shifted rapidly from month to month. And not since the impeachment trial of Justice Samuel Chase, Taney's confrontation with Lincoln over habeas corpus, and Congress's rebuff to the justices in *Ex Parte McCardle* (1869) had the Supreme Court provoked sharper opposition from the political branches of both the national and state governments, a storm that climaxed in 1937 with President Roosevelt's daring and abortive effort to "pack" the high bench with additional justices.

And finally, few eras in the history of the Court have fomented more sustained and contentious debate among legal scholars over both its reputation and legacy. Many traditional accounts of these years emphasize the importance of 1937 and argue that the Hughes Court executed a sudden constitutional revolution, an abrupt departure from earlier rulings when it came under intense political pressure from Roosevelt and Congress. Revisionist interpretations stress a more gradual constitutional evolution during the decade, one with doctrinal roots that reached back to the jurisprudence of the Taft and White eras. From this perspective, the 1937 term of the Hughes Court assumes less importance than both earlier and later years when the Court majority articulated new approaches to both the Due Process Clause and the Commerce Clause. Some commentators continue to stress the importance of external pressures upon the Court's jurisprudence, while others point to the internal dynamics of legal reasoning and the more astute lawyering of the Roosevelt administration and its allies after 1935. The Court's confrontation with the political branches may have been one episode in a larger crisis touching the very nature and legitimacy of judicial power itself in the United States, a crisis left unresolved in these years and even beyond.

Between 1930 and 1940 the Hughes Court took the judicial ax to fourteen congressional statutes and seventy-eight enacted by the states, a figure that appears quite large until one compares it to the vetoes wielded by its predecessors and successors. The White Court and Taft Courts, for example, each struck down 12 federal statutes, but invalidated 107 and 131 state laws, respectively. By contrast, the Warren Court overturned 25 federal enactments and 150 state laws, while the totals for the Burger Court were 34 and 192, the most in the Court's entire history through the 1990s. The more recent Rehnquist Court, by comparison, struck down all or portions of 25 federal laws in five years from 1995 to 2000. And in its first four years (1986–1990) that tribunal vetoed 52 state statutes or constitutional provisions.

Based on these crude comparisons, the Hughes Court does not appear to have been swept away by extreme judicial activism. But, of course, Hughes and his brethren functioned during the most serious and sustained economic crisis in the United States since the Civil War, and its judicial ax fell especially hard upon several federal and state programs intended to combat the manifold manifestations of that crisis—high unemployment, bank failures, massive deflation, falling commodity prices, and their attendant social unrest. Between 1935 and 1936 an often-divided bench struck down eight out of ten measures advanced by President Roosevelt and Congress, in addition to a bundle of state statutes designed to combat the effects of the economic crisis, the most important of which was New York's minimum wage law.

Over the course of the decade, however, the justices sustained a large number of governmental programs at both the federal and state levels. And while expanding the scope of Congressional authority, the Court also reduced the intrusiveness of federal courts into areas of state law by overturning *Swift v. Tyson*, a precedent from 1842 that had permitted federal judges to ignore local common law decisions. The Hughes Court also gave the states greater latitude in regulating aspects of interstate commerce that did not require the imposition of a single uniform national standard, discriminate against other states, or burden the national marketplace (*South Carolina State Highway Dept. v. Barnwell Bros.* [1938]). In short, the Hughes Court simultaneously enlarged the boundaries of federal authority, both legislative and judicial, but also confirmed the ample authority of the individual states in many areas touching the nation's economic life.

Tables 1.2 and 1.3 offer a quick look at the caseload of the Hughes Court by year, the number of unanimous decisions, cases decided by one-vote majority, and the number of cases in which justices filed either a dissenting or concurring opinion.

The Court's confrontation with the New Deal in 1935–1936, however, provoked the president's historic proposal to restructure the federal courts in 1937, the Judicial Procedures Reform Act. Faced with the prospect of additional judicial vetoes of administration programs, FDR's advisers presented him with a range of responses to tame the Hughes Court. Some proposed a constitutional amendment requiring the Court to vote unanimously when striking down an act of Congress or, in another variation, allowing Congress to override the Court by a two-thirds vote in both chambers. Roosevelt, however, chose a measure once suggested by then Attorney General James McReynolds in 1913 and took delight in the fact its origins came from one of his chief antagonists on the Court. As presented to Congress, FDR's bill proposed to expand the membership of the Supreme Court from nine to a maximum of fifteen if justices who reached the age of seventy did not retire within six months. Additionally, the plan would have permitted Roosevelt to appoint at least fifty judges to all levels of the federal court system.

In fairness to Roosevelt, the plan also contained other significant provisions, including the expediting of constitutional questions directly to the Supreme Court from lower tribunals and a requirement that federal judges refrain from issuing injunctions against federal statutes unless first granting a hearing on the law to attorneys representing the United States. This last measure seemed imminently reasonable in light of the scores of injunctions granted since 1934 against New Deal statutes by federal district judges, virtually all of them Republican appointees.

Table 1.2 Unanimous and One-Vote Decisions

Term	No. of Cases	No. Unanimous	Percent Unanimous	One-vote Decisions
1930	166	148	.892	6
1931	150	124	.827	2
1932	168	141	.839	3
1933	158	132	.835	6
1934	156	134	.859	8
1935	145	119	.821	7
1936	149	118	.792	13
1937	152	106	.697	3
1938	139	89	.640	6
1939	137	95	.693	4
1940	165	118	.715	5

Table 1.3 Dissenting and Concurring Opinions

Term	No. of Cases	No. w/Dissenting Opinions	No. w/Concurring Opinions
1930	166	13	2
1931	150	16	1
1932	168	17	1
1933	158	18	4
1934	156	11	7
1935	145	20	4
1936	149	17	2
1937	152	26	11
1938	139	35	11
1939	137	20	5
1940	165	27	5

Against the advice of several advisers, Roosevelt disingenuously argued that his proposed expansion of the judicial branch, including the Supreme Court, would advance efficiency because a heavy caseload had clogged the arteries of the federal courts. In a joint letter to the Senate Judiciary Committee, the chief justice and Brandeis demolished the president's spurious justification, which had not in any event fooled many members of Congress, the press, or the public. Roosevelt also contended that the Supreme Court would benefit from an infusion of younger jurists, men more in tune with the times, a taunt that infuriated Justice Brandeis, then eighty years old, who believed he had supported the president to the limits of constitutional authority. Amidst cries of executive tyranny, FDR's plan encountered fierce opposition in Congress. The chairman of the House Judiciary Committee, Hatton Summers of Texas, announced his immediate disgust with the plan. "Boys," he told colleagues, "this is where I cash in my chips" (Parrish 1992, 371). On the Senate side many of the president's faithful allies took the lead in attacking the plan, notably liberal Montana Democrat Burton K. Wheeler. In another ironic twist of fate, Wheeler had previously sponsored a constitutional amendment giving Congress authority to reverse the Court by a two-thirds vote, but in 1937 he used all of his influence on the Senate Judiciary Committee to kill FDR's bill. Roosevelt found his major allies among the more conservative members of his own party such as Carter Glass of Virginia and Majority Leader Joe Robinson of Arkansas. Congressional Republicans enjoyed the spectacle of Roosevelt tormented by those who had formerly backed the president's legislative agenda.

Roosevelt's plan, most scholars now agree, had little chance of adoption from the beginning, a fact not lost upon the chief justice and his colleagues. The full Senate buried the plan in July 1937 by sending it back to Wheeler's committee, which had previously reported against it by a vote of ten to eight, with the observation that it would destroy judicial independence and "make the Constitution what the executive or legislative branches of the Government say it is" (Senate Report No. 711, 1937, 27). A month later, Roosevelt signed a very watered-down reorganization measure that reformed lower-court procedures, but did not allow for the addition of Supreme Court justices. FDR's scheme failed for many reasons, including growing fears in Congress and the public about executive despotism; continued reverence for the Court as an institution, despite its past vetoes of the New Deal; the sudden death of Senator Robinson in the middle of the legislative battle; and the Court's endorsement of key reform legislation in early 1937.

Roosevelt would have been better advised to support and expedite the Supreme Court Retirement Act, which he finally signed into law in March 1937 and which permitted justices to retire in senior status at full pay rather than resign. Similar legislation to encourage judicial retirements had run afoul of Roosevelt's frequent desire to trim government expenditures and balance the budget. In May Justice Van Devanter, long anxious to step down, became the first to take advantage of the new retirement program and in so doing gave Roosevelt what he desired—an opportunity to change the complexion of the Hughes Court. Justice Sutherland, plagued by serious back ailments, soon followed Van Devanter.

Before their departure, however, Hughes and Roberts further derailed Roosevelt's reorganization bill. By narrow five-to-four votes, the justices simultaneously sustained landmark pieces of federal and state legislation, including the National Labor Relations Act, the Social Security Act, and a new minimum wage law from Washington. As Senator and future Justice James Byrnes of South Carolina remarked at the time of these decisions: "Why run for a train after you've caught it?" (Leuchtenburg 1963, 237). The crisis of the Hughes Court, the New Deal, and the Great Depression passed into history. The Hughes Court cautiously sanctioned the arrival of the modern welfare state by abandoning the Due Process Clause of the Fourteenth

Amendment and the dormant Commerce Clause as major weapons in the judicial arsenal aimed at the states' economic policies, by affording broad scope to the Article I powers of Congress, and by deferring to the administrative expertise of the growing federal regulatory apparatus.

The year 1937, dominated by the "court-packing" fight and the Court's endorsement of critical New Deal reforms, has loomed so large in histories of the era that it has tended to oversimplify the convoluted course of constitutional development during the decade. The appointments of Hughes and Roberts, for example, raised the hopes of many progressives that the Court would begin to display a more tolerant attitude with respect to legislative intervention into the marketplace, but such hopes were not immediately realized. In a series of cases in 1931 touching the authority of the Interstate Commerce Commission to control railroad reorganization fees and freight car rental charges and rates, Hughes and Roberts joined the four conservatives in striking down the regulatory efforts.

A year later, over a powerful dissent by Brandeis, the majority, including Hughes and Roberts, struck down an Oklahoma law that imposed strict licensing provisions on new entrants into the ice business, a regulation intended to stop cutthroat competition and price cutting in the industry (*New State Ice Co. v. Liebmann* [1932]). And in *Liggett v. Lee* (1933) the justices also invalidated a Florida statute that attempted to tax chain stores at a higher rate than small, owner-operated establishments. Again, Brandeis, always eager to endorse a wide range of social and economic experiments in what he called the laboratories of the individual states, dissented.

As the ICC cases as well as *Liebmann* and *Liggett* indicated, the holdover justices from the Taft era—Van Devanter, McReynolds, Sutherland, and Butler—remained a formidable obstacle to a more liberalized jurisprudence on issues touching property rights and contracts. Often voting as a block on key economic issues, they needed only a single additional justice to carry the Court, leverage they continued to use until 1937 when Hughes and Roberts finally cast their lot permanently with Brandeis, Stone, and Cardozo. At the same time it should be noted that even Van Devanter, McReynolds, Sutherland, and Butler, usually branded as antigovernment reactionaries, voted to sustain more state and federal regulatory laws during the decade than they voted to strike down. In 1937, for example, Van Devanter and Sutherland joined Cardozo's opinion upholding the old-age benefit provisions of the Social Security Act, perhaps the premier symbol of the emerging New Deal welfare state (*Helvering v. Davis* [1937]). And even Butler and McReynolds found nothing constitutionally objectionable in key spending programs of the New Deal such as the Public Works Administration and the Home Owners' Loan Corporation. The largest funding agency of the Roosevelt years, the Reconstruction Finance Corporation, never suffered a constitutional setback.

The chief justice and Roberts maintained an uneasy relationship with the Four

Horsemen. They defected sharply from the conservative block in 1934–1935 in three cases that signaled before 1937 a major shift in the Court's reception of depression-generated legislation. In January 1934, speaking through the chief justice, the majority sustained Minnesota's emergency mortgage moratorium law against the challenge that it violated the ban on state action impairing the obligation of contracts (*Home Building & Loan Ass'n v. Blaisdell* [1934]). In sustaining this obvious debtor-relief law, Hughes engaged in a remarkable feat by distinguishing prior decisions that had nullified similar measures, some reaching back to the Marshall era. He also appalled colleagues like Sutherland and McReynolds by suggesting that the meaning of constitutional language such as "no state shall impair the obligations of contract," depended upon a social context that might change over time.

Two months later, Roberts swept away nearly a century of precedent when the same five-to-four majority (including Hughes, Stone, Brandeis, and Cardozo) upheld a New York law that set minimum prices to be charged for milk (*Nebbia v. New York* [1934]). Since *Munn v. Illinois* (1877), the justices had restricted the states' regulatory authority under the Fourteenth Amendment to "businesses affected with a public interest," a limited category that embraced traditional public utilities or enterprises wielding unusual market power, but which left most areas of the economy, defined as private enterprise, immune to price fixing and other forms of market intervention. But in *Nebbia*, Roberts erased the ancient judicial distinction between public and private by allowing the legislature to define "business affected with a public interest" and to engage in regulation so long as the proposal was "reasonable" and carried out through appropriate means. The Four Horsemen, who dissented, rightly regarded this judicial innovation as one that opened wide the doors to legislative control of the economy. *Blaisdell* and *Nebbia*, it can be argued, represented a significant shift in constitutional doctrine equal to any that came later.

Early in 1935, in a decision that provoked Justice McReynolds to declare, "the Constitution . . . that has meant so much to us, is gone" (Schlesinger 1958, 260), the Hughes-led majority, including Roberts, sustained the New Deal's monetary initiative that abrogated clauses in private contracts requiring payment in gold, thereby devaluing the dollar and easing somewhat everyone's debt burdens. The Court refused to extend the congressional ban to gold payments fixed in United States government bonds and other federal contracts, but limited the ability of plaintiffs to recover significant damages (*Gold Clause Cases: Norman v. Baltimore and Ohio Railroad Co.; Nortz v. United States;* and *Perry v. United States* [1935]).

But even as the chief justice and Roberts joined Stone, Brandeis, and Cardozo to sustain the New Deal's monetary experiments, storm clouds gathered that forecast very rough seas ahead for the Roosevelt administration. In the National Industrial Recovery Act (NIRA), passed during the first hundred days of the New Deal to cope with falling prices, cutthroat competition, and unemployment, Congress had authorized the president to prohibit shipments in interstate commerce of petroleum produced in violation of state regulations that capped output, so-called hot oil. A month before the *Gold Clause Cases* came down, however, in *Panama Refining Co. v. Ryan* (1935) a nearly unanimous Court, speaking through Hughes, declared this section of the NIRA unconstitutional on grounds that Congress had improperly delegated authority to the executive, leaving too much discretion in his hands, a constitutional boundary that the Court had seldom guarded with rigor in the past. The decision drew a sharp dissent from Cardozo, who argued that Congress had not left the president totally at large and without guidance in the statute. "Separation of powers between the Executive and Congress is not a doctrinaire concept to be made use of with pedantic rigor," he cautioned. "There must be sensible approximation, there must be elasticity of adjustment, in response to the practical necessities of government."

In May 1935 the Court handed Congress and the president major defeats. First, by a narrow five-to-four vote, with Roberts writing for himself and the Four Horsemen, the justices struck down the Railroad Retirement Act passed a year earlier in which Congress had mandated a comprehensive pension system for railroad workers to be funded by the companies (*Railroad Retirement Board v. Alton* [1935]). Despite a line of cases dating back to the turn of the century in which the Court had upheld Congress's authority to regulate all aspects of the interstate rail business, including labor relations, liability for injuries, intrastate rates, and safety equipment, Roberts held that the pension plan bore only a limited, indirect relationship to interstate commerce. Temporarily resurrecting the public/private distinction he had cast overboard with respect to state regulation in *Nebbia*, Roberts placed the pension plan outside the scope of the railroads' public duties that threatened or burdened interstate commerce. The plan violated due process because it forced employers to make an involuntary contribution to the welfare of their employees without the companies or the public receiving a reciprocal benefit, such as increased safety.

Roberts's analysis in *Alton* departed so fundamentally from the Court's historic Commerce Clause jurisprudence touching the railroad industry, much of it authored by Hughes himself, that the chief justice dissented—along with Brandeis, Cardozo, and Stone. The latter expressed great disbelief in the opinion, calling it "the worst performance of the Court since the Bake Shop case [*Lochner v. New York* (1905)].... How arrogant it must all seem to those unaccustomed to judicial omniscience in the interpretation of the Constitution" (Parrish 1982, 261).

Two weeks after *Alton*, on May 27, 1935, "Black Monday" from the perspective of the New Dealers, the justices unanimously struck down the remainder of the National Industrial Recovery Act, overturned the Frazier-Lemke Farm Mortgage Moratorium Act, and denied to the president power to remove a member of the Federal Trade Commission without the consent of Congress.

In the NRA case, *Schechter Poultry Corp. v. United States* (1935), the entire bench agreed with Hughes that Congress had improperly delegated legislative authority to the president and through him to the private trade associations authorized to adopt and enforce codes of fair competition binding against others in particular industries. Even Cardozo, who had dissented in *Panama Refining Co.*, noted that the entire NRA statute condoned "delegation run riot."

But Hughes also ruled that because the chickens processed by the Schechter Brothers' live poultry business in Brooklyn never left New York City, the prices and wages set by the company constituted local production and bore only an "indirect" or trivial relationship to interstate commerce. Since at least the 1880s the Court had drawn a distinction, sometimes sharp, between production or manufacturing that preceded interstate commerce and commerce itself. The former remained beyond federal jurisdiction. Only in cases when the local economic activity "obstructed" or otherwise "burdened" interstate commerce because of its potential for monopoly or other market distortions had the justices sustained federal regulation. Although the Schechter's chickens arrived at their plant from outside New York City, they were processed and consumed locally, which placed them beyond the reach of congressional authority. Cardozo, writing separately, cautioned his brethren about the difficulty of judges drawing such sharp conceptual distinctions with respect to the boundaries of interstate commerce.

Again without dissent, Brandeis wrote that the 1933 Farm Mortgage Moratorium Act had stepped over the Fifth Amendment's constitutional ban on "taking property without just compensation," because it gave debtors rights in property that had belonged to creditors prior to the statute. But neither he nor others in the majority explained how Congress could impair existing private contracts (and property rights) as they had done in the *Gold Clause Cases*, without also running afoul of the "takings" and "just compensation" provisions of the Fifth Amendment.

Brandeis enjoyed another triumph in the third unanimous decision of May 27, *Humphrey's Executor v. United States* (1935), in which the justices denied the president authority to remove unilaterally a member of the Federal Trade Commission, a ruling that sharply limited the broader removal power granted to the executive by the Taft Court a decade earlier in *Myers v. United States* (1926). That earlier case, Justice Sutherland pointed out, concerned the removal of a purely executive appointee, a postmaster, not the appointee to an independent regulatory agency such at the FTC. Brandeis, who had dissented in *Myers* and had become by 1935 deeply alarmed by the centralizing ambitions of FDR and the New Deal, welcomed the limits now placed on the president.

Aside from *Alton* and Cardozo's few caveats in *Panama Refining Co.* and *Schechter*, the judicial vetoes of the New Deal in the spring of 1935 did not reflect a sharp ideological division on the Hughes Court. Brandeis had manifested as much skepticism about the statutes as McReynolds or Butler. Roosevelt immediately denounced the chief justice's interpretation of the commerce power as "the horse-and-buggy definition of interstate commerce" (Schlesinger 1958, 286), although his best advisers had warned him that the *Schechter* litigation presented one of the weakest possible tests of the NIRA, a law under attack in Congress for spawning monopoly and rising prices. The president made matters worse when he compared the NIRA decision to the *Dred Scott* case (1857), in which the Taney Court had vetoed congressional efforts to restrict slavery in the territories and barred African Americans from citizenship, not a happy comparison from the perspective of the justices.

In a final blast at the Court for its decision in *Schechter*, Roosevelt noted that although the Court ruled wages and hours in the live poultry industry beyond federal jurisdiction, it had in the past found sufficient federal jurisdiction to sustain damages against a local of the United Mine Workers for a violent strike against Arkansas coal producers (*Coronado Coal Co. v. United Mine Workers* [1925]). The president failed to point out, however, that the *Coronado* case had been before the Supreme Court twice and only on the second occasion did the justices find compelling evidence that the union leaders had intended the strike to prevent the movement of coal into interstate commerce. In the earlier decision, *United Mine Workers v. Coronado Coal Co.* (1922), rejecting the argument of the operators, they held that "coal mining is not interstate commerce, although it may affect it by reducing the amount of coal carried in that commerce," a view not repudiated in 1925 and one that even Brandeis and Stone endorsed. In another ironic twist, Charles Evans Hughes had represented the coal operators in the first *Coronado* case and suffered a rebuff on the interstate commerce claim. Also in 1925, the Taft Court justices had sustained a New York law regulating the kosher meat industry against allegations that it constituted an interference with interstate commerce (*Hygrade Provision Co. v. Sherman* [1925]).

Brandeis, who enjoyed relationships with many of the younger attorneys working for the New Deal through Frankfurter, expressed great satisfaction with the Court's rulings against the administration in the spring of 1935. "These three decisions change everything," he told Ben Cohen. "The President has been living in a fool's paradise" (Parrish 1982, 262). He also lectured Tom Corcoran: "This is the end of this business of centralization and I want you to go back and tell the President that we're not going to let this government centralize everything. It's come to an end" (Parrish 1982, 260–261). As for the young lawyers who had come to Washington, Brandeis advised, "[T]ell them to go home, back to the states. That is where they must do their work" (Parrish 1982, 260–262). The NIRA, Brandeis believed, had been captured by big business and promoted monopoly. He harbored the same hostility to the New Deal's Agricultural Adjustment Act, which, he argued, rewarded the most prosperous farmers, led to the eviction of sharecroppers, and took money out of the pockets of consumers before wages had been increased.

But not even Brandeis, fearful of centralization, monopoly, and an aggrandizing executive, endorsed the burst of judicial negatives fired against the New Deal and the states in the following term. In February 1936 the Court gave the New Deal its only victory since the *Gold Clause Cases*, when it upheld the authority of Congress to create the Tennessee Valley Authority, construct dams, and sell electric power as a "by-product" of the property it had acquired (*Ashwander v. Tennessee Valley Authority* [1936]). But the suit had been brought by a minority shareholder of a private utility who hoped to block the purchase of power, a ruse that drew a stinging concurrence from Brandeis, who argued that the justices should not litigate such nonadversary proceedings. Nor should they, he added, determine the validity of a law unless the plaintiff had been injured by its enforcement or pronounce a constitutional conclusion if other grounds existed for deciding the case.

But *Ashwander* afforded small comfort in the midst of decisions that overturned the New Deal's agricultural program, scuttled federal efforts to regulate the bituminous coal industry, reprimanded the new Securities and Exchange Commission, and voided several state laws, one on the basis of a moribund constitutional provision never before invoked to invalidate a statute. The shaky consensus of 1935 broke down, with Stone and Cardozo, usually joined by Brandeis, firing off angry dissents at the majority, a block of five or six that included Roberts and sometimes the chief justice. In an effort to counter this offensive, the three dissenters began to meet regularly before the weekly conference in order to discuss pending cases, marshal their resources, and map strategy.

The first sign of a new judicial aggressiveness came in December 1935, when Hughes and Roberts joined the Four Horsemen to strike down a provision in the Vermont income tax laws that imposed a higher levy on the interest earned on loans made outside the state than on similar loans made inside Vermont. In *Colgate v. Harvey* (1935), the majority ruled the provision invalid on grounds of the Privileges and Immunities Clause of the Fourteenth Amendment, an extraordinary conclusion, because that particular clause in the Reconstruction-era amendment had never been deployed by the Court to invalidate a state law and had been treated as a constitutional derelict since the *Slaughterhouse Cases* (1873). In the spring of 1935, Stone had complained to Frankfurter, "We are getting new doctrine now faster than I can absorb it" and Frankfurter denounced the *Colgate* decision as "the end of the limit" (Parrish 1982, 263, 265). The worst was yet to come.

The Agricultural Adjustment Act (AAA) of 1933 had imposed a tax on food processors for the purpose of funding benefit payments to farmers who participated in the government's voluntary crop reduction program aimed at curbing agricultural surpluses and thereby raising farm income.

For a majority of six, Roberts declared the "Triple A" unconstitutional in one of the era's more bizarre opinions filled with contradictory reasoning. *United States v.*

Butler simultaneously empowered Congress and crippled it. At the threshold, probably influenced by Hughes, Roberts made a sweeping constitutional concession by declaring that Congress could spend "public moneys for public purposes," including "the general welfare," unbounded by the specific grants of authority in Article I, Section 8. In a stroke, Roberts had placed constitutional blessing upon a host of existing and future New Deal spending programs, including public works, power generation, rural electrification, export subsidies, mortgage assistance, and the recapitalization of private banks.

But what Roberts and Hughes gave away initially, they immediately withdrew by adhering to the venerable distinction between "commerce," which Congress could regulate and "production," which occurred prior to commerce. Predictably, Roberts placed agriculture—like coal mining—on the states' side of that line. What Congress could not directly control under one constitutional provision such as the Commerce Clause, it could not indirectly control through others, including taxation and spending, although Roberts had conceded that the Constitution placed few restrictions on the latter.

The Triple A's revenue provision also contained another fatal flaw, Roberts argued. The tax, he said, was not a true tax, designed to raise revenue, but a "penalty" intended to coerce farmers into federal programs outside the scope of Congress's authority. A year earlier, Roberts had written the Court's opinion in *United States v. Constantine* (1935), which struck down a federal tax on dealers who sold liquor in violation of state laws. With the repeal of the Prohibition Amendment, Roberts reasoned, Congress had lost authority to regulate the liquor trade and could not via such taxation "usurp the police powers of the States." He now applied that reasoning to agricultural production. Across the United States farmers might be suffering similar economic misfortune, he concluded, but their individual production remained subject only to state, not federal, regulation.

Cardozo, joined by Stone and Brandeis, had dissented in *Constantine* on the grounds that the tax levied by Congress against dealers who sold liquor contrary to state law represented "not repression, but payment commensurate with the [illicit] gains" received through such traffic. He also cited cases in which the Court had sustained prohibitive taxes on products such as oleomargarine and questioned whether the justices should engage in psychological speculation concerning the motives of Congress. Justice Stone, unable to contain his contempt for Roberts's arguments in *Butler*, echoed Cardozo's sentiments, but used much harsher language. The Triple A decision, he said, remained "contradictory and destructive . . . a tortured construction of the Constitution" that produced "absurd consequences" for the country. He reminded the majority sharply that the courts were not the only institutions authorized to govern the United States.

In April, with Sutherland leading the charge and Hughes and Roberts in tow, the Court blocked an effort by the Securities and Exchange Commission to pursue an investigation against a person who had attempted to market securities of dubious value, but quickly withdrew his application when the agency subpoenaed his financial records. Sutherland compared the SEC's pursuit of the elusive financier to the "intolerable abuses" of the Elizabethan Star Chamber, but Cardozo, speaking for himself as well as Stone and Brandeis, ridiculed such hyperbole and believed the decision gave comfort to "knaves intent upon obscuring and suppressing the knowledge of their knavery" (*Jones v. Securities and Exchange Commission* [1936]).

A month later, one legacy of *Ashwander* became very clear, when Sutherland and the same five justices overturned the Bituminous Coal Conservation Act through which Congress sought to stabilize prices, wages, and labor conditions in the coal industry by means of local boards composed of operators, unionists, and public representatives. In addition to controlling prices and production through district boards, the law guaranteed collective bargaining for the miners and stipulated that when the unions and two-thirds of the producers reached agreement on wages and hours those terms would bind the entire industry.

In a suit brought by a stockholder, *Carter v. Carter Coal Company* (1936), Sutherland and the majority again invoked the traditional distinction between "production" and "commerce" to hold that the mining of coal remained as before on the production side of the federalism boundary. Labor relations, including wage levels in the industry, had only an "indirect" effect upon interstate commerce and lay therefore beyond the power of Congress. While conceding that the coal industry suffered from an epidemic of strikes, price cutting, and the curtailment of production that touched the entire nation, Sutherland nonetheless argued that "the evils are all local evils over which the federal government has no legislative control." The source of the effect, not its magnitude, placed the industry's distress in the hands of the states. "The effect [upon interstate commerce] does not become direct by multiplying the tonnage, or increasing the number of men employed. . . . The relation of employer and employee is a local relation. . . . Such effect as they may have upon commerce, however extensive it may be, is secondary and indirect."

Although the framers of the Bituminous Coal Conservation Act had taken pains to separate the price and production provisions from the labor clauses, Sutherland held them all invalid, a bit of judicial overreaching that provoked a sharp rebuke from the chief justice. From Hughes's perspective and probably Roberts's as well, *Nebbia* had already opened the door to price fixing by both the states and the federal government by eroding the distinction between private enterprise and "business affected with a public interest." It had not, however, confronted the separate federalism issue imprisoned within the "production" versus "commerce" categories. Remaining squarely within the traditional framework of analysis, Hughes and Roberts endorsed Sutherland's burial of the labor provisions. "If the people desire to give Congress the power to regulate industries within the State and the relations of employers to employees," he declared, "they are at liberty to declare their will in the appropriate manner, but it is not for this Court to amend the Constitution by judicial decision." For himself, Brandeis, and Stone, Cardozo chastised the majority for its blindness to economic reality and its cramped conception of the commerce power, which, he argued was "as broad as the need that evokes it."

What Stone called "this fateful term" ended in June, when Roberts joined Butler, Sutherland, McReynolds, and Van Devanter in reaffirming "freedom of contract" as the fundamental rule of the Constitution and invalidated New York's minimum wage law for women and minors. Any legislative effort to force employers into making such payments, Butler wrote in *Morehead v. New York ex rel. Tipaldo* (1936), violated their liberty and confiscated their property without due process of law. In the wake of *Carter Coal*, the Court had now created a "twilight zone" with respect to wage issues where neither the federal government nor the individual states appeared able to act, a condition that drew criticism not only from Roosevelt and the Democrats, but from many Republicans as well. Former President Hoover urged that "something . . . be done to give back to the states the powers they thought they already had" (Schlesinger 1958, 489). The Republican Party's national platform in 1936 called for a Constitutional amendment to overturn the *Tipaldo* decision. Hughes joined Stone, Cardozo, and Brandeis in dissent.

The fall of 1936, however, brought Roosevelt's stunning reelection victory and sit-down strikes in the American auto industry during December and January 1937, climaxed by General Motors's surrender to the United Automobile Workers on February 11, 1937. A week earlier, Roosevelt had sent his "court-packing" bill to Congress. In March the United States Steel Corporation, a bastion of antiunion efforts since the turn of the century, also agreed to recognize the steelworkers' union, a capitulation that signaled a fundamental transformation in labor-management relations. In March 1937 as well a new majority on the Hughes Court, including the chief justice and Roberts, appeared to retreat from many of the limiting constitutional doctrines espoused only six months earlier. Most contemporary observers attributed this sudden about-face to the external pressures bearing down on the justices, either FDR's election, the social conflict manifested in the sit-down strikes, the president's plan to revamp the judiciary, or a combination of all of them.

On March 29, with Hughes writing for the majority that now included Roberts, the Court sustained Washington's minimum wage law for women and minors, a statute virtually identical to the New York law overturned nine months earlier. As *Nebbia* had sounded the death knell for "business affected with a public interest," *West Coast Hotel v. Parrish* (1937) now entombed "freedom of contract" as a fundamental limit on the states' police powers. Hughes had dissented in *Tipaldo*, because he believed the New York statute could be distinguished from the federal law invalidated a decade earlier in *Adkins*. Now he neatly placed the Washington statute in the category of earlier laws, some dating back to the 1890s, that had limited contractual freedom and received the Court's blessing.

In the present case, Hughes suggested, the Court restored the proper contours of the due process limitation, one departed from in several earlier decisions, notably *Adkins v. Children's Hospital.* As he had done in *Blaisdell,* the chief justice placed constitutional principles within an evolving social framework of meaning, a technique that subtly altered the content of those principles. "Liberty in each of its phases," Hughes wrote, "has its history and connotation." The Constitution, he noted, protected liberty, "but the liberty safeguarded is liberty in a social organization which requires the protection of law against the evils which menace the health, safety, morals and welfare of the people." *Adkins*, authored by Justice Sutherland, had been an unfortunate detour from the "true . . . principles governing the regulation by the State of the relation of employer and employed."

Two weeks later Hughes again spoke for the majority, when the Court sustained the sanctions of the National Labor Relations Act against four enterprises, including the giant Jones & Laughlin Steel Corporation, all of which had refused to recognize or bargain in good faith with unions certified as the representatives of employees by the new labor board. Jones & Laughlin had spurned recognition of the Amalgamated Association of Iron and Tin Workers of America at its plants in Pittsburgh and Aliquippa, Pennsylvania. The company's refusal to bargain, prelude to a strike that would ripple through the economy, constituted "an unfair labor practice" under the law. And Congress had a right to prohibit such acts that "directly burden or obstruct interstate or foreign commerce."

Invoking many prior rulings that had located federal jurisdiction within a so-called stream of commerce or current of commerce, Hughes turned back the argument that the steelmakers' local labor conflict lay beyond the control of Congress. The mere fact that such "burdens or obstructions" arose from a local labor dispute, the chief justice pointed out, did not render them immune from the reach of congressional power. Rejecting Sutherland's language in *Carter Coal,* Hughes declared, "It is the effect upon commerce, not the source of the injury which is the criterion." Moreover, the "close and intimate effect" that brought a subject within federal power "may be due to activities in relation to productive industry although the industry when separately viewed is local." Without overruling them, Hughes forcefully distinguished both *Schechter* and *Carter Coal* as irrelevant to the present case because neither presented an issue of obstructing or burdening interstate commerce. In *Schechter* interstate commerce had ended at the kosher plant. In *Carter Coal* it had not yet begun.

The Four Horsemen agreed with Hughes that the National Labor Relations Act could be applied to the Washington, Virginia, and Maryland Coach Company, a traditional interstate common carrier, which had been found in violation of the statute, but they vigorously dissented in *Jones & Laughlin* and in two other NLRB cases that involved manufacturers of clothing and trailers. Relying as usual upon the "commerce" versus "production" distinction and spurning Hughes's invocation of "burdens" and "obstructions," they rejected the application of federal law to those enterprises they regarded as both local and wholly private (*Washington, Virginia & Maryland Coach Co. v. National Labor Relations Board; National Labor Relations Board v. Friedman-Harry Marks Clothing Co.;* and *National Labor Relations Board v. Fruehauf Trailer Co.* [1937]).

In May, invoking a broad interpretation of Congress's spending powers, the Court sustained the taxing and spending plans embodied in the unemployment compensation and old-age pension provision of the Social Security Act. The unemployment scheme levied an excise tax on employers, based on a percentage of their employee's wages, with the funds deposited in the United States Treasury. Employers who contributed to a state-run unemployment fund, one subject to strict federal standards with proceeds deposited in Washington, could credit their payments against the federal tax (*Steward Machine Co. v. Davis* [1937]). In dissent, the Four Horsemen condemned this mechanism of federal standards and disbursements as an assault upon state sovereignty, but even Van Devanter and Sutherland hinted that slight modifications of the program could draw their endorsement.

The latter program, funding pensions as well as federal assistance to the blind, disabled, and women with dependent children, captured even the support of Sutherland and Van Devanter, with only Butler and McReynolds left to dissent against Cardozo's view that "when money is spent to promote the general welfare, the concept of welfare or the opposite is shaped by Congress, not the states. So if the concept be not arbitrary, the locality must yield" (*Helvering v. Davis* [1937]).

Many contemporary observers of the Court's behavior between March and June 1937 believed that the justices, especially Hughes and Roberts, had succumbed to the political heat generated by Roosevelt's victory at the polls, or to the president's "court-packing" proposal. Charles Wyzanski, a young attorney who argued the *Jones & Laughlin* case before the Court, quipped to Isador Lubin that "the President's castor oil seemed to work." Lubin replied, "Yes, after some labor pains the Court gave birth to quintuplets" (Parrish 1982, 271). After the Washington minimum wage decision came down, Frankfurter told the president he felt "like finding some honest profession to enter" (Parrish 1982, 271). Following *Jones & Laughlin*, Justice Stone commented acidly, "in order to reach the result . . . in these cases it was necessary for six members of the Court either to be overruled or to take back some things they subscribed to in the Guffey Coal Act case" (Parrish 1982, 271).

Scholarly opinion since the 1930s has questioned some or all of these conclusions, without, however, undermining entirely the political influence hypothesis. Defenders of Hughes and Roberts, for example, note the timing of the decisions and place considerable emphasis upon the unique fact situations and procedural posture of each case to argue that neither justice made a dramatic jurisprudential leap. The evidence is considerably stronger in this regard for Hughes than for Roberts, but the behavior of both justices remains something of a mystery.

Roberts's decisive vote in *West Coast Hotel v. Parrish*, for example, cannot be studied in isolation from the role of the chief justice in the two minimum wage cases. That vote came after the November election, but months before Roosevelt unveiled his plan for the federal judiciary. The "court-packing" measure, therefore, can be ruled out as a decisive variable. Nor does the 1936 election appear to have been a critical turning point. Roosevelt had gained strength in the off-year congressional elections of 1934, but the justices hammered the New Deal a year later. And when FDR lost congressional support in 1938, the Court continued to support administration programs such as the Fair Labor Standards Act.

Decades after the minimum wage decision, Roberts maintained in a memorandum and letter to Felix Frankfurter that he had been prepared to overrule *Adkins* in the earlier New York litigation, but attorneys for the state had failed to present that issue, preferring instead to distinguish their law from the one struck down in 1923. The chief justice, unwilling as always to overrule a prior decision unless absolutely necessary, dissented from Butler's opinion, but on the grounds that the New York law could be distinguished from the earlier federal statute. *Adkins* did not control. When the state of Washington later invited the Court to reconsider *Adkins*, Roberts welcomed the opportunity to overturn it and supported Hughes's opinion that did so while sustaining the new minimum wage law.

But Roberts's explanation does not square with all the known facts or resolve several puzzles. In their petition for a rehearing, New York's counsel specifically asked the justices to reconsider *Adkins*. On the other hand, Washington's brief also attempted to distinguish its statute from the federal law and did not ask the Court to overrule *Adkins*, yet both Hughes and Roberts took that step uninvited. Roberts and Hughes had no difficulty a year later joining an opinion by Brandeis that overruled a venerable precedent dating from 1842, although neither party raised the issue in their briefs or arguments (*Erie Railroad Co. v. Tompkins* [1938]).

Assuming he knew of Roberts's desire to bury *Adkins* in *Tipaldo*, why did Hughes hold out against the overruling in 1936? Why did the chief justice depart from his usual method of distinguishing cases in *West Coast Hotel?* And if he felt so strongly that it was time to revisit the minimum wage issue in 1936, especially in light of his own opinion in *Nebbia*, why did Roberts not write a concurring opinion in *Tipaldo* instead of joining Butler's full-throated reaffirmation of *Adkins?* If Roberts was the key to Hughes's vote or visa versa, the failure of the two justices to effectively communicate in 1936 may account for the outcome that led most contemporaries to assert that in the minimum wage decisions there had been "a switch in time that saved nine." Personal relations among the justices on the Hughes Court impressed many observers as very formal, a condition that may account for the absence of serious dialogue between the austere chief justice and his younger colleague.

Roberts's votes in both the labor board cases and Social Security cases present fewer interpretative problems, although many contemporaries believed he had departed sharply from views endorsed in *Carter Coal* and *Butler*. But Cardozo relied on *Butler*'s sweeping conception of "the general welfare" as the foundation of his opinion in *Helvering v. Davis* and nothing said about the distinction between "commerce" and "production" with respect to coal mining excluded the application of another time-honored concept, a "current of commerce," to steel producers or companies manufacturing clothing and trailers.

The chief justice presents a far less complicated puzzle. As his dissent in *Tipaldo* confirmed, Hughes had never elevated "freedom of contract" to the status of a constitutional dogma that barred state regulation of private agreements. Private contracts demanding payment in gold could not trump the power of Congress to manage the nation's monetary system. As indicated by his earlier views on debt peonage in *Bailey v. Alabama* (1911), he adopted a realistic view of bargaining relationships in the marketplace and remained alert to their potential for oppression. Private contracts, he ruled on another occasion, could not bar recovery by an injured railroad worker for the negligence of an employer (*Chicago, Burlington & Quincy Railroad Co. v. McGuire* [1911]). For Hughes, the only difficulty in *West Coast Hotel v. Parrish* remained Justice Sutherland, author of *Adkins*, but he presented a psychological rather than a doctrinal hurdle.

Nor did Hughes have to bend his jurisprudential principles very far in order to sustain the jurisdiction of the National Labor Relations Board in *Jones & Laughlin*. He had dissented from Roberts's views in *Alton* and authored the opinion in the landmark *Shreveport Rate Case* (1914), which held that "wherever the interstate and intrastate transactions . . . are so related that the government of the one involves the control of the other, it is Congress, and not the State, that is entitled to prescribe the final and dominant rule." Even in *Carter Coal*, Hughes had left himself an exit when it came to the scope of the commerce power, enough wiggle room to sustain Congress when the appropriate facts presented themselves, as they did in 1937 thanks to the careful selection of cases and litigation strategy by administration lawyers. *Jones & Laughlin* bore slight resemblance to the *Schechter Brothers*.

The departure of Van Devanter in the summer of 1937, followed by Sutherland in early 1938, brought New Dealers Hugo Black and Stanley Reed to the Court and secured the directions announced in *West Coast Hotel* and *Jones & Laughlin*. In 1941 the Court unanimously sustained the last reform measure of the New Deal, the Fair Labor Standards Act of 1938. Justice Stone's opinion in *United States v. Darby Lumber Co.* (1941) extended the reach of Congress's power to regulate matters of production and labor conditions beyond what Hughes had sanctioned in *Jones & Laughlin.* And by so doing, the Court relegated *Hammer v. Dagenhart* (1918) and *Carter Coal* (1936) to the ash heap of constitutional limitations. Reluctantly, even Hughes went along with this near coup de grace to the venerable distinction between "commerce" and "production," something he had studiously avoided in 1937.

But whether one speaks of a constitutional revolution or a constitutional evolution, the result of the Court's behavior by the end of the decade had been to undermine in both the popular imagination and academic discourse the lingering belief in judges as infallible oracles, who discovered preexisting legal rules rather than making new law. The intellectual assault on the idea of judges as the passive transmitters of fixed legal rules embedded in the Constitution or prior decisions had been gathering momentum since the late nineteenth century, when Holmes argued that the life of the common law, and by implication, the life of public law as well "had not been logic, but experience" (Holmes 1923, 1–2).

By the 1930s the Supreme Court had established several competing and often conflicting lines of precedent that gave the justices a range of choices when they confronted constitutional questions of federal and state power to regulate economic and social life. Was the Constitution to be read basically as a document of fetters, intended to limit governmental authority? Or, on the contrary, was it a document of powers, intended to equip government to deal with the manifold crises of change in the twentieth century? Depending upon how an individual justice answered that fundamental question, he would adopt a broad or narrow conception of government's role with respect to taxation, spending, the regulation of commerce, and the police power. Did one apply the distinction between "production" and "commerce" when analyzing the scope of Congress's authority "to regulate commerce among the states," or did one invoke the equally useful metaphor of a "stream" or "current" of commerce, a continuous flow of economic transactions over which Congress had jurisdiction? What economic enterprises were to be included in the magic category of "business affected with a public interest," subject to wide state regulation, including prices and wages, while those outside this category remained immune to such controls?

Although the Hughes Court justices did not always align themselves neatly along "liberal" and "conservative" lines in every important constitutional case, a number of generalizations can be made. Van Devanter, McReynolds, Sutherland, and Butler generally privileged judicial over legislative power and manifested a high degree of skepticism concerning the role of government, whether federal or state, except in areas touching criminal justice and freedom of expression. They also tended to believe that the Constitution itself contained absolute conceptual boundaries with respect to such issues as federalism or the separation of powers and that judges were capable of distinguishing these categories and their boundaries with a high degree of intellectual precision.

Justices such as Holmes, Brandeis, Stone, Cardozo, Frankfurter, Black, Douglas, and Murphy, willing to sanction a much expanded role for government at all levels, asserted a far less imperial role for the judiciary in its relationship to the political branches, but often made exceptions when state power bore down on individuals outside a purely economic context. And they were far less confident about the capacity of judges to discern absolute boundaries in the constitutional text. Justices Hughes and Roberts, less bound by the conceptualism that shaped the outlook of a Sutherland or a Butler, displayed more frequent regard for the orientation of this second group, but also thirsted at times for the intellectual security afforded by the other.

Without question, the end of the Hughes era marked the triumph of subversive ideas about the law and the judicial role. In the first four decades of the twentieth century, advocates of sociological jurisprudence such as Roscoe Pound and later legal realists Jerome Frank and Karl Llewellyn demonstrated the social context and consequences of various legal rules, attacked the notion of law as an objective science, dismissed the distinction between facts and values, and argued that judges usually had sovereign choice when electing the rule that applied to the case before them. The belief in timeless, essential principles of law, many realists avowed, remained a fantastic myth, propagated by judicial imperialists but refuted by the actual behavior of judges. Law was little more than the immediate legal decisions made by fallible human officials in a constantly shifting social, moral, and economic environment.

Try as they might to reconcile present rulings with past decisions and to portray constitutional interpretation as a seamless, rational process, the justices of the Hughes Court could not easily escape the realist critique of judicial power. Their behavior, in fact, struck many as confirming the realist argument. How was it possible for nine judges to interpret the meaning of the Commerce Clause or the Contracts Clause so differently? How could Justice Sutherland have been correct about the meaning of due process in *Adkins* and Hughes also correct in *West Coast Hotel?* If constitutional interpretation was so subjective, the only antidote appeared to be the rigorous insistence upon judicial restraint, strict deference to the elected, political branches. The Court had begun that approach already in the field of foreign relations.

While the Hughes Court struggled throughout the depression decade to reconcile constitutional limitations with the need for bold domestic experiments designed to cope with the economic crisis, it displayed far less hesitation in sustaining far-reaching exercises of presidential authority governing the nation's external relations with other countries. Although the Court scrutinized carefully congressional delegation of authority to the executive in the management of domestic economic issues and often invoked the reserved powers of the states as an additional limitation upon federal programs initiated by the White House, the justices dispensed with such restraints when Roosevelt functioned as the nation's leader abroad.

The architect of broad presidential authority in foreign affairs in the 1930s was none other than Justice Sutherland, who usually regarded similar deference to the executive with respect to domestic issues as a dangerous threat to individual liberty and states' rights. But in *United States v. Curtiss-Wright Export Corp.* (1936), sustaining an executive order banning arms sales during the Chaco War between Bolivia and Paraguay in the 1930s, Sutherland rested the external sovereignty of the United States on the very fact of nationhood rather than the Constitution itself and extended to the president the "very delicate, plenary and exclusive power . . . as the sole organ of the Federal government in the field of international relations." Moreover, Sutherland and the majority concluded, the states had no foreign powers to surrender and federalism, enshrined in the Tenth Amendment, remained irrelevant in the conduct of American foreign relations.

A year later, in *United States v. Belmont* (1937), Sutherland and the Court elaborated further on these doctrines that deconstitutionalized foreign affairs by upholding Roosevelt's executive agreements with the Soviet Union that gave the confiscatory decrees of the communist government legal effect in states such as New York, despite protests that such an agreement, not authorized by any congressional action, took property without compensation and undermined the sovereignty of state courts. "We do not pause to inquire," Sutherland wrote, "whether in fact there was any policy of the State of New York to be infringed, since we are of opinion that no state policy can prevail against the international compact here involved." While the liberals and moderates on the Hughes Court set the constitutional foundation for the welfare state, Sutherland erected doctrines that undergirded the imperial presidency of World War II and the Cold War.

The economic crisis of the 1930s and its constitutional resolution, rooted in profound questions concerning the scope of the commerce, taxing, and spending powers of the federal government and the Due Process Clauses of the Fifth and Fourteenth Amendments, tended for a long time to define the entire impact and legacy of the Hughes Court. But this emphasis upon the Court's confrontation with the president and Congress and the dramatic events of 1937, whether defined as a revolution or not, obscured other, less sudden shifts in the constitutional architecture—important breakthroughs in civil liberties and civil rights that both anticipated and set the foundation for the rights revolution of the Warren and Burger years. Invoking the Due Process and Equal Protection clauses of the Fourteenth Amendment, the Hughes Court extended additional provisions of the Bill of Rights to the states; set new standards for the conduct of state criminal trials; and challenged "separate but equal," the core of racist jurisprudence since *Plessy v. Ferguson* (1896).

The landmark in this other "constitutional revolution" of the Hughes era came not in 1937 but a year later when a unanimous Court, speaking through Justice Stone, handed down *United States v. Carolene Products Co.* with its now famous Footnote 4, a decision that proclaimed deference to legislatures in matters of commercial and economic affairs, but heightened judicial scrutiny for laws that tread upon the Bill of Rights, abridge political participation, or discriminate against "discrete and insular minorities." Eight months after *Carolene Products*, Hughes himself, speaking for five others, ordered the admission of Lloyd L. Gaines, an African American, to the all-white law school at the University of Missouri. Brushing aside the state's offer to pay the plaintiff's tuition to an out-of-state institution and its intention to develop soon a separate law school for blacks, Hughes found Missouri in violation of the Fourteenth Amendment and the "separate but equal" requirement of *Plessy*. Without repudiating racial segregation, *Missouri ex rel. Gaines v. Canada* (1938) signaled that the standard of "separate but equal" would be strictly interpreted and the ensuing costs of compliance raised for white Southerners.

With Hughes providing the initiative, the justices also began to methodically dismantle the machinery of discrimination erected by Southern states against African American suffrage. In *Nixon v. Condon* (1932), over dissents by the Four Horsemen, the Court ruled that political party officials, although authorized to act under a state statute, violated the Equal Protection Clause when they barred African Americans from participating in primary elections. And in 1939 Frankfurter and five justices overturned Oklahoma voter registration procedures in *Lane v. Wilson* (1939), which exempted all persons who had voted in 1914 from a required literacy test. Because nearly all those who voted in 1914 were white, the law presented African Americans with greater hurdles at the ballot box. This "grandfather clause," the Court ruled, violated the Fifteenth Amendment ban on racial discrimination.

African American voters suffered one setback in 1935, when the Court ruled unanimously that the Texas Democratic Party had not violated the Fourteenth Amendment when it chose to bar African Americans from membership and thus from participating in the party's primary elections. Writing for the Court in *Grovey v. Townsend* (1935), Roberts defined the party as a wholly private association that had acted without the authority of state law, a category that placed it beyond the reach of the Fourteenth Amendment. In Hughes's last term on the Court, however, the justices limited *Grovey* in *United States v. Classic* (1941) by ruling that Congress had authority under Article I to regulate primary elections when they functioned as an integral part of the process of selecting candidates for federal office. And three years later, in the middle of the Second World War, the Stone Court would flatly overrule *Grovey* in *Smith v. Allwright* (1944).

Hughes may have helped to apply the constitutional brakes to economic reforms prior to 1937, but as the racial discrimination cases indicate, he put his foot on the accelerator of change when it came to civil liberties and civil rights. In the spring of 1931, Hughes spoke for the Court on two occasions that set the tone for the remainder of the decade and laid the foundation for *Carolene Products*. First, in

Stromberg v. California (1931), the Court struck down as impermissibly vague a statute that punished persons who displayed a red flag as a symbol of opposition to organized government. The language of the California enactment, Hughes noted, conceivably permitted criminal sanctions against persons who displayed any banner advocating changes in government, even through nonviolent methods.

A month later, incorporating for the first time the press guarantee of the First Amendment into the liberty provision of the Fourteenth Amendment, the Court struck down a Minnesota statute that had authorized judges to enjoin publications deemed to have printed malicious or defamatory articles in the past. Writing for himself and four others in *Near v. Minnesota* (1931), Hughes voided the Minnesota law as a prior restraint of the press, an action forbidden even by the common law.

The *Near* decision drew dissents from the Four Horsemen, with McReynolds and Butler also voting against the majority in *Stromberg*, an alignment that clearly suggests that the more conservative members of the Hughes Court who usually wept copious tears over the government's invasion of economic rights prior to 1937, did not always rally to the banner of liberty when it touched other interests. On the other hand, the Court spoke with one voice in 1936, when in *Grosjean v. American Press* (1936) it struck down a Louisiana law, inspired by Governor Huey "Kingfish" Long, that imposed a selective 2 percent gross receipts tax on newspapers having a circulation larger than 20,000 per week. The only newspapers subject to the tax had been strong critics of Long's regime. The justices voided a similar Arizona law that had targeted the press in *Arizona Publishing Co. v. O'Neil* (1938) and in that same year also overturned a city ordinance that had prohibited distribution on public streets of handbills or literature of any kind without written permission from the city manager. That broad ban, wrote Hughes in *Lovell v. City of Griffin* (1938), also constituted a prior restraint.

The incorporation of other First Amendment guarantees into the Fourteenth Amendment's Due Process Clause took a further step forward in early 1937, when Hughes wrote for a unanimous bench in *DeJonge v. Oregon* (1937), reversing a conviction under the state's criminal syndicalism law and holding the right of peaceable assembly "equally fundamental" to those of freedom of speech and press. The states could not, Hughes wrote, make it a crime to organize and participate in a meeting at which no illegal action was discussed, even a meeting held under the auspices of an organization such as the Communist Party whose goal remained the forcible overthrow of the government.

Two years later, with McReynolds and Butler in dissent, the Court reaffirmed the essentials of *DeJonge* in *Hague v. Congress of Industrial Organizations* (1939) when it ruled that federal, state, and local governments could not arbitrarily prohibit the right to speak and assemble in public. The municipal ordinance voided in *Hague* had required persons and organizations to secure a permit from the director of public safety in Jersey City before holding public meetings or distributing printed materials in the city's streets, parks, and other public places. The ordinance had been used by Jersey City's mayor, Frank "I am the Law" Hague, to arrest and otherwise harass labor organizers and union gatherings.

A year before Hughes retired, the justices added another provision of the First Amendment to the Fourteenth Amendment incorporation package, when it overturned a Connecticut law in *Cantwell v. Connecticut* (1940) that gave state officials broad discretion in issuing permits to persons soliciting for religious causes and encouraged selective prosecution under a general breach of the peace ordinance. When Connecticut convicted a sidewalk preacher under this general ordinance that swept "a great variety of conduct under a general and indefinite characterization," wrote Roberts, it infringed the constitutional guarantee of the free exercise of religion.

In one of his last opinions as chief justice, Hughes wrote for a unanimous Court to make clear that the Court's robust defense of the First Amendment and its application to the states through the Fourteenth did not imply an absolute right to freedom of expression. The guarantee of freedom of speech, he wrote in *Cox v. New Hampshire* (1941), did not bar a state from setting the time, place, and manner of demonstrations or parades on the public streets, so long as the regulations were narrowly drawn and administered in a nondiscriminatory manner.

Before the Hughes era, the Supreme Court had granted the states broad discretion in the operation of their criminal justice systems by refusing to read the Fourteenth Amendment's Due Process Clause as a significant limitation on local police methods, prosecutions, and sentences. But a Court that granted Congress broad national authority over the economy, and further nationalized the Bill of Rights by applying First Amendment guarantees to the states, did not hesitate to incorporate other provisions respecting criminal justice as well. America's long ordeal with racism provided the occasion for this profound constitutional innovation in federalism. Not until *Moore v. Dempsey* (1923) did the justices rule in a habeas corpus proceeding that the Sixth Amendment and the Due Process Clause of the Fourteenth guaranteed the right to a fair trial in a state court. In that landmark case, five African Americans had been convicted and sentenced to death in Arkansas, where the constant threat of mob violence dominated the proceedings. Writing for all but McReynolds and Sutherland, Justice Holmes declared the trial little more than a sham, a judicially approved lynching, and when the states could not guarantee minimal fairness, federal courts had a clear obligation to "secure to the petitioners their constitutional rights."

The trial of eight African American youths convicted and sentenced to death in Scottsboro, Alabama, for rape provided the occasion for the Hughes Court to significantly extend the principles first enunciated in *Moore*. In the first Scottsboro case, *Powell v. Alabama* (1932), the Court overturned these convictions for failure of the trial court to provide the defendants with effective counsel. The two attorneys who represented the defendants at Scottsboro had no opportunity to investigate the case and consulted their clients for only thirty minutes before the trial began. This procedure, wrote Justice Sutherland for all but Justices Butler and McReynolds, violated due process.

In the second Scottsboro case, *Norris v. Alabama* (1935), Hughes wrote for a unanimous bench in setting aside the conviction because African Americans had been systematically barred from service on both the grand and the trial jury. A year later, in *Brown v. Mississippi* (1936), the justices also reversed without dissent the conviction of another African American who had been convicted on the basis of a confession obtained through torture. The use of such involuntary statements to convict the defendant, Hughes declared, was a clear denial of due process. And in *Johnson v. Zerbst* (1938), the Court put new bite into the Sixth Amendment by ruling that federal courts had an affirmative obligation to provide defendants with counsel, unless the right had been explicitly waived.

There were limits, however, to the enthusiasm of Hughes and his brethren for imposing new standards of criminal procedure on the states through the Fourteenth Amendment. Speaking through Cardozo, they reached such boundaries in the cases of Herman "Red" Snyder and Frank Palka, both under sentence of death. Snyder had been convicted of the murder of a gas station attendant during the course of a holdup in Massachussetts, but near the conclusion of his trial the prosecution had taken the jury to the crime scene without the defendant being present. Most states, Massachusetts excepted, regarded such exclusion as reversible error because a viewing by the jury constituted part of the trial itself. Brandeis had stayed Snyder's execution on the grounds that barring him from the crime scene raised a serious constitutional issue, but Cardozo and four others (Stone, Hughes, McReynolds, and Van Devanter) rejected Snyder's argument that his presence during all stages of the trial constituted the very essence of due process and fundamental fairness guaranteed by the Fourteenth Amendment. The Court should not, Cardozo wrote in *Snyder v. Massachusetts* (1934), allow "gossamer possibilities of prejudice . . . to nullify a sentence . . . and set the guilty free."

Palka, whose name was misspelled in the official Supreme Court report of his case, had been convicted of second-degree murder and sentenced to life in prison for a homicide and robbery in Bridgeport, Connecticut, but a provision in state law permitted the unhappy prosecutor, who sought the death sentence, to appeal the trial judge's rulings to the state's Supreme Court of Errors "upon all questions of law arising on the trial of criminal cases." That court agreed the trial judge had committed reversible error and that Connecticut could try Palka a second time. At his new trial in 1936, the new jury convicted Palka of first-degree murder and the judge sentenced him to death. Palka's appeal to the Hughes Court a year later raised the critical issue of whether Connecticut had violated the double jeopardy provision of the Fifth

Amendment, applicable to the states through the Due Process Clause of the Fourteenth Amendment.

With only Butler dissenting, Cardozo and the majority rejected this incorporation thesis in *Palko v. Connecticut* (1937) by arguing that only certain selective rights had been absorbed into the concept of due process, such as freedom of speech and press, what he called "principles of justice so rooted in the traditions and conscience of our people as to be ranked fundamental." The promise that an individual would not be tried twice for the same crime fell outside this category, because it was not of "the very essence of a scheme of ordered liberty." Connecticut, Cardozo reasoned, had done no more than seek a trial free of errors.

The arrival of Roosevelt justices beginning in 1937 secured both the triumph of the New Deal in the Hughes Court and of judicial restraint as its guiding ideological orientation. Despite the admonition of Justice Stone in the *Carolene Products* footnote, this development did not augur well for the immediate fate of noneconomic issues coming before the justices. Indications of a new conservative tone came with Cardozo's opinion in *Palko* and Hughes's parting statement on the First Amendment in *Cox*, but the real turning point came with the first "flag salute" case, *Minersville School District v. Gobitis* (1940). That decision also demonstrated how the gathering storm of a world at war had displaced the Great Depression as the central focus of political events.

The West Virginia school district, seeking to advance patriotism and national solidarity in a community with a polyglot population, required all students to salute the American flag each day. Those who refused faced expulsion from the classroom and their parents were then subject to prosecution for encouraging truancy. Members of the Jehovah's Witness sect violated the regulations and asserted the constitutional claim that their participation was "forbidden by command of scripture" and thus protected by the Free Exercise Clause of the First Amendment, incorporated into the Fourteenth.

The Hughes Court, speaking through Justice Frankfurter, handed down its decision at a time when German troops had overrun France. "Time and circumstances are surely not irrelevant considerations in resolving the conflicts that we do have to resolve in this case," he wrote, with obvious reference to the flames devouring Europe and soon to touch the United States. With only Stone, the author of *Carolene Products*, in dissent, the Court sustained the school board's policy as a reasonable effort to promote what Frankfurter called "the ultimate foundation of a free society . . . the binding tie of cohesive sentiment." Stone told Frankfurter, however, "I cannot overcome the feeling that the Constitution tips the scales in favor of religion."

Roosevelt would soon tell Americans that "Dr. Win-the-War" had replaced "Dr. New Deal." But that change had already arrived at the Hughes Court with Frankfurter's opinion in *Gobitis*, a harbinger of the extreme judicial deference to the political branches that led the Court in the future to sanction both the Japanese American relocation and the anticommunist repression of the late 1940s and early 1950s. But against that sad legacy of the Hughes era must be weighed another: its robust commitment to what Stone had labeled "preferred freedoms," its steady reformation of the nation's flawed criminal justice system, and its tentative, but unmistakable, attack upon the odious doctrines of racial supremacy and segregation. That legacy, too, would be revived by Earl Warren and his brethren in the not-too-distant future.

References and Further Reading

THE GREAT DEPRESSION AND THE NEW DEAL

Badger, Anthony J. 1989. *The New Deal: The Depression Years, 1933–1940.* New York: The Noonday Press.

Degler, Carl. 1959. *Out of Our Past: The Forces That Shaped Modern America.* New York: Harper & Row.

Gordon, Colin. 1994. *New Deals: Business, Labor, and Politics in America, 1920–1935.* New York: Cambridge University Press.

Kennedy, David. 1999. *Freedom from Fear: The American People in Depression and War, 1929–1945.* New York: Oxford University Press.

Leuchtenburg, William E. 1963. *Franklin D. Roosevelt and the New Deal, 1932–1940.* New York: Harper & Row.

McElvaine, Robert S. 1984. *The Great Depression: America 1929–1941.* New York: Times Books.

Parrish, Michael E. 1970. *Securities Regulation and the New Deal.* New Haven, CT: Yale University Press.

———. 1992. *Anxious Decades: America in Prosperity and Depression, 1920–1941.* New York: Norton.

Schlesinger, Arthur M., Jr. 1958. *The Age of Roosevelt: The Coming of the New Deal.* Boston: Houghton Mifflin.

———. 1960. *The Age of Roosevelt: The Politics of Upheaval.* Boston: Houghton Mifflin.

Watkins, T. H. 1999. *The Hungry Years: A Narrative History of the Great Depression in America.* New York: Henry Holt.

THE HUGHES COURT

Congressional Record, 71st Cong., 2d Sess., 73, February 12, 1930, 3373.

Corwin, Edward S. 1938. *Court over Constitution: A Study of Judicial Review as an Instrument of Popular Government.* Princeton, NJ: Princeton University Press.

———. 1941. *Constitutional Revolution, Ltd.* Claremont, CA: Pomona College.

Cushman, Barry. 1998. *Rethinking the New Deal Court: The Structure of a Constitutional Revolution.* New York: Oxford University Press.

Danelski, David J., and Joseph S. Tulchin, eds. 1973. *The Autobiographical Notes of Charles Evans Hughes.* Cambridge, MA: Harvard University Press.

Gunther, Gerald. 1994. *Learned Hand: The Man and the Judge.* New York: Alfred A. Knopf.

Holmes, Oliver Wendell, Jr. 1923. *The Common Law.* Boston: Little, Brown.

Jackson, Robert H. 1941. *The Struggle for Judicial Supremacy: A Study of a Crisis in American Power Politics.* New York: Alfred A. Knopf.

Kaufman, Andrew L. 1998. *Cardozo.* Cambridge, MA: Harvard University Press.

Lash, Joseph P. 1975. *From the Diaries of Felix Frankfurter.* New York: Norton.

Leuchtenburg, William E. 1995. *The Supreme Court Reborn: The Constitutional Revolution in the Age of Roosevelt.* New York: Oxford University Press.

Murphy, Paul. 1972. *The Constitution in Crisis Times 1918–1969.* New York: Harper & Row.

Parrish, Michael E. 1978. "The Hughes Court, the Great Depression, and the Historians." *The Historian* 40: 286–308.

———. 1982. *Felix Frankfurter and His Times: The Reform Years.* New York: Free Press.

Pepper, David A. 1998. "Against Legalism: Rebutting an Anachronistic Account of 1937." *Marquette Law Review* 82: 63.

Polenberg, Richard. 1997. *The World of Benjamin Cardozo: Personal Values and the Judicial Process.* Cambridge, MA: Harvard University Press.

Purcell, Edward A., Jr. 2000. *Brandeis and the Progressive Constitution: Erie, the Judicial Power, and the Politics of the Federal Courts in Twentieth Century America.* New Haven, CT: Yale University Press.

Pusey, Merlo. 1963. *Charles Evans Hughes.* 2 vols. New York: Columbia University Press.

Urofsky, Melvin I., and David W. Levy, eds. 1991. *"Half Brother, Half Son": The Letters of Louis D. Brandeis to Felix Frankfurter.* Norman: University of Oklahoma Press.

White, G. Edward. 2001. *The Constitution and the New Deal.* Cambridge, MA: Harvard University Press.

2

The Justices

One member of the Hughes Court graduated from Harvard College in 1861, fought in the Civil War as a second lieutenant in the Massachusetts Twentieth Volunteers, and was wounded three times. Another lived to see the end of America's misadventure in Vietnam in the spring of 1975 and sat on the Court for thirty-six years, longer than any justice in history. In one of his last dissenting opinions, this justice upheld the right of an underground newspaper that distributed antiwar literature near military bases to resist a congressional subpoena designed to force disclosure of the paper's financial records.

The Civil War veteran was Oliver Wendell Holmes Jr., who sat with Hughes from 1930 to 1932. The second in 1975 was William Orville Douglas, who joined the Hughes Court two years before the chief justice retired. The membership of the Hughes Court, in short, included justices whose entire tenure on the Supreme Court spanned three-quarters of the twentieth century. Either as young men or old they witnessed every American military engagement from Bull Run to the evacuation of Saigon. Collectively, they lived through the Spanish-American War, two world wars, a Great Depression, and carried memories of presidents from Lincoln to Jimmy Carter.

At the time of its greatest influence in the mid to late 1930s, however, the Hughes Court comprised justices whose intellectual roots could be traced to three eras in the nation's political and social development. Justices who emerged from the often-labeled Progressive years of Theodore Roosevelt, William Howard Taft, and Woodrow Wilson included Holmes, Hughes, Brandeis, Cardozo, Van Devanter, and McReynolds. From the years of Republican ascendancy after World War I came Sutherland, Butler, Stone, and Roberts. And, finally, the New Deal Roosevelt justices arrived after 1937—Black, Reed, Frankfurter, Douglas, and Murphy. This chapter examines, in order of their appointment, the backgrounds and impact of those fifteen justices who sat with Hughes from 1930 to 1941.

Justices of the Progressive Era

Oliver Wendell Holmes Jr.

Justice Holmes celebrated his eighty-eighth birthday the year Charles Evans Hughes became chief justice and no member of the Court felt greater relief at the first conference where the new leader presided. Since the illness and death of William Howard Taft, the duty of guiding the justices' deliberations had fallen to Holmes as the senior associate. Although still mentally vigorous and capable of dispatching opinions with his customary gusto, the duties had taken their physical toll on the man many regarded as the greatest living American jurist. He continued to accept young secretaries each year sent from the Harvard Law School by Professor Frankfurter, but as he often remarked to the latter, "I reserve liberty to die or resign" (Parrish 1982, 161).

Theodore Roosevelt's first appointment to the Court in 1902, Holmes had become twenty-eight years later a judicial icon to those who called themselves progressives or liberals, although he shared little of their faith in the capacity of political institutions to ameliorate the human condition, which he usually regarded as nasty, brutish, and short. Intellectually, Holmes shared more with social Darwinists like William Graham Sumner than with social gospelers like Walter Rauschenbusch. His reputation as a progressive rested almost entirely on his willingness to allow majorities, what he called "dominant opinion," to work their will upon the law without judicial interference, even if the result might "take the country to hell." He made an exception in those cases in which legislative majorities attempted to shut down competition in ideas, his evolutionist beliefs there coming to the support of the First Amendment in much the same way as they influenced his skepticism about the antitrust laws and other efforts to redirect the cruel forces of the marketplace.

A member of the Supreme Judicial Court of Massachusetts since 1883 and its chief justice since 1899, Holmes initially attracted Roosevelt's attention because of his dissenting opinions in cases involving tort actions against labor unions engaged in boycotts and picketing. These opinions drew criticism from the Bay State's respectable classes, who equated such union tactics with socialism. Although the new justice soon disappointed his White House patron when it came to several Sherman Anti-Trust cases, he cemented his progressive reputation forever by articulating both a broad conception of Congress's authority to regulate interstate commerce in *Swift & Co. v. United States* (1905) and an equally latitudinarian view of the states' police powers in areas of contract and property, *Lochner v. New York* (1905).

Holmes seldom departed from the views he expressed in his *Lochner* dissent, views grounded in his own skepticism about the ultimate answers to complex social problems. "My agreement or disagreement has nothing to do with the right of a majority to embody their opinions in law," he said of New York's effort to limit the hours of

Oliver Wendell Holmes Jr.

bakery workers. "[A] constitution is not intended to embody a particular economic theory. . . . It is made for people of fundamentally differing views, and the accident of our finding certain opinions natural and familiar or novel and even shocking ought not to conclude our judgment upon the question whether statutes embodying them conflict with the Constitution of the United States."

In addition to his own war-induced fatalism and reverence for the common law tradition that stressed the influence of social experience over pure logic, Holmes had been influenced by the academic writing of James Bradley Thayer of the Harvard Law School, whose 1893 essay, "The Origin and Scope of the American Doctrine of Constitutional Law," soon became a founding text for those who believed in judicial restraint. The authority of the courts to strike down acts of the legislature, Thayer declared "a great and stately jurisdiction," but he feared the tyranny of judicial review as well and urged the courts to stay their hand unless the legislators "have not merely made a mistake, but have made a very clear one—so clear that it is not open to rational question" (Thayer 1893, 129–130).

Like Thayer, Holmes gave voice to similar judicial deference in 1930, when he dissented in *Baldwin v. Missouri* as the McReynolds-led majority, including the new chief justice, invoked the Due Process Clause of the Fourteenth Amendment to void the state's attempt to levy an inheritance tax on personal property held by Missouri banks in the name of a deceased Illinois resident. "I have not yet adequately expressed the more than anxiety that I feel at the ever increasing scope given to the Fourteenth Amendment in cutting down what I believe to be the constitutional rights of the States," he wrote. "As the decisions now stand, I see hardly any limit but the sky to the invalidating of those rights if they happen to strike a majority of this Court as for any reason undesirable. I cannot believe that the Amendment was intended to give us *carte blanche* to embody our economic or moral beliefs in its prohibitions."

Holmes's repeated articulation of what would become known as the "rational basis test" with respect to economic legislation endeared him to New Dealers and progressives in the 1930s as they sought to invoke the affirmative powers of state and national governments against the manifold crises of the Great Depression. Holmes's skepticism about the abuses of judicial power, especially by federal judges, also underlay his fierce opposition to the venerable decision of *Swift v. Tyson* (1842) in which Justice Joseph Story had armed the national judiciary with the authority, absent a specific state statute, to promulgate their own common law rules in diversity cases, a result that ignored local court decisions, promoted forum shopping by litigants, and created conflicting legal principles of law governing such areas as tort liability and contracts.

For Holmes, the notion of a judge-made federal common law apart from that of the individual states, something akin to the "brooding omnipresence in the sky" that he had ridiculed decades earlier, offended both his legal positivism and his belief in judicial restraint. He vented his hostility to *Swift* in *Black and White Taxicab Co. v. Brown and Yellow Taxicab Co.* (1928), two years before Hughes joined the Court. Fighting competition in Kentucky and faced with unfavorable state law, a Kentucky taxicab company assigned its assets to a new corporation chartered in Tennessee. Then able to claim diversity jurisdiction, the new company sued for an injunction against its competitor in the Kentucky federal court, which granted the relief. The Supreme Court affirmed over Holmes's dissent, which Stone and Brandeis joined. Holmes denounced as a "fallacy" the concept of "a transcendent body of law outside of any particular State but obligatory within it unless and until changed by statute." The *Swift* ruling, he concluded "has resulted in an unconstitutional assumption of powers by the Courts of the United States."

Holmes's dissent in *Black and White Taxicab* gave further ammunition to Justice Brandeis, long an opponent of *Swift* and diversity jurisdiction, who believed that Story's 1842 ruling had added to the legal arsenal by means of which giant corporations evaded wholesome state regulations and continued their exploitation of consumers and workers. A decade after *Black and White Taxicab* and one year after the Hughes Court sustained major national regulatory power in *Jones & Laughlin* and the *Social Security Cases*, Brandeis gave Holmes a posthumous victory when he mobilized a majority in *Erie Railroad Co. v. Tompkins* (1938) to overturn *Swift* and attempt to cabin federal judicial authority in diversity cases.

Holmes's legacy lived on as well in other areas. His "clear and present danger" test for speech protected by the First Amendment, first articulated in *Schenck v. United States* (1919) but spurned by the Taft Court during the 1920s, experienced a rebirth during the Hughes years. Writing for a majority of five in *Herndon v. Lowry* (1937), Justice Roberts reversed the conviction of a black communist labor organizer in Georgia who had been charged under a law that made it a crime to persuade anyone to participate in an insurrection against the organized government. The statute swept too broadly, Roberts wrote, because Georgia needed to show more than that Herndon's words and actions might tend to incite an insurrection at some future time. Such abridgement of freedom of speech and assembly, Roberts wrote, could not stand unless there existed "a reasonable apprehension of danger to organized government."

With few exceptions, notably the great First Amendment cases of World War I and the 1920s, Holmes seldom contested the uses of the state's police power, whether directed at social ills such as substandard wages, hereditary mental defects, or criminality. Such judicial deference made him at times insensitive to civil liberties in procedural contexts that troubled others. His last opinion as a justice, *Dunn v. United States* (1932) exhibited this characteristic. Tried on three counts of violating the National Prohibition Act—maintaining a common nuisance by keeping liquor for sale at a specified place, unlawful possession of liquor, and unlawful sale of the same—the defendant had been acquitted on the second and third counts, but found guilty on the first. He challenged the logical consistency of that verdict, because possession of liquor—the evidence required for the second and third counts—was also necessary for the first. Holmes and the majority brushed this objection aside and affirmed the conviction over a powerful dissent by Justice Butler. This deferential side of Holmes's jurisprudence would find fresh expression on the Court with the appointment of Felix Frankfurter in 1939.

Willis Van Devanter

Willis Van Devanter, like Holmes a Republican, nominated in 1910 by another Republican, William Howard Taft, rose to political and legal influence in a world far removed from the Brahmin establishment of Boston and Harvard University that shaped his colleague Holmes. Van Devanter was a product of the rugged frontier society of the territory and state of Wyoming in the late nineteenth century. There, cattle barons, horse thieves, absentee landlords, and railroads such as the Union Pacific and Burlington dominated the landscape. While Holmes sipped tea with New England's literary lions in the 1890s, Van Devanter hunted real grizzly bears with Buffalo Bill in the Bighorn Mountains. In 1926, much to his embarrassment, the justice would be cited by a game warden in Virginia for shooting ducks along the Potomac River without the license stamps required by the federal Migratory Bird Act.

A protege of Wyoming's powerful territorial governor and one of its first United States senators, Francis E. Warren, Van Devanter moved rapidly up the political ladder in Wyoming. He served as city attorney of Cheyenne, a member of the territorial legislature, and chief justice of the territorial supreme court, while simultaneously providing legal services to Warren's land and livestock company and the Union Pacific Railroad, which had become the object of numerous congressional investigations into the company's extensive acquisitions of land, coal deposits, and water rights. Like Senator Warren, a frequent critic of President Roosevelt's conservation initiatives, Van Devanter believed that Western resources should be exploited rather than locked up under federal regulations. Before moving to Washington to join the McKinley administration in 1897, Van Devanter developed a keen grasp of the law relating to public lands, irrigation, and Indian affairs that made him an ideal candidate to run the legal staff in the Department of the Interior. In 1903 Roosevelt named him to the Eighth Circuit Court of Appeals, and seven years later Taft sent his name to the Senate to fill the vacancy created by the president's elevation of Edward White to the chief justiceship.

In his 26 years on the Supreme Court, 9 of them during Hughes's tenure as chief justice, Van Devanter participated in over 5,000 opinions, but he authored only 360 for the Court, dissented 4 times and wrote a single concurrence. By comparison, Holmes wrote 873 opinions in 29 years and dissented 72 times; Butler wrote 325 in 16 years, while dissenting on 35 occasions; Sutherland wrote 23 dissents in 15 years.

Willis Van Devanter

These figures indicate that Brandeis hit the mark when he noted in 1929 that Van Devanter "can act quickly if there is no decision to write. But if this job involves one, the time will doubtless be long" (Urofsky and Levy 1991, 380). The justice may have suffered from writer's block, as Brandeis suggested, but no one seems to have been more comfortable with his colleagues and the general direction of the Court in the long time span from 1910 to 1937. Only Taft wrote fewer dissents during this entire period and he sat for only eight years.

Van Devanter remained often in the shadows, content to let others justices speak for him—behavior that made it difficult to delineate his own jurisprudential stance on many issues. An expert on technical questions of jurisdiction, equity, and admiralty, the justice rowed his boat with muffled oars and usually made his greatest contributions behind closed doors. "No one could fully appreciate his value," Brandeis wrote in 1937, "who has not observed his work in conferences, particularly in the days of White and of Taft, and who has not watched his performance in Court" (Urofsky and Levy 1991, 597). Along with Chief Justice Taft, he played the major role in drafting the proposals that ultimately became the Judiciary Act of 1925, the second most significant statute in the history of the federal courts, which limited appeals of right and gave the justices broad discretion over their docket. And Van Devanter's signature on the Hughes-Brandeis letter to the Senate Judiciary Committee in 1937 helped to kill Roosevelt's "court-packing" measure.

Often critical of the work of the Hughes Court, Judge Learned Hand usually placed Van Devanter in the same ideological camp with Sutherland, Butler, and McReynolds, whom he branded pejoratively as "the mastiffs" based on their perceived eagerness to wield the judicial ax against major initiatives of the New Deal. But Van Devanter and the other mastiffs alone did not strike down New Deal statutes such as the National Recovery Act and, as his vote on the old-age pension provisions of the Social Security Act suggests, Van Devanter did not always march in lockstep with those justices labeled as conservative. Along with Sutherland, he voted to put the stamp of constitutional approval upon the "socialistic" Tennessee Valley Authority and its ability to sell excess power generated by a TVA-owned dam in competition with private enterprise (*Ashwander v. Tennessee Valley Authority* [1936]).

In one of his earlier opinions for the Court in 1911, Van Devanter gave ample scope to the power of Congress to regulate interstate commerce when he rejected the arguments of the railroads that Congress could not require the use of certain safety devices on railway cars used only within a single state (*Southern Railway Co. v. United States* [1911]). He also wrote for a unanimous bench a year later when the justices sustained Congress's second attempt to impose liability upon the nation's railroads for injuries sustained by their interstate employees (*Employers' Liability Cases II* [1912]). The companies had argued that issues of tort liability and labor relations lay beyond Congress's authority to regulate interstate commerce. A few years later, Van Devanter joined the Court's opinion that extended coverage of this law even to a cook who prepared meals for railroad carpenters while they repaired bridges for the company (*Philadelphia, Baltimore & Washington Railroad v. Smith* [1919]). And the former railroad attorney likewise endorsed Hughes's opinion in 1930 when the justices upheld the Railway Labor Act of 1926, which required the companies to recognize and bargain with the union representing railway and steamship clerks (*Texas & New Orleans Railroad Co. v. Brotherhood of Railway and Steamship Clerks* [1930]; and *Virginia Railway Co. v. System Federation No. 40* [1937]).

Broad federal regulation of the railroads could be sustained on the grounds that these common carriers functioned throughout interstate commerce and enjoyed substantial public benefits, and that the regulations (including compensation for injured employees and union recognition) prevented the disruption of vital public services that could obstruct commerce. In 1937 Van Devanter even voted to sustain the jurisdiction of the New Deal's National Labor Relations Board over the Washington, Virginia and Maryland Coach Company, which had been found guilty of unfair labor practices in failing to recognize the employees' union and bargain in good faith (*Washington, Virginia & Maryland Coach Co. v. National Labor Relations Board* [1937]).

Van Devanter sanctioned federal regulation of commercial activities via the commerce power beyond common carriers, however. He joined Taft and later Brandeis in opinions that upheld the Packers and Stockyards Act, including the authority of the secretary of agriculture to fix the rates charged for services in the yards as well as the fees charged by commission men who sold livestock in interstate commerce (*Stafford v. Wallace* [1922]; and *Tagg Bros. & Moorhead v. United States* [1930]). Likewise, he joined the majority that extended federal regulations to the Chicago Board of Trade under the Grain Futures Act (*Chicago Board of Trade v. Olson* [1923]). Such economic activities, he agreed, resembled public utilities and affected the public interest because they lay athwart the current of interstate commerce.

But Van Devanter also shared with other justices a belief that even within an undoubted sphere of federal jurisdiction, such as the authority "to regulate commerce among the states," there remained a core of private rights protected from government intrusion by other constitutional provisions. One such provision could be found in the Due Process Clauses of the Fifth and Fourteenth Amendments, which prohibited the deprivation of life, liberty, and property. Those liberties protected, the Court had ruled since the 1880s, included the liberty to make contracts concerning wages and prices, subject only to the state's police power to protect the health, welfare, and morals of the community.

Van Devanter therefore dissented when the Court narrowly upheld the Adamson Act in which Congress avoided a threatened nationwide strike in the railroad industry by mandating an eight-hour day for employees with no reduction in wage levels from what had been the customary ten-hour day. Lawyers for the United States argued that disputes over wages often produced an interference with the free flow of commerce that Congress had authority to prevent (*Wilson v. New* [1917]). Congress and the president might believe the nexus existed between wages and the free flow of commerce, but in Van Devanter's constitutional universe, the Due Process Clause of the Fifth Amendment barred them from imposing such a wage contract. Not surprisingly, he voted with Justice Roberts in 1935 when another narrow majority struck down the federal retirement law for railway employees. Like wages, he reasoned, a mandatory pension program might bear some relationship to labor peace in the industry, but Congress lacked authority to impose it because of the Due Process Clause (*Railroad Retirement Board v. Alton*). Critics of Van Devanter and other justices who subscribed to this interpretation of the Due Process Clause as a constitutional limitation pointed out how hard it was to reconcile these decisions with all of those that upheld the authority of Congress to fix railroad rates, also an obvious interference with freedom of contract between the carriers, shippers, and the public.

Consistent with this interpretation of the Due Process Clause, Van Devanter even voted to deny the federal government authority to impose rent controls on property within the District of Columbia during the housing emergency created by World War I (*Block v. Hirsh* [1921]). And he also voted to strike down both federal and state minimum wage laws (*Adkins v. Children's Hospital* [1923]; *West Coast Hotel v. Parrish* [1937]), as well as efforts to fix prices or services for economic activities outside the magic category of "business affected with a public interest" (*O'Gorman & Young v. Hartford Fire Insurance Co.* [1931]; *Nebbia v. New York* [1934]). He found no warrant, of course, for government efforts to alter the terms and conditions of mortgage contracts during the depression years (*Home Building & Loan Ass'n v. Blaisdell* [1934]), or to void the gold clauses in public or private contracts (*Gold Clause Cases* [1935]).

For a justice who viewed the Constitution as generally a restraint upon the power of the state, especially when it tread upon that sphere of private economic choice guarded by the Due Process Clause, Van Devanter displayed little consistent sympathy for plaintiffs who suffered other forms of intrusion and oppression by government. Two years before Hughes ascended the bench as chief justice, Van Devanter wrote for a near-unanimous Court that sustained provisions of a New York law requiring the local Buffalo provisional chapter of the Knights of the Ku Klux Klan to disclose its membership list, rules, and regulations. The law also provided that any person who belonged to an organization that had failed to comply with these disclosure requirements could be charged with a misdemeanor (*New York ex rel. Bryant v. Zimmerman* [1928]). His opinion rejected both equal protection and due process challenges to the law, although labor unions, corporations, and most fraternal organizations had been excluded from its coverage. Only Justice McReynolds dissented on the grounds that the New York litigation had not raised a substantial federal question.

Early in Hughes's tenure, Van Devanter endorsed the chief justice's 1931 opinion reversing the conviction of Yetta Stromberg, who had been convicted along with others for possession and display of a red flag at the Pioneer Summer Camp in California. Categorizing the flag as symbolic speech, the majority for the first time invoked the liberty provision of the Fourteenth Amendment's Due Process Clause to overturn a conviction on the grounds that the California ban swept too broadly and prohibited constitutionally protected speech. Only Butler and McReynolds dissented.

Van Devanter balked, however, at following Hughes further down the path of incorporating specific guarantees of the Bill of the Rights into the Due Process Clause of the Fourteenth Amendment and applying them against the states. In the landmark decision *Near v. Minnesota* (1931), the chief justice mobilized four other justices to support such a conclusion, when they stuck down Minnesota's Public Nuisance Abatement Act, also known as the Minnesota Gag Law, which had permitted a state judge to prohibit the publication of a newspaper if, in light of past contents, he found the paper to be "obscene, lewd, and lascivious" or "malicious, scandalous and defamatory." The Minnesota law, invoked by a state judge against a notorious anti-Catholic, anti-Jewish publication known as the *Saturday Press*, represented a clear prior restraint of publication, Hughes argued, and "it is no longer open to doubt that the liberty of the press . . . is within the liberty safeguarded by the due process clause of the Fourteenth Amendment from invasion by state action." Van Devanter joined Butler's dissent, which rejected Hughes's prior restraint analysis and viewed the statute as a legitimate police power regulation designed to abate behavior found to be a public nuisance, little different from shutting down houses of prostitution. Van Devanter may have regarded the *Saturday Press*, published by the unsavory J. M. Near, as little different from the Klan member prosecuted in New York. Order and social decency, he believed, trumped a free but licentious press.

Six years after *Stromberg* and *Near*, however, shortly before his retirement, Van Devanter appears to have abandoned the fight against further incorporation of the Bill of Rights through the Due Process Clause of the Fourteenth Amendment. He joined Hughes's opinion that overturned the conviction of Dirk DeJonge, who had been convicted under Oregon's criminal syndicalism law for helping to conduct a meeting organized by the Communist Party in Portland to protest the shooting of striking longshoremen by local police. Although no one at the peaceful meeting advocated violence or the overthrow of the government, DeJonge had been convicted solely for the possession of the party's literature, which the prosecution argued promoted criminal syndicalism. Hughes's landmark opinion placed the First Amendment right of peaceable assembly for the first time within the zone of liberty protected by the Fourteenth Amendment (*DeJonge v. Oregon* [1937]).

That same term, however, Van Devanter wrote a dissent for himself, Sutherland, Butler, and McReynolds, that protested the majority's reversal of the conviction of the communist labor organizer Angelo Herndon, sentenced to twenty years in prison in Georgia for inciting a riot. Invoking the "clear and present danger" test, Justice Roberts for the majority placed Herndon's conduct and speeches within the protected core of the First Amendment and rejected the state's and Van Devanter's contention that the defendant's militant organizing efforts threatened imminent violence. For Van Devanter and the dissenters, Herndon presented a more serious threat to the status quo than those who simply displayed a red flag or attended an otherwise peaceful communist meeting in Portland. Roberts, on the other hand, characterized the Georgia law as a "dragnet which may enmesh anyone who agitates for a change of government," a right protected by the First Amendment and the Fourteenth (*Herndon v. Lowry* [1937]).

On issues touching criminal justice and race, Van Devanter often displayed a tendency to break away from Butler and McReynolds. He joined Sutherland's opinion in *Powell v. Alabama* (1932), the first of the so-called Scottsboro cases, where seven justices voted to reverse the convictions of eight African American youths convicted of rape and sentenced to death in a judicial proceeding characterized by a defense attorney who had been given no chance to conduct an investigation into the charges. Five years later, Van Devanter again joined Hughes when the justices unanimously reversed the second conviction of one Scottsboro defendant, Clarence Norris, on the grounds that the state had violated the Equal Protection Clause of the Fourteenth Amendment by systematically excluding African Americans from both the grand jury that indicted him and the trial jury that convicted him and sentenced him to death (*Norris v. Alabama* [1935]).

The issue of a constitutionally protected sphere of private choice, a major theme in Van Devanter's approach to economic regulation, surfaced for him as well in cases involving the right to vote for African Americans. In order to reduce the impact of minority votes, the Texas legislature barred African Americans from voting in the primary elections conducted by the state's Democratic Party. In 1927 the Supreme Court unanimously struck down that law as a violation of the Fourteenth Amendment's Equal Protection Clause (*Nixon v. Herndon* [1927]). Undaunted, the Texas legislature delegated the authority to fix the qualifications of all primary voters to the executive committee of the Democratic Party, which immediately adopted rules limiting the vote to whites. In Cardozo's first opinion for the Hughes Court, five justices declared this method of barring African American voters also to be a violation of the Fourteenth Amendment on the grounds that the legislature's delegation to the party constituted sufficiently prohibited "state action." Van Devanter joined McReynolds's dissent, which argued that the Texas Democratic Party remained a private association that could define its own membership and voting privileges (*Nixon v. Condon* [1932]).

When the Texas legislature finally withdrew statutory support entirely from the Democratic Party a few years later, however, the Hughes Court unanimously upheld the party's refusal to extend voting rights to an African American, although the denial of the ballot had been made ultimately by a state elections official who conducted the actual primary. Now echoing McReynolds, the majority ruled the party a private association. And the conduct of the elections official, Justice Roberts argued, was insufficient to implicate the state in prohibited racial discrimination (*Grovey v. Townsend* [1935]).

James Clark McReynolds

As president, Woodrow Wilson made two monumental blunders, both of which came back to haunt his party and American liberals in the 1930s. The biggest, of course, was his refusal to compromise any provisions in the Treaty of Versailles and to insist that Democrats in the Senate do likewise—a decision that doomed the treaty, killed participation in the League of Nations by the United States, weakened the organization's machinery for collective security, and emboldened aggressor nations from Italy to Japan. His second was the nomination of James Clark McReynolds to the Supreme Court in the summer of 1914, an elevation designed to remove the irascible Tennessean from his post as attorney general of the United States, where he had alienated subordinates, other cabinet officials, and members of Congress by his abrasive response to their criticism—most of it warranted.

Cost overruns in the construction of a new Department of Justice building began before McReynolds's tenure. Wild rumors could not be substantiated that his agency spied on federal judges or failed promptly to prosecute the relative of a prominent Democrat for violating the Mann Act, the federal law that prohibited the transportation of women across state lines for "immoral purposes." But McReynolds's response to these charges usually lacked tact, prudence, and cunning, attributes of character with which he had not originally been endowed and that only became magnified during the next twenty-seven years of his tenure on the Court. Although he usually enjoyed McReynolds's support on constitutional questions, Chief Justice Taft soon regarded him as "selfish to the last degree," a person who "seemed to delight in making others uncomfortable," a man with "no high sense of duty" and possessing "less of a loyal spirit to the Court than anybody" (White 1976, 180).

Three years after joining the Court, McReynolds wrote for a majority of five in *Adams v. Tanner* (1917) to overturn a Washington state initiative that had sought to prohibit employment agencies from collecting fees from workers to whom they had furnished either employment or information leading to such employment. Even "useful occupations" might be regulated by the states' police powers, McReynolds conceded, when their nature or location proved injurious or offensive to the public. And the states might prohibit entirely any business that was "inherently vicious and harmful," but the people of Washington in approving its Employment Agency Law had violated the liberty provisions of the Fourteenth Amendment by an "arbitrary and oppressive" enactment that would prohibit individuals from engaging in a "useful

James Clark McReynolds

business." By equating the states' police powers narrowly with the authority to abate public nuisances and by drawing the distinction between "useful" and "nonuseful" occupations, McReynolds had erected a formidable barrier to any state regulation of prices or wages, exclusive of those businesses "affected with a public interest" or in which the state itself remained a party to the contract. For the remainder of his tenure, McReynolds never strayed from this fundamental belief that the Constitution generally proscribed government regulation of those economic activities deemed "useful" and wholly private from a judicial perspective, legislative findings to the contrary notwithstanding.

In 1923 and 1925 McReynolds authored two opinions for the Taft Court that appeared to vault him into the front ranks of those protecting civil liberties, opinions that his defenders continue to invoke as examples to leaven his otherwise reactionary reputation. In the first, *Meyer v. Nebraska* (1923), the justices struck down a law inspired by the anti-German hysteria of World War I that prohibited the teaching in private or public schools of any language other than English to children who had not passed the eighth grade. The plaintiff, a German language instructor in the Zion Parochial School, challenged the law on Fourteenth Amendment grounds and McReynolds agreed by citing "those privileges long recognized at common law as essential to the orderly pursuit of happiness by free men." At the top of this list, he ranked "the right of the individual to contract" and "to engage in any of the common occupations of life," followed by the right "to acquire useful knowledge, to marry, establish a home and bring up children, [and] to worship God according to the dictates of his own conscience."

In the second case, *Pierce v. Society of Sisters* (1925), the Court enjoined enforcement of Oregon's Compulsory Education Act, which required attendance in public schools for all children between the ages of eight and sixteen, a measure intended to shut down private institutions, especially those with a religious orientation that served the state's foreign-born population. Relying upon *Meyer* and the threat posed by the law both to parental supervision of education and "the right of schools and teachers . . . to engage in a useful business," McReynolds held the statute invalid under the Fourteenth Amendment.

Later justices would place emphasis upon McReynolds's invocation of marriage, procreation, and child rearing in order to enlist *Meyer* and *Pierce* as precedent in cases involving access to birth control, reproductive freedom, and parental supervision over the education of their children, but McReynolds saw the issues as fundamentally ones involving economic liberty, especially freedom of contract, little different from *Adams v. Tanner* (1917), except that Nebraska had "attempted to interfere with the calling of modern language teachers" and Oregon had infringed "the right of schools and teachers . . . to engage in a useful business." As authority in *Meyer*, he cited *Adams* as well as a string of freedom-of-contract decisions from *Allgeyer v.*

Louisiana (1897) to *Adkins v. Children's Hospital* (1923). In *Pierce,* he called upon *Hitchman Coal & Coke Co. v. Mitchell* (1917), a radical freedom-of-contract decision that crippled union organizing efforts by the United Mine Workers.

Justice Sutherland, the author of *Adkins* and a frequent ally of McReynolds in many cases touching economic freedom, joined a dissent by Holmes in the companion case to *Meyer,* a plea for judicial restraint that stressed the legitimate legislative goal of promoting a "common tongue," the reasonable method adopted to further that objective, and the fact that the Iowa law presented "a question upon which men . . . might differ" (*Bartles v. Iowa* [1923]). As this ironic division among the justices suggests, McReynolds, not Sutherland or Van Devanter, carried the torch of judicial imperialism forward into the New Deal era.

From the *Gold Clause Cases* in 1935 until the Court's 1940 decision upholding the Bituminous Coal Conservation Act of 1937 (*Sunshine Anthracite Coal Co. v. Adkins*), McReynolds registered consistent and adamant dissents against the New Deal's entire legislative agenda, which he argued either constituted a "taking" of property prohibited by the Fifth Amendment, exceeded the authority of Congress to regulate commerce among the states, or invaded the powers reserved to the states by the Tenth Amendment. Upon occasion he found a federal statute invalid on all three constitutional grounds. Dissenting in the *Gold Clause Cases,* he compared the president of the United States to the Roman emperor Nero. And dissenting against the unemployment compensation provisions of the Social Security Act, the justice objected to such "a novel and vast field of legislation . . . providing for the care and support of those among the people of the United States who by any form of calamity become fit objects of public philanthropy" (*Steward Machine Co. v. Davis* [1937]).

McReynolds displayed little more toleration for state efforts to cope with the economic dislocations of the depression decade. When a majority of the Hughes Court, led by Brandeis and including the new junior justice, Owen Roberts, sustained a New Jersey law regulating the commissions paid to fire insurance agents by their companies, McReynolds joined Van Devanter's dissent in which the latter argued that "the right to regulate a business [fire insurance rates] does not necessarily imply power to fix the scale for services therein" (*O'Gorman & Young v. Hartford Fire Insurance Co.* [1931]). What McReynolds and the dissenters feared in *O'Gorman* came true three years later, when Roberts wrote for the majority in *Nebbia v. New York,* upholding the state's minimum price regulations for the sale of milk at retail, a decision that ultimately laid the foundation for the successful defense of state and federal minimum wage legislation at the decade's end. McReynolds, predictably, resisted a development that in his judgment signaled the triumph of governmental regimentation and the extinction of economic freedom.

For someone who composed soaring rhapsodies on the theme of economic liberty, McReynolds, unlike other conservative members of the Hughes Court, remained consistently tone deaf to cries for liberty in other constitutional contexts. He dissented in the landmark First Amendment cases, including *Stromberg v. California* (1931), *Near v. Minnesota* (1931), *Herndon v. Lowry* (1937), and *Hague v. C.I.O.* (1939). The plight of the Scottsboro defendants did not draw his support for Justice Sutherland's majority opinion in *Powell v. Alabama* (1932). He voted to sustain Missouri's racially segregated law school (*Missouri ex rel. Gaines v. Canada* [1938]), as well as Oklahoma's revised voter registration requirements that continued to bar African Americans from the polls (*Lane v. Wilson* [1939]). When the justices ruled that the Sixth Amendment required the federal government to provide counsel to criminal defendants, McReynolds joined Butler in dissent.

McReynolds, a lifelong bachelor, generously supported young victims of the Nazi air war against England, donated $10,000 to the Save the Children Campaign, and left a substantial bequest in his will to the Children's Hospital in Washington, D.C., the very institution that he had helped to protect from minimum wage legislation in 1923. But throughout his tenure on the Court, he continued to display rude, boorish behavior toward numerous colleagues, especially Brandeis and Cardozo—behavior that many attributed not only to ideological differences, but, with some justification, to McReynolds's racial insensitivity and barely concealed anti-Semitism.

In February 1936 Chief Justice Hughes wrote for a majority of his Court in sustaining the authority of the Tennessee Valley Authority to enter into contracts for the sale of excess electricity generated by a TVA-operated dam. Ruling that construction of the dam fell within Congress's undoubted power to improve navigation and provide for the common defense, Hughes concluded that Congress also possessed unfettered authority to dispose of government property, in this case, electric power. The challenge to the TVA contract with a private utility had come from a minority shareholder, who claimed that the agreement violated the Constitution and threatened financial injury to the corporation (*Ashwander v. Tennessee Valley Authority* [1936]).

The decision drew a sharp dissent from McReynolds, joined by Sutherland, Van Devanter, and Butler, who regarded it as another green light for government intrusion into the sacred sphere of private enterprise, an undertaking not specifically authorized by Article I of the Constitution that also diluted the value of the shareholder's corporate interest. "If under the thin mask of disposing of property the United States can enter into the business of generating, transmitting and selling power," McReynolds wrote, "an easy way has been found for breaking down the limitations heretofore supposed to guarantee protection against aggression."

Louis Brandeis

Hughes's opinion in *Ashwander* also inspired a famous concurring opinion from Justice Brandeis, who, while agreeing with the chief justice on the scope of congressional power, set down seven reasons why the Court in *Ashwander* and other cases

Louis Brandeis

should avoid "passing upon a large part of all the constitutional questions pressed upon it for decision." The Court, Brandeis declared, should not pass upon the constitutionality of legislation in "friendly, non-adversary, proceedings" such as the stockholder's claim before them; the Court should not anticipate a question of constitutional law in advance of the necessity of deciding it; the Court should not formulate a rule of law broader than required by the precise facts of the case; the Court should not reach a constitutional issue if other grounds existed for disposing of the case; the Court should not pass upon the validity of a statute when the complaint arose from one who has failed to demonstrate injury from its operation; the Court should not pass upon the constitutionality of a law at the instance of one who has availed himself or herself of its benefits; and where the validity of an act of Congress is drawn into question, the justices should first ascertain whether a construction of the statute is fairly possible by which the constitutional question can be avoided.

The contrasting approaches of McReynolds and Brandeis to the issues raised in the first TVA litigation provide a striking illustration of the wide jurisprudential gap that separated President Wilson's first appointment from his second. McReynolds remained forever the judicial imperialist, unshakable in his faith that the courts remained the ultimate repository of wisdom about both constitutional and policy matters. He seldom shirked the task of wielding the judicial ax against legislative majorities and their programs that challenged entrepreneurial prerogatives. Brandeis, to the contrary, devoted his entire judicial career to the task of curbing the judicial appetite for power, a stance that furthered his own robust faith in the democratic process and his fear of concentrated power, whether exercised by giant corporations, an overweening judge, or a charismatic president like Franklin Roosevelt. His law clerks took to calling him "Isaiah" in honor of the Old Testament prophet who often called upon his people to reject the temptations of the present and restore the values of the past. "I never realized how serious Brandeis always was," recalled Justice Stone at the time of his death. "There is little that I can recall of him in the lighter vein" (Baker 1984, 184).

Born into the comfortable, cultured world of German immigrants in late-nineteenth-century Louisville, Kentucky, Brandeis compiled a distinguished record at the Harvard Law School, entered private practice in St. Louis and later Boston, where he represented many commercial clients and earned a substantial income before the age of forty. By the first decade of the new century, however, he had earned the reputation as "the people's attorney" by virtue of his legal efforts, often assumed without fee, on behalf of consumers, workers, and small businessmen who battled the growing power of monopolistic capitalism. He defended Oregon's ten-hour law for women before the Supreme Court, devised the plan for savings bank life insurance in Massachusetts, blocked J. P. Morgan's plan to consolidate the major railroads in New England, and brought labor peace to the New York garment industry.

Brandeis's nomination to the Court in 1916 provoked the sharpest confirmation battle prior to the Senate's defeat of Judge John J. Parker in 1930. Past and present leaders of the American Bar Association lined up to oppose his appointment. Brandeis, they argued, lacked something called "judicial temperament," because as a lawyer he had taken vigorous positions against corporate mergers, criticized railroads for their inefficiencies, and favored social legislation to limit the hours of work and impose minimum wages. Opponents of Judge Parker denounced him for a decision upholding a yellow-dog contract, a devise widely used by employers to defeat union organizing efforts by requiring workers to promise not to join a union as a condition to employment. Brandeis's opponents had found him "unqualified" to serve on the Court for the opposite reason: he has displayed in private practice too much solicitude for the working man and unions. And indeed, over the next decades while on the Court, Brandeis would do all in his power, on and off the bench, to eliminate the yellow-dog contract from American law along with the injunctive power of federal judges so often deployed against labor unions (*Hitchman Coal & Coke Co. v. Mitchell* [1917]).

Brandeis's long campaign against the yellow-dog contract and labor injunction, which ultimately bore fruit in the 1932 Norris-LaGuardia Act that curbed federal equity jurisdiction in labor-management disputes, mirrored his concurrence in *Ashwander.* Both reflected his desire to cabin federal judicial power and nourish democracy by affirming legislative supremacy and dispersing power across a wide spectrum of public and private institutions. His robust defense of the First Amendment supplemented these commitments as well. If legislatures attempted to silence dissent through sedition laws, he believed, they choked off debate and attempted to impose a monopoly on public discourse in the same way that J. P. Morgan had attempted to dominate the railroads of New England. The framers of the Constitution and the Bill of Rights, he argued in his most celebrated defense of the First Amendment, believed "in the power of reason as applied through public discussion." They therefore "eschewed silence coerced by law—the argument of force in its worst form. Recognizing the occasional tyrannies of governing majorities, they amended the Constitution so that free speech and assembly should be guaranteed" (*Whitney v. California* [1927]).

But with the exception of limitations upon speech, press, and assembly, Brandeis remained prepared to grant legislatures, especially those at the state level, broad latitude to structure America's economic relationships. "It is one of the happy incidents of the federal system," he wrote early in the depression years, "that a single courageous state may, if its citizens choose, serve as a laboratory and try novel social and economic experiments without risk to the rest of the country" (*New State Ice Co. v. Liebmann* [1932]). Even the latitudinarian Holmes believed Pennsylvania had gone too far in restricting the mining of coal on corporate property in situations where the mining threatened existing dwelling units, but Brandeis would have sustained the statute as a reasonable exercise of the state's police power, one that did not require compensation for the diminished value of the company's property. "The State merely prevents the owner from making a use which interferes with the paramount rights of the public," he wrote in dissent (*Pennsylvania Coal Co. v. Mahon* [1922]). Brandeis blamed Holmes's law clerk for "accentuating the tendency of age to conservatism" (Urofsky and Levy 1991, 132).

When the Florida legislature adopted a business tax graduated according to the number of stores owned by a single chain in more than one county, a majority on the Hughes Court struck down the law on equal protection grounds. That decision drew from Brandeis one his most passionate dissents against judicial nullification of a state's economic policy, especially since the Florida law had been aimed at what he often referred to as "the curse of bigness." The great disparities in personal income, Brandeis argued, had been one factor leading to the economic depression and that disparity arose from the concentration of wealth and power held by a few corporations and their stockholders. By failing to control the size and power of corporations, he declared, the states had created a "Frankenstein monster," institutions capable of dominating government and imposing upon the American people "the rule of a plutocracy" (*Liggett v. Lee* [1933]). Brandeis's attack upon corporate bigness was so extreme that even Cardozo, who also dissented in *Liggett,* declined to join the opinion.

That same year, Brandeis dissented again when the Hughes Court majority struck down a state law revoking the charter of any corporation that removed a law suit from local into federal courts (*Mortensen v. Security Insurance Co.* [1933]). Such "forum shopping," he believed, allowed giant corporations to escape state scrutiny and find relief in the national courts manned by judicial conservatives.

As an enemy of bigness and an apostle of localism, Brandeis remained decidedly ambivalent about Roosevelt's New Deal. Frankfurter, his closest ally in the legal academy, advised the president on a regular basis and Frankfurter's students, many former Brandeis law clerks, took up positions in the administration as well. Through Frankfurter and his acolytes, especially Benjamin V. Cohen and Thomas Corcoran, Brandeis carried on running dialogues about programs of the administration that both pleased and dismayed him. He seldom hesitated to offer advice on policy, behavior that made him unusual among his brethren and that probably transgressed strict notions of the separation of powers. The initial programs of the New Deal, for instance, especially the National Recovery Act and the Agricultural Adjustment Act, inspired his contempt. Under the guise of curbing competition, boosting prices, and allowing workers to unionize, Brandeis believed, the NRA sanctioned cartels, usually dominated by the largest corporations. The Triple A, by offering cash subsidies to the largest farmers who took land out of production, devastated tenant farmers and sharecroppers while passing on the cost to urban consumers. "The evidence begins to indicate that the Kunststucke [clever tricks] (including both NRA and AAA) are having the effect of retarding recovery," he concluded to Frankfurter, early in 1934 (Urofsky and Levy 1991, 541). He voted with Hughes to strike down the former, but held his nose to join Stone's dissent in the Triple A case, put off by Roberts's narrow reading of the taxing and spending power and his invocation of the Tenth Amendment as a limit on congressional authority. "The whole AAA production curtailment policy will prove disastrous," he predicted (Urofsky and Levy 1991, 562).

Brandeis joined Hughes's opinion in the *Gold Clause Cases* as well, but privately expressed almost as much outrage as McReynolds over the government's repudiation of its financial obligations. "The action on the gold clause," he fumed, "is terrifying in its implications. A declaration of bankruptcy, or composition, is honorable if warranted by existing conditions. . . . If the Government wished to extricate itself from the assumed emergency, taxation would have afforded an honorable way out" (Urofsky and Levy 1991, 523).

From the beginning of Roosevelt's presidency, Brandeis expressed fears that the economic emergency would lead to unchecked executive power. When FDR abruptly rejected American participation in efforts to stabilize international exchange rates, a decision that caught even many of his closest advisers off guard, Brandeis suggested the decision "may be a manifestation of the disintegrating effect of absolute power on mind and character." At the end of 1933 he took "some comfort in the thought that each day brings Congress' convening nearer. It was a terrible thing to vest absolute power in one man" (Urofsky and Levy 1991, 524–525, 534). He readily joined Sutherland's opinion in *Humphrey's Executor v. United States* (1935), reversing Roosevelt's dismissal of a member of the Federal Trade Commission. He likewise endorsed Hughes's opinion striking down the NRA, especially that portion that stressed improper delegation of legislative power by Congress to the executive.

Brandeis had always favored heavy taxation on large incomes, inheritances, estates, and corporations as the method for curtailing the "curse of bigness" and monopoly. He also favored substantial public works projects funded by progressive taxes as an important stimulus for economic recovery. The justice found much to admire, therefore, in many of Roosevelt's new initiatives in 1935 and 1936, especially FDR's "soak-the-rich" revenue proposals, the Public Utilities Holding Company Act, the $4.8 billion commitment to the Works Progress Administration and the Social Security Act. He took special pride in the unemployment insurance features of the latter, based in large measure upon the Wisconsin model shaped by his youngest daughter, Elizabeth, and her husband, Paul Raushenbush.

But Brandeis's enthusiasm for FDR cooled again in 1937 when the president launched his ill-conceived plan to "pack" the federal bench, a decision that revived for the justice all of his earlier anxieties about Roosevelt's lust for power. The justice's long and fruitful relationship with Frankfurter went into the deep freeze as well when the latter did not speak out against the Judicial Reorganization Act publicly, supported FDR behind the scenes, and blamed the Court for bringing the crisis upon itself. Frankfurter, in turn, criticized Brandeis for joining Hughes's letter to the Senate Judiciary Committee that refuted the president's arguments in favor of the legislation. The Brandeis-Frankfurter relationship remained fragile even at the time of the latter's appointment to the Court, when a few of the law professor's supporters suggested that Brandeis's refusal to retire had delayed Frankfurter's nomination because FDR had been hesitant to nominate another New Englander and a Jew.

Of all his many opinions over nearly a quarter century, Brandeis probably took the greatest pride and satisfaction in one of his last from the Hughes era—*Erie Railroad Co. v. Tompkins* (1938). It expressed his deepest beliefs about the importance of limiting federal judicial authority, nourishing decentralized policy making, and curbing the power of giant corporations. In *Erie* he mobilized a majority to achieve finally what he and Holmes had struggled to accomplish for decades: overruling the 1842 decision of *Swift v. Tyson*, which had given federal courts authorization to ignore state common law decisions and to promulgate their own independent federal rules. Although neither party in *Erie* had specifically asked the justices to reconsider *Swift*, Brandeis and the majority ruled that there was no federal common law, that federal courts in each state would be bound by the decisional rules of the highest state court on all issues involving state law, and that the Taney Court had acted unconstitutionally in *Swift*, a conclusion that even some of Brandeis's supporters thought unnecessarily provocative.

In the wake of *Erie*, Brandeis hoped that either through legislation or judicial decision it might be possible to go even further in restricting the diversity jurisdiction of the federal courts, which he regarded as another litigation tool usually manipulated solely for the benefit of big business. Despite fits and starts, the Hughes Court ultimately confirmed a broader presence of federal power—legislative, judicial, and executive—in American life than ever before. Brandeis, one of the last authentic voices of progressivism on that Court, often cautioned against that general trend. Passionate about economic inequality and injustice, he hoped to eradicate them through means that empowered individuals to take responsibility for change at the state and local levels of government above all.

Justices of the Harding-Coolidge Era

George Sutherland

Their critics during the 1930s branded Van Devanter, McReynolds, Sutherland, and Butler "the mastiffs," the "Battalion of Death," or somewhat later, "The Four Horsemen," an obvious reference to riders in the Book of Revelations who brought war, famine, pestilence, and death to a world wallowing in sin. Likewise, it was said, the Four Horsemen of the Hughes Court smote the constitutional sinners of the Great

George Sutherland

Depression, the New Dealers in Washington, and other reformers at the state level who transgressed the boundaries of America's sacred legal text.

But the Four Horsemen, we have seen, did not always ride alone. Important measures of the New Deal, notably the "hot oil" provisions of the National Recovery Act and the NRA itself, fell under the constitutional ax wielded by a near-unanimous bench. On the same day it struck down the NRA, moreover, the justices also without dissent voided the federal Frazier-Lemke Act, which compelled mortgagees to surrender property free of any lien without full payment of the debts, in effect destroying preexisting creditor property rights (*Louisville Bank v. Radford* [1935]). That same day, the justices also agreed that Roosevelt could not fire a member of the Federal Trade Commission without the approval of Congress (*Humphrey's Executor v. United States* [1935]).

Nor did the Four Horsemen always ride together. Only McReynolds and Butler held the old-age pensions of the Social Security Act beyond the taxing and spending powers of Congress (*Helvering v. Davis* [1937]), voted to sustain California's "red flag" statute (*Stromberg v. California* [1931]), refused to reverse the convictions of the Scottsboro defendants (*Powell v. Alabama* [1932]), and did not believe Missouri had violated the constitutional rights of Lloyd Gaines by refusing his admission to their all-white state law school (*Missouri ex rel. Gaines v. Canada* [1938]).

In brief, at least two of the Four Horsemen, Van Devanter and Sutherland, sometimes broke ranks with their conservative brethren and voted with the Court's more liberal justices on both economic issues as well as those touching civil liberties and civil rights. Of the two, George Sutherland, a son of the Utah frontier, compiled the more interesting and paradoxical record. Upon his retirement in 1938, Sutherland received the following accolade from Justice Brandeis, often his opponent on constitutional issues and whose appointment Sutherland had opposed in 1916 as a member of the United States Senate: "Sutherland's resignation, at this time," Brandeis noted, "was like all his other acts, animated solely by sense of patriotic duty. He felt that he would soon be unable to do the work which he thinks he should do (in fact, he has done more than his share) and he felt that there should be ample time for F. D.[R.] [Franklin Roosevelt] and the Senate to consider his successor and get him worked in before the end of the Term" (Urofsky and Levy 1991, 606–607).

Despite historical legend, no rigid philosophy of laissez-faire dominated Sutherland's approach to the issues of law and politics, despite a year of legal education at the University of Michigan in the 1880s under Dean Thomas McIntyre Cooley, perhaps the leading exponent of constitutional limitations. Unlike McReynolds, his other colleague from the resource-rich but capital-scarce West, Sutherland displayed from the beginning of his public life a robust appreciation for utilizing government as an instrument of economic development. The future Republican senator backed William Jennings Bryan's crusade for the recoinage of silver in 1896, an obvious boon to the state's mining industry. As a member of Utah's first state senate at the turn of the century, he likewise sponsored legislation that endowed both mining companies and irrigation districts with the powers of eminent domain, a grant of public authority that enabled these private, profit-oriented institutions to exploit the region's limited water resources even at the expense of other property owners. Moving to Washington, D.C., first as a congressman and later as a senator, Sutherland and Utah's other political kingmaker, Reed Smoot, championed high tariffs that sought to protect the state's sugar beet farmers from the rigors of foreign competition.

As a Republican senator, Sutherland likewise supported those forms of government regulation that made the costs of doing business more predictable, eliminated unscrupulous fly-by-night firms from the market, and gave his region's farmers and businessmen some leverage over absentee corporations, especially the railroads and Eastern banking interests. In this regard, he voted for federal workmen's compensation that rationalized the archaic system of industrial accident law on interstate railroads; LaFollette's Seamen's Act that imposed uniform safety and health standards on the maritime industry; the Pure Food and Drug Act that cracked down on the purveyors of worthless patent medicines and adulterated food products; the Postal Savings Act that provided competition with Eastern lenders and promoted capital formation in Utah; and the Hepburn Act that gave the Interstate Commerce Commission authority to fix "reasonable" railroad rates, a perpetual goal of Western shippers in their long-standing battle against the major lines that dominated their commerce. And he remained a strong supporter of women's suffrage as well.

Out of simple partisanship and a belief that the passion for reform had become unchecked, Sutherland fought critical parts of Wilson's New Freedom agenda, including the Federal Reserve Act, the Clayton Anti-Trust Act, and the Federal Trade Commission Act. The first federal income tax also incurred his opposition. For Sutherland, government encouragement of business was one thing, redistributing the rewards of the market quite another. Efforts to inject more democracy into the political system, notably the initiative, referendum, and recall, also drew his scorn and he became one of the first casualties of the Seventeenth Amendment, which gave Utah voters a direct voice in choosing their U.S. senator in 1916.

Nominated to the Court in 1922 by his former Senate colleague, Warren G. Harding, after returning to private legal practice, serving as president of the American Bar Association, and as an advisor to the Department of State during the International Conference on the Limitation of Naval Armaments, Sutherland's tenure on the Taft Court in the 1920s provided a clear forecast, with one exception, of his response to the constitutional crisis generated by the Great Depression. The exception came in the arena of foreign affairs, where Sutherland's views on national and executive authority during the Roosevelt years prepared the foundation for expanded presidential power in the late twentieth century—an ironic development considering the dedication the Utah jurist displayed in other contexts for limiting the scope of federal and presidential power.

In *Massachusetts v. Mellon* (1923) and the companion case of *Frothingham v. Mellon* (1923), Sutherland for a unanimous bench turned back challenges to the Federal Maternity Act, the first significant federal grant-in-aid program through which the national government offered funds to the states for the purpose of "promoting the welfare and hygiene of maternity and infancy." Congress required states choosing to receive the federal money to comply with federal regulations and match the federal appropriation. The state of Massachusetts and taxpayer Frothingham sought to invalidate the law on the grounds that the Constitution did not authorize Congress to undertake matters relating to the welfare of mothers and infants, that the statute violated the Tenth Amendment, and, further, that it took the taxpayer's property without due process of law. Sutherland ruled, however, that neither the state nor the taxpayer had standing to challenge the congressional appropriation; the state because it did not pay a tax and was under no obligation to accept the grant, and the taxpayer because her interest in any federal appropriation was too remote and she could not claim any immediate personal injury.

Without reaching the underlying constitutional issues, Sutherland had disposed of a limitation on the taxing and spending powers of Congress that would reach full fruition during the New Deal. Roberts's opinion in the Triple A case, *United States v. Butler* (1936), although resurrecting the Tenth Amendment barrier to congressional action, extended Sutherland's framework further with an expansive definition of the spending power on behalf of "the general welfare." That doctrine would finally undergird the Hughes Court's endorsement of the taxing and spending mechanisms for the retirement provisions in the Social Security Act, which Sutherland supported in 1937. And in one of his final opinions before retiring in 1938, Sutherland wrote for a unanimous court that rejected a challenge by private utilities to federal grants offered to municipal governments for the construction of electric transmission and distribution systems. The utilities, he affirmed, had no more standing to challenge these appropriations than Mrs. Frothingham in 1923. Moreover, the companies had suffered no injury other than "the damage of lawful competition," and the local government was under no obligation to accept the funds (*Alabama Power Co. v. Ickes* [1938]). With his consistent endorsement of Congress's spending power via the grant-in-aid, soon to become the most powerful engine of expanding federal authority, Justice Sutherland, otherwise the nemesis of the big government, could lay claim to sponsoring the luxurious growth of the post–World War II welfare state.

Three years after the *Mellon* decision, Sutherland also displayed a captious view of the state's police powers when he wrote the landmark opinion in *Euclid v. Ambler Realty Co.* (1926), which upheld a city's zoning ordinance that excluded apartment houses from certain neighborhoods. Those challenging the ordinance argued that it violated due process by denying to property owners the right to derive the maximum beneficial use from their property, a view shared by three members of the Court, McReynolds, Butler, and Van Devanter, but which Sutherland flatly rejected. In a broad ruling that served as the foundation of modern zoning regulations, he held that so long as the classification of land use was "fairly debatable," the Court would accept the judgment of the local legislative body, a close approximation to what would be later called a rational basis test.

A zoning ordinance, of course, subjected the free market to legislative fiat and sanctioned some redistribution of the income that would have been produced in the absence of those rules, but Sutherland could accept such a framework that set only broad boundaries upon property rights similar to the common law of nuisance and that did not attempt a naked reallocation of rewards produced by market forces. By accepting the venerable distinction between "business affected with a public interest" and those economic transactions deemed entirely "private," he never wavered from his belief that legislative efforts to fix either wages or prices violated the economic liberty protected by the Due Process Clauses of the Fifth and Fourteenth Amendments. Congress could not prescribe minimum wages, even for women, whom, he argued, had gained political equality with the adoption of the Nineteenth Amendment (*Adkins v. Children's Hospital* [1923]). Nor could the states regulate the fees charged by employment agencies (*Ribnik v. McBride* [1928]). In the absence of what he called "a grave emergency," Sutherland wrote in *Ribnik*, "the fixing of prices for food or clothing, of house rentals or of wages to be paid, whether minimum or maximum, is beyond legislative power."

To no one's surprise, Sutherland dissented in *O'Gorman* and *Nebbia*, in which Brandeis and Roberts began the dismantling of the "public-private" distinction, and he adhered to these views when the Court finally overruled *Adkins* to sustain Washington's minimum wage statute in 1937. Minnesota's mortgage moratorium law, Congress's abrogation of the gold clause in private contracts, and Hughes's opinions that sustained both laws likewise drew his dissent. *Home Building & Loan Ass'n v. Blaisdell* (1934) became one of his most eloquent dissents and, in the judgment of many constitutional scholars, offered a devastating critique of Hughes's interpretation of the Contracts Clause. Brandeis, no stranger to dissenting opinions, called it one of the finest opinions he had ever read, although he declined to join it.

Sutherland resisted congressional encroachments upon the states by reading the Tenth Amendment as a barrier to many national initiatives (*Carter v. Carter Coal Co.* [1936]), and cabined the president's removal power in *Humphrey's Executor*, but he left the executive largely unfettered by Congress or the states when conducting the nation's foreign relations. In *United States v. Curtiss-Wright Export Corp.* (1936), Sutherland spoke for a near-unanimous bench (only McReynolds dissented) in upholding the indictment of corporate officials who had been charged with violating a congressional resolution that gave Roosevelt authority to impose an arms embargo, backed by criminal sanctions, at any time he judged the decision would "contribute to the establishment of peace" between the two warring countries. Sutherland not only sustained this broad delegation of decision making to the president, he described the power of the executive in foreign affairs as "plenary and exclusive" and even argued that the nation's authority to act in the international arena rested upon "inherent" sovereignty outside the constitutional structure itself. A year later, Sutherland further "deconstitutionalized" the president's authority to act in foreign affairs when he wrote for five members of the Hughes Court to sustain the Roosevelt-Litvinov pact. That landmark executive agreement had normalized diplomatic and trade relations between the United States and the Soviet Union and transferred economic assets confiscated by the Bolshevik government in 1918 to the United States government, including those held by American financial institutions subject to state laws of property and contract. Although two federal courts had ruled that the executive agreement violated the public policy of New York state and constituted a taking of property without due process, Sutherland swept those concerns aside in *United States v. Belmont* (1937) with the observation that "no state policy can prevail against the international compact here involved," including those provisions that recognized the confiscation decrees of a communist government. This sweeping assertion of federal and presidential power over the states in the area of international affairs provoked a concurrence from Justice Stone, joined by Brandeis and Cardozo, the three members of the Hughes Court most accepting of national and executive authority in the domestic context.

In the same manner that he drew a sharp constitutional distinction between "public" and "private" spheres of economic life, Sutherland carved out an equally clear boundary between "foreign" and "domestic" affairs. Up to the water's edge, Congress could not delegate to the president the authority to ban "hot oil" or sanction codes of fair competition without running afoul of the Constitution, although that document did not speak with clarity about delegation. Nor could Congress seek to regulate the output of agricultural products or coal without treading upon the powers reserved to the states by the Tenth Amendment. But abroad, Congress could delegate to the president, "the sole organ of the federal government in the field of international relations," and the president, acting without a formal treaty, but simply through an executive agreement, could bypass Congress and override the states entirely.

During his Senate years, Sutherland had played a significant role in the revision and codification of the federal criminal code, but prior to the Hughes era, in comparison to other justices he displayed considerable indifference to questions of individual rights in this growing field of constitutional jurisprudence. The case of *Moore v. Dempsey* (1923) offered a shocking example of Southern justice tainted by racism and mob intimidation when an all-white jury in Arkansas sentenced six African American sharecroppers to death for their part in a violent confrontation in Phillips County that had left five whites and hundreds of blacks dead. The defendants claimed that the trial had been dominated by a mob and that witnesses had been tortured to force confessions against them.

By a vote of six to two, with Holmes writing the opinion, the Taft Court ordered a habeas corpus hearing and ruled that such mob domination had deprived the trial court of jurisdiction and the defendants of due process. *Moore v. Dempsey* represented the first occasion in which the Supreme Court had overturned a state criminal conviction and marked the beginning of stricter federal scrutiny of state convictions through the federal writ of habeas corpus. Sutherland, however, joined by McReynolds, dissented on the grounds that the decision would lead to greater federal interference in state criminal proceedings, a forecast that proved accurate over the next decade, with Sutherland sometimes leading the charge.

When the Taft Court extended the scope of warrantless searches to automobiles used in violation of the prohibition laws, Sutherland dissented against what he regarded as an assault on the Fourth Amendment (*Carroll v. United States* [1925]), but he joined the majority five years later in placing wiretapping outside the protection of that same constitutional provision. And he refused to join Hughes's landmark opinion that struck down Minnesota's gag law aimed at newspapers deemed defamatory of public officials (*Near v. Minnesota* [1931]).

A year after *Near*, however, Sutherland extended the scope of federal scrutiny over state criminal trials that he had denounced a decade earlier in *Moore v. Dempsey.* Breaking with McReynolds and Butler, he wrote for the majority in the first Scottsboro case, in which the Court reversed the convictions of eight indigent Alabama black youths convicted of rape. Alabama, he wrote, had denied the defendants effective legal counsel, an essential element of a fair trial, guaranteed by the Due Process Clause of the Fourteenth Amendment (*Powell v. Alabama* [1932]). Without suggesting that the Sixth Amendment's right-to-counsel provision applied to the states as well as to the federal government, Sutherland's *Powell* opinion became the foundation for the Court's requirement that the states provide counsel to criminal defendants in "special circumstances" involving indigent and illiterate defendants who faced capital charges.

When the Court overturned the conviction of Clarence Norris in the so-called second Scottsboro case three years later on the grounds that Alabama had consistently excluded African Americans from both grand and trial juries, Sutherland also signed on to Hughes's opinion (*Norris v. Alabama* [1935]). He likewise joined the unanimous decision in *Brown v. Mississippi* (1936), a near reprise of *Moore v. Dempsey* that excluded involuntary confessions obtained through torture. That same year, Sutherland also wrote a vigorous First Amendment opinion for a unanimous bench in *Grosjean v. American Press Co.* (1936), in which the justices struck down a Louisiana gross receipts tax on newspaper advertising that had been structured in such a way as to apply only to thirteen of the state's 163 publications. That discriminatory and selective tax, Sutherland wrote, sought to punish the press and constituted a prior restraint.

Of all the Four Horsemen, who often invoked constitutional liberty as the grounds for their decisions, especially in cases touching issues of property and contract, only Sutherland could claim the mantle of general philosophical consistency. By the 1930s, more often than not, his conception of constitutional liberty embraced far more than the freedom to barter, truck, and exchange.

Pierce Butler

Pierce Butler, a Minnesotan who had spent most of his legal career as a county prosecutor or representing railroad interests such as the Chicago, St. Paul, Minneapolis and Omaha Company, owed his appointment in 1922 to the assiduous lobbying of Chief Justice Taft and Justice Van Devanter, both of whom hoped their candidate would solidify the conservative tilt of the Court that continued to face the annoying dissents of Holmes and Brandeis. Taft made certain that Butler, a Roman Catholic, enjoyed the support of his archbishop and "attended to" a key member of the Senate Judiciary Committee as the nomination moved forward (Baker 1984, 306).

Butler did not disappoint Taft. Described once by Holmes as "a monolith . . . there are no seams the frost can get through," Butler was a man of imposing physical size and dogmatic philosophical beliefs who detested overruling precedents (Danelski, "Pierce Butler," in Urofsky 1994, 82). Along with McReynolds, his frequent ally in dissent, Butler truly deserved membership in what Judge Hand referred to as "the Battalions of Death," those justices on the Supreme Court who resisted tenaciously both the programs of the New Deal and the revolution in civil liberties and civil rights law promoted by Chief Justice Hughes. Beginning with the "hot oil" case in January 1935 (*Panama Refining Co. v. Ryan*) and continuing through the second Agricultural Adjustment Act decision (*Mulford v. Smith*), handed down in 1939, eleven months before his death, Butler voted to sustain only three significant measures associated with Roosevelt and the New Deal, a record of negativity surpassed only by McReynolds. He joined Hughes's opinion upholding the authority of the TVA to sell surplus power in competition with private utilities (*Ashwander v. Tennessee Valley Authority* [1936]); endorsed Sutherland's sweeping affirmation of the president's authority to embargo arms in *United States v. Curtiss-Wright Export Corp.* (1936); and voted to sustain the Ashurst-Summers Act, which made it a federal offense to transport convict-made goods into any state where the sale or possession of such goods violated local law (*Kentucky Whip & Collar Co. v. Illinois Central Railroad Co.* [1937]). But as the Hughes Court began to sustain antidepression legislation after 1937, Butler authored more and more dissenting opinions, twenty in 1938 and thirty-two during his final term, a number second only to McReynolds.

Pierce Butler

In Butler's jurisprudential world, one in place long before the 1930s, the Constitution of the United States mandated an untrammeled marketplace, free of government regulation except for those economic entities such as utilities that fell within the narrow category of "businesses affected with a public interest." When the legislature in Pennsylvania, for example, banned the use of unsterilized "shoddy" in bedding material as a threat to public health, Butler led the Taft Court in striking down the statute as an "arbitrary" restriction upon entrepreneurial liberty (*Weaver v. Palmer Bros. Co.* [1926]).

Neither state nor federal efforts to cope with the economic crisis of the 1930s found favor with Butler when, as often occurred, such efforts curbed market forces by restricting property rights or freedom of contract. He revealed the depths of this fundamentalism even before the economy collapsed when he dissented in *Euclid v. Ambler Realty* (1926), the landmark zoning opinion written by Sutherland. While the latter argued that the ordinance protected passive owners and existing property values from devaluation, Butler focused on the restrictions that would be imposed upon those seeking to maximize the value of their property through further development. It came as no surprise, therefore, when Butler voted against Minnesota's mortgage moratorium; New York's attempt to stabilize the dairy industry; or Congress's efforts to do the same with respect to agricultural commodities, coal mining, and labor relations.

Butler's opinion in *Morehead v. New York ex rel. Tipaldo* (1936), affirming *Adkins v. Children's Hospital* (1923) that struck down the state's minimum wage law for women, became his signature statement on the laissez-faire Constitution: "The state," he wrote, "is without power by any form of legislation to prohibit, change or nullify contracts between employers and adult women workers as to the amount paid. Any measure that deprives employers and adult women of freedom to agree upon wages, leaving employers and men free to do so, is necessarily arbitrary, a violation of due process." Although Butler anchored much of this opinion on the requirement of legal equality for women, he opposed such paternalism with respect to male workers as well.

Like his colleague McReynolds, Butler wrote vigorous opinions defending the economic rights of the individual against the encroachments of government, but displayed far less judicial activism when the confrontation between the state and the individual came in the context of issues such as the First Amendment, racial discrimination, or the criminal justice system. Some exceptions, however, deserve analysis. A Democrat, a Catholic, a critic of the national prohibition laws and the enforcement machinery they promoted, Butler often reprimanded federal agents for conducting illegal searches and seizures (*United States v. Lefkowitz* [1932]), and wrote a separate dissent in *Olmstead v. United States* (1928), which held wiretapping to be a violation of the Fourth Amendment.

Butler's defenders have noted as well that in several notable criminal cases, he manifested a scrupulous concern for the liberty interests of criminal defendants. In 1934, for example, he joined Roberts, Brandeis, and Sutherland in dissent when a Cardozo-led majority upheld the conviction and death sentence of Herman "Red" Snyder in Massachusetts, who had alleged that the state's failure to include him in the jury's visit to the crime scene violated due process. Butler rejected the conclusion that this constituted harmless error (*Snyder v. Massachussetts* [1934]).

Three years later, he dissented alone without comment when another Cardozo-led Court upheld the conviction of Frank Palka, who had been tried twice in Connecticut for the same crime and sentenced to death on the second occasion when prosecutors utilized a state statutory rule that allowed them to appeal a trial judge's procedural errors (*Palko v. Connecticut* [1937]).

And, finally, in one of his last majority opinions for the Court in 1939, Butler wrote to reverse the convictions of three men under a New Jersey law that defined a "gangster" as any person "not engaged in any lawful occupation . . . known to be a member of any gang consisting of two or more persons," who, in addition, had been convicted at least three times "of being a disorderly person" or who had been convicted of "any crime in this or any other state." The state wished to punish such "gangsters" with fines of $10,000, twenty years in prison, or both. The statute, Butler affirmed, was "so vague, indefinite and uncertain" as to violate due process (*Lanzetta v. New Jersey* [1939]).

The particular facts of *Snyder*, *Palko*, and *Lanzetta* probably account for Butler's stance because he generally remained very adverse to endorsing the adoption of broad new rules to govern criminal procedures either at the state or federal levels. It seems unlikely that he agreed with the claim of Palka's attorneys that the Fifth Amendment's double jeopardy provision had been "incorporated" within the Due Process Clause of the Fourteenth Amendment, an argument that the Court had adopted only with respect to the speech, press, and assembly provisions of the First Amendment. And Butler had dissented in both *Stromberg* (1931) and *Near* (1931). He dissented as well in *Powell v. Alabama* (1932) in which the Court took a major step toward requiring counsel in state capital cases involving "special circumstances." He also dissented in *Johnson v. Zerbst* (1938), which mandated the appointment of counsel in all federal criminal prosecutions.

Far fewer exceptions characterized Butler's approach to issues of race and civil liberties. He not only wrote the unanimous opinion in *Breedlove v. Suttles* (1937), which affirmed the validity of Georgia's annual poll tax that effectively reduced the African American electorate, but he voted to uphold the all-white Democratic Party primary in Texas (*Nixon v. Condon* [1932]), as well as the revised "grandfather clause" that barred blacks from voting in Oklahoma (*Lane v. Wilson* [1939]). And he joined McReynolds in dissent in *Missouri ex rel. Gaines v. Canada* (1938).

As an active member of the University of Minnesota Board of Regents prior to his appointment, Butler had waged successful campaigns against faculty members he regarded as holding radical economic or political views, which he defined as including those who advocated municipal ownership of street railways. In the more turbulent times of the 1930s, punctuated by militant voices on the far left and right, those who advocated other than orthodox opinions received little support from him.

With the exception of *DeJonge v. Oregon* (1937) and *Grosjean v. American Press Co.* (1936), both unanimous decisions, Butler sided with the forces of law and order against political dissenters like Yetta Stromberg and Angelo Herndon (*Herndon v. Lowry*). In the decade of the Great Depression, a majority of the justices on the Hughes Court cautiously but methodically allowed for the expansion of governmental authority over the nation's economic arrangements while simultaneously curbing the state's power over individual rights. Justice Butler consistently opposed both historic trends.

Harlan Fiske Stone

Harlan Fiske Stone, on the other hand, sensed the turn in the constitutional tide in the late 1920s, generally welcomed it, hastened it along the new course during the depression decade, and succeeded Hughes as chief justice in 1941. The son of a New Hampshire farmer, Stone had risen to become a chair professor of law and dean of the Columbia University Law School and a member of the influential Wall Street firm of Sullivan and Cromwell. He had been tapped in 1924 by his old Amherst classmate President Calvin Coolidge to clean up the scandal-ridden Department of Justice, one of several federal departments victimized by the friends and appointees of the late President Harding. As attorney general of the United States, Stone quickly restored the department's morale and placed in charge of the Bureau of Investigation an energetic young bureaucrat named J. Edgar Hoover, who shared his passion for orderly administration. When the long-ailing Joseph McKenna finally stepped down in 1925, Coolidge named Stone to his seat.

Stone's ties to Sullivan and Cromwell, whose clients included powerful New York financial institutions such as J. P. Morgan and Company, inspired a flurry of criticism in the Senate from Western and Southern members, including the redoubtable old progressive from Nebraska, George Norris. Chief Justice Taft, however, never one to take a passive role on appointments to his Court, urged Coolidge to nominate Stone, "the strongest man . . . in New York that was entitled to the place," because he feared the president might choose either New York Court of Appeals Judge Benjamin Cardozo or federal Judge Learned Hand. Taft regarded both Cardozo and Hand as potential allies for Brandeis and Holmes and therefore dangerously "unsound" with respect to constitutional interpretation (Baker 1984, 306). Taft came to regret his endorsement of Stone when "the strongest man in New York" soon gravitated into the orbit of the chief justice's ideological opponents.

Harlan Fiske Stone

In 1915, while a professor and practitioner in New York, Stone had written critically of legal reformers who urged judges to respond creatively to contemporary social evils. He took this to mean that judges "should consciously endeavor to mould [sic] the rules of law to conform to their own personal notion of what is the correct theory of social organization and development" (Mason 1979, 29). Stone deplored this conception of the judicial role, especially with regard to constitutional questions, because he shared Holmes's famous observation in the *Lochner* case that "a constitution is not intended to embody a particular economic theory, whether of paternalism and the organic relation of the citizen to the State or of laissez faire." Such agnosticism about the judicial role distinguished him from Taft, McReynolds, Van Devanter, and Butler, all of whom subscribed to the view that the Constitution mandated a particular economic philosophy, the one they shared that stressed minimal interference by government into economic relationships.

Stone's belief that judges should eschew injecting their values into the constitutional text placed him at odds even with other members of the Court whose general orientation he shared. When Brandeis circulated his long, passionate dissent against the curse of bigness and the overweening power of corporations in the Florida anti-chain-store case (*Liggett v. Lee* [1933]), Stone declined to join it and wrote his own criticism of the majority's decision. "I think," he told Brandeis candidly, "you are too much an advocate of this particular legislation. I have little enthusiasm for it, although I think it constitutional. In any case, I think our dissents are more effective if we take the attitude that we are concerned with power and not with the merits of its exercise" (Mason 1979, 142).

Three years later Stone directed even more pungent and public criticism at Justice Roberts's opinion for the majority in the first Triple A case (*United States v. Butler* [1936]). He found it unfathomable how Roberts could on the one hand affirm the broad spending authority granted to Congress, yet deny that the national legislature could use such power to relieve the economic distress of farmers because of the Tenth Amendment. He ridiculed Roberts's opinion as "a tortured construction of the Constitution," one that "hardly rises to the dignity of argument," and one that appealed to minds "accustomed to believe that it is the business of courts to sit in judgment on the wisdom of legislative action."

Like Brandeis, he voted to sustain the New Deal's initial agricultural policy in *Butler*, although he believed the program wrongheaded, especially vicious with respect to the displacement of poor sharecroppers, and one that promoted scarcity in a time of hunger and privation. A year earlier, he joined the majority in the *Gold Clause Cases* as well, although privately he deplored the government's breach of its contractual obligations. He vowed never to purchase another government bond, but of all the members of the Court he appeared the most willing to accept that Congress had the authority even to regulate the value of money when it came to its own securities.

In 1941, the year he followed Hughes as chief justice, Stone relished the opportunity to bury the Tenth Amendment as a limitation on Congress's powers under Article I, which he did with gusto in *United States v. Darby Lumber*, the unanimous decision that sustained the New Deal's Fair Labor Standards Act mandating minimum wages and maximum hours. With Roberts on the bench with him, but without overruling or even mentioning *Butler*, Stone made it clear that "the [Tenth] amendment states but a truism that all is retained [by the states] which has not been surrendered [to the national government]. . . . From the beginning and for many years the amendment has been construed as not depriving the national government of authority to resort to all means for the exercise of a granted power that are appropriate and plainly adapted to the permitted end."

By the end of the Taft years, Stone had also manifested equal impatience with what he regarded as abstract doctrinal categories that the justices had evolved over many years in order to limit governmental action at both the state and national levels. The concept of "business affected with a public interest," usually invoked to bar state regulation of most economic activities, struck him as one such shibboleth in an economy of increasing interdependence and complexity. Likewise he questioned the usefulness of the doctrine that Congress might regulate local economic activities that "directly" affected interstate commerce, but could not touch those whose impact remained "indirect." These abstract categories, he wrote, were "too mechanical, too uncertain in . . . application, and too remote from actualities, to be of value" (*DiSanto v. Pennsylvania* [1927]).

Stone joined Brandeis's opinion in *O'Gorman & Young v. Hartford Fire Insurance Co.* (1931), which hastened the demise of "business affected with the public interest," and readily joined Roberts's opinion three years later in *Nebbia v. New York* (1934) that finally demolished the concept as a significant limitation upon state legislative policy. And while he joined Hughes in striking down the National Recovery Act, he rejected the "direct/indirect" formula as a limitation on Congress's authority under the Commerce Clause in the bituminous coal conservation case (*Carter v. Carter Coal Co.* [1936]), joined Hughes's opinion upholding the National Labor Relations Act a year later, and ignored the distinction entirely in *Darby Lumber*.

Stone's willingness to abandon old doctrinal categories such as the distinction between "direct" and "indirect" effects upon interstate commerce and his support for a broad reading of Congress's Article I powers in cases such as *United States v. Butler*, did not mean he was prepared to sacrifice the interests of the states in the federal structure. Next to Brandeis, he displayed consistent attentiveness to the autonomous regulatory role of the states and resisted invoking the commerce power as a limitation upon state power in the absence of congressional intent. When the Taft Court overturned a Pennsylvania law designed to license steamship agents and protect immigrants from fraud on the grounds that the state had tread upon Congress's authority over foreign commerce, Stone's dissent criticized the majority for ignoring "interests peculiarly local," and failing to consider "all the facts and circumstances, such as the nature of the regulation, its function, the character of the business involved, and the actual effect on the flow of commerce" (*DiSanto v. Pennsylvania* [1927]).

A decade later his views prevailed for a unanimous Court in *South Carolina Highway Dept. v. Barnwell Bros.* (1938), in which the Court upheld a statute that prohibited the use on the state's highways of motor trucks and semitrailer motor trucks whose width exceeded ninety inches and whose weight included loads above 20,000 pounds. That law had been challenged and invalidated by a lower federal court on grounds that it constituted an unreasonable restriction upon interstate commerce. But because Congress had not legislated with respect to such issues and the state law did not discriminate against interstate commerce, Stone wrote, "the judicial function . . . stops with the inquiry whether the state legislature . . . has acted within its province, and whether the means of regulation chosen are reasonably adapted to the end sought." *Barnwell* reflected Stone's deepest commitment to judicial restraint with respect to economic policy choices and, next to Brandeis's opinion in *Erie v. Tompkins*, the strongest statement from the Hughes Court concerning the importance of affirmative federalism that empowered the states to manage such affairs.

No member of the Hughes tribunal, including the chief justice and Brandeis, did more to shift the image of the Supreme Court away from that of an institution generally hostile to economic reforms over to one broadly committed to the vindication of other civil rights and liberties. But even in this area of striking constitutional evolution, Stone often exhibited an unwillingness to write his own values into the law. In 1931, for example, he joined Hughes's dissent in the case of two Canadian-born pacifists denied United States citizenship because they refused to take an unqualified oath to bear arms on behalf of the country. Five members of the Court, including Roberts and Sutherland, upheld the Immigration Service's ruling that such refusal threatened the nation's security and very survival (*United States v. Macintosh* and *United States v. Bland* [1931]). Fifteen years later, in his last opinion as chief justice, Stone dissented when the new Court majority, adopting the views he himself endorsed in 1931, overturned those two earlier decisions. His dissent noted that Congress had not legislated to change the Court's interpretation of the naturalization statute and for the majority to do so "is to discourage, if not to deny, legislative responsibility" (*Girouard v. United States* [1946]).

But where statutory interpretation was not at issue, Stone vigorously endorsed the landmark civil rights and civil liberties rulings of the Hughes era from *Stromberg* and *Near* in 1931 to *United States v. Classic* (1941). He wrote the most famous footnote in the Court's history in *United States v. Carolene Products* (1938), the foundation of the concept of "preferred freedoms," by arguing that legislation restricting the political process, voting rights, specific provisions of the Bill of Rights, or that which was hostile to "discrete and insular minorities" should be subjected to "more exacting judiciary scrutiny" than laws regulating "ordinary commercial transactions." And he applied this concept eloquently in the first flag salute case as the lone dissenter against Frankfurter's opinion sustaining the ritual against First Amendment claims (*Minersville School District v. Gobitis* [1940]). A life-long Republican, but one of the few justices who voted to sustain key New Deal measures, even when he disagreed with their policy implications, Justice Stone became a logical successor to Hughes in 1941. At that time Roosevelt sought to built a broad, nonpartisan coalition following his reelection to the third term and with war looming for the United States in Europe and Asia.

Mr. Hoover's Court

In the twilight of his tenure as chief justice, William Howard Taft feared for the future of the Court and the Constitution should he lose through death or retirement his majority of Sutherland, Van Devanter, McReynolds, Sanford, and Butler. As he told Justice Butler in the fall of 1929, only the "continued life of enough of the present membership" could "prevent disastrous reversals of our present attitude. With Van and Mac and Sutherland and you and Sanford, there will be five to steady the boat. . . . We must not give up at once" (Mason 1956, 75). By "our present attitude," of course, the chief justice meant that body of decisions since the First World War that had limited the scope of both federal and state authority over the nation's economic arrangements. Several months later, he expressed little confidence that the new president, Republican Herbert Hoover, would perpetuate the correct attitude should he fill vacancies on the high tribunal. "The truth is," he told Horace Taft, "that Hoover is a Progressive, just as Stone is, and just as Brandeis is and just as Holmes is" (Mason 1979, 72). And to his brother Charles he lamented that "if a number of us died, Hoover would put in some rather extreme destroyers of the Constitution" (Mason 1979, 70–71).

Discounting Taft's hyperbole, his prediction proved more than accurate about the new president and his three appointments over the next three years—Hughes, Roberts, and Cardozo. Even as secretary of commerce under Harding and Coolidge, Hoover had never enjoyed the full confidence of rank-and-file Republicans, who regarded him as far too anxious to use governmental power for the promotion of enterprise, especially when he urged a large federal public works program as an antidote to unemployment during the postwar recession of 1920–1921. The Great Engineer, the super administrator of the wartime food program, and architect of refugee relief efforts in Belgium, the president brought impeccable progressive credentials to the White House and no one seemed more fit to lead the country through a crisis. At the Paris Peace Conference, John Maynard Keynes had praised him as the ablest member of Wilson's entourage. Until he announced his party affiliation, Hoover had been the choice of many Democrats, including Brandeis, to head the party's presidential ticket in 1920. Hoover's three appointments, far more than Roosevelt's after 1937, changed fundamentally the Court's jurisprudence in the decade of depression.

Charles Evans Hughes

Charles Evans Hughes had three great virtues: He looked like a chief justice. He managed the Court, especially during oral argument and during conference, with an iron hand wrapped in a velvet glove. And, by the standards of his time, he was very liberal. With piercing eyes set above an impressive grey mustache and beard, Hughes struck Robert Jackson and others as the closest they would ever come to meeting God. Theodore Roosevelt, a sometime political rival and ally in New York, called him "Charles the Baptist," a sobriquet that described both his religious persuasion and the moral rectitude that characterized his public life from governor of the Empire State to secretary of state.

At the beginning and end of his tenure, Hughes earned high marks from many of his colleagues for his management of both oral arguments and the justices' Saturday conferences at which votes were taken and opinions assigned. On days of oral argument, Hughes commanded the courtroom with a blend of graciousness and rigor that held attorneys, even those peppered with vexing questions from the other justices, to their allotted time of one hour. He did not hesitate to cut off a startled advocate in midsentence. So, too, during conference, Hughes seldom allowed discussion to stray off the issues at hand. "My admiration of the C. J.'s performance at conference continues unabated," Brandeis reported in 1931 (Urofsky and Levy 1991, 457).

During the conflict-ridden years of 1935–1937, Professor Frankfurter often criticized Hughes and held him responsible for the constitutional impasse between the Court, the president, and Congress. Once on the same Court with Hughes, however, Frankfurter became effusive in his praise for how the chief justice ran the conference. He resembled, Frankfurter often said, Arturo Toscanini conducting a symphony orchestra. Hughes set the agenda, crisply summarized the key points at issue in each case, and offered his views about how they should be resolved. He then allowed each justice to speak, promoting "that austerity of atmosphere which I thought so admirable in a scrupulous observance of each man's saying his say in turn without an interruption" (Lash 1975, 52).

As conflict among the justices and with the Roosevelt administration escalated in the middle of the 1930s, the chief justice's management style came in for increasing criticism from other justices. When the majority voted to strike down the Agriculture Adjustment Act, Stone complained that "the main question in the case was decided practically without discussion and with no analysis or consideration of the relation of conditional gifts for a national purpose to the spending power conferred

Charles Evans Hughes

upon Congress." The unfortunate result, he concluded, had been "inadequate discussion and great haste in the production and circulation of the opinions" (Cushman 1999, 95). Even Brandeis in these tense days remarked that "sometimes our conferences would last six hours and the Chief Justice would do almost all the talking" (Cushman 1999, 95).

With the formidable Hughes remaining aloof on Olympus, other members of his Court organized discussion and strategy groups outside the formal conference, a practice begun by the Four Horsemen and soon followed by Stone, Brandeis, and Cardozo. But even these intellectual alliances did not overcome the extreme isolation among the justices and their small group of clerks, with each office functioning like an autonomous law firm. The isolation must have been especially acute for Justice Roberts, who appears not to have been included in either group. Outside the formal conferences, the austere Hughes eschewed ad hoc discussions with other members of the Court, a posture of rigorous independence that forestalled politicking for votes, but also prevented fruitful collaboration and compromise and may have contributed to misunderstandings in critical situations such as the minimum wage case, *Morehead v. New York ex rel. Tipaldo*, in 1936.

Those members of the Senate who attacked Hughes's nomination as chief justice in 1930 focused on his representation of powerful corporate and financial clients after his tenure in the Department of State to argue that he could not defend the interests of ordinary citizens before the Court. Had these critics instead assessed his record as an associate justice from 1910 to 1916, they would have reached a different conclusion. Hughes's approach to constitutional issues then foreshadowed his later work as chief justice. He crafted a strikingly liberal-progressive record, demonstrated in cases dealing with contracts, interstate commerce, and criminal justice.

Hughes indicated early in his judicial career that shibboleths such as "freedom of contract" held little attraction for him. That abstract principle often hid the realities of gross inequalities in a bargaining relationship. Moreover, private contracts presupposed a viable social order for their enforcement and such agreements could not trump many public policies designed to ensure that stability. In the famous Alabama debt peonage case, *Bailey v. Alabama* (1911), over a dissent by the redoubtable Holmes, he struck down on Thirteenth Amendment grounds the state's statute that authorized the jailing of a party who refused to perform a contract for personal service after accepting some advance payment. In Hughes's judgment, this law sanctioned slavery masquerading as voluntary consent.

That same year, he wrote to sustain the recovery for negligence of Charles McGuire against the Chicago, Burlington and Quincy Railroad, when the railroad raised the defense of McGuire's acceptance of benefits under his contract of membership in the company's relief department. "Freedom of contract is a qualified and not an absolute right," Hughes wrote then, in language strikingly similar to that he would use in *West Coast Hotel v. Parrish* (1937) a quarter-century later. "Liberty implies the absence of arbitrary restraint, not immunity from reasonable regulations and prohibitions imposed in the interests of the community" (*Chicago, Burlington & Quincy Railroad Co. v. McGuire* [1911]).

In 1915 Hughes joined Justice Day's dissent in *Coppage v. Kansas*, in which the majority invalidated a Kansas statute designed to abolish employers' use of yellow-dog contracts, which impeded union activities. Again spurning "freedom of contract" arguments, Hughes argued in dissent that such antiunion devises made a sham of contractual freedom by restricting employees' freedom of association. And in one of his first opinions as chief justice in 1930, Hughes silently buried *Coppage* and the legitimacy of yellow-dog contracts when the Court sustained provisions in the Railway Labor Act of 1926 that required railroad management to bargain with representatives chosen by their employees "without interferences, influence or coercion exercised by either party" (*Texas & New Orleans Railroad Co. v. Brotherhood of Railway and Steamship Clerks* [1930]).

When the landmark Oregon minimum wage law for women came before the Court first in 1916, Hughes voted in conference to sustain the law, but resigned to run for the presidency before the case could be reargued. With Brandeis, who had participated in the litigation, recused from participating, the justices affirmed the lower court by an equally divided bench, but could not therefore establish a binding precedent (*Stettler v. O'Hara* [1917]). Had a majority endorsed the Oregon law in 1917, *Adkins v. Children's Hospital* (1923) would not have blocked similar legislation until 1937. Even in the face of *Adkins*, Brandeis kept the Hughes position alive during the Taft years by dissenting when the Court struck down minimum wage laws from Arizona and Arkansas (*Murphy v. Sardell* [1925]; *Donham v. West-Nelson Manufacturing Co.* [1927]).

When Hughes's own Court revisited the minimum wage issue in *Morehead v. New York ex rel. Tipaldo* (1936), at the height of growing criticism over its invalidation of New Deal measures, the chief justice faced two obstacles presented by the legacy of *Adkins*. Justice Sutherland, the author of *Adkins*, as well as Justices Butler, Van Devanter, and McReynolds, who had helped form the majority in 1923, remained on the Court, all prepared to reaffirm its validity. Furthermore, lawyers representing New York, calculating the odds against them, attempted to distinguish their statute from the federal law struck down in *Adkins*. That approach found favor with Hughes, who dissented in *Tipaldo* because it permitted him to reaffirm support for a minimum wage law without overturning the *Adkins* precedent, a course he often found unpalatable. The storm of criticism against the Court that followed *Tipaldo*, including a rebuke from former President Hoover, finally left the chief justice with no option but overruling *Adkins* a few months later, when it became clear that four others were prepared to cut the Gordian knot (*West Coast Hotel v. Parrish* [1937]).

Hughes's willingness to see private contracts as always embedded in a web of broader social and economic relationships that sustained them permitted him during the depression to author two opinions that stirred the wrath of his conservative colleagues: *Home Building and Loan Ass'n v. Blaisdell* (1934), upholding Minnesota's mortgage moratorium law; and the *Gold Clause Cases* (1935), sustaining Congress's Article I powers over monetary policy. This did not mean, however, that Hughes generally subordinated private contracts to legislative power, especially when the statute went too far in tipping the balance in favor of debtors and stripping creditors of their rights. He joined Brandeis's opinion striking down the Frazier-Lemke Act, aimed at providing relief to farm mortgagors (*Louisville Bank v. Radford* [1935]), but voted to uphold a revised version of the law that swept less broadly (*Wright v. Mountain Trust Bank* [1937]). And shortly after *Blaisdell*, the chief justice also wrote the Court's opinion striking down an Arkansas law that had attempted to place the assets in life insurance policies beyond the reach of creditors. His careful effort to distinguish the Minnesota mortgage moratorium from the Arkansas statute drew support from all but Sutherland, Van Devanter, Butler, and McReynolds, who had dissented vehemently in the earlier case (*W.B. Worthen Co. v. Thomas* [1934]).

Before resigning from the Court in 1916, Hughes also set a broad foundation for the exercise of Congress's power under the Commerce Clause in two cases touching railroad rates, but which could be expanded to allow national regulation of other intrastate activities that affected interstate commerce. In the first, known as the *Minnesota Rate Cases* (1913), he wrote to uphold the intrastate rates fixed by the state's commission against a strong challenge that they burdened interstate commerce and usurped Congress's authority. In the course of that opinion, however, he made clear that "the authority of Congress extends to every part of interstate commerce and to every instrumentality or agency by which it is carried on and . . . its regulation is not to be denied or thwarted by the commingling of interstate and intrastate operations." A year later, he reaffirmed these expansive ideas in the *Shreveport Rate Case* (1914), which sustained Congress's authority to regulate intrastate rail rates if they are so intertwined with local ones that it is impossible to regulate one without the other.

In 1896 the conservative majority on the Supreme Court had invoked the Commerce Clause as grounds for enforcing an injunction against Eugene Debs and striking railroad workers whose boycott against the Pullman Company threatened the disruption of rail traffic to and from Chicago. "The strong arm of the national government may be put forth to brush away all obstructions to the freedom of interstate commerce or the transportation of the mails," declared Justice David Brewer. A half-century later, Hughes employed similar language in sustaining the right of railroad employees to choose bargaining representatives "without interference, influence or coercion." In the landmark case of *Texas & New Orleans Railroad Co. v. Brotherhood of Railway and Steamship Clerks* (1930), the new chief justice gave wide scope to the power of Congress to protect interstate commerce from obstructions by "facilitat[ing] the amicable settlement of disputes which threaten the service of the necessary agencies of interstate transportation," a principle broad enough to soon encompass labor-management conflicts that threatened other aspects of interstate commerce apart from transportation.

And Hughes invoked the same metaphors in 1937 when five justices voted to uphold the collective bargaining requirements of the landmark National Labor Relations Act as applied against major manufacturers of steel (*National Labor Relations Board v. Jones & Laughlin Steel Corp.* [1937]); men's clothing (*National Labor Relations Board v. Friedman-Harry Marks Clothing Co.* [1937]); and trailers (*National Labor Relations Board v. Fruehauf Trailer Co.* [1937]). Thus did the antilabor injunction against Eugene Debs provide additional support for the emancipation of labor in the 1930s, an emancipation driven by militant labor organizers in the CIO, engineered by Senator Robert Wagner and the New Deal, and confirmed by a narrow majority on the Hughes Court.

Hughes's willingness to sustain government regulation of wages, hours, and prices against attacks grounded in substantive due process and his similar support for federal statutes that sought to protect interstate commerce from alleged burdens or obstructions did not mean that he entertained the radical notion that all restraints had been lifted from state and federal regulatory efforts or that the commerce power remained unbounded by other constitutional provisions. While endorsing the minimum price regulations in *Nebbia* (1934) against a due process challenge, Hughes joined Roberts in striking down another portion of New York's milk control laws that allowed producers without well-advertised brand names to sell milk for one cent less than those with well-advertised trade names, a differential intended to protect the industry's weakest members. But that provision offended equal protection, Roberts argued, by giving one class of producers "an economic advantage . . . at an arbitrary date" (*Mayflower Farms v. Ten Eyck* [1936]).

The chief justice likewise joined Brandeis in sustaining New Jersey's regulation of the commissions paid to agents by fire insurance companies (*O'Gorman & Young v. Hartford Fire Insurance Co.* [1931]), but he departed from Brandeis when it came to the Oklahoma law that barred new competition in the ice business (*New State Ice Co. v. Liebmann* [1932]). In Hughes's constitutional universe, the state might discipline the market by regulating the prices charged by public or private businesses, but it could not close the market completely and thereby shut down the channels of opportunity.

Nor did Hughes, despite his latitudinarian conception of federal power to protect and regulate commerce among the states, abandon the venerable distinction between commerce and production embedded in the Court's jurisprudence since *Kidd v. Pearson* (1888) and *United States v. E.C. Knight* (1895). This distinction, often ridiculed by critics, usually placed the manufacture or production of goods beyond the reach of federal power, unless such activities took place within a distinct "stream of commerce" or constituted a "direct" or "substantial" impact upon interstate commerce. No member of the Hughes Court broke entirely free of these conceptual categories when considering the scope of Congress's authority to regulate commerce among the states, although Stone and Cardozo came the closest to doing so.

From the perspective of most justices who served on the Court in the first four decades of the twentieth century, the distinction between commerce on the one hand and production/manufacturing on the other played a fundamental role in their conception of American federalism. That federalism, most assumed, had been enshrined in the Tenth Amendment, which cabined the scope of national jurisdiction and preserved the autonomy of the states. They could not imagine a constitutional world influenced by macroeconomic theory, where even the most localized forms of behavior by businessmen, financiers, or farmers could be conceptually linked to national commerce among the states.

Hughes certainly shared this perspective on the commerce power, which is why he found the New Deal's attempt to fix wages and labor standards in the kosher poultry (*Schechter Poultry Corp. v. United States* [1935]) and bituminous coal industries (*Carter v. Carter Coal Co.* [1936]) beyond Congress's authority, yet supported federal price controls on coal shipped in interstate commerce (*Carter Coal* [1936]) and raised no objection when Congress imposed marketing quotas on the amount of farm products shipped in interstate commerce. With the greatest reluctance, the chief justice joined Stone's opinion in *United States v. Darby Lumber Co.* (1941), which upheld the New Deal's Fair Labor Standards Act and made federal wage and hours regulations applicable to all employees engaged "in commerce" or "in the production of goods for commerce." By overruling *Hammer v. Dagenhart* (1918) in *Darby,* Stone virtually erased the commerce/production distinction and attempted to defang the Tenth Amendment as a limitation upon the commerce power, a result eventually achieved by Justice Jackson's opinion in *Wickard v. Filburn* (1942), a year after Hughes's retirement.

The failure of lawyers in the early years of the New Deal to fully appreciate these inherited conceptual categories governing interpretations of interstate commerce accounted in large measure for their lack of success before Hughes and his brethren. As Hughes remarked to Senator Burton K. Wheeler during the "court packing" controversy: "The laws have been poorly drafted, the briefs have been badly drawn and the arguments have been poorly presented. We've had to be not only the Court but we've had to do the work that should have been done by the Attorney General" (Swindler 1970, 72). This assessment of the administration's litigation talent had been shared by Brandeis, who remarked to Frankfurter in the summer of 1933: "Our Court will apparently be confronted, in a time of greatest need of help, with a Department of Justice as incompetent as was that of Mitchell Palmer" (Urofsky and Levy 1991, 523). The administration's simple failure to publish its "hot oil" regulations in 1933 confirmed this judgment and gave opponents further ammunition against the statute.

Even when he endorsed the New Deal's use of the commerce power, Hughes remained unwilling to ignore other defects in the administration's early statutes. When, for example, Justice Roberts joined Sutherland, Van Devanter, Butler, and McReynolds to strike down the federal Railroad Retirement Act partially on grounds that the law exceeded Congress's authority to regulate commerce among the states, the chief justice wrote a blistering dissent demolishing what he called an "unwarranted limitation upon the commerce clause of the Constitution." Few aspects of the railroad industry, he believed, remained immune to federal regulation. But like Roberts, he found other provisions in the statute to be violations of due process, especially the one mandating pension benefits to those employed by the railroads only one year before the law became effective, including some who had been fired for cause, some who had been retired, and some who had resigned to take other employment (*Railroad Retirement Board v. Alton Railroad Co.* [1935]). As Hughes suggested in his dissent in *Alton*, Congress later in the decade proved capable of rewriting a railroad pension law that enjoyed the support of management and the unions and remained immune to similar due process challenges.

While prepared to leave the president with broad discretion in the conduct of the nation's foreign relations, even when his actions overrode state law, Hughes and his Court looked with far greater skepticism upon congressional enactments that left the executive at large when it came to managing the domestic economy. On at least three occasions (*Panama Refining*, *Schechter Poultry*, and *Carter Coal*), a majority of the justices believed that Congress had transgressed the separation of powers by delegating unbounded legislative power to the president. In *Schechter Poultry*, Cardozo condemned the policy as "delegation run riot." Critics of the justices then and later noted that the Supreme Court had seldom invoked such grounds to void earlier congressional statutes, but New Deal measures often carried delegation into uncharted terrain. In the case of both the National Recovery Act and the Bituminous Coal Conservation Act, the statutes permitted the president to further delegate rule-making authority over production and prices to private industry groups and trade associations, in effect transferring public power to private interests. Even the first Agricultural Adjustment Act, struck down on other grounds, had given large farm producers, organized by county, effective power to determine acreage allotments. This policy may have been necessitated by the primitive level of the federal government's administrative machinery spawned by decades of hostility to a strong state sector, but the result still permitted the brazen use of national authority for private ends. The invalidation of the NRA and the Guffey Coal Act did not bring an end to this kind of delegation. In the Taylor Grazing Act, for example, Congress gave the Western livestock raisers a virtual blank check to promulgate the rules for their own utilization of the public lands.

In addition to the delegation issue raised in cases such as *Schechter*, Hughes manifested considerable skepticism concerning the growing rule-making power granted by Congress to administrative agencies, the new "fourth branch of government," which grew luxuriously during the New Deal years. As early as 1932, while upholding Congress's revision of compensation features in the Longshoremen's and Harbor Workers' Act and the legislature's decision to create non-Article III courts to hear such cases, Hughes mobilized a majority to reject provisions in the statute that denied further judicial review by Article III tribunals. That provision, he wrote, would "sap judicial power as it exists under the Federal Constitution, and . . . establish a government of a bureaucratic character alien to our system" (*Crowell v. Benson* [1932]). Although no friend of big government, Brandeis, joined by Cardozo and Stone, dissented against what he regarded as the flouting of Congress's choice of forums and one that "would impair the entire administrative process" by encouraging federal judges to hold trials *de novo*, second-guessing more competent experts (*Crowell v. Benson* [1932]).

The chief justice soon retreated from the extreme standard of judicial oversight of administrative agencies announced in *Crowell* by holding that the findings of fact by compensation commissioners should be "deemed . . . conclusive" by federal courts "when supported by evidence" (*Voehl v. Indemnity Insurance Co.* [1933]). In 1936, however, he joined Justice Sutherland's scathing rebuke of the new Securities and Exchange Commission, which had continued to investigate the activities of a notorious stock swindler after he had withdrawn his registration statement to avoid a further inquiry (*Jones v. Securities and Exchange Commission* [1936]).

In the same term as *Jones*, Hughes also rebuked the secretary of agriculture for failing, in his judgment, to give livestock brokers a "full hearing" before fixing their commission fees (*Morgan v. United States* [1936]). And when Roosevelt's appointees after 1937 began to extend greater deference to administrative agencies, Hughes raised his voice in protest. In 1940, for example, when Frankfurter and the majority ruled that due process did not require an independent judicial determination of facts in rate-fixing cases, even against claims of confiscation, Hughes dissented with McReynolds and Roberts (*Railroad Commission v. Rowan and Nichols Oil Co.* [1940]).

Hughes's devotion to the institutional image and integrity of his tribunal served him well during the battle against Roosevelt's "court-packing" legislation, but his quest for consensus and his distaste for conflict among the justices may have led him at times to endorse views that contradicted his own judicial style and constitutional logic. Some critics believed that he often cast his vote in closely divided cases in order to avoid five-to-four decisions that gave the appearance of a badly fractured bench and a legal system riddled with subjectivity. As tensions rose inside the Court during the months of controversy with the Roosevelt administration in 1935–1937, Justice Stone often blamed the chief justice for deepening the crisis by appeasement of the Sutherland-McReynolds-Butler-Van Devanter bloc. He referred to Hughes as "that inventive genius" who "has so often of late distorted the body of our law. If the inventor would only sponsor his invention in public, I think, I could write a really effective dissent, but prudence seems to warn against any unnecessary exposure to attack" (Parrish 1982, 318–319). Later he complained to Frankfurter, "I think there has never been a time in the history of the Court when there has been so little intelligible, recognizable pattern in its judicial performance. . . . The worst of it is that the one that you find it most difficult to understand [Hughes] is the one chiefly responsible" (Parrish 1982, 318–319).

No decision of the Hughes Court sparked more criticism from Stone and Frankfurter as an example of "inventive genius" than *Colgate v. Harvey*, decided in 1935, the same year the justices struck down the Triple A and New York's minimum wage law. In *Colgate*, six members of the Court, led by Sutherland and including Hughes, invalidated a section of Vermont's revenue code that taxed the income earned by the state's residents from loans made outside Vermont, but exempted similar income earned from loans made within the state. That distinction, wrote Sutherland, violated the privileges and immunities of United States citizens protected by the Fourteenth Amendment "to loan . . . money and make contracts with respect thereto in any part of the United States." As Stone noted in his dissent, since the adoption of the Fourteenth Amendment in 1868, the Court had never struck down a state law by invoking the Privileges and Immunities Clause, although at least forty-four cases had challenged state legislation on those grounds. Sutherland's unprecedented interpretation, Stone feared, added another weapon to the Court's arsenal of vetoes and "would enlarge judicial control of state action and multiply restrictions upon it to an extent difficult to define." He complained to Frankfurter that "we are getting new doctrine now faster than I can absorb it" (Parrish 1982, 263).

Even before his tenure as an associate justice, Hughes manifested a striking commitment to the defense of civil liberties and civil rights. During the worst excesses of the Red Scare in 1919–1920, he spoke out against the decision of the New York legislature to oust five elected socialists and he later chaired the bar association committee appointed to defend them. He denounced the Palmer Raids, the federal government's massive campaign to deport radical aliens, as one "savor[ing] of the worst practices of tyranny" (Parrish 1982, 126).

The lawyer and associate justice who defended the claims of socialists and radical aliens became the chief justice who authored some of the most important civil liberties opinions prior to the era of Earl Warren, notably *Stromberg* and *Near* (1931) and *DeJonge v. Oregon* (1937). Cautious with respect to expanding the role of the federal executive and legislature on issues of economic policy, Hughes showed little hesitation when it came to enlarging the role of the federal judicial branch as the guardian of First Amendment rights.

Shortly before leaving the Court in 1916, Hughes joined Holmes in dissenting against the majority's refusal to grant relief to Leo Frank, who had been convicted of murder and sentenced to death by the Georgia court in an atmosphere of anti-Semitism and mob domination at his trial. While the majority endorsed the decision of the state supreme court that Frank had failed to demonstrate undue prejudice reaching the threshold of a denial of due process, Hughes and Holmes wanted federal courts to hear all the evidence in Frank's case without regard to the opinion of the Georgia Supreme Court and "to declare lynch law as little valid when practiced by a regularly drawn jury as when administered by one elected by a mob intent on death" (*Frank v. Mangum* [1915]). In his *Frank* dissent, Hughes helped to plant the seeds for that expanded federal scrutiny of state criminal proceedings that his Court carried forward two decades later in cases such as *Powell v. Alabama* (1932); *Mooney v. Holohan* (1935), which broadened the reach of habeas corpus to attack constitutionally defective state trials; and *Brown v. Mississippi* (1936), which restricted the use of coerced confessions. As chief justice, Hughes also encouraged the expansion of the Court's *in forma pauperis* docket, which allowed indigent prisoners to raise challenges to their state criminal convictions.

Owen Roberts

No member of the Hughes Court and perhaps no Supreme Court justice in history left a more ambiguous legacy and stirred more controversy during and after his tenure than Owen Roberts, the Pennsylvanian confirmed by the Senate in 1931 following Hoover's abortive attempt to put Judge John J. Parker of North Carolina on the bench. Faulted by many critics for lacking a consistent judicial philosophy, Roberts wrote one of the decade's most progressive opinions with respect to the scope of government's authority to regulate private markets (*Nebbia v. New York* [1934]) as well as two of the era's most restrictive opinions (*Railroad Retirement Board v. Alton Railroad Co.* [1935] and *United States v. Butler* [1936]). And his approach to issues of civil liberties and civil rights often baffled observers when he displayed similar contradictions.

Of all his votes during the decade, none raised more questions than those in the two minimum wage cases handed down in 1936 and 1937, decisions that for many years remained central to historical interpretations of the Hughes Court, the Great Depression, and the New Deal. In the first, *Morehead v. New York ex rel. Tipaldo*, decided on June 1, 1936, Roberts joined Butler, Sutherland, Van Devanter, and McReynolds in striking down the state statute mandating minimum wages for women and children as a violation of liberty of contract protected by the Due Process Clause of the Fourteenth Amendment. That decision drew rebukes from all of the nation's leading newspapers and even the Republican Party's platform in 1936.

Owen Roberts

Nine months later, five months after Roosevelt's crushing reelection victory and one month following his introduction of the plan to "reorganize" the federal judiciary, Roberts voted with Hughes, Cardozo, Stone, and Brandeis to sustain Washington's similar minimum wage statute for women (*West Coast Hotel v. Parrish* [1937]). Small wonder that for many years thereafter these two votes earned the epithet of "a switch in time that saved nine," based on the assumption that Roberts had bowed to the political storm gathering around the Court and that his about-face had helped to kill FDR's court-packing legislation. Frankfurter at the time denounced Roberts's "somersault" as one "incapable of being attributed to a single factor relevant to the professed judicial process. . . . It is very, very sad business" (Parrish 1982, 271).

Before long, however, it became clear that Roberts had voted to uphold the Washington law several months prior to FDR's announcement of his court-packing plan, and that only Justice Stone's illness had delayed its announcement until March 1937. Then, several years before his death in 1955, Roberts attempted a fuller explanation of his apparent "switch" in a memorandum prepared for Justice Frankfurter, who had become one of his closest friends and staunchest defenders in the years after 1937. According to Roberts, he had been prepared to overrule the precedent of *Adkins v. Children's Hospital* (1923) and sustain the New York law, but lawyers for the state had not requested a reconsideration of *Adkins* in their briefs or arguments. Furthermore, the chief justice, not eager to overrule *Adkins*, endorsed New York's strategy and expressed his willingness to distinguish the new statute from the one invalidated in *Adkins*. Under these circumstances, Roberts believed he had no choice but to join the Four Horsemen in affirming the 1923 decision. When Washington's attorneys asked the Court to reconsider *Adkins*, however, Roberts joined Hughes, Cardozo, Stone, and Brandeis in overturning that landmark of freedom of contract.

Roberts's retrospective attempt to justify his votes in the two cases left many unpersuaded. They note, for example, that New York's lawyers requested a rehearing and urged a reconsideration of *Adkins*. Furthermore, attorneys for Washington state, following much the same strategy as New York, also sought to distinguish their law from the earlier statute and did not ask the Court to revisit *Adkins*. If Roberts had been prepared to overrule *Adkins* in *Morehead*, why did he not state that position in a concurring opinion instead of joining Butler's rousing reaffirmation of freedom of contract, a principle he had all but repudiated in *Nebbia* two years earlier? And if procedural scruples stayed his hand in *Morehead*, why did they not present a similar obstacle in later cases such as *Erie Railroad Co. v. Tompkins?*

Roberts's opinion in *Nebbia* appeared to sanction expanded state regulation of markets and prices, a point noted by Justice Stone in his dissent in *Morehead*, but the Pennsylvanian had displayed in other cases a strong distaste for more direct forms of income redistribution by the government, notably in *Railroad Retirement Board v. Alton* (1935) and *United States v. Butler* (1936). Minimum wage legislation, the paradigmatic example of state-mandated income redistribution, may for that reason have offended Roberts's conception of due process far more than price controls. If one rejects both the court-packing theory as well as Roberts's own procedural explanation for his "switch," there still remain several other possibilities: the justice felt the pressure of Roosevelt's reelection; he changed his mind about minimum wage legislation; he remained confused and conflicted about the issue; or some combination of these. The truth may never be known, but the minimum wage decisions cast a perpetual cloud over Roberts's career. At the time of his resignation from the Court in 1945, two Roosevelt-appointed justices, Hugo Black and William O. Douglas, refused to endorse a tribute to him written by Chief Justice Stone that included the statement: "You have made fidelity to principle your guide to decision" (Mason 1956b, 765).

While Roberts's votes in the two minimum wage cases have drawn the most attention, a like puzzle surrounds the position of the chief justice. He may have hesitated to confront Sutherland and overrule *Adkins* in *Morehead*, although if Roberts is to be believed, there were then four votes, including his own, prepared to do so. Five months later in *West Coast Hotel*, Hughes did not hesitate to inter *Adkins*, although a similar distinction might have been made between the two statutes. What changed the chief justice's mind? Never wedded to the abstraction of freedom of contract, Hughes may have misunderstood Roberts's willingness to overrule *Adkins* in July 1936, but finally grasped the situation in December. This is a plausible explanation, although one that does not shed great credit on Hughes's leadership skills because public reaction to the two decisions inflicted serious damage upon the Court's reputation.

Whether motivated by political pressures outside the Court or intellectual currents flowing from within the institution, Roberts also displayed a capacity for altering his views on the scope of national powers over the economy. He rejected Congress's effort to manage agricultural surpluses through taxation and direct subsidy payments to farmers (*United States v. Butler* [1936]), but three years later he wrote for the majority, over the dissent of Butler and McReynolds, to sustain the second New Deal agricultural program that limited the amount of any farm commodity shipped in interstate commerce (*Mulford v. Smith* [1939]). The doctrinal categories were, of course, different, but realist critics noted that both laws clearly limited agricultural production, an economic activity Roberts had placed firmly beyond national authority in *Butler* because of the Tenth Amendment. And finally, a year after Hughes retired, Roberts joined Justice Jackson's far-reaching opinion in *Wickard v. Filburn* (1942) that upheld penalties levied under the 1938 agricultural adjustment law against a single farmer who had produced for his own consumption more wheat that he had been allotted by the secretary of agriculture.

Until the spring of 1937, Roberts displayed a similar addiction to abstract constitutional labels in other Commerce Clause cases, notably the "direct/indirect" distinction used by Hughes in *Schechter* (1935) or the "commerce/production" line drawn by Sutherland in *Carter Coal* (1936). He endorsed both opinions that significantly curbed the New Deal. On the other hand, he joined Hughes in upholding the National Labor Relations Act in 1937, in which the chief justice's opinion rested upon a wholly different line of precedents and dismissed the relevance of *Schechter* and *Carter Coal* altogether. Some of Roberts's defenders have argued that he displayed here, as in the minimum wage cases, a rigid devotion to procedural fairness and fine doctrinal distinctions. His critics at the time and later suggested that he may have been motivated as well by political forces swirling around the Court, especially Roosevelt's reelection mandate in 1936 and the burst of sit-down strikes that paralyzed the nation's automobile industry.

Roberts's penchant for often framing constitutional issues in hard conceptual categories, an approach shared by other justices and attacked throughout the decade by legal realists, exposed him to criticism on other fronts apart from those focusing on economic regulation. In *Nixon v. Herndon* (1927) and again in *Nixon v. Condon* (1932), the Court struck down Texas statutes that sanctioned the exclusion of African Americans from the primary elections conducted by the Democratic Party. But when the Texas Democratic Party, responding to the second decision, adopted a resolution limiting its membership to "white citizens," the Court, speaking through Roberts, rejected the claim of a constitutional violation because Texas had not made the rule or selected the entity that imposed it (*Grovey v. Townsend* [1935]). Roberts and the Court treated the "white citizens" rule as a form of private choice beyond the reach of the Fourteenth and Fifteenth Amendments, which barred only state-sanctioned forms of discrimination.

At least one contemporary commentator ridiculed Roberts's reasoning in *Grovey* as "singularly unconvincing" and "a rarefied atmosphere of dialectic far removed from political reality." Roberts had detached the primary from the election, made the Texas Democratic Party in charge "an exclusive club—and, off to such an ipse dixitical start, the conclusion comes easy. It is hard to magnify the tragedy of the decision" ("Black Justice," *The Nation* 1935, 140, 497) Although he displayed sensitivity to racial discrimination in other contexts during the Hughes years, voting with the majority in *Powell v. Alabama* (1932), *Norris v. Alabama* (1935), and *Missouri ex rel. Gaines v. Canada* (1938), Roberts did not deviate from the views he expressed in *Grovey* and dissented when the Stone Court finally overturned that precedent and struck down the all-white primary in 1944 (*Smith v. Allwright*).

Very little ambiguity characterized Roberts's position in civil liberties cases. In addition to joining Hughes in *Stromberg* and *Near*, he wrote for the Court to sustain the free speech claim in *Herndon v. Lowry* (1937) and vindicated the right to public assembly in *Hague v. Congress of Industrial Organizations* (1939). He likewise authored the Court's opinion in *Cantwell v. Connecticut* (1940) in which the justices for the first time incorporated the First Amendment guarantee of the free exercise of religion into the Fourteenth Amendment's Due Process Clause when they reversed the conviction of a Jehovah's Witness who had solicited door-to-door without obtaining a permit from the state secretary of public welfare. The states may not punish a sidewalk preacher for breach of the peace under a general ordinance, Roberts wrote, or one that leaves too much discretion to officials who apply it.

Apart from his controversial role in the minimum wage cases, Roberts is most often recalled as the author of *Betts v. Brady,* the 1942 right-to-counsel decision in which the majority held that due process required the appointment of legal counsel to aid criminal defendants only in "special circumstances" involving capital offenses and when the defendants themselves suffered from illiteracy and poverty. The decision effectively excluded many poor, noncapital defendants from legal assistance in state courts and was not overruled until *Gideon v. Wainwright* (1963). But while Roberts eschewed fixing a broad constitutional rule in cases such as *Betts* or *Palko v. Connecticut* (1937), he often displayed considerable sensitivity to procedural violations in specific criminal cases. He dissented vigorously in *Snyder v. Massachusetts* (1934), for example, where Cardozo and the majority rejected the defendant's claim that excluding him from the crime scene during the jury's visit to the site with the prosecution violated due process.

Justice Roberts played a significant role in another constitutional controversy whose origins are to be found in the final year of the Hughes era. Soon after the Japanese bombed Pearl Harbor on December 7, 1941, Roosevelt persuaded the justice to become chairman of the official government inquiry into why the attack had been so successful. The commission found that there had been "dereliction of duty" by Major General Walter C. Short, the army commander in Hawaii and by Admiral Husband E. Kimmel, navy commander, but did not recommend a court martial for either man.

The Roberts report also alleged, without any documentation, that Hawaii-based espionage agents, including Japanese American citizens, had assisted in the successful raid. Other investigators, including the FBI, rejected such espionage claims as without foundation, but Roberts's report helped to fuel the anti-Japanese sentiments in the U.S. military and among West Coast politicians that led to the eventual exclusion and detention of 120,000 Japanese American citizens. However, when the Supreme Court upheld the exclusion regulations and, by implication, the detention program, in *Korematsu v. United States* (1944), Roberts joined the dissenters, a statement of regret, perhaps, for the unfounded accusations he had made three years before.

Benjamin Cardozo

Aside from Holmes, no jurist came to the Supreme Court in the twentieth century with a larger reputation for legal acumen than Benjamin Cardozo, who had sat upon the New York Court of Appeals for eighteen years, six as its chief judge. From that

Benjamin Cardozo

position he had authored opinions that transformed the common law and published several collections of lectures that made him one of the most widely read jurists in American history. Responding to a personal letter of praise from Cardozo, Holmes paid a similar tribute to the New Yorker: "The only ground that warrants a man for thinking that he is not living in a fool's paradise, if he ventures such a hope, is the voice of a few masters, among whom you hold a conspicuous place" (Rauh 1979, 10).

Cardozo's appointment added a strong voice to the progressive wing of the Court, but he remained unhappy in Washington during his brief six-year tenure there. Compared to the close, congenial relations among the state judges in Albany, he found the climate of the Supreme Court cold and remote, with each justice laboring largely in isolation. "There is nothing like the genuine debate—the painstaking and willing interchange of views—that gave my old court whatever strength it had," he complained as early as 1932. "I don't believe that I'll ever have the influence here that I had at Albany" (Kaufman 1998, 480). He was right. Either out of jealousy or court politics, Hughes assigned Cardozo, the most junior justice, very few landmark opinions. Yet behind the scenes, Cardozo's memoranda and unpublished opinions made major contributions to constitutional development and the opinions he did write, often in dissent, forecast the doctrinal structure of the advancing welfare state dominated by the executive branch and its administrative arm.

In the Minnesota mortgage moratorium case, *Home Building & Loan Ass'n v. Blaisdell* (1934), for example, Hughes's initial opinion for the majority rested on the distinction between a law that impaired a mortgagee's substantive rights and one that merely altered the remedy. Cardozo attempted to push the chief justice toward a more affirmative defense of the state's law in a proposed concurring opinion whose core emphasized the requirement that courts interpret constitutional provisions such as the Contracts Clause in light of changing social and economic circumstances "beyond the experience or the thought of a century ago." The gospel of laissez-faire, Cardozo added, "may be inadequate in the great society that we live in to point the way to salvation, at least for economic life." A private contract between two individuals should not be allowed to trump the authority of the state to maintain the entire structure of economic life "on which the good of all depends" (Kaufman 1998, 501).

Cardozo admitted that his approach to the Contracts Clause might be inconsistent with "things that men said in 1787 when expounding . . . the newly written constitution," but perhaps not inconsistent with what the Founding Fathers would believe in 1934 if called upon to interpret "in light of our whole experience the constitution that they framed for the needs of an expanding future" (Kaufman 1998, 502). No member of the Hughes Court wrote a more radical statement of constitutional interpretation rejecting the notion that jurists should simply apply the so-called original intention of the document's framers. Cardozo's declaration can be contrasted with Justice Roberts's naive statement in *Butler* that all the justices did when determining the validity of any law was to place "the Constitution next to the statute which is challenged and to decide whether the latter squares with the former." Roberts, unlike Cardozo, assumed that constitutional provisions had unambiguous meanings and that both history and experience remained irrelevant factors in interpretation. Cardozo never published his concurring opinion in *Blaisdell,* but his draft encouraged Hughes to make the observation that while a national emergency did not enhance constitutional powers, such an emergency might be the occasion for the exercise of such powers. And Hughes also incorporated Cardozo's belief that a promised exchange between private parties could not frustrate efforts to protect the general welfare, an approach Hughes soon applied in the *Gold Clause Cases* as well.

Cardozo also forced a major revision of the Court's initial approach to its important First Amendment decision, *Grosjean v. American Press Co.* (1936), which arose in a challenge to Louisiana's tax on the advertising receipts of newspapers with a circulation of over 20,000 copies per week. As lawyers for the newspapers, the lower court and Justice Sutherland viewed the matter, Louisiana's legislature had violated the Equal Protection Clause of the Fourteenth Amendment because it made the taxation turn on the size of circulation. Fearful that this use of the Equal Protection Clause could be invoked against other forms of state taxation and regulation, Cardozo's proposed concurrence spurned Sutherland's argument and rested the law's unconstitutionality squarely on the First Amendment. Sutherland rewrote his majority opinion based on Cardozo's First Amendment analysis and *Grosjean* thus became another civil liberties landmark for the Hughes Court.

In his general posture of judicial deference to the political branches and his skepticism about rigid conceptual categories of constitutional analysis, Cardozo shared much of the same mental universe as Justice Stone, perhaps his closest social and intellectual colleague on the Court. Although an admirer of Brandeis, he often found the latter's zeal for particular causes, whether Zionism or attacks on "the curse of bigness" to be either personally distasteful or beyond the bounds of judicial propriety. Among all of the justices, Cardozo appeared the most sympathetic to the general goals of the New Deal, although he, too, objected at times to its slapdash approach to constitutional questions. Unlike many of his colleagues, he welcomed the growing reliance of government upon administrative agencies, given broad rulemaking authority by the legislature. And his pragmatic, flexible approach to issues arising under the commerce power, usually stated in dissent, laid the foundation for the more expansive doctrines that emerged in *Jones & Laughlin* (1937), *Darby Lumber* (1941), and *Wickard v. Filburn* (1942).

One of Cardozo's clearest statement of judicial restraint came in *Mayflower Farms v. Ten Eyck* (1936), one in a series of New York's milk control laws that gave producers without well-established trade names a slight price advantage. Despite the ruling in *Nebbia* (1934) granting state legislatures broad authority to impose price regulations upon the industry, the majority struck down this provision as a violation of equal protection. Writing for himself, Brandeis, and Stone, Cardozo noted that "hardships, great or little, were inevitable, whether the field of the differential was narrowed or enlarged." But more important, he added, "the legislature, and not the court, has been charged with the duty of determining their comparative extent."

He first displayed similar deference to administrative rule making in *Norwegian Nitrogen Products Co. v. United States* (1933), in which the plaintiff challenged hearing procedures adopted by the United States Tariff Commission, the advisory body to the president that had been given broad authority by Congress to raise or lower duties in order to equalize differences in the cost of production in the United States and elsewhere. Writing for seven other justices, Cardozo rejected the argument that the commission was bound to follow formal judicial standards that required, for example, cross-examination of its investigators by complaining parties. These administrative officers had been "clothed by statute with discretionary powers," he wrote, and "their resolve is not subject to impeachment for unwisdom without more. It must be shown to be arbitrary."

Alone among the nine justices, Cardozo voted to sustain the discretion given to the president under Section 9(c) of the National Recovery Act, the so-called hot oil provisions. He rejected Hughes's analysis that Congress had left the president at large, with unbounded and unchecked authority to ban oil produced in violation of state-imposed quotas. "Discretion is not unconfined and vagrant," he pleaded. "It is canalized within banks that keep it from overflowing." The concept of the separation of powers between president and Congress, he concluded, "is not a doctrinaire concept to be made use of with pedantic rigor. There must be sensible approximation, there must be elasticity of adjustment, in response to the practical necessities of government" (*Panama Refining Co. v. Ryan* [1935]). And when Sutherland and the majority compared the behavior of the Securities and Exchange Commission to the techniques employed by the Court of Star Chamber, Cardozo ridiculed his colleague's verbal excesses (*Jones v. Securities and Exchange Commission* [1936]).

Even Cardozo declined to endorse the scope of delegation granted to the president by the National Recovery Act or to apply the wage and hours provisions of the NRA's Live Poultry Code to the Schechter brothers' New York slaughterhouse. But he felt obliged to add a caveat to Hughes's rather broad denunciation of the government's attempt to invoke the commerce power as grounds for the prosecution. Cardozo agreed that the Court had to draw some boundary between the scope of Congress's power and those myriad local economic activities that might conceivably influence interstate commerce, but he was not enamored by the "direct/indirect" test invoked by Hughes in *Schechter* or by the "commerce/production" formula often deployed to veto federal authority. "There is a view of causation that would obliterate the distinction between what is national and what is local in the activities of commerce," he wrote, but "the law is not indifferent to considerations of degree." For him, the critical issue became whether the impact of the economic activity was predominately local or not (*Schechter Poultry Corp. v. United States* [1935]).

When the majority invoked the "commerce/production" distinction to strike down the price regulations of the Guffey Coal Act, Cardozo dissented against such reliance upon abstract categories and reminded his colleagues again that "the law is not indifferent to considerations of degree." The Kentucky and West Virginia coal producers sold only 25 percent of their production intrastate, but he noted substantial competition between intrastate coal sales and interstate coal sales in both states, and there was no evidence that interstate sales would not be prejudicially affected if the local prices were maintained at a lower level. In short, the bituminous coal industry could be easily distinguished from the small live poultry industry. Here were extensive local productive activities that had a substantial impact upon interstate commerce and Congress had provided more than adequate documentation to that effect when adopting the system of regulation (*Carter v. Carter Coal Co.* [1936]).

Cardozo rejoiced when Hughes and Roberts provided the necessary votes to sustain the National Labor Relations Act in 1937, but to his law clerk he expressed amazement and some regret that Hughes's opinion, relying upon a different line of precedents, failed to explain how the outcome in *Jones & Laughlin* could be justified without confronting the core of Sutherland's opinion in *Carter Coal.* Stone expressed somewhat similar views to Frankfurter. "In order to reach the result which was reached in these cases," he said, "it was necessary for six members of the Court either to be overruled or to take back some things they subscribed to in the Guffey Coal Act case" (Parrish 1982, 271).

In the same year that five of the justices followed Hughes's reasoning to sustain the National Labor Relations Act, Cardozo wrote an opinion in *Holyoke Water Power Co. v. American Writing Paper Co.* (1937) that pointed in the direction of a fresh approach to the reach of federal authority under its Article I powers. The case, one of many arising under Congress's abrogation of the gold clause in private and public contracts, involved a lease providing for payment of rent in a quantity of gold equal to $1,500 in gold coin of the United States of 1894 or the equivalent in United States currency. When the lessee went bankrupt, the lessor sued to recover the commodity value of the gold. The lessor also argued that this covenant was so exceptional that to enforce it would not jeopardize the new national monetary policy.

Cardozo dismissed both claims, but especially the second one. "A particular covenant, if viewed in isolation," he wrote, "may have a slight, perhaps trivial, influence upon the effectiveness and symmetry of a new monetary policy. The aggregate of many covenants, each contributing its mite, may bring the system to destruction. . . . Rivulets in combination make up a stream of tendency that may attain engulfing power" (*Holyoke Water Power Co.* [1937]). As he had begun to argue in *Carter*

Coal, Cardozo stressed that a series of seemingly discrete local events might have a profound, cumulative impact upon the nation's welfare. Here, although articulated in a case removed from the Commerce Clause, lay the seeds of doctrinal growth that would reach fruition years after Cardozo's death when Stone wrote *Darby Lumber* (1941) and Jackson penned *Wickard v. Filburn* (1942).

Although his opinion in *Butler* had cabined Congress's spending power with the Tenth Amendment, Justice Roberts had at least uncoupled the national purse from the specific enumerated provisions of Article I. Overturning one New Deal program, *Butler* ultimately opened the door wide to even greater ones, but it required Cardozo's two landmark opinions in the Social Security Act cases to realize its full potential. After Cardozo finished his analysis to sustain the unemployment compensation features of the law in *Steward Machine Co. v. Davis* (1937), as well as the old-age benefits provisions in *Helvering v. Davis* (1937), the Tenth Amendment no longer served as an impediment to the federal spending power. These two opinions anchored the growth in federal grant-in-aid programs to the states, programs that soon became the single most potent force of national policy making and governmental centralization.

Cardozo's posture of judicial deference extended to issues touching criminal justice and civil liberties. Except in First Amendment cases that raised questions of freedom of speech or press such as *Grosjean* (1936), *Herndon v. Lowry* (1937), and *DeJonge* (1937), state legislatures and courts enjoyed considerable latitude from Cardozo when administering punishment and otherwise restricting personal autonomy. In *Hamilton v. Regents* (1934), for example, he rejected the claim of conscientious objector students who argued that the university's compulsory military science courses infringed upon the free exercise of their religion. Cardozo refused to endorse Justice Butler's majority opinion, which included a rousing endorsement of every citizen's duty to bear arms. Instead, Cardozo drew a distinction between military instruction and compulsory military service. Mere course work in military science, he argued, constituted a modest burden upon the student's religious scruples. But he concluded his concurring opinion in *Hamilton* with a reprise of his beliefs stated in cases such as *Blaisdell* that private interests could not paralyze important public policies: "[t]he right of private judgment has never yet been so exalted above the powers and the compulsion of the agencies of government. One who is a martyr to a principle—which may turn out in the end to be a delusion or an error—does not prove by his martyrdom that he has kept within the law." Stone and Brandeis joined this paean to state authority.

Neither in New York nor Washington did Cardozo display much sympathy for criminal defendants, especially in a case such as *Snyder v. Massachusetts*, in which the evidence of guilt seemed conclusive and the alleged errors by the state appeared minor in comparison. He was not easily moved by defendants who claimed they were the victims of an unreasonable searches and seizures or self-incrimination. And in his most famous criminal justice opinion, endorsed by all of the justices except Butler, he turned away Frank Palka's attack upon a Connecticut law that allowed the state to allege judicial errors in its appeal of the jury's verdict convicting him of second-degree murder, then try Palka a second time, convict him of first-degree murder, and sentence him to death (*Palko v. Connecticut* [1937]).

Palka and his attorney asked the Supreme Court to make a substantial doctrinal leap by holding that his second conviction constituted double jeopardy, barred by the Due Process Clause of the Fourteenth Amendment in the same way that the Fifth Amendment prohibited the federal government from twice trying a defendant for the same crime. By 1937 the Supreme Court had ruled that certain provisions of the Bill of Rights, notably freedom of speech, press, and assembly, limited the states as well as the federal government by virtue of the Fourteenth Amendment. The justices had also applied the just compensation provision of the Fifth Amendment to eminent domain proceedings in the states and required the states to provide legal assistance to indigent defendants in capital cases such as those in the Scottsboro proceedings. But the Supreme Court had also rejected on three occasions the claim that other specific guarantees of the Bill of Rights relating to criminal procedures (grand jury indictments, twelve-person juries, and self-incrimination) also applied to the states by virtue of the Fourteenth Amendment's command that "no person shall be deprived of life, liberty or property without due process of law."

Cardozo rested his opinion in *Palko* upon this inherited foundation of "selective incorporation" of the Bill of Rights. The only provisions of the Bill of Rights applicable to the states through the Fourteenth Amendment, he wrote, were those "of the very essence of a scheme of ordered liberty," such as freedom of speech or press. Outside this magic category lay other immunities and privileges "of value and importance," including indictment by grand jury, self-incrimination, and—in Palka's case—double jeopardy. But to abolish these, he concluded, would not violate "a principle of justice so rooted in the traditions and conscience of our people as to be ranked as fundamental." The Court's newest member, Justice Black, would soon protest against this doctrine of "selective incorporation" that immunized the states from much of the Bill of Rights, but Cardozo's selective approach continued to dominate the Court's Fourteenth Amendment criminal procedure jurisprudence through the Warren years.

Roosevelt's Justices

With Justice Van Devanter's retirement in 1937, Franklin Roosevelt began to fill vacancies on the Hughes Court with loyal New Dealers who for the remainder of the chief justice's tenure continued to ratify the constitutional victories gained by the administration and its allies in cases such as *West Coast Hotel*, *Jones & Laughlin*, and *Steward Machine Co.* Roosevelt's new justices through the summer of 1941—Hugo Black, Stanley Reed, Felix Frankfurter, William O. Douglas, and Frank Murphy—all left important judicial legacies and soon came to dominate the Supreme Court, but they generally made their lasting contributions in the years and decades after Hughes stepped down. Only a slight hint of the conflicts that came to shape the Court after 1941 could be glimpsed in the months before the United States entered the Second World War.

With the exception of Justice McReynolds, who continued to hold aloft the banner of extreme laissez-faire as late as the spring of 1940, the Hughes Court swiftly abandoned the field of economic policy making to the political branches of the states and the federal government, a posture of judicial restraint with respect to "ordinary commercial transactions" advocated by Justice Stone and confirmed by the unanimous vote to sustain the Fair Labor Standards Act in *Darby Lumber* (1941) during Hughes's final term. But fresh issues touching civil liberties and civil rights, beginning with the first flag salute case, *Minersville School District v. Gobitis* (1940), began to expose important cleavages among the justices who soon constituted Mr. Roosevelt's Court presided over by Chief Justice Stone.

Hugo Black

Hugo Black, FDR's first confirmed justice, survived the brief tempest raised by revelations concerning his prior membership in the Alabama Ku Klux Klan and soon indicated his disagreement with several landmarks of constitutional interpretation. A champion of the workingman and organized labor and one of the leading critics of big business during his tenure in the United States Senate, Black urged the exclusion of corporations from the protections afforded to "persons" by the Fourteenth Amendment, a doctrine dating back to the late nineteenth century.

A bitter critic of substantive due process, which he held responsible for the judicial veto of social legislation, Black also began to rethink his endorsement of Cardozo's opinion in *Palko* with its reaffirmation of "selective incorporation" of the Bill of Rights into the Fourteenth Amendment. Cardozo's approach, he believed, resembled substantive due process in that it left judges untethered and allowed them to impose their own subjective values upon the constitutional text. He soon advocated "total incorporation" of the first eight amendments in the Bill of Rights as the final, definitive meaning of due process in the Fourteenth Amendment, a radical position in the 1940s that Black advocated for essentially the conservative ends of containing judicial power.

Initially tarred with the brush of bigotry because of his Klan membership, Black soon shouldered much of the burden of the Court's growing attack upon the South's racist criminal justice system. In 1940 he wrote to reverse the convictions of four

Hugo Black

African Americans sentenced to death for murder in Florida whose confessions had been coerced and secured "under circumstances filled with terror" in violation of the Fourteenth Amendment (*Chambers v. Florida*). That term also he spoke for a unanimous Court in overturning the death sentence for rape of a black defendant in Texas, whose indictment had been secured by a grand jury from which African Americans had been systematically excluded (*Smith v. Texas* [1940]).

Stanley Foreman Reed

Stanley Foreman Reed, the second of Roosevelt's nominees, played a far less dramatic, but nonetheless influential, role on the Court by virtue of his incremental approach to judging that made him often the "swing" vote in closely divided cases. If the Kentuckian had any guiding legal philosophy it was one colored by judicial restraint, a product of his negative experience defending New Deal statutes before the Hughes Court as a special assistant to the attorney general and later solicitor general of the United States.

In the first post he successfully defended the administration's decision to abandon the gold standard, but in the second he managed to win the TVA case (*Ashwander v. Tennessee Valley Authority* [1936]), while losing both *Schechter* and *Butler*. As solicitor general he could also lay claim to victory in the landmark *Jones & Laughlin* case, although lawyers for the National Labor Relations Board prepared the briefs and led the oral argument. A moderate Democrat, but a loyal New Dealer, Reed earned the president's affection by his stalwart defense of the doomed "court-packing" bill before a hostile Senate Judiciary Committee. With ten years of government experience stretching back to the Hoover era, he became a logical if not inspired choice to take the seat vacated by George Sutherland. Over the course of his tenure, which lasted until 1957, Reed proved to be the most conservative of FDR's eight appointees, especially with respect to issues of civil liberties, civil rights, and criminal justice.

Reed's parsimonious approach to the judicial role emerged in 1938 when he authored a concurring opinion in *Erie v. Tompkins*. For the majority, Justice Brandeis's tour-de-force rejected the idea of a federal general common law and declared unconstitutional a Supreme Court decision dating from 1842. While he agreed that Justice Story had misconstrued Section 34 of the original Judiciary Act and that his opinion in *Swift v. Tyson* (1842) ought to be disapproved, Reed balked at Brandeis's resort to constitutional interpretation and his assertion that due to *Swift* the federal courts had pursued an unconstitutional course of conduct for nearly 150 years. He also rejected Brandeis's suggestion that Congress might be without power to declare what rules of substantive law should govern the federal courts.

On questions touching the scope of federal power to regulate commerce among the states or to protect the rights of working men and women to organize unions under the protective umbrella of the National Labor Relations Board, Reed repre-

Stanley Foreman Reed

sented a significant shift in favor of the New Deal's approach to economic policy. He became a dependable vote to sustain NLRB findings of unfair labor practices and to affirm rulings of the Wage and Hours Division of the Labor Department with respect to the coverage of the federal minimum wage. In *United States v. Appalachian Electric Power Co.* (1940), he wrote for the majority to uphold the exclusive licensing authority of the Federal Power Commission over dam projects on the New River, a waterway that both the utility and West Virginia claimed to be nonnavigable and therefore beyond federal jurisdiction.

In the major civil liberties decisions of the late Hughes era, Reed could usually be found voting with the majority. He endorsed Roberts's opinion in *Cantwell v. Connecticut* (1940) overturning the petitioner's conviction on free exercise grounds, but also voted with Frankfurter a month later to sustain the conviction of religious dissenters in the first flag salute case, *Minersville School District v. Gobitis* (1940). In 1945, over a powerful dissent by Justice Black, he wrote the Court's opinion upholding the decision of the Illinois bar association to deny admission to a conscientious objector (*In re Summers* [1945]). As the Court began to move in a more liberal direction under the influence of Black, Douglas, Murphy, and Jackson, however, Reed usually found himself in dissent against that trend. He dissented in *Pollock v. Williams* (1944), for example, in which the Jackson-led majority dealt another blow to the Southern regime of debt peonage.

Felix Frankfurter

No Roosevelt nominee came to the Hughes Court after 1937 with a more passionate devotion to judicial restraint than Felix Frankfurter, a protege of Justice Brandeis and a confidant of Justice Holmes to whom he had dispatched many law clerks from his post as a professor at the Harvard Law School. While Hugo Black, for example, sought to restrict judicial activism and subjectivity by an absolutist interpretation of the Bill of Rights and "total incorporation" of their provisions into the Due Process Clause of the Fourteenth Amendment, Frankfurter had once urged the complete abolition of that clause so often invoked by judges to invalidate social legislation. He had argued the losing side in *Adkins v. Children's Hospital* (1923) and during the Taft and Hughes years kept up a steady fusillade of criticism whenever the justices wielded the judicial ax. Caught between his devotion to both Brandeis and Roosevelt, he finally cast his vote with the president, never spoke out publicly against the court-packing plan, and offered FDR advice behind the scenes. The Court, he believed, bore greater responsibility for the crisis of 1935–1937 than the administration, and when the justices finally endorsed New Deal reforms such as the Wagner Act and Social Security, Frankfurter accused them of naked political opportunism.

Once on the bench Frankfurter argued that the only secure foundation of judicial restraint resided in each justice's capacity to observe strict procedural limitations

Felix Frankfurter

and to put aside all personal beliefs in the interests of a self-imposed agnosticism that bowed to the choices made by legislatures. He spurned Black's positivism as an illusion of judicial restraint and viewed the latter's theory of "total incorporation" as dangerously activist because it would impose a single standard of criminal justice upon the states. For one who had once denounced the Due Process Clause, he became its chief defender against Black's attempt to restrict it with the Bill of Rights. Like Black, however, he had his own set of absolutes that often emerged in cases involving the Fourth Amendment. Of all Roosevelt's appointees, he remained the most committed to a federalism that stressed the important role of the states, a legacy of Brandeis's influence.

Combining judicial restraint with a strong belief in the utility of administrative agencies and expertise, Frankfurter easily endorsed the expanding regulatory apparatus of the new welfare state fashioned by federal and state governments after 1937. To this extent, he endorsed Justice Stone's "rational basis test" for weighing the constitutionality of economic policies as set down in *Carolene Products* (1938). But he extended his vision of judicial restraint to issues of civil liberties and criminal procedure and rejected Stone's emphasis in *Carolene Products* upon "preferred freedoms" that should enjoy unusual judicial scrutiny and protection. The Constitution, he argued, did not contain such a hierarchy of values and to endow judges with their creation risked a new regime of discredited judicial activism.

Frankfurter's academic learning and prestige gave him a commanding position on the Hughes Court next to the chief justice and Stone until June 3, 1940. On that day, his majority opinion came down in the first flag salute case, *Minersville School District v. Gobitis*, a rigid example of judicial restraint influenced by Cardozo's earlier opinion in *Hamilton v. Regents* (1934), which had rejected the religious claims of conscientious objectors to compulsory military science instruction. Now, against similar First Amendment objections raised by Jehovah's Witnesses, Frankfurter sustained a school board's decision to impose a mandatory flag salute. Only Stone, faithful to his views in *Carolene Products*, dissented.

The outcry from civil libertarians over *Gobitis*, including criticism from many of Frankfurter's own proteges, stunned its author. And numerous episodes of physical assault against dissenting Witnesses, including efforts to coerce them into kissing the American flag, quickly followed in the summer of 1940. When Frankfurter returned to the Court in the fall, he encountered Justice Douglas, who informed him that he and Justice Black had concluded that their support of his *Gobitis* opinion had been a terrible mistake, a position they announced publicly in *Jones v. Opelika* (1942). Frankfurter's brief moment of Court leadership had passed.

William Orville Douglas

A few months short of his forty-first birthday when he took Brandeis's seat in 1939, William Orville Douglas became the second youngest person to sit on the Supreme

William Orville Douglas

Court. A product of the legal realist movement at Columbia University and Yale Law School, where he had both been educated and taught following a short career with a major Wall Street firm, Douglas came to the New Deal in 1934 as one of the first members of the new Securities and Exchange Commission and succeeded Joseph P. Kennedy and James Landis as its chairman in 1936. As head of the SEC, Douglas preached the virtues of regulated capitalism and business-government cooperation while promoting modest reforms on the New York Stock Exchange and overseeing the initial reorganizations of major public utilities mandated by the Public Utilities Holding Company Act.

Douglas's New Deal credentials, like those of Black, Reed, and Frankfurter, were genuine. Federal and state efforts to maintain and expand the welfare state and its regulatory machinery enjoyed his firm support. In one of his first opinions for the Court, he wrote to sustain the constitutionality of the New Deal's second coal conservation act, the successor to the statute invalidated in *Carter Coal.* The new law imposed a stiff federal tax on coal sold in interstate commerce, but exempted from payment those producers who agreed to enforce industrywide price and production regulations (*Sunshine Anthracite Coal Co. v. Adkins* [1940]). In addition, he became one of the Court's leading experts on corporate law and bankruptcy.

Douglas soon aligned himself with Black on most issues touching civil liberties, an alliance first cemented in the aftermath of the *Gobitis* decision and in other cases involving the Jehovah's Witnesses. A major critic of Frankfurter's philosophy—indeed their differences became quite vitriolic—Douglas also never adopted Black's strict positivism that would have stifled his flair for liberal judicial creativity. In 1942, for example, he wrote for the Court in *Skinner v. Oklahoma,* striking down a state law that provided involuntary sterilization for certain felons and announcing for the first time that individuals had certain "fundamental interests," such as procreation, with which the state could not interfere unless it asserted a compelling need. Two decades later, building on *Skinner,* he announced a new constitutional right of privacy in the landmark birth control case, *Griswold v. Connecticut* (1965).

Frank Murphy

Not many years after he replaced Pierce Butler in 1940, followers of Justice Frank Murphy and the Supreme Court began to describe his influence as "justice tempered by Murphy." A devout Catholic and the former New Deal governor of Michigan, Murphy had lost his bid for reelection when he refused to call out state troopers to break up the sit-down strikes. He had served briefly as attorney general of the United States and did not covet appointment to the bench out of the sincere belief that others were probably more qualified. For nine years, until his sudden death in 1949, however, he became the Court's most reliable liberal voice across a wide spectrum of issues, including social welfare, civil liberties, civil rights, and criminal justice. And his

Frank Murphy

death, coupled with the passing of Justice Wiley Rutledge in the same year, gave President Truman two appointments that changed the complexion of Roosevelt's Court and ushered in one of the most reactionary periods in the institution's history.

Often eschewing technical legal language in favor of broad declarations of humanitarianism, Murphy quickly moved out of Frankfurter's orbit into the camp of Black and Douglas, an alliance that Frankfurter soon labeled "the Axis" (Lash 1975, 197–198). He gave clear expression to his judicial philosophy in *Falbo v. United States* (1943), when he declared that "the law knows no finer hour than when it cuts through formal concepts and transitory emotions to protect unpopular citizens against discrimination and persecution." In his short tenure with Hughes, he wrote a landmark opinion on labor law and the First Amendment by holding peaceful picketing within the scope of the Bill of the Rights (*Thornhill v. Alabama* [1940]). Deeply patriotic, but rebuffed by Roosevelt when he sought the post of secretary of war, Murphy's military zeal did not warp his sense of justice. He prepared a dissent that became a critical concurrence in the first Japanese American case (*Hirabayashi v. United States* [1943]), denounced their exclusion from the West Coast as the "legalization of racism" (*Korematsu v. United States* [1944]), and protested the procedures used by the American military in the postwar trial of Japanese General Yamashita (*In re Yamashita* [1946]).

References and Further Reading

Arkes, Hadley. 1994. *The Return of George Sutherland: Restoring a Jurisprudence of Natural Rights.* Princeton, NJ: Princeton University Press.

Baker, Leonard. 1984. *Brandeis and Frankfurter: A Dual Biography.* New York: Harper & Row.

"Black Justice." 1935. *The Nation* 140 (April 17): 477.

Cushman, Barry. 1999. "Lost Fidelities." *William and Mary Law Review* 41 (December): 95.

Danelski, David J., and Joseph S. Tulchin, eds. 1973. *The Autobiographical Notes of Charles Evans Hughes.* Cambridge, MA: Harvard University Press.

Kaufman, Andrew. 1998. *Cardozo.* Cambridge, MA: Harvard University Press.

Lash, Joseph P., ed. 1975. *From the Diaries of Felix Frankfurter: With a Biographical Essay and Notes.* New York: Norton.

Mason, Alpheus T. 1956a. *Brandeis: A Free Man's Life.* New York: Viking.

———. 1956b. *Harlan Fiske Stone: Pillar of the Law.* New York: Viking.

———. 1979. *The Supreme Court from Taft to Burger.* Baton Rouge: Louisiana State University Press.

Novick, Sheldon. 1989. *Honorable Justice: The Life of Oliver Wendell Holmes.* Boston: Little, Brown.

Parrish, Michael E. *Felix Frankfurter and His Times: The Reform Years.* New York: Free Press, 1982.

Pusey, Merlo J. 1963. *Charles Evans Hughes.* 2 vols. New York: Columbia University Press.

Rauh, Joseph L., Jr. 1979. "A Personal View of Justice Benjamin N. Cardozo: Recollections of Four Cardozo Law Clerks." *Cardozo Law Review* 1: 10.

Strum, Philippa. 1984. *Louis D. Brandeis: Justice for the People.* Cambridge, MA: Harvard University Press.

Swindler, William F. 1970. *Court and Constitution in the 20th Century: The New Legality, 1932–1968.* Indianapolis and New York: Bobbs-Merrill.

Thayer, James B. 1893. "The Origin and Scope of the American Doctrine of Constitutional Law." *Harvard Law Review* 7: 129.

Urofsky, Melvin I., ed. 1994. *The Supreme Court Justices: A Biographical Dictionary.* New York: Garland.

Urofsky, Melvin I., and David W. Levy, eds. 1991. *"Half Brother, Half Son": The Letters of Louis D. Brandeis to Felix Frankfurter.* Norman: University of Oklahoma Press.

White, G. Edward. 1976. *The American Judicial Tradition: Profiles of Leading American Judges.* New York: Oxford University Press.

———. 1999. *Justice Oliver Wendell Holmes: Law and the Inner Self.* New York: Oxford University Press.

3

Major Decisions

One of the most influential constitutional scholars of our century, Edward S. Corwin, whose ideas about expanding the size of the Supreme Court found their way into President Roosevelt's ill-fated court-packing proposal, entitled one of his contemporary accounts of the Hughes era *Constitutional Revolution, Ltd.* (1941), a title suggesting that the universe of constitutional discourse underwent a sea change in the years from 1930 to the summer of 1941 when the chief justice stepped down. More recently, scholars such as Bruce Ackerman have likewise suggested that the New Deal–Hughes Court years constituted one of the fundamental moments of constitutional "transformation," when, even in the absence of formal amendment, the scope and meaning of critical constitutional provisions underwent major alterations by the justices in response to social and political pressures buffeting the Court.

This conception of the Hughes Court places great emphasis upon the decisions between 1934 and 1937 that unshackled legislative and executive power to reshape the rewards and penalties of the American economic system, a system battered and shaken by the worst depression in the nation's history. Without question, decisions such as *Nebbia v. New York* (1934), *West Coast Hotel v. Parrish* (1937), and *National Labor Relations Board v. Jones & Laughlin Steel Corp.* (1937) formally emancipated both state and federal governmental authority from constitutional constraints that had limited their regulatory functions over the previous half century. But those constraints, it now seems equally clear, had been weakened significantly during the progressive movement prior to World War I and even during the years of so-called constitutional fundamentalism under Chief Justice Taft. The depression decade provided the occasion for their final interment through a slow ritual that might have been shortened had the Court not been often sharply divided and, like most courts, unwilling to break too suddenly from the doctrinal grooves laid down in the past. No constitutional revolution in our history—not even *Brown v. Board of Education* (1954) or *Roe v. Wade* (1973), to note only the two most obvious examples—arose in a doctrinal vacuum, unattached to historical roots in the Court's own jurisprudence.

In short, the Hughes Court finally confirmed the revolution in the relationship between the state and the American economy, one made ad hoc, piece by piece, at least since the eras of Theodore Roosevelt and Woodrow Wilson. But the long-standing scholarly focus upon its decisions touching government and the economy obscured a second revolution in constitutional law carried out during these years that had profound importance for the structure of American federalism and individual rights: the revolution in criminal procedure and the extension of guarantees in the Bill of Rights to the states. While this revolution, too, had sources even in the White and Taft years, the Hughes Court hastened it along in dramatic fashion.

The Scope of Judicial Power

Not long after the Civil War, Chief Justice Salmon P. Chase wrote a classic statement concerning the fundamental importance of jurisdiction to the functions of the Supreme Court: "Without jurisdiction," he declared, "the court cannot proceed at all in any cause. Jurisdiction is the power to declare the law, and when it ceases to exist, the only function remaining to the court is that of announcing the fact and dismissing the cause" (*Ex parte McCardle* [1869]). Article III of the Constitution vests in Congress the authority to create federal courts inferior to the Supreme Court and to fix their jurisdiction as well as the appellate jurisdiction of the Supreme Court itself, which is subject to "such Exceptions, and under such Regulations as the Congress shall make."

The most controversial exercise of this authority came during Reconstruction, when Congress stripped the Supreme Court of its jurisdiction to hear appeals under the Habeas Corpus Act for fear that the justices might rule against the legislature's military governments in the South (*Ex parte McCardle* [1869]). A less stunning, but no less important, example of Congress's role in federal jurisdiction came during Hughes's tenure when Congress passed and President Hoover signed the Norris-LaGuardia Act in 1932, which restricted the authority of courts of the United States to issue restraining orders or injunctions in "a case involving or growing out of a labor dispute." It also provided that so-called yellow-dog contracts (employment contracts in which workers agreed not to join or organize a labor union) "shall not be enforceable in any court of the United States and shall not afford any basis for the granting of legal or equitable relief by any such court."

In passing the Norris-LaGuardia statute, Congress responded to the growing strength of the labor movement in the 1930s and to the mounting criticism leveled at the federal courts, including the Supreme Court, for restricting strikes and union organizing drives by means of injunctions and decisions that upheld the legality of yellow-dog contracts. When the law came before the Supreme Court for a constitutional test later in the decade, Justice Roberts, writing for the majority, sustained it with the observation that "there can be no question of the power of Congress thus to define and limit the jurisdiction of the inferior courts of the United States" (*Lauf v. E.G. Skinner & Co.* [1938]). Only Justices Butler and McReynolds, still eager for the federal courts to maintain an unfettered role in labor-management disputes, dissented.

While Congress could and did legislate with respect to questions of federal jurisdiction, the Supreme Court itself exercised the most significant day-to-day influence over this threshold issue through another provision in Article III of the Constitution that limits the jurisdiction of federal courts, including the Supreme Court, to "cases" and "controversies" involving certain subject matter (a claim arising, for example, under the Constitution, federal statutes, or treaties) or certain parties (for example, the United States, a state, or citizens of different states). In its interpretation of "cases" and "controversies," the Hughes Court confronted and generally resolved new questions regarding federal jurisdiction in favor of an enlarged vision of its power to decide, but not without strong dissent from justices such as Brandeis and later, Frankfurter.

Chief Justice Jay and a minority of his colleagues wrote to President Washington in 1790 that in their opinion the statutory requirement of riding circuit imposed by Congress was unconstitutional, but the justices soon adopted the practice of refusing to issue such advisory opinions and adhered to the "cases or controversies" limitation upon their judicial power as an essential component of the separation of powers in the Constitution itself. The Supreme Court would decide only concrete adversarial disputes, not hypothetical or speculative ones. In 1911 the Court affirmed this posture in *Muskrat v. United States.* Seeking to determine the validity of certain laws it had passed concerning Indian tribal lands, Congress by statute had authorized certain Indians to sue the United States in order to obtain a ruling on the question. Speaking through Justice William Day, the Court dismissed the suit for want of jurisdiction: no actual "case" or "controversy" existed because all parties were in reality working together to ascertain the constitutionality of the law and not to resolve any actual conflict over legal rights or concrete interests.

In the twilight of the Taft years, Brandeis, ever anxious to place boundaries on federal judicial power, reaffirmed the core of *Muskrat* in *Willing v. Chicago Auditorium Ass'n* (1928), in which the parties, having commenced but failed to conclude negotiations, sought the assistance of a lower federal court in removing a cloud upon title to land leased by the association, which intended to tear down an existing auditorium and build a new one on the property. Charles Evans Hughes, who represented the lessors and bondholders against the association, argued that the lower court had properly dismissed the suit, a position endorsed by Brandeis, who ruled that the proceeding did not constitute "a case or controversy within the meaning of Article 3 of the Constitution. . . . No defendant has wronged the plaintiff or has threatened to do so." What the plaintiff sought, he noted, "is simply a declaratory judgment. To grant relief is beyond the power of the federal judiciary." In *Willing*, however, Justice Stone wrote a concurring opinion in which he made clear his belief that Congress might confer on the federal courts jurisdiction to render declaratory opinions when they appeared to be "the appropriate remedy" and to review such judgments by state courts when they involved "a federal question."

That very issue came before Hughes and the justices five years later in *Nashville, Chattanooga & St. Louis Railway Co. v. Wallace* (1933), a suit brought under Tennessee's Uniform Declaratory Judgments Act in which the railroad sought a judicial declaration that a state tax violated both the Commerce Clause and the Fourteenth Amendment, claims rejected by the state's supreme court. Writing for a unanimous court that included Brandeis, Stone began his opinion by asserting that the justices would look to the substance not the form of the litigation to determine whether or not it presented "a case within the appellate jurisdiction." Noting that in the "ordinary course of judicial procedure" courts usually rendered a judgment that required an award of process or execution to carry out their decision, he cited numerous instances in which the Supreme Court had exerted its judicial power without such consequences: adjudicating boundary disputes between states; reviewing judgments of the Court of Claims; in suits to determine matrimonial or other status; and bills to quite title when plaintiffs rested their claims on adverse possession. By analogy, Tennessee's declaratory judgment statute fit into this category and presented a "case" or "controversy" suitable for review.

Tennessee's Uniform Declaratory Judgment Act, Stone argued, had simply changed the form or method of procedure by which federal rights could be brought to final adjudication in the state's courts, and because states remained free to determine their own judicial procedures, such a change in form did not preclude review by the Supreme Court of the United States. Of course, Stone concluded, the litigation to meet the test of a "case" must have "the essentials of an adversary proceeding, involving a real, not a hypothetical controversy." In this respect the litigation could be distinguished from that present in both *Muskrat* and *Willing.* Having resolved the jurisdictional question, the Court affirmed the judgment of the Tennessee Supreme Court on the constitutionality of the tax. Even Brandeis no doubt recognized that if the Court failed to sustain the Tennessee law and, by implication, similar declaratory judgment statutes in other states, the ultimate power of decision on federal questions would often be lodged in state courts, a result that raised a troubling problem with respect to the federal system and the Supremacy Clause.

The Court's decision in *Wallace*, sustaining the procedures of the Tennessee Declaratory Judgment Act, hastened the passage of congressional legislation in 1934 that extended similar authority to the federal courts. The Federal Declaratory Judgment Act of that year provided that "in a case of actual controversy, except with respect to Federal taxes, any court of the United States . . . , upon the filing of an appropriate pleading, may declare the rights and other legal relations of any interested party seeking such declaration, whether or not further relief is or could be sought. Any such declaration shall have the force and effect of a final judgment or decree and shall be reviewable as such" (28 U.S.C. §§ 2201, 2202). Had Congress here attempted to revise the jurisdiction of the federal courts beyond the "case" or "controversy" boundaries fixed in the Constitution?

Three years later, in the same term that it sustained the National Labor Relations Act and the Social Security Act, the Hughes Court answered that question in the negative when it upheld the federal statute in *Aetna Life Insurance Co. v. Haworth* (1937) by stressing that Congress had limited its scope to "cases of actual controversy," thereby making it operative only as to those disputes that fit the traditional constitutional definitions found in Article III. The case arose when the insured claimed and the insurance company denied that he had become totally disabled and hence relieved of the obligation to continue payment of premiums. The chief justice's opinion took great pains to emphasize that the law did not give the federal courts jurisdiction to resolve what he described as disputes "of a hypothetical or abstract character" or ones that were "academic or moot." To qualify, the controversy had to be "real and substantial . . . admitting of specific relief through a decree of a conclusive character, as distinguished from an opinion advising what the law would be upon a hypothetical state of facts."

The language of the statute and Hughes's interpretation of it in *Haworth* gave the federal courts abundant possibilities for either enlarging their roles or adhering to the traditional jurisdictional limitations set out in Article III. The presence of an "actual controversy" would always seem to exist in every situation in which one of the parties could maintain a legal action for coercive relief. How then to determine when declaratory relief seemed appropriate? The *Haworth* case involved the legal consequences of past events, which could be fixed with such definiteness so as to pose clear legal issues, but could the plaintiffs obtain a declaration of the legal consequences of conduct that had not yet taken place? And since the statute said a federal court "may" render a declaratory judgment in "a case of actual controversy," what were the parties to make of a court's refusal to extend relief? Did the court find an "actual controversy" lacking or did it believe declaratory relief inappropriate? These thorny jurisdictional issues, unsettled by the Hughes Court, would be puzzled out by its successors on a case-by-case basis.

In addition to the "case" or "controversy" limitation upon access to the federal courts, the Supreme Court had historically emphasized that such cases could be brought only by persons directly involved in or affected by the dispute, what the justices defined as another threshold question of legal "standing." In private litigation, of course, where the questions of personal injury or interest are usually very clear, the problem of "standing" seldom arises. The issue of "standing" becomes complicated in cases in which governmental actions are challenged as unconstitutional and in which the relationship between the plaintiff and the challenged state policy may be more indirect. Issues of "standing" in major constitutional cases had often sparked sharp division among the justices in the past and the Hughes Court proved to be no exception to this tradition.

The Taft Court, for example, had placed sharp limits on the standing of states and individual taxpayers to contest federal spending programs in *Massachusetts v. Mellon* and *Frothingham v. Mellon* (1923) by arguing that states were not obliged to accept the federal largess and that individual taxpayers whose funds had become commingled with others' were too remote to claim direct injury arising from a government program. Six years later, however, a majority on the Taft Court allowed a suit to commence against the policies of a state corporation's commission in circumstances that seemed equally remote to three dissenters.

Oklahoma's legislature had declared cotton ginning to be a public utility and placed such enterprises under the licensing authority of the state's corporation commission with the requirement that additional gins could not be licensed without a showing of public necessity. The Mitchell Gin Company obtained a license under this law, but a later revision of the statute permitted cooperatives to obtain similar permits without a showing of public necessity. Mitchell Gin sued to enjoin the commission from issuing licenses to such cooperatives, alleging that they would compete with it and that the revised statute violated the Equal Protection Clause of the Fourteenth Amendment. Writing for the majority, Justice Sutherland upheld Mitchell Gin's standing to litigate and the injunction against the corporation commission.

In his dissent, joined by Brandeis and Holmes, Justice Stone doubted that the plaintiff had standing to bring the challenge. "It seems to me that a fallacy, productive of unfortunate consequences, lurks in the suggestion that one may maintain a suit to enjoin competition of a business solely because hereafter someone else might suffer from an unconstitutional discrimination and enjoin it," he wrote (*Frost v. Corporation Commission* [1929]).

The programs of the New Deal's massive Tennessee Valley Authority (TVA) provoked a sharp debate among the justices over the question of standing during Hughes's tenure. In *Ashwander v. Tennessee Valley Authority* (1936), preferred stockholders in the Alabama Power Company sought to enjoin a contract between the company and the TVA, a contract that provided for the purchase by the Authority of company transmission lines and real property for an interchange of power and mutual restrictions on the areas to be served in the sale of power. The stockholders argued that the contract exceeded the powers of the federal government and would inflict financial injury upon the company. The majority, led by Hughes, ruled that the stockholders had standing to bring the suit, but sustained the contract on the grounds that the government had the authority to dispose of the power generated from its property at Wilson Dam on the Tennessee River.

Although he joined in sustaining the contract, Brandeis, joined by Roberts, Stone, and Cardozo, wrote one of the most memorable concurring opinions in the Court's history on the scope of the judicial power, one that stressed the passive virtues of judicial restraint and that began with an attack upon the standing of the plaintiffs to sue. After pointing out that the management of the Alabama Power Company had broken no laws, complied with all conditions of the company's charter, and that the contract contained substantial benefits to the company, Brandeis observed that the plaintiffs owned about one-three-hundred-and-fortieth of the preferred stock and that the Court had never accorded standing to stockholders under similar circumstances: "Their rights are not enlarged because the Tennessee Valley Authority entered into a transaction pursuant to an act of Congress. . . . Ordinary stockholders have no standing to interfere with the management. Mere belief that corporate action, taken or contemplated, is illegal gives the stockholders no greater right to interfere than is possessed by any other citizen. Stockholders are not guardians of the public."

Brandeis concluded by listing what he described as "a series of rules under which [the Supreme Court] has avoided passing upon a large part of all constitutional questions pressed upon it for decision":

> 1. The Court will not pass upon the constitutionality of legislation in a friendly, non-adversary proceeding, declining because to decide such questions is legitimate only in the last resort, and as a necessity in the determination of real, earnest and vital controversy between individuals. . . .
> 2. The Court will not anticipate a question of constitutional law in advance of the necessity of deciding it. . . .
> 3. The Court will not formulate a rule of constitutional law broader than is required by the precise facts to which it is to be applied. . . .
> 4. The Court will not pass upon a constitutional question although properly presented by the record, if there is also present some other ground upon which the case may be disposed of. . . .
> 5. The Court will not pass upon the validity of a statute upon complaint of one who fails to show that he is injured by its operation. . . .
> 6. The Court will not pass upon the constitutionality of a statute at the instance of one who has availed himself of its benefits. . . .
> 7. When the validity of an act of the Congress is drawn in question, and even if a serious doubt of constitutionality is raised, it is a cardinal principle that this Court will first ascertain whether a construction of the statute is fairly possible by which the question may be avoided. (*Ashwander v. Tennessee Valley Authority* [1936])

At the top of Brandeis's inventory of rules promoting judicial restraint in constitutional litigation stood his admonition not to pass upon such questions in "a friendly, non-adversary proceeding." Three months after *Ashwander*, the Court appeared to do just that when it heard the case of *Carter v. Carter Coal Co.* (1936) and struck down the Guffey Coal Act, with Cardozo, Stone, and Brandeis dissenting. The challenge to the New Deal statute had been brought by the president of the coal company against the company and its officers, one of whom was the plaintiff's own father.

But Brandeis's concurrence in *Ashwander*, although ignored in *Carter Coal*, may have tempered the Court's enthusiasm for relaxing standing requirements. After *Ashwander*, the justices had occasion to reaffirm more traditional standing limits in other cases involving the TVA. In *Alabama Power Co. v. Ickes* (1938), for example, Justice Sutherland drew upon the logic of *Frothingham* when the Court rebuffed efforts by power companies to enjoin loans made by the federal government's Public Works Administration to municipalities who intended to use the funds for building generating facilities and transmission lines. Both as competitors and taxpayers, the companies alleged that Title II of the National Industrial Recovery Act, which authorized the loans, was unconstitutional and that the uses of the loans would inflict economic injury upon them. Sutherland denied them standing to sue: "If such a suit can be maintained," he wrote, "similar suits by innumerable persons are likewise admissible to determine whether money is being loaned without lawful authority for uses which, although hurtful to the complainants, are perfectly lawful. The supposition opens a vista of litigation hitherto unrevealed."

A year later, Justice Roberts invoked the traditional common law rule that a business does not have an interest in freedom from competition. The court denied standing to other power companies that attempted to challenge the constitutional authority of the TVA to produce electricity and sell it to industrial users and municipalities who competed with them. Conceding that the companies would likely suffer genuine economic harm from the TVA's activities, Roberts and the majority reasoned that they would not suffer "legal" injury because one could not claim a "legal right" to be free from lawful competition. The companies had no more standing to block competition from the TVA than they would to enjoin competition from other private utilities. Only Justices Butler and McReynolds, the dying voices of orthodox laissez-faire, dissented (*Tennessee Electric Power Co. v. Tennessee Valley Authority* [1939]).

The Hughes Court recognized, however, the authority of Congress to modify judge-made rules of standing in much the same way that Congress controlled the jurisdiction of the federal courts. A provision in the Federal Communication Act of 1934, for example, allowed appeals from license orders by both applicants and "any other person aggrieved or whose interests are adversely affected by a decision of the Commission granting or refusing any such [license] application" (47 U.S.C. § 402[b]). In *Federal Communications Commission v. Sanders Bros. Radio Station* (1940), the justices sustained the provision with the observation that Congress "may have been of the opinion that one likely to be financially injured by the issue of a license would be the only person having a sufficient interest to bring to the attention of the appellate court errors of law."

Apart from the *Ashwander* case, the most contentious debate over standing during the Hughes years arose in 1939, when a bare majority of the justices, led by Hughes and Stone, ruled that state legislators in Kansas who had voted against ratification of the federal Child Labor Amendment could seek Supreme Court review of the state court's refusal to enjoin other state officials from certifying Kansas's ratification. The legislators' central constitutional argument, rejected by the state court, focused on the role played by the Kansas lieutenant governor, who broke a tie vote in the state senate that made ratification possible, but who was not, they claimed, a member of the state legislature as defined in the Constitution of the United States.

The Hughes Court majority, accepting the determination of the state court, recognized the standing of state senators to litigate this issue in order to protect their official vote. But, in addition, the majority upheld their standing to argue that the ratification had been invalid because of the state's previous rejection of the amendment and because the proposed amendment had been outstanding for more than a reasonable time and was no longer susceptible of ratification (*Coleman v. Miller* [1939]).

The majority's eagerness to resolve this thorny issue drew a strong dissent from Frankfurter, joined by Roberts, Black, and Douglas, who focused on both the issue of standing and what he believed to be the Court's tradition of avoiding so-called political questions best left to other forums because not appropriate for disposition by judges. The Kansas legislators, Frankfurter declared, "have no more standing in these claims of unconstitutionality . . . then they would have standing here to attack some Kansas statute claimed by them to offend the Commerce Clause. By as much right could a member of Congress who voted against the passage of a bill because moved by constitutional scruples urge before this Court our duty to consider his arguments of unconstitutionality" (*Coleman v. Miller* [1939]).

Consistent with the long-standing tradition, the Hughes Court displayed great deference to interpretations of state statutes and state constitutional provisions offered by state supreme courts, a posture reinforced by the arrival of justices like Frankfurter. The Court also refused to invoke federal judicial power in situations in which the decisions of state courts rested upon independent state constitutional grounds that did not conflict with the Constitution of the United States and in cases in which plaintiffs had failed to exhaust their remedies under state law. In addition, the justices declined to exercise federal judicial authority when state courts had not rendered an authoritative interpretation of local laws.

The 1941 case of *Railroad Commission v. Pullman*, with Frankfurter writing for a unanimous court, displayed the justices' commitment to comity and abstention. A three-judge federal panel, notable—as Frankfurter observed—for their collective distinction, had enjoined the enforcement of a regulation of the Texas state railroad commission. That regulation required all Pullman cars operating in Texas to be "continuously in charge of employees having the rank and position of Pullman conductors," a revision of existing company policies that had placed some Pullman cars under the control of porters, who, unlike conductors, were African American. The porters and Pullman company challenged the regulation on grounds that it violated both the Equal Protection Clause and the Commerce Clause. The federal judges, however, ruled only that the commission lacked authority to impose such a regulation under all relevant Texas statutes. Despite obvious sympathy for the plight of the plaintiffs and respect for the federal jurists, Frankfurter and the Court reversed the judgment on the grounds that federal intervention had been premature and ordered the case sent back to the Texas Supreme Court for an interpretation of the relevant state's laws.

Separation of Powers

Although the first three articles of the Constitution allocate certain responsibilities to Congress, the president, and the federal judiciary, nowhere does the document assert a fundamental rule mandating a separation of powers as set forth by "the celebrated Montesquieu," the French political theorist of the eighteenth century who argued that there were only three functions of government—legislative, executive, and judicial—which had to be kept separate and exercised by distinct bodies in order to avoid a dangerous concentration of power.

A more accurate description of the constitutional structure would stress checks and balances and the sharing of authority among the three branches of the federal government. No congressional measure can become law without the president's signature. A presidential veto of legislation, in turn, may be overridden by a two-thirds vote in both houses of Congress. The president negotiates treaties and nominates federal judges, but the Senate must advise and consent to both. The House is given the sole power of impeachment, but impeachments are tried by the Senate, and if the president is put to trial there, the chief justice of the United States presides.

As the above examples suggest, the government of the United States would cease to function effectively without a high degree of cooperation among its three principle branches and a strict application of Montesquieu's dictum would not facilitate that important objective. Early in its history, the Supreme Court recognized this fact when Chief Justice Marshall wrote: "The difference between the departments [of the federal government] undoubtedly is, that the legislature makes, the executive executes, and the judiciary construes the law; but the maker of the law may commit something to the discretion of the other departments, and the precise boundary of this power is a subject of delicate and difficult inquiry, into which a court will not enter unnecessarily" (*Wayman v. Southard* [1825]).

Marshall made that observation in affirming the authority of Congress to settle upon the federal courts the power to promulgate rules of practice, although that task could be construed strictly as falling outside the "case" or "controversy" boundaries of the judicial power fixed in Article III. And as his words suggested, the issue of delegation, the extent to which Congress, "the maker of the law[,] may commit something to the discretion of the other departments" became the rubric under which the Supreme Court came to analyze the question of the separation of powers. Until the years of Hughes's chief justiceship, the Court generally adopted a relaxed view of the delegation issue, but the legislative programs of the early New Deal changed that environment.

From the early years of the republic, the justices sustained numerous congressional laws vesting broad discretion in the president to implement foreign policy and foreign trade policies, even though these had important domestic consequences. Between 1813 and 1892, for example, the Court sustained the right of Congress to authorize the president under certain conditions to reinstate the Non-Intercourse Act and to prohibit the free entry of certain items of trade when he determined that a foreign government had imposed unreasonable tariffs on American imports (*The Brig Aurora v. United States* (1813); *Field v. Clark* [1892]). In 1904 the justices upheld a statute that gave the secretary of the treasury authority to appoint a board of tea inspectors to set grading standards for that product and that barred the import of tea failing to meet those standards (*Buttfield v. Stranahan* [1904]). And a year before the stock market crash, the Taft Court upheld provisions in the Fordney-McCumber Act, which authorized the president to boost or reduce tariff duties by as much as 50 percent in order to equalize production costs between the United States and other nations (*J. W. Hampton Jr. & Co. v. United States* [1928]).

The *Hampton* case called forth a ringing declaration from Chief Justice Taft about the importance of the separation of powers: "It is a breach of the national fundamental law if Congress gives up its legislative power and transfers it to the President, or to the Judicial branch, of if by law it attempts to invest itself or its members with either executive or judicial power." But this stalwart defender of constitutional fundamentals concluded by noting: "In determining what it [Congress] may do in seeking assistance from another branch, the extent and character of that assistance must be fixed according to common sense and the inherent necessities of the governmental coordination."

Prior to the 1930s, the Court had also upheld the authority of Congress to delegate substantial rule-making power to new independent regulatory agencies such as the Interstate Commerce Commission (*Interstate Commerce Commission v. Brimson* [1894]) and the Federal Reserve Board (*First National Bank v. Fellows* [1917]) and to endow the secretary of war with broad authority to remove bridges from the waters of the United States when he found such structures to be an "unreasonable" obstruction to the free navigation of the waters (*Louisville Bridge Co. v. United States* [1917]).

Only rarely did the justices invoke the language of separation of powers or improper delegation to nullify governmental actions on constitutional grounds. And those cases provoked sharp division on the Court. In 1920, over four dissents, the majority ruled that Congress had improperly delegated its authority by permitting the application of state workmen's compensation laws to injuries within the maritime and admiralty jurisdictions, in effect delegating its constitutional and legislative authority over those matters to the states (*Knickerbocker Ice Co. v. Stewart* [1920]). And in *Myers v. United States* (1926), with three justices in dissent, it voided a congressional effort to protect certain postmasters from removal by the president on the grounds that the legislature had tread too deeply upon the prerogatives of the executive. The power to remove federal officials confirmed by the Senate, the majority ruled, remained distinct from the shared power of the president and the Senate over their appointment.

Then, in the space of a year and a half, from January 7, 1935, until May 18, 1936, a majority of the justices on the Hughes Court rolled out the twin cannons of separation of powers and invalid delegation in decisions that struck down four actions of the New Deal, an unprecedented use of these doctrinal weapons not repeated by the Court until the 1980s. In rapid succession they overturned the "hot oil" provisions of the National Recovery Act (*Panama Refining Co. v. Ryan* [1935]); sharply limited the scope of the decision in *Myers* by limiting the president's authority to fire members of a independent regulatory agency (*Humphrey's Executor v. United States* [1935]); and invalidated Title I, the heart of the National Industrial Recovery Act (*Schechter Poultry Corp. v. United States* ([1935]). A year later, over three dissents, they invoked invalid delegation and a restricted interpretation of the Commerce Clause to hold invalid the Bituminous Coal Conservation Act (*Carter v. Carter Coal Co.* [1936]).

The "hot oil" decision struck many observers at the time and since as the least principled of the Court's blows against the early New Deal. The congressional statute held invalid in this case prohibited the shipment in interstate commerce of oil produced in violation of state quota laws and placed federal enforcement in the hands of the secretary of the interior. Congress, in effect, had delegated its authority to regulate commerce among the states to the oil-producing states, but this was little different than the Webb-Kenyon Act of 1916 in which Congress had prohibited the shipment of intoxicating liquor into states where it had been banned. The White Court had sustained that law in *Clark Distilling Co. v. West Maryland Railway Co.* (1917). Nor did the authority vested in the secretary of the interior seem much different from that delegated by Congress in the past when it accepted such broad terms as "public interest" and "public convenience" as meeting constitutional standards (*Radio Commission v. Nelson Brothers Co.* [1933]).

In *Humphrey's Executor*, by contrast, the justices drew a more reasonable distinction between the president's removal power with respect to postmasters, traditionally a patronage position, and his authority to oust members of independent regulatory bodies such as the Interstate Commerce Commission, Federal Trade Commission, or the Federal Reserve Board, for which Congress had historically fixed the terms of appointment to overlap those of a president. The very concept of an independent regulatory body—officials immune to the immediate winds of political change—would have been seriously eroded by an extension of *Myers* beyond its immediate facts.

The statutes invalidated in *Schechter* and *Carter Coal* presented a different constellation of delegation issues, ones that transcended the president and officers of the executive branch such as the secretary of the interior. Both statutes allowed administrators such as General Hugh Johnson, head of the National Recovery Administration (NRA), to utilize numerous private interest groups—trade associations, coal producers, and labor unions—in the drafting and enforcement of regulations that carried the force of law against their competitors. In the case of the many code authorities created under the NIRA to set the rules of the market, those businessmen who reached Washington first usually wrote the regulations, a practice that soon gave rise to cries of monopoly by those excluded. In short, Congress had effectively delegated considerable legislative power over commerce to wholly private, unelected groups and individuals. This is what Cardozo meant when he characterized the NRA structure as "delegation run riot."

The New Deal's resort to private interest groups as instruments of regulation, sometimes justified as a positive example of "grassroots democracy," arose in large measure from the primitive development of the federal government's administrative capacity, long weakened by the rhetoric of laissez-faire, the fear of active government, and parsimonious budgets. The NIRA and the Guffey Coal Act were not the only federal programs characterized by the delegation of decision making to private interests, a process that often masked the domination of the powerful. The initial Agricultural Adjustment Act, struck down by the Court on Tenth Amendment grounds in 1936, delegated authority to the largest producers and landowners, who determined acreage allotments, received the biggest government subsidies, and evicted poor sharecroppers and tenants.

When FDR's judicial appointments began to influence the Hughes Court after 1937, the majority brushed aside invalid delegation challenges to federal statutes in cases only marginally different from those held unconstitutional several years before. In *Currin v. Wallace* (1939), for example, Hughes and the majority sustained the Tobacco Inspection Act that authorized the secretary of agriculture to establish action markets where tobacco was to be graded and inspected prior to shipment in interstate commerce. Inspectors, drawn from the industry, could prohibit the secretary from designating a market unless two-thirds of the growers favored it in a referendum. This provision did not constitute unconstitutional delegation, Hughes argued, because Congress had merely "placed a restriction upon its own regulation by withholding its operation as to a given market" until a referendum supported it.

Two-thirds of the milk producers in a designated area enjoyed the same authority to ratify price regulations proposed by the secretary of agriculture under the Agricultural Marketing Act, which the justices upheld in *United States v. Rock Royal Cooperative* (1939). The secretary's regulations also exempted cooperatives from the uniform pricing scheme imposed upon other milk handlers and allowed the coops to cast the votes of all their members or patrons. Justice Reed and the majority sustained these provisions against an invalid delegation attack by holding them consistent with the declared policy of Congress to restore the purchasing power of agricultural commodities. Hughes and Roberts dissented, not on grounds of invalid delegation, but because the regulations gave an unreasonable advantage to large milk handlers in violation of due process.

Provisions of the Bituminous Coal Conservation Act of 1937 exempted from a prohibitive federal tax those coal producers, but not others, who subscribed to regulations set by twenty-three operator-dominated district boards whose minimum coal prices were later ratified by the National Bituminous Coal Commission, a government agency. Rejecting a challenge to this statute on grounds of invalid delegation, Justice Douglas neatly placed the commission, not the coal operators, at the center of the regulatory scheme. "Since law-making is not entrusted to the industry," he observed, "this statutory scheme is unquestionably valid" (*Sunshine Anthracite Coal Co. v. Adkins* [1940]). Only Justice McReynolds dissented.

In 1936, over the views of three dissenters, the Court rebuked the administrative practices of the new Securities and Exchange Commission, which Congress had charged broadly with regulating the underwriting, marketing, and trading of stocks and bonds (*Jones v. Securities and Exchange Commission* [1936]). That judicial reprimand to the burgeoning "fourth branch" of government, the regulatory commissions expanded and created by the New Deal, proved exceptional. Thereafter, and especially when Roosevelt's appointees joined the bench, the Hughes Court endorsed broad delegation language by Congress and displayed unusual deference to the judgments of independent regulatory agencies such as the SEC, the Federal Communications Commission, and the Federal Power Commission (*Electric Bond & Share Co. v. Securities and Exchange Commission* [1939]); *Federal Communications Commission v. Broadcasting Co.* [1940]).

At the same time that the majority on the Hughes Court employed what for some appeared to be a cramped view of congressional delegation when it came to the early domestic programs of the New Deal in 1935–1936, the justices continued the established constitutional trend of endorsing very broad delegation authority when it came to the president's role in foreign affairs. Justice Sutherland's opinion in *United*

States v. Curtiss-Wright Export Corp. (1936) flatly rejected the charge that Congress had given the president "unfettered discretion" to enforce its authorized embargo on arms sales in Latin America; drew a sharp distinction between delegation issues in domestic as opposed to foreign affairs; and concluded, finally, that the president had "plenary" powers in the field of foreign affairs arising from Article II of the Constitution and not dependent upon congressional delegation at all! A year later, Justice Sutherland and the Court added another powerful weapon to the president's foreign affairs arsenal when they confirmed the constitutional validity of Roosevelt's executive agreement made with the Soviet government, an agreement made without the consent of the Senate or even in response to a congressional directive (*United States v. Belmont* [1937]). Congress and the Supreme Court, of course, had always displayed great deference to the president's conduct of international relations and *Curtiss-Wright* and *Belmont* confirmed once again that there were "two presidencies" embedded in constitutional doctrine—a domestic one, whose conduct would be more carefully monitored, but also a foreign affairs president, who functioned largely outside the boundaries of separation of powers and federalism.

When it came to its own role in carrying out congressional mandates, the Court also displayed a very tolerant view of the separation of powers and delegation. In 1933, acting pursuant to its authority in Articles I and III, Congress gave the Supreme Court authority to prescribe rules to govern procedures and practice in federal criminal cases after a verdict, including appeals. The justices drafted a set of rules quickly, which took effect in the spring of 1934, without further congressional scrutiny or approval.

Also in 1934, after years of lobbying by members of the elite bar, Chief Justice Taft, and Attorney General Homer Cummings, Congress passed without opposition legislation authorizing the Supreme Court to prescribe rules of federal procedure in civil cases. A year later, Hughes and his Court delegated this vital task to a committee headed by William D. Mitchell of New York, a former solicitor general of the United States, with instructions to prepare a draft of the proposed rules. Mitchell's committee, in turn, drew upon the views of other federal judges, law professors, and practitioners in crafting the final version of what became the Rules of Civil Procedure. Following cosmetic revisions by the Supreme Court, the Rules of Civil Procedure went into force in 1938, sixty days after they were presented to Congress without its veto.

The United States now had a uniform system of pleading and practice for the federal courts as well as rules governing procedure and practice in criminal cases after a verdict. Cummings also pushed for and secured by 1940 congressional approval for the Supreme Court to prescribe criminal rules prior to and including the verdict, a process completed during the Second World War with the assistance of another advisory committee chaired by Arthur T. Vanderbilt.

In these instances, some observers noted, the Supreme Court technically stepped outside the "case" or "controversy" limitation upon federal judicial power. Further, the justices delegated the task of forging the rules of federal procedure and practice to private interests and they ultimately gave approval to the fundamental framework of litigation through which constitutional issues were presented. Not every member of the Hughes Court endorsed the process set in motion by Cummings and Congress. "I asked C. J. [Hughes] to advise A. G. [Cummings] that I do not approve of their adoption," Brandeis told Frankfurter, with reference to the proposed Rules of Civil Procedure. "I am sure several others feel as I do, but thought they must be silent as the Court was committed. Will anything be done in Congress to prevent them becoming operative?" (Urofsky and Levy 1991, 606).

Without dissent, the Hughes Court also adopted a posture of vigilance when it appeared that Congress and the president attempted to tamper with judicial independence by means of the purse strings. As part of his initial New Deal program, FDR pushed through Congress the so-called Economy Act of 1933, a law designed to reduce federal expenditures and trim the growing budget deficit inherited from the Hoover years. A section in the statute trimmed the compensation for federal judges who did not resign, but chose retirement, pursuant to provisions in the Federal Judicial Code.

In an opinion by Justice Roberts, the Court struck down that provision on grounds that it violated Article III, which prohibited any reduction in the compensation of federal judges "during their continuance in office." Because retired federal judges "continued in office" under the Judicial Code, Roberts argued, any reduction in their retirement compensation violated Article III, even though the reduced compensation remained greater than the salary fixed at the time of their appointment (*Booth v. United States* [1934]). Roberts and the Court did not explain how to square this ruling with *Stuart v. Laird* (1803), in which the Marshall Court had upheld the authority of Congress to abolish federal judicial offices, including, of course, the compensation to be paid to the ousted incumbents.

Federalism

Writing for the Court majority more than three decades after his appointment in 1937, Justice Hugo Black paid tribute to what he called "the ideals and dreams of 'Our Federalism.'" That concept, he explained, "does not mean blind deference to 'State's Rights' any more than it means centralization of control over every important issue in our National Government and courts. The Framers rejected both these courses. What the concept does represent is a system in which there is sensitivity to the legitimate interests of both State and National Governments, and in which the National Government, anxious though it may be to vindicate and protect federal rights and federal interests, always endeavors to do so in ways that will not unduly interfere with the legitimate activities of the States" (*Younger v. Harris* [1971]).

Like other justices before and after him, Black attempted to define "Our Federalism" as that delicate balance between "the legitimate interests of both State and National Governments," in which neither "state's rights" nor "centralization" achieved complete hegemony. He called his vision of American federalism an ideal and a dream, however, which suggests an abstraction never fully realized in historical experience. And indeed, throughout its history, the Supreme Court has moved back and forth between the twin poles of federalism, one moment giving broad scope to national authority, while at others emphasizing the constitutional limits upon that authority and the necessity for protecting the autonomy of the states.

The years of Hughes's chief justiceship are rightly viewed as one of the more important watersheds in the history of constitutional federalism, the time when the Court officially abandoned something called "dual federalism" that emphasized the rigid, impermeable boundaries between federal and state power and substituted a more fluid "cooperative federalism" in which the role of national institutions (legislative, executive, and judicial) soon predominated.

In one area of constitutional doctrine, the change is clearly illustrated by the demise of intergovernmental tax immunities. In 1842 the Supreme Court struck down a Pennsylvania tax upon the salary of the captain of a U.S. revenue cutter on the grounds that such a state levy constituted an interference with the Article I powers of Congress "to lay and collect taxes, duties, imposts, etc., and to regulate commerce" (*Dobbins v. Erie County* [1842]). Thirty years later, the Court closed this circle in *Collector v. Day* (1871) when it invoked the Tenth Amendment and ruled that the federal income tax could not be levied on the salaries of state officers. Justice Nelson there gave voice to the strict theory of "dual federalism": "The States within the limits of their powers not granted, or, in the language of the Tenth Amendment, 'reserved,' are as independent of the general government as that government within its sphere is independent of the States." In 1939, with only McReynolds and Butler in dissent, the Hughes Court overturned both *Dobbins* and *Collector* to eliminate most intergovernmental tax immunities at a time of serious economic decline when both the states and the federal government struggled to balance their budgets with new sources of revenue (*Graves v. New York ex rel. O'Keefe* [1939]).

Apart from the issue of intergovernmental tax immunities, however, the Supreme Court until the second decade of the twentieth century did not invoke federalism principles, especially the Tenth Amendment, as a significant limitation upon the Article I powers of Congress. Quite the opposite: In 1904, speaking through Justice White, the Court sustained a prohibitive federal tax on oleomargarine that had been challenged on both due process and Tenth Amendment grounds. "Undoubtedly both the Fifth and Tenth Amendments qualify, in so far as they are applicable, all the provisions of the Constitution," White wrote, "[but] nothing in those amendments operates to take away the grant of power to tax conferred by the Constitution upon Congress" (*McCray v. United States* [1904]).

The justices also allowed Congress to override state policies in a number of important areas, usually invoking its authority to regulate commerce among the states or the Court's own judicially created mandate to protect interstate commerce from discriminatory local regulations. Invalidating a state law that conflicted with Congress's regulation of the infant telegraph industry, the Court gave breathtaking scope to the national legislature's writ by declaring that it "operates on every foot of territory under its jurisdiction. It legislates for the whole nation, and is not embarrassed by State lines" (*Pensacola Telegraph Co. v. Western Union* [1878]).

In similar fashion the Court struck down state railroad rates that impinged on interstate operations (*Wabash, St. Louis & Pacific Railway v. Illinois* [1886]) as well as state laws designed to protect local producers from the competition generated by large, integrated corporations (*Barber v. Minnesota* [1890]). Dismissing federalism concerns, the Court affirmed Congress's authority to ban lottery tickets from interstate commerce as well as tainted meat and adulterated food and drugs (*Champion v. Ames* [1903]; *Hipolite Egg Co. v. United States* [1911]). The Justice Department could also utilize the federal antitrust law against a price-fixing conspiracy by meatpackers in the Chicago stockyards when their activities took place within a continuous "steam of commerce" (*Swift & Co. v. United States* [1905]). Even when the justices struck down the first federal Employers' Liability Act because Congress had extended coverage beyond the railroads' interstate employees, they did not invoke the Tenth Amendment as grounds for their decision (*Employers' Liability Cases (I)* [1908]).

The aggressive use of federal power during the second Wilson administration, culminating in the wide range of national regulations deployed during the First World War, produced a judicial backlash beginning in 1918 that resurrected the Tenth Amendment as a significant limitation upon Congress's enumerated powers. In rapid succession, often with divided votes, the justices struck down the federal Child Labor Act of 1916 as well as the Child Labor Tax Act of 1919, in both cases ruling that the Tenth Amendment trumped Congress's authority to regulate local economic activities either through the Commerce Clause or the taxing power (*Hammer v. Dagenhart* [1918]; *Bailey v. Drexel Furniture Co.* [1922]).

And although the Court sustained the Packers and Stockyards Act of 1921, which gave the secretary of agriculture authority to regulate transactions in the local stockyards, including the rates charged for services and the fees levied by those making sales of stock in interstate commerce (*Stafford v. Wallace* [1922]), the justices soon overturned the Futures Trading Act, which sought to regulate sales of grain futures on local boards of trade by taxing such sales at a prohibitive rate and then exempting from the tax all sales that complied with federal regulations (*Hill v. Wallace* [1922]).

In the Packers and Stockyards Act, the Court ruled, Congress had not usurped local authority because it sought to regulate a "more or less constant practice [the sale of livestock] . . . [that] threatens to obstruct or unduly burden the freedom of interstate commerce." In the Futures Trading Act, the Court held by contrast, the sales of grain futures on boards of trade were not per se interstate commerce, although such sales obviously affected the interstate market in grain. This nice distinction, which Chief Justice Taft and others believed essential to the very essence and preservation of the federal system, did not persuade everyone.

Nor did the justices who sang praises to federalism appear to display much sympathy for the autonomy of local governments a few years later when they sustained a federal injunction against the Sanitary District of Chicago for diverting water from Lake Michigan in excess of a specified amount. "This is not a controversy among equals," wrote Holmes for a unanimous bench. "The United States is asserting its sovereign power to regulate commerce and to control navigable waters within its jurisdiction. . . . There is no question that this power is superior to that of the States to provide for the welfare or necessities of their inhabitants" (*Chicago Sanitary District v. United States* [1925]).

The Hughes Court inherited a range of doctrines touching basic issues of federalism and the American economy notable for their complexity, nuance, and contradiction. These circumstances left the justices with unusual opportunity for choice in a political environment generating new demands for national action, but the opportunity for choices also exposed them to criticism on the grounds of judicial subjectivity and arbitrariness. The Tenth Amendment had been invoked to limit congressional and federal authority in certain areas and at certain times (taxation and interstate commerce), but dismissed in circumstances (taxation and interstate commerce) that appeared nearly identical. Often the amendment had been deployed to protect local, entrepreneurial choice from federal control (*Hammer v. Dagenhart* [1918]), but not always (*Stafford v. Wallace* [1922]). Sometimes it appeared to empower state and local governments (*Collector v. Day* [1871]), while at other times it buried their interests beneath arguments for federal supremacy (*Barber v. Minnesota* [1890]; *Chicago Sanitary District v. United States* [1925]).

Decisions such as *Erie v. Tompkins* (1938), requiring federal judges to apply the substantive law of the states in diversity cases, and *South Carolina State Highway Department v. Barnwell Bros.* (1938), permitting local variations in transportation regulations, conveyed a strong judicial commitment to the role of the states in the federal system. But throughout Hughes's tenure his Court's solicitude for federalism did not always extend to the activities of the states as states. When Arizona sought to enjoin the construction of Hoover Dam until the secretary of the interior submitted plans and specifications for the project to the state's own engineers for approval, the justices, led by Brandeis with only McReynolds in dissent, dismissed the claim (*Arizona v. California* [1931]). California's state-run railroad was held financially liable for penalties incurred by its violation of the Federal Safety Appliance Act (*United States v. California* [1936]). That same year, with the chief justice and three others joining Cardozo's dissent, the justices ruled that Congress could not extend the benefits of voluntary bankruptcy proceedings to subdivisions of the states, even though the federal statute required the states to consent to those proceedings (*Ashton v. Cameron County Water District* [1936]). The Court also allowed state-owned property to be condemned by the federal government under its power of eminent domain even though the state intended to use the same property for its own water and conservation projects (*Oklahoma v. Atkinson Co.* [1941]). And Pennsylvania could not enforce an alien registration law that conflicted with provisions in federal regulations (*Hines v. Davidowitz* [1941]), a ruling that drew dissents from the unusual trio of Hughes, Stone, and McReynolds.

Under Hughes's leadership, the states also began to experience unprecedented federal judicial scrutiny of their policies with respect to civil liberties, criminal procedure, and civil rights. By selectively incorporating more of the specific provisions of the Bill of Rights into the Due Process Clause of the Fourteenth Amendment (*Near v. Minnesota* [1931]); by subjecting local criminal trials to greater surveillance under that same provision (*Powell v. Alabama* [1932]); by encouraging utilization of federal habeas corpus provisions to test the constitutionality of state convictions (*Mooney v. Holihan* [1935]); and by invoking both the Equal Protection Clause and the Fifteenth Amendment against state-sponsored racial discrimination, the Court instituted a profound revolution in federal-state relations.

The Hughes Court ultimately affirmed federal supremacy in the economic sphere when it rejected Tenth Amendment challenges to the National Labor Relations Act, the Social Security Act, the Guffey-Vinson Bituminous Coal Act, and the Fair Labor Standards Act. By sustaining a federal program of tax relief for those coal producers who adhered to national standards in *Sunshine Anthracite Coal Co. v. Adkins* (1940), the Court silently overturned *Hill v. Wallace* (1922). And when putting the stamp of constitutional approval on the Fair Labor Standards Act, it gave a swift burial to *Hammer v. Dagenhart* (1918) in Justice Stone's ringing reaffirmation of the views of Hamilton and Marshall concerning the relationship of the Tenth Amendment to Article I: "The [Tenth] amendment states but a truism that all is retained which has not been surrendered" (*United States v. Darby Lumber Co.* [1941]). But the road to *Darby* and federal supremacy over the basic rules of the national marketplace had been a bumpy and twisting one for the Hughes Court prior to 1937, a journey that inspired pungent criticism and helped to provoke the confrontation with the president and Congress.

When the Hughes Court first confronted the relationship of the Tenth Amendment to other constitutional provisions, the issue arose not in the context of Article I, but with respect to ratification of the Prohibition Amendment (Eighteenth) and its enforcement statute, the Volstead Act. Article V of the Constitution invests Congress with two options for ratification of proposed amendments: either by three-fourths of the states' legislatures or by conventions in three-fourths of the states. In the case of the Eighteenth Amendment as with earlier ones, Congress chose the former, but a federal district court ruled this method unavailing by invoking the Tenth Amendment as a limitation upon Congress's Article V powers: Because the Eighteenth Amendment touched vital questions of personal liberty, the district court held, it could only be ratified by the people in state conventions.

In reversing this bizarre ruling, Justice Roberts, writing for a unanimous court, seemed to confirm an interpretation of the Tenth Amendment more consistent with *McCray* than with *Hammer v. Dagenhart.* "The Tenth Amendment," he wrote, "was intended to confirm the understanding of the people at the time the Constitution was adopted, that powers not granted to the United States were reserved to the States or to the people. It added nothing to the instrument as originally ratified and has no limited and special operation . . . upon the people's delegation by Article V of certain functions to the Congress" (*United States v. Sprague* [1931]).

If the Tenth Amendment did not function as a limitation upon Congressional choice in Article V, one might have assumed after *Sprague* that the amendment did not likewise serve as a limitation upon Congress's choices under Article I, specifically the powers to tax, spend, and regulate commerce among the states, and "to make all laws which shall be necessary and proper for carrying into execution the foregoing powers." But four years after *Sprague*, Roberts rolled out the Tenth Amendment as a fundamental barrier to a taxing scheme mandated by Congress that, in addition to raising revenue, aided the states in enforcing their liquor-control laws following the repeal of the Eighteenth Amendment. Above the usual $25 federal excise tax on retail dealers in malt liquor, the statute imposed an additional $1,000 special excise tax on those dealers who violated state law.

Roberts and the majority voided the special excise tax, noting that its true purpose was not fiscal, but an attempt to aid in the enforcement of local criminal laws. And such a federal penalty constituted "a clear invasion of the police power, inherent in the states, reserved from the grant of powers to the federal government." In his dissent, joined by Brandeis and Stone, Cardozo chided the majority for probing the motives of the national legislature: "Thus the process of psychoanalysis has spread to unaccustomed fields" (*United States v. Constantine* [1935]).

And one year after *Constantine*, the author of *Sprague* again relied upon the Tenth Amendment to overturn the federal tax designed to bring the nation's agricultural surpluses under some measure of control through the first Agricultural Adjustment Act

(*United States v. Butler* [1936]) and he soon joined the majority that invoked the amendment as well in striking down the Guffey Coal Act (*Carter v. Carter Coal Co.* [1936]).

In the spring of 1937, however, on the same day he added his vote to those who sustained Washington's minimum wage law (*West Coast Hotel v. Parrish*), Justice Roberts abandoned the Tenth Amendment limitations endorsed in *Constantine*, *Butler*, and *Carter Coal*. In the National Firearms Act of 1934 Congress had imposed a $200 annual licensing fee on all dealers in firearms. In addition to raising modest income for the federal treasury, the statute also arose from federal efforts to do something about the rising tide of gun-related criminal violence, especially bank robberies, then plaguing the United States. The licensing provisions clearly assisted state, local, and federal law enforcement officials in their war against the likes of Pretty Boy Floyd and John Dillinger. Noting that the tax produced "some revenue," Justice Stone observed that the Court would not speculate as to the motives of Congress or the extent to which the tax "may operate to restrict the activities taxed." And because "an offensive regulation" did not attend the levy, it could be distinguished from those invalidated in *Constantine* and *Butler* as "within the national taxing power" (*Sonzinsky v. United States* [1937]). There were no dissents.

By 1941 Justice Roberts endorsed Stone's complete burial of the Tenth Amendment in *Darby*, thereby reaffirming what he had said about the Tenth Amendment a decade earlier in *Sprague*. But in the interim, the court-packing debacle had taken place and Roosevelt had reconstructed the Court. Roberts's fluctuating, inconsistent reading of that amendment and its relationship to the federal system, a reading often expressed for the majority, had played a significant role in precipitating that crisis in 1935–1936 and eroding confidence in the Court's fidelity to its own precedents.

Government and the Economy

Fundamental constitutional questions touching federalism during the Hughes era remained ever entwined with the Court's interpretation of Congress's powers in Article I of the Constitution, especially the scope of its authority to tax and spend, regulate commerce among the states, and whether federal statutes resting upon those provisions invaded the reserved powers of the states, often catalogued as the police power. In turn, both the reach of these Article I provisions as well as the states' police power—usually invoked to regulate the health, welfare, and morals of the community—remained subject to a broad array of other constitutional limitations, notably the Commerce Clause itself, the Contracts Clause, as well as that captious provision in the Fifth and Fourteenth Amendments that prohibited the deprivation of life, liberty, or property "without due process of law." In short, the ability of either the federal government or the states to impose legal restraints upon the behavior of individuals in the national or local marketplace remained sharply constrained at the beginning of Hughes's tenure, but less so at its conclusion.

Until the adoption of the Fourteenth Amendment following the Civil War, the Contracts Clause in Article I, Section 10 of the Constitution, which prohibited the states from passing laws "impairing the Obligations of Contracts," remained, in addition to the Commerce Clause, the most potent source of federal judicial supervision over local regulations designed to govern economic relationships. Intended by the Framers as a restraint upon legislative majorities extending financial relief to hard-pressed debtors, the provision had been invoked often by the Court in the nineteenth century to that purpose in addition to protecting corporate charters from unilateral legislative revision (*Dartmouth College v. Woodward* [1819]) and limiting the states' capacity to alter its own contractual obligations (*Fletcher v. Peck* [1810]).

The economic collapse of the 1930s, which destroyed the income of millions of homeowners, small businessmen, and farmers, inspired a wide range of new state laws intended to aid these casualties of the marketplace. Most of these statutes, favoring debtors rather than creditors, faced constitutional challenges resting on the Contracts Clause and forced the Hughes Court to confront issues as old as the Marshall era.

Although the Contracts Clause does not limit the scope of federal legislative power, the Hughes Court invoked the just compensation provision of the Fifth Amendment to reach much the same result in 1934 in *Lynch v. United States*, a decision that suggested a rough road ahead for economic reforms that disrupted contractual expectations. In the Economy Act of 1933, promoted by Roosevelt, Congress abrogated the renewal of all term insurance contracts originally issued under the War Risk Insurance Act of World War I. With Justice Brandeis leading the charge, the justices for the third time in Hughes's tenure struck down an act of Congress. The insurance policies issued by the government, Brandeis argued, had created vested property rights that Congress could not destroy without paying just compensation, even though Congress had attempted in the Economy Act to take away the right to sue the federal government.

At the very end of the 1934 term, however, the Court moved in a different direction when it handed down *Home Building & Loan Ass'n v. Blaisdell*, a landmark Contracts Clause decision that gave new heart to many of those urging expanded government intervention to cushion the economic fall while simultaneously provoking denunciations of judicially sanctioned communism. It proved to be neither, but Hughes's opinion for a narrow majority of five indicated at least a willingness to view the Minnesota mortgage moratorium law and the constitutional provisions challenging it through the prism of the social and economic conditions then prevailing. Hughes placed the individual mortgage contract within the broad context of the state's duty to maintain the integrity of the economic and legal structure that made all contracting possible.

In *Lynch*, decided the same term, Congress had attempted to erase entirely its contractual obligations for renewal term insurance. But Minnesota's legislature, instead of impairing the obligations of contracts, the chief justice argued, had affirmed the importance of those obligations by modestly altering the remedies available to creditors. In so doing, the state had saved the entire system of contracting from collapse. Hughes offered a sophisticated conception of the social context of private contracts that harkened back to his views as an associate justice and bordered upon legal realism. As a piece of historical analysis capable of invoking solid precedents, the chief justice's opinion frankly paled in comparison to Sutherland's powerful dissent, but it was far better constitutional statesmanship.

For all of the contention it appeared to arouse among the justices, *Blaisdell* did not usher in a era of judicial softheartedness toward hard-pressed debtors who secured relief from sympathetic state legislators. Quite the opposite: Four months after upholding the Minnesota law, Hughes and the majority struck down an Arkansas statute that had attempted to place the assets in life insurance policies beyond the reach of creditors. Noting that in *Blaisdell* the Court had insisted that such relief "must be limited by reasonable conditions related to the emergency," the chief justice distinguished the Arkansas law as "neither temporary nor conditional." That effort drew a sharp concurrence from Sutherland, joined by Butler, Van Devanter, and McReynolds, who saw no difference between the two measures and they continued to denounce Hughes's invocation of an economic emergency (*W. B. Worthen Co. v. Thomas* [1934]).

Arkansas, a state staggering under the impact of the collapse of the cotton economy and the Dust Bowl, fared little better a year later when the justices unanimously invalidated a series of its laws designed to assist the state's debtors by extending their time for payment, lowering penalties for late payments, and slowing the appeals process for creditors. Writing for the Court, the liberal icon Cardozo again distinguished the remedies sustained in *Blaisdell* from those struck down in the present case, which he characterized as "without moderation or reason." Nor, he added, should even the Arkansas decision be taken to "exclude the possibility that the bounds [of state power] are even narrower" (*W. B. Worthen Co. v. Kavanaugh* [1935]).

The Arkansas decisions indicated that even in the wake of the *Blaisdell* decision, the Hughes Court, including Stone, Brandeis, and Cardozo, declined to declare the venerable Contracts Clause a constitutional derelict. The justices remained prepared to defend this essential rampart of capitalism in situations in which state legislatures, seeking to assist debtors, acted "without moderation or reason or in a spirit of oppression." But with the Court displaying a more tolerant attitude toward economic regulations generally after 1937 and with the addition of Roosevelt justices, litigants faced an uphill battle when attempting to overturn state laws by invoking the Contracts Clause. They would bear the burden of persuading the Court that the state had acted unreasonably.

In Hughes's last term, for example, a New York bank challenged a new state law that allowed judges in determining the amount of a default judgment to fix the "fair and reasonable market value" by deducting from the amount of the debt either such market value or the sale price, whichever was higher. Under the New York law in force at the time of the mortgage contract, the mortgagee would have had the right to the full amount of the difference between the debt and the sale price. Citing decisions from the Marshall era and noting that the economic emergency present in *Blaisdell* had passed, lawyers for the mortgagee argued that New York had impaired the contract. Speaking for a unanimous bench that spurned all of these complaints, Justice Douglas opined that "we cannot permit the broad language which those early decisions employed to force legislatures to be blind to the lessons that another century taught" (*Gelfert v. National City Bank* [1941]).

The Contracts Clause lost considerable potency during the Hughes years as a significant limitation upon the state's choice of economic policy, and a similar fate befell the Fourteenth Amendment's Due Process Clause, which, since the end of the nineteenth century, had become the chief weapon in the arsenal of courts seeking to maximize the scope of private choice in the market by limiting the states' police powers. The Supreme Court had never employed that captious provision to strike down every state law that tread upon the freedom of persons to barter and exchange. Even during the tenure of Fuller, White, and Taft, the justices had sustained more state laws challenged on due process grounds than they had eviscerated. But they had erected some significant doctrinal hurdles for the states to overcome in this regard and their decisions had fallen with special force upon laws seeking to advance the economic interests of ordinary wage earners, a pattern that gave rise to justifiable complaints about the class prejudices of the justices.

For a state law to survive due process attack in the view of most justices before 1934, the statute had to be directed against an economic activity deemed "affected with a public interest," a rather narrow category of enterprises. This limit the Court had decreed as early as *Munn v. Illinois* (1877), when it sustained the state's regulation of maximum rates for grain elevator companies that held a virtual monopoly over the service. But, in addition, the regulation had to be "reasonable," rather than "unreasonable, unnecessary and [an] arbitrary interference with the right of the individual to his personal liberty," as Justice Rufus Peckham put it so emphatically in *Lochner v. New York* (1905). The justices measured the standard of reasonableness, of course, not the legislature.

Employing this subjective yardstick of reasonableness, the Court majority had permitted the states to limit the hours of work in underground mines (*Holden v. Hardy* [1898]) as well as for women employed in laundries (*Muller v. Oregon* [1908]), but not for adult men employed in bakeries (*Lochner*). An equally divided Court sustained an Oregon minimum wage law in 1917, but a reconstituted bench found such a statute lacked reasonableness five years later (*Adkins v. Children's Hospital* [1923]). They also condemned as unreasonable a compulsory arbitration scheme for resolving labor-management disputes (*Wolff Packing Co. v. Court of Industrial Relations* [1923]). And even in the case of businesses "affected with a public interest," the justices curbed legislative and administrative decisions by requiring that all rates fixed for railroads and other utilities guarantee a profit, based upon the reproductive cost of the enterprise (*Smyth v. Ames* [1898]).

Marshaling a slim majority of five, the Hughes Court methodically chipped away at this inherited due process limitation beginning in 1931 with *O'Gorman & Young v. Hartford Fire Insurance Co.*, which sustained a legislative regulation of the commissions paid to insurance agents by their companies. *Nebbia* three years later effectively eliminated "business affected with a public interest" as a due process barrier to price regulations mandated by the state, and the walls came tumbling down on minimum wage statutes with *West Coast Hotel v. Parrish* (1937), despite the brief procedural detour taken in *Morehead v. New York ex rel. Tipaldo* (1936).

In the wake of *West Coast Hotel*, the justices all but banished the Due Process Clause in both the Fourteenth and Fifth Amendments from their arsenal of substantive limitation upon legislative policy in the broad area of what Stone referred to as "ordinary commercial transactions" (*United States v. Carolene Products* [1938]). If the legislature attempted to prevent a judicial inquiry into the rational basis for the statute, Stone declared, the law might violate due process, but then only if the court could not determine some rational basis "within the contemplation of the legislature." Even such a minuscule dose of judicial scrutiny over economic affairs proved too much for a New Dealer like Justice Black, who declined to endorse that portion of Stone's opinion. Somewhat later he asserted the new orthodoxy that emerged from the ashes of the decade's constitutional struggles: "Whether the legislature takes for its textbook Adam Smith, Herbert Spencer, Lord Keynes, or some other," Black wrote for a unanimous court, "is no concern of ours" (*Ferguson v. Skrupa* [1963]).

By 1944, with the infusion of New Deal justices, the Court majority also retreated from its traditional role of supervising the rate-making decisions of state and federal regulatory agencies when it overruled *Smyth v. Ames* as the controlling doctrine with respect to the setting of utility rates (*Federal Power Commission v. Natural Gas Pipeline* [1942]; and *Federal Power Commission v. Hope Natural Gas* [1944]).

The burial of the Due Process Clause by the Hughes Court did not mean, however, that the justices eliminated as well other constitutional limitations upon the economic policy choices of the states. Despite dissents by Cardozo, Stone, and Brandeis, the Equal Protection Clause of the Fourteenth Amendment continued upon occasion to serve the majority as a restraint upon the states' regulatory activities, a posture announced in *Colgate v. Harvey* (1935), in which six votes overturned part of a Vermont tax exemption for in-state loans. That decision did not survive the arrival of Roosevelt justices, who overruled it five years later in *Madden v. Kentucky* (1940), with Justices Roberts and McReynolds in dissent. Two years after upholding the price regulations in *Nebbia* (1934), however, Roberts and the majority struck down on grounds of equal protection an amendment to New York's regulatory regime that allowed milk producers without a well-advertised trade name to sell at prices below those with well-advertised trade names (*Mayflower Farms v. Ten Eyck* [1936]). On the same day, the Court rejected a similar equal protection challenge to the differential treatment of producers contained in the original New York regulations (*Borden's Farm Products v. Ten Eyck* [1936]).

Like its predecessors, the Hughes Court also continued to apply the Commerce Clause as a constitutional mandate, enforced by the federal courts, to protect the national market from burdens and obstructions from whatever source. The justices invoked this so-called dormant Commerce Clause in the absence of congressional legislation to void state laws that sought to protect local producers by discriminating against their out-of-state competitors.

Portions of New York's milk regulations survived a due process challenge and even one bottomed on the Equal Protection Clause but ran afoul of the Commerce Clause in *Baldwin v. G.A.F. Seelig, Inc.* (1935). A section of the 1933 New York law prohibited sales in New York of milk from another state if the milk had been purchased below the price set for similar purchases within New York. New York, claiming that its law had only an "incidental" impact on interstate commerce, justified the regulation as a necessary exercise of its police power to maintain an adequate supply of milk that would be jeopardized if the income of dairy farmers collapsed. For the Court, Cardozo rejected this reasoning. "Let such an exception be admitted, and all that a state will have to do in times of stress and strain is to say that its farmers and merchants and workmen must be protected against competition from without, lest they go upon the poor relief lists or perish altogether."

Of course, not every such state law, challenged on grounds of the dormant Commerce Clause, failed to pass constitutional scrutiny. The Public Utilities Commission of Ohio, invoking highway congestion, refused to grant a certificate of public convenience and necessity to a trucker who wished to operate a motor vehicle over state Route 20, which extended from Cleveland to the Ohio-Michigan state line with a final destination in Flint, Michigan. The aggrieved trucker asserted his rights under the Commerce Clause and the Equal Protection Clause of the Fourteenth Amendment. But speaking for a unanimous bench in *Bradley v. Public Utilities Commission*

(1933), Brandeis rejected both arguments and sustained Ohio's police power to promote the safety of its highways, a power later extended to South Carolina's width and weight limit on all trucks using its highways (*South Carolina State Highway Dept. v. Barnwell Bros.* [1938]).

State regulation of the insurance business, long sanctioned by the Court, continued to survive even in the face of statutes that clearly intruded upon business transactions beyond the state's borders. In 1940 the justices sustained a Virginia law that prohibited a licensed insurance company from writing policies except through resident agents, who could not share more than half of their commissions with nonresident brokers. "The mere fact that state action may have repercussions beyond state lines," wrote Justice Frankfurter, "is of no judicial significance so long as the action is not within that domain which the Constitution forbids" (*Osborn v. Ozlin* [1940]).

Even local milk regulations could sometimes survive constitutional attack. Like New York, Pennsylvania invoked the police power for its own milk control law, which set a minimum price to be paid by dealers to milk producers. The state's milk control board sought to extend these regulations to a New York dealer who bought milk from Pennsylvania producers for shipments out of state. The Hughes Court, speaking through Justice Roberts, sustained the Pennsylvania regulations and rejected the contentions that they constituted "a prohibited burden on interstate commerce." To find otherwise, Roberts argued, would permit the state's milk dealers to destroy the regulations by claiming that all or a portion of the milk they purchased was destined to another state. The affected activity, Roberts argued, was "essentially local in Pennsylvania," where only a small fraction of the milk produced actually left the state (*Milk Control Board v. Eisenberg Farm Products* [1939]).

In his *Eisenberg* opinion, Roberts attempted to distinguish the result from *Baldwin*, an effort that did not persuade all observers of the Court's work, who noted that the justice's long-standing attempts to arbitrate between the states' police powers and the dormant Commerce Clause continued to produce an ever-shifting line between those regulatory schemes that placed a prohibited burden on the national marketplace and those that did not. Justices Frankfurter, Black, and Douglas summarized the frustrating nature of this task near the end of the Hughes era in 1940: "Judicial control of national commerce—unlike legislative regulations—must from inherent limitations of the judicial process treat the subject by the hit-and-miss method of deciding single local controversies upon evidence and information limited by the narrow rules of litigation. Spasmodic and unrelated instances of litigation cannot afford an adequate basis for the creation of integrated national rules which alone can afford that full protection for interstate commerce intended by the Constitution" (*McCarroll v. Dixie Greyhound Lines* [1940]).

Similar complexities confronted the Hughes Court in its efforts to draw the line between permissible state taxes on business enterprises and other prohibited levies that obstructed or burdened interstate commerce at a time when the revenue demands of government grew in response to the depressed economy. Even before it overturned the long-standing ban on intergovernmental tax immunities in *Graves v. New York ex rel. O'Keefe* in 1939, the Court demonstrated heightened sensitivity to the states' revenue crisis when plaintiffs challenged local levies by invoking the Commerce Clause.

In 1933, for example, Hughes led the Court in sustaining a Minnesota personal property tax levied May 1, "tax day," against eleven head of cattle sold the following day to out-of-state buyers. Citing the Court's long "current of commerce" rulings, the plaintiff claimed the tax had improperly taxed goods in interstate commerce. Not so, declared Hughes, who noted that the cattle were not in transit on the day of the tax. "But because there is a flow of interstate commerce which is subject to the regulating power of the Congress, it does not necessarily follow that . . . a state may not lay a nondiscriminatory tax upon property which, although connected with that flow . . . has come to rest . . . within the state" (*Minnesota v. Blasius* [1933]).

Justice Cardozo, whose opinion in *Baldwin v. G.A.F. Seelig* (1935) condemned New York's attempt to apply its milk price regulations to other states as a "protective tariff," adopted a somewhat more tolerant approach to state taxation schemes that also took away the competitive advantage some states might have enjoyed in an unrestricted national market. In *Henneford v. Silas Mason Co.* (1937), he wrote for the Court to uphold a Washington "use of chattels" tax applied to goods purchased in other states and used in Washington. The levy did not apply to any article that had already been subjected to a sales or use tax of at least 2 percent. Washington's plan survived a challenge under the Commerce Clause in the Court's view because it sought to promote equality in the national market by canceling only a single tax advantage enjoyed by out-of-state sellers and thus permitted some continuing price competition.

In 1941, Hughes's last term, the Court also upheld a state law that compelled an out-of-state company to collect use taxes on all sales at its retail stores, including interstate mail-order sales made at the same location, on the assumption that the mail-order business had been aided by the local retail business (*Nelson v. Sears Roebuck & Co.* [1941]).

Prior to 1938 the Supreme Court had routinely struck down state taxes on gross receipts generated by interstate sales on the grounds that such levies constituted a "direct burden on interstate commerce." Justice Stone, who led the attack on the inherited conceptual categories of "direct" versus "indirect" with respect to other issues arising under the Commerce Clause, also attempted to discard these formulas in the taxation field by easing the restrictions on gross receipts taxes imposed by the states so long as they were reasonably apportioned. Over dissents by McReynolds and Butler, Stone advanced his so-called multiple burdens test in *Western Livestock v. Bureau of Revenue* (1938), in which the majority upheld a New Mexico tax for the privilege of doing business imposed on the gross receipts of a trade journal that, although published in the state, had a significant interstate circulation and received revenues from out-of-state advertisers. The state calculated the privilege tax on the basis of advertising space sold to all customers, both intrastate and interstate.

Stone conceded that the Court had in the past invalidated local taxes measured by gross receipts from interstate commerce, especially those levied by states on transportation companies. Such taxes, if adopted by a multiplicity of states, threatened both to disadvantage interstate enterprises relative to the tax burden carried by local ones and to impose a substantial tariff on interstate commerce generally. Stone distinguished the New Mexico tax on the trade magazine published in its state, however, because "the tax is not one which in form or substance can be repeated by other states in such manner as to lay an added burden on the interstate distribution of the magazine."

If the states believed that Stone and the Court had given them a green light in *Western Livestock* to impose various forms of gross receipts taxes upon companies operating across state boundaries they were sorely mistaken. A year after *Western Livestock*, the justices struck down a 1 percent Indiana tax on a local manufacturer's gross receipts from products shipped on orders taken from buyers in other states and foreign countries. Without apportionment between the receipts derived from intrastate as opposed to interstate transactions, Justice Roberts wrote, the Indiana levy contained the fatal defect of encouraging other states to act likewise, thus risking "a double tax burden to which intrastate commerce is not exposed" (*Adams Manufacturing Co. v. Storen* [1938]).

A Washington state "business activities" tax on the gross income of a local company engaged in marketing throughout the country apples and pears grown in Washington and Oregon did not survive, however (*Gwin, White & Prince v. Henneford* [1939]). Stone, for the Court, again condemned the levy for a lack of apportionment and the threat of multiple burdens. A year later, however, Stone mobilized a majority to sustain a New York City 2 percent levy upon the amount of the receipts from "every sale" in the city, with sellers directed to collect the tax. The majority, with Hughes, Roberts, and McReynolds dissenting, sustained the tax against a company that mined coal in Pennsylvania and maintained a New York sales office from which it sold the coal to local consumers. Because the ultimate burden fell upon New Yorkers who bought the coal as measured by the sale price and because the tax was "conditioned upon events occurring within New York," Stone argued, the levy did not constitute a prohibited levy upon interstate commerce. Hughes's long dissent noted that "the tax as here applied is open to the same objections as a tariff upon the entrance of the coal into the State of New York, or a state tax upon the privilege of doing interstate business, and in my view it cannot be sustained without abandoning principles long established and a host of precedents soundly based" (*McGoldrick v. Berwind-White Coal Mining Co.* [1940]).

Determined to defend both the revenue-generating powers of the states and the free trade ideal for interstate commerce, Hughes and his brethren failed to articulate a magic formula capable of subsuming the myriad taxation schemes generated by the Great Depression. Their use of such concepts as "multiple burdens" or "local incidents" to justify some state taxes while overturning others failed to convince many critics. And at least one new Roosevelt justice, Hugo Black, urged the Court to abandon these efforts in the interests of judicial restraint and deference to Congress. Beginning in *Adams Manufacturing Co.*, Black argued that the Court had usurped the national legislature's function when it insisted upon an apportionment or allocation formula for the Indiana tax and that "possible future unfair burdens" did not constitute a persuasive constitutional reason for invalidating the measure.

Another New Dealer, Justice Frankfurter, later summarized the failure of the Hughes Court, as well as its predecessors and successors, to bring rational order to the tension between the power of the states to tax and the limitations upon that power imposed by the Commerce Clause. "To attempt to harmonize all that has been said in the past would neither clarify what has gone before nor guide the future," he wrote. "Suffice it to say that especially in this field opinions must be read in the setting of the particular case and as the product of preoccupation with their special facts" (*Freeman v. Hewit* [1946]).

The Hughes Court strove with considerable success to emancipate state lawmakers—legislators, judges, and administrators—from many of the constitutionally imposed restraints that had limited their choice of economic policies since the late nineteenth century. By 1941 the states possessed a wider range of options with respect to the sources from which they could raise revenue. By that year, too, few areas of local economic life—from minimum wages to utility rates and land-use decisions—remained immune to the reach of the states' police powers, now sheltered by a generous use of the rational basis test. The Due Process Clause of the Fourteenth Amendment had been largely defanged and many local aspects of interstate commerce, absent federal preemption, remained subject to state control. *Erie v. Tompkins* (1938) held out the further promise that federal judges would pay greater deference to state law in civil litigation arising through diversity jurisdiction.

But despite *Erie* (1938), *Nebbia* (1934), and *West Coast Hotel v. Parrish* (1937), the states as architects of economic policy still functioned within a series of judicially imposed constitutional restraints of major significance, including the Commerce Clause and the requirement of equal protection of the laws. Moreover, they faced on the eve of World War II a federal government newly endowed by the Hughes Court with an arsenal of substantive powers, especially those relating to taxation, spending, the regulation of interstate commerce, and the conduct of foreign relations, that would promote far greater centralization in the future than had been imagined under the New Deal.

Faced with the historic choice of whether the Constitution was a document of limitations or a charter of powers, the Hughes Court ultimately opted for the latter when it came to the scope of federal authority over the nation's basic economic arrangements. The road to that final destination in 1941 seemed to many contemporaries one of twists and turns, the view certainly of President Roosevelt and the New Dealers, who bridled at the decisions that struck down their initial recovery measures such as the Railroad Retirement Act, the NIRA, the Frazier-Lemke Farm Mortgage Moratorium Act, the Triple A, and the Guffey Coal Act.

Unwilling to accept any responsibility for the fate of these statutes, even when their judicial allies joined the majority, the New Dealers simply blamed the Court for the constitutional impasse that seemed to have developed by 1937. They did not immediately see that short-term defeats often contained the doctrinal seeds of major victories such as occurred in *United States v. Butler* (1936), which invalidated the AAA, but also yoked Congress's taxing and spending powers to the General Welfare Clause with language broad enough to encompass an extraordinary range of future federal initiatives, including Social Security.

Similar to the situation they faced with respect to the states' police powers and the Fourteenth Amendment, the Hughes justices inherited a series of precedents that both limited and expanded the scope of Congress's authority under Article I, conceptual categories that often baffled lay observers because of their apparent contradictions. A striking example was the Court's approach to the Commerce Clause and the extent to which the inherent structure of the federal system, the Due Process Clause of the Fifth Amendment, or the Tenth Amendment limited what Congress might do when invoking it as the justification for economic policies.

On the one hand, rooted in the *E.C. Knight* decision of 1895, the Court had attempted to draw a clear distinction between interstate commerce and what it labeled "production" or "manufacturing," those economic activities, usually located within a state, that preceded interstate commerce. The former, either by virtue of the federal structure itself or the Tenth Amendment, remained beyond Congress's authority. Utilizing those conceptual limitations, a majority of the justices had overturned a federal antitrust prosecution against a company with a monopoly of sugar refining facilities (*United States v. E.C. Knight*) as well as efforts to bar the products of child labor from interstate commerce (*Hammer v. Dagenhart* [1918]).

The Court had also articulated a distinction between those local economic activities that affected interstate commerce only "indirectly" and those whose impact was "direct." Congress might, for example, impose strict liability upon railroads for injuries to employees working directly in interstate commerce, but not for injuries to those who merely supported such employees, such as ticket agents or machine shop repairmen. Nor could Congress prohibit railroads from utilizing yellow-dog contracts because such a ban violated freedom of contract, protected by the Due Process Clause, and the majority could not discern any relationship between membership in a labor organization "and the carrying on of interstate commerce" (*Adair v. United States* [1908]). On the other hand, the national legislature could authorize the fixing of purely local, intrastate railroad rates when they had a direct impact upon the longer, interstate tariff because Congress had the duty "to keep the highways of interstate communication open to interstate traffic upon fair and equal terms. . . . [and] injury upon that commerce, or some part thereof, furnishes abundant ground for Federal intervention" (*Shreveport Case* [1914]).

Beginning with the case of *In re Debs*, decided in the same term as *E.C. Knight*, the Court had also ruled unanimously that "the strong arm of the national government may be put forth to brush away all obstructions to the freedom of interstate commerce." Congress might also bar from interstate commerce certain traffic or commodities, such as lottery tickets, tainted food products, and stolen automobiles. Further, if economic activities took place within a "current of commerce" or "stream of commerce," such as a conspiracy to fix prices at the stockyards or the fees levied by commission men who sold livestock there, Congress could act, in the Court's words, "to protect that commerce from being restrained by methods, whether old or new, which would constitute an interference" (*Standard Oil Company v. United States* [1911]).

In common with other practitioners of the literary arts, Supreme Court justices invoked particular metaphors and images when explaining their grounds for decision. Chief Justice Hughes remained especially fond of the language found in his own *Shreveport* opinion and many others that emphasized the responsibility of Congress to keep the channels of interstate commerce "open," and free from "all obstructions," and "interferences" that might "burden" it. Hughes found it easy, therefore, to sustain provisions of the Railway Labor Act of 1926, which allowed employees to choose their bargaining representatives (i.e., union representatives) "without interference, influence or coercion" by the railroads, because Congress had the authority to "facilitate . . . the settlement of disputes which threaten the service of the necessary agencies of interstate transportation" (*Texas & New Orleans Railroad Co. v. Brotherhood of Railway and Steamship Clerks* [1930]).

Texas & New Orleans Railroad silently overruled *Adair* and disposed of liberty of contract and the Due Process Clause as a limitation upon Congress's authority to regulate interstate commerce. Without much hesitation, the chief justice also voted to sustain the Railroad Retirement Act four years later on similar grounds and he chided Justice Roberts for his failure to see the obvious relationship between the pension plan invalidated and Congress's effort to guarantee the freedom of interstate commerce by removing another potential "obstruction," "burden," or "interference" from its path. From these railroad cases, Hughes extracted the reasoning that anchored his decisive opinion in *Jones & Laughlin*, which sustained Congress's authority to broadly remove the burden of all labor disputes that might threaten the freedom of interstate commerce. By 1937 the threat posed to that commerce from large-scale strikes and labor disruptions had become far greater than in 1930.

Nonetheless, *Jones & Laughlin* involved a big step for Hughes and the majority, because the cases that employed the metaphors of "obstruction," "interference," or "burden" to sustain the commerce power had arisen usually in relation to the railroad industry and/or economic activities that involved rates, prices, or buying and selling, not industrial manufacturing, mining, or agriculture per se. The line of cases that stressed a distinction between "production" or "manufacturing" and "commerce" as well as those that emphasized "direct" as opposed to "indirect" effects, still retained their vitality. Hughes and others invoked them to strike down the NIRA's live poultry code, the crop restrictions of the Agricultural Adjustment Act, and the production and labor features of the first Bituminous Coal Conservation Act.

Hughes and Justice Roberts manifested greater willingness to sustain the marketing restrictions of the Second Agricultural Adjustment Act (*Mulford v. Smith* [1939]) as well as the taxing mechanism mandated by Congress in the revised coal conservation statute (*Sunshine Anthracite Coal Co. v. Adkins* [1940]), which indicates that the inherited intellectual framework of Commerce Clause analysis exercised a powerful influence on virtually all of the justices, wholly apart from external political and economic pressures or the addition of new members. Only Justices Butler and McReynolds dissented in *Mulford* and McReynolds stood alone in *Sunshine Anthracite*, but both Hughes and Roberts had great difficulty accepting Stone's opinion in *Darby Lumber* (1941), which sustained the authority of Congress to regulate "production for commerce" and overruled *Hammer v. Dagenhart.*

With only McReynolds in dissent, Stone had also led the Hughes Court when it brushed aside the Due Process Clause of the Fifth Amendment as a substantive limitation upon Congress's exercise of the commerce power (*United States v. Carolene Products Co.* [1938]). That decision, combined with those removing any lingering doubt about the scope of the federal taxing and spending power, prepared the way for an expansion of federal authority via Article I not seriously questioned by the Supreme Court until the 1990s.

New Directions in Civil Liberties

When Hughes convened his court for the first time in the winter of 1930, American constitutional law remained at a critical crossroads with respect to the issues broadly defined as civil liberties, above all those touching freedom of expression and the free exercise of religion as set forth in the First Amendment or included within the concept of "liberty" protected by the Fourteenth. Over the next decade, the Hughes-led justices significantly expanded the scope of governmental powers with respect to economic policy, what Justice Stone called "ordinary commercial transactions," by invoking a minimal level of judicial scrutiny, labeled the "rational basis test" (*United States v. Carolene Products Co.* [1938]). So doing, the justices struck off many of the judicially constructed fetters that had limited government's role in the economy.

In that same opinion's famous Footnote 4, however, Stone suggested that the justices ought to require government to meet a much higher standard of review when legislation appeared to violate specific guarantees of the Bill of Rights, denied individuals access to the ballot box, or discriminated against "discrete and insular minorities" who lacked significant political influence. Stone's footnote soon entered the constitutional lexicon as the "preferred freedoms" doctrine, one that appealed to Roosevelt appointees such as Black, Douglas, and Murphy and one that came to represent the general orientation of the Earl Warren–led bench in the 1960s. But Stone's footnote proved to be more than a forecast of the distant jurisprudential future. In 1938 it captured the direction already charted by the Hughes Court, which between 1930 and 1941 became the most self-conscious defender of civil liberties prior to the Warren era by imposing new limits upon the exercise of governmental authority.

The First World War had spawned both some of the most repressive laws in the nation's history with respect to speech and press while at the same time it sowed the seeds for a rebirth of libertarian values associated with the First Amendment. The war years brought federal espionage and sedition prosecutions and postal censorship in addition to state criminal anarchy statutes, all aimed at individuals and groups who opposed the war, militant labor organizations such as the Industrial Workers of the World, and the quarreling factions of the Communist Party. But the war years also launched the American Civil Liberties Union, dedicated to defending freedom of expression, plus a series of dissenting opinions by Holmes and Brandeis that stressed the need to limit governmental restraints upon expression to those words and conduct that threatened a "clear and present danger" to the nation's safety.

Between 1918 and 1921 a majority of the justices gave "clear and present danger" a restrictive interpretation and employed the so-called bad tendency test that permitted the punishment of ideas likely to produce social harm. They easily sustained the convictions of antiwar leaders, pacifists, and assorted political radicals under both federal and state statutes. If the First Amendment offered little protection for those charged under federal law, the Fourteenth Amendment appeared to offer even less. The Court upheld a conviction under a Minnesota law that prohibited public speaking against enlistment and the teaching of pacifism. That decision provoked a vigorous dissent from Brandeis, who noted that the Court had often invoked the

Fourteenth Amendment against wage and hours legislation and even "incorporated" the Just Compensation Clause of the Fifth Amendment into its limitations upon the states (*Chicago, Burlington & Quincy Railroad Co. v. City of Chicago* [1897]). "I cannot believe," he wrote, "that the liberty guaranteed by the Fourteenth Amendment includes only liberty to acquire and enjoy property" (*Gilbert v. Minnesota* [1920]).

Brandeis won this historic doctrinal war four years later, however, when in the course of his opinion affirming the conviction of Benjamin Gitlow under New York's criminal anarchy law, Justice Sanford for the Court announced that "we may and do assume that freedom of speech and press—which are protected by the First Amendment from abridgement by Congress—are among the fundamental personal rights and 'liberties' protected by the due process clause of the Fourteenth Amendment from impairment by the States" (*Gitlow v. New York* [1925]). By "incorporating" the First Amendment guarantees of speech and press into the Due Process Clause, *Gitlow* represented a huge victory for civil liberties. At the same time, the opinion set back the quest for limits upon governmental restrictions by invoking the "bad tendency" test and declaring the "clear and present danger" standard inapplicable in situations where the legislature itself defined certain ideas (rather than certain conduct) as so dangerous that they merited immediate suppression.

There matters stood when Hughes came to the Court. Only once since the war had the justices overturned the conviction of a political dissenter on due process or First Amendment grounds. In that case, *Fiske v. Kansas* (1927), the justices found merely that the one document used by the state to secure a conviction under its criminal syndicalist law—the preamble to the constitution of the IWW—did not advocate the use of force, violence, or other unlawful acts. As applied to Fiske, therefore, the Kansas statute constituted an "arbitrary and unreasonable exercise of the police power," according to Justice Sanford. At the same time, however, the Sanford-led majority upheld the California conviction of Anita Whitney, whose only offense had been to join and meet with the Communist Labor Party, an organization formed to teach criminal syndicalism. That decision provoked a powerful dissent in the form of a concurrence by Brandeis, who reaffirmed his and Holmes's commitment to the "clear and present danger" test with the added caveat that "even imminent danger cannot justify resort to prohibition [of speech and press] . . . unless the evil apprehended is relatively serious" (*Whitney v. California* [1927]).

Hughes, joined by Roberts, Brandeis, Holmes, Stone, Sutherland, and Van Devanter, began modestly enough in 1931 by reversing the conviction of Yetta Stromberg, found guilty for violating a California law that prohibited the public use or display of a red flag, a symbol condemned by the legislature as indicating opposition to organized government. Without specifically invoking the First Amendment, Hughes condemned the statute for overbreadth since its prohibition, which also threatened peaceful, nonviolent uses of the flag, violated due process. Yet the opinion's avoidance of a broad First Amendment analysis hid somewhat its more radical implications, noted by the two dissenters, McReynolds and Butler. For the first time, the Court had extended the protections of the First Amendment via the Fourteenth to include symbolic speech (*Stromberg v. California* [1931]).

A month after *Stromberg*, the trend became more clear when Hughes marshaled five votes to lift an injunction against a Minnesota newspaper, the *Saturday Press*, imposed by a state judge under a state "gag" law that permitted judicial suppression of publications deemed lewd, obscene, malicious, or defamatory. In previous cases, notably *Toledo Newspaper Co. v. United States* (1918) and *Milwaukee Social Democratic Publishing Co. v. Burleson* (1921), which provoked dissents by Holmes and Brandeis, the Supreme Court majority had displayed remarkably little concern for the First Amendment interests of the press by sustaining a contempt conviction as well as censorship by the postmaster general. In *Near*, however, Hughes invoked the ancient authority of Blackstone ("liberty of the press consists in laying no previous restraints upon publication"), the First Amendment, and the Fourteenth to strike down the Minnesota statute, the first occasion on which the Court specifically enforced the press clause against either a state or federal law. With only limited exceptions, Hughes wrote, an injunction against publication constituted an unconstitutional prior restraint, a far greater danger to freedom of expression than other sanctions, because it altogether prevented ideas from entering the arena of public discourse (*Near v. Minnesota* [1931]). Aware of the important constitutional turn now taken, one that allowed an unsavory, anti-Catholic, anti-Semitic, and antiblack publication to continue, Sutherland, Butler, Van Devanter, and McReynolds dissented.

Stromberg and *Near* represented the first skirmish in a longer campaign by Hughes and a majority of the justices to strengthen First Amendment protections for speech and press at the expense of the state's traditional police powers. In 1936, without dissent, the Court overturned a Louisiana gross receipts tax that purposefully fell upon the state's largest newspapers, the publications most critical of Huey Long's gubernatorial regime. Such a discriminatory tax, wrote Justice Sutherland, was "a deliberate and calculated device . . . to limit the circulation of information" (*Grosjean v. American Press Co.* [1936]). And again invoking the First Amendment rule against prior restraint announced in *Near*, the Court soon overturned a city ordinance that prohibited the distribution or sale of circulars, magazines, handbooks, or pamphlets without written permission of the city manager. Prior restraint applied to more than newspapers, Hughes wrote, and to distribution as well as to publication. Vesting such broad powers of censorship in a single official constituted an unconstitutional procedure (*Lovell v. City of Griffin* [1938]).

These decisions provided the momentum for the landmark rulings in *Bridges v. California* and *Times-Mirror Co. v. Superior Court* (1941), decided several months after Hughes had stepped down to be replaced by Harlan Stone. In *Bridges*,

Justice Black and five others reversed contempt convictions against the militant labor leader Harry Bridges and the *Los Angeles Times* on grounds that their published comments had not constituted a "clear and present danger" to pending judicial proceedings, the first time the justices had invoked that lofty standard to protect freedom of the press. How Hughes might have voted in *Bridges* remains a matter of speculation, but both Roberts and Stone, who had formed the majority in cases such as *Near* and *Lovell*, joined Frankfurter's dissent against Black's sweeping affirmation of the First Amendment.

Under Hughes, the Supreme Court extended constitutional protection to the press far beyond its predecessors, but the justices also insisted that this protection did not immunize the institution from other important social obligations. Like other economic enterprises, newspapers could not escape nondiscriminatory, general tax liabilities (*Giragi v. Moore* [1937]). On a similar theory, the Court held that the First Amendment did not bar nondiscriminatory application of the National Labor Relations Act to a major news organization. The new federal law might alter their labor relations and even raise the cost of doing business, but it did not affect the impartial distribution of the news (*Associated Press v. National Labor Relations Board* [1937]).

The Supreme Court did not apply the "clear and present danger" test to government actions touching the press until the *Bridges* decision. But that libertarian doctrine influenced speech cases somewhat earlier during Hughes's tenure, notably during the years from 1937 to 1941, when the justices handed down six important freedom of expression rulings, all but one overturning state restrictions.

DeJonge v. Oregon (1937), with Hughes writing for a unanimous bench, vindicated Brandeis's concurrence in *Whitney* and all but erased that precedent from the constitutional canon. The justices reversed the conviction of Dirk DeJonge, convicted under Oregon's version of a criminal syndicalism law, which made participation in any organization that advocated the overthrow of established government a felony. DeJonge had conducted public meetings in Portland under the auspices of the Communist Party to protest police shootings of striking longshoremen and their raids against the union hall and workers' homes. The Oregon Supreme Court had affirmed his conviction despite the absence of any evidence at trial indicating that DeJonge or anyone at the meeting had advocated unlawful action. Communist Party sponsorship alone had been sufficient.

In reversing DeJonge's conviction and holding that Oregon's interpretation of its law infringed freedom of expression, Hughes for the first time ruled that "the right of the people peaceably to assemble," guaranteed by the First Amendment, was a fundamental right, one "incorporated" within the meaning of the "liberty" protected by the Due Process Clause of the Fourteenth Amendment. "Peaceable assembly," the chief justice wrote, "cannot be made a crime. The holding of meetings for peaceable political action cannot be proscribed. Those who assist in the conduct of such meetings cannot be branded as criminals on that score" (*DeJonge v. Oregon* [1937]).

The second major freedom of expression decision of the 1937 term left the justices sharply divided. Angelo Herndon was every white Southerner's nightmare. An African American member of the Communist Party, he arrived in Georgia with the goal of recruiting new members for the organization. In addition to holding three meetings in the state, Herndon distributed an official party pamphlet entitled "The Communist Party Position on the Negro Question," which advocated self-determination for those living in the South's "black belt" and the establishment of a separate black-dominated government in the United States. The party's membership applications affirmed its role as the guardian of the working class and the personification of "proletarian revolution." Because Georgia did not have a criminal anarchy statute, the state charged and convicted Herndon for violating a pre–Civil War Georgia law designed to forestall slave insurrections, which made it a crime for anyone to attempt to persuade others to participate in an insurrection against organized government.

The Georgia Supreme Court interpreted the statute as permitting a finding of guilt if Herndon intended an insurrection "to happen at any time, as a result of his influence." Writing for the majority of five to overturn the conviction, Justice Roberts took a major step toward eradicating the "bad tendency" test from First Amendment jurisprudence. The Georgia statute, he declared, was so vague and indefinite as to be invalid under the standard set in *Stromberg.* It did not give the judge and jury any guidance for appraising the circumstances and character of the defendant's utterances and conduct in order to determine whether they created "a clear and present danger of forcible obstruction of a particular state function." As construed and applied to Herndon, he concluded, the Georgia law "amounts merely to a dragnet which may enmesh anyone who agitates for a change in government if a jury can be persuaded that he ought to have foreseen his words to have some effect on the future conduct of others" (*Herndon v. Lowry* [1937]).

The Four Horsemen, invoking the "bad tendency" test, argued that Herndon's possession and distribution of the self-determination plan by itself indicated his support for insurrection because such a change "could not be effected otherwise." Roberts and his supporters, however, had given new life to the "clear and present danger" test in *Herndon,* which stands as the Hughes Court's most libertarian statement on due process and the First Amendment. When he compared all of the major sedition defendants since World War I, including Eugene Debs, Gitlow, and Whitney, the foremost student of the First Amendment, Professor Zechariah Chafee, concluded that only one—Angelo Herndon—probably created a "clear and present danger" of unlawful acts under the circumstances surrounding his words. Herndon sought to change the intolerable conditions under which most Southern Negroes lived in the 1930s (Chafee 1941).

After *Herndon*, the balance of First Amendment/due process decisions by the Hughes Court became almost predictable. In 1939 five justices upheld an injunction against the enforcement of a Jersey City ordinance that banned all public meetings and the distribution of printed materials in the city's streets, parks, and other public places without a permit from a "director of public safety." Jersey City mayor Frank "I am the Law" Hague and his administration had used the ordinance selectively against union meetings and union organizers. Justice Roberts and two others defined the parks and streets as public forums protected by the First Amendment as part of the privileges and immunities of citizens. Stone and the chief justice, concurring, invoked *DeJonge* and *Lovell* as authority: the arbitrary authority exercised by the city's director of public safety infringed the right to peaceable assembly guaranteed by the Fourteenth Amendment's Due Process Clause (*Hague v. Congress of Industrial Organizations* [1939]).

And a year later, speaking through Justice Murphy with only McReynolds in dissent, the justices gave the labor movement a second major First Amendment victory in *Thornhill v. Alabama* (1940), when they declared picketing a form of protected expression under the First and Fourteenth Amendments, invoked the "clear and present danger" standard, and struck down a state statute that had imposed a blanket prohibition on all such activities. The government might regulate picketing by labor organizations that interfered with the "privacy, the lives, and the property of its residents," Murphy wrote, but its suppression could be justified "only where the clear danger of substantive evils arises under circumstances affording no opportunity to test the merits of ideas . . . in the market of public opinion."

In his final term and in his last important statement on freedom of expression, the chief justice who had been the principal architect of its expanded protection, elaborated on the boundaries suggested in *Thornhill*. In *Cox v. New Hampshire* (1941), Hughes wrote for a unanimous court to establish the right of the government to make reasonable regulations concerning the time, manner, and place of speech, so long as the regulations did not prevent expression or favor some speakers over others. The justices sustained a Manchester ordinance as applied to a group of Jehovah's Witnesses, who marched with placards to publicize their local meetings, but refused to obtain the license or pay the fee required of every parade or procession upon the city's streets. By interpreting the ordinance as a police regulation designed to ensure traffic safety and orderly use of the streets, Hughes attempted to make it clear that the licensing and fee requirements did not infringe upon the First Amendment, including speech and the free exercise of religion, because the conviction of the Witnesses had not been for conveying a message or holding a meeting.

Alma Lovell raised another question of liberty. A member of the Jehovah's Witnesses' sect, she refused to abide by the city ordinance that required the city manager's written permission for the distribution of pamphlets, leaflets, and magazines, she declared she had been sent by "Jehovah to do His work" and that compliance with the ordinance constituted "an act of disobedience to His commandment." Her attorneys challenged the Griffin, Georgia, ordinance on broad First and Fourteenth Amendment grounds, including the claim that it violated "the free exercise of religion" protected by the First Amendment.

In *Lovell v. Griffin* (1938), Hughes and the Court, however, studiously avoided any discussion of Lovell's religious claim or the Free Exercise Clause and invalidated the ordinance as an arbitrary restriction on freedom of the press. Lovell's religion was not even mentioned in the course of the opinion. Hughes and his majority eagerly incorporated freedom of speech and press within the compass of the Fourteenth Amendment's Due Process Clause, but displayed much greater caution when it came to the great religion clauses of the First Amendment. And even after holding the free exercise of religion to be among the fundamental liberties protected by the Fourteenth Amendment, the justices construed that liberty narrowly and allowed the states to override it initially on grounds of promoting national unity on the eve of American involvement in the Second World War.

Religious claims had seldom trumped the police powers of the states or the federal government before the 1930s, as the justices sustained criminal statutes that prohibited the practice of polygamy (*Reynolds v. United States* [1890]) and *Davis v. Beason* [1889]), and laws mandating compulsory vaccinations (*Jacobson v. Massachusetts* [1905]). In the case of polygamy, sanctioned by the Mormon Church, or vaccinations, resisted by followers of Christian Science, the justices attempted to draw a distinction between belief and conduct. The state might not compel, coerce, or punish religious ideas, but when these beliefs produced conduct that threatened the health, welfare, or morals of the community, such conduct could be regulated and, in some instances, prohibited. This framework generally tipped the constitutional balance in favor of the state as indicated by the first major decision by the Hughes Court, *Hamilton v. Regents of the University of California* (1934).

The student plaintiffs in *Hamilton* belonged to the Methodist Episcopal Church, whose General Conference supported their pacifism and conscientious objection to military training and service as contrary to the teaching of the church and Jesus Christ. The Regents of the University of California, however, denied them exemption from such training in "rifle marksmanship . . . musketry, combat principles, and the use of automatic rifles" and suspended them from the institution until they agreed to complete these mandatory graduation requirements administered by the War Department of the United States.

Writing for six of his colleagues, including Hughes, Justice Butler dismissed the plaintiffs' religious claims grounded in both the Privileges and Immunities Clause and the Due Process Clause of the Fourteenth Amendment and sustained the regents' policy. The liberty protected by the Fourteenth Amendment, Butler conceded, "undoubtedly . . . does include the right to entertain the beliefs, to adhere to the principles and to teach the doctrines on which these students base their objections," but California had not drafted them or called them to attend its public university. Their claim amounted to no more than an assertion that "the due process clause . . . confers the right to be students . . . free from obligation to take military training as one of the conditions of attendance." As the federal and state governments owed a duty to the people to maintain peace and order, "every citizen owes the reciprocal duty . . . to support and defend government against all."

Justice Cardozo's concurrence, joined by Stone and Brandeis, assumed "for present purposes that the religious liberty protected by the First Amendment against invasion by the nation is protected by the Fourteenth . . . against invasion by the states," but it did not afford the plaintiffs further constitutional comfort. Cardozo drew a distinction between instruction in courses and actual military service, which ignored the mandatory requirement of training in various weapons whose only purpose could be combat. Further, he wrote, instruction in military science "is not instruction in the practice or tenets of a religion," nor was it "an interference by the state with the free exercise of religion when the liberties of the Constitution are read in the light of a century and a half of history." Were the Court to sanction this exemption, he feared, conscientious objectors would next refuse to contribute taxes to the support of war. Finally, Cardozo ridiculed the plaintiffs' beliefs when he warned that "one who is a martyr to a principle—which may turn out in the end to be a delusion or an error—does not prove by his martyrdom that he has kept within the law."

Two years after *Lovell*, which had ignored the free exercise claim, and Stone's *Carolene Products* footnote, which suggested closer judicial scrutiny of laws that especially burdened "discrete and insular minorities," the justices for the first and only time during Hughes's tenure struck down a state law on grounds that it violated the free exercise of religion. In *Cantwell v. Connecticut* (1940), a unanimous bench overturned the conviction of a Jehovah's Witness, his words and literature usually laced with anti-Catholicism in Catholic neighborhoods, who had failed to secure a permit from the state director of public welfare before soliciting funds and preaching door to door. The justices had voided a similar ordinance in Irvington, New Jersey, the year before, without the necessity of raising a free exercise claim (*Schneider v. Irvington* [1939]). For the Court, Roberts condemned the Connecticut statute because it vested in a public official discretion to determine which causes were religious in much the same manner as the ordinance struck down in *Hague* left control of public parks to the unfettered judgment of a director of public safety. Further, Roberts wrote, the states could restrict the free exercise of religion only through statutes narrowly drawn and applied in a nondiscriminatory manner. And they could not punish sidewalk preachers under general "breach of the peace" laws, even when their speech offended other religions, unless the speech threatened a "clear and present menace to public peace."

Two weeks after *Cantwell*, with German tanks sweeping through the Ardennes and 330,000 British and French troops retreating from the beaches of Dunkirk, the justices inflicted a punishing blow upon the Free Exercise Clause in *Minersville School District v. Gobitis* (1940), when they rebuffed the claims of Jehovah's Witnesses and sustained a mandatory flag salute for school children, including provisions that expelled nonparticipants and punished parents or guardians who held them out of school in protest. If ever external political events shaped the content of an opinion, it was this one, written by Justice Frankfurter and endorsed by seven of his brethren, including the chief justice.

Invoking the prestige of Cardozo and the logic he employed earlier in *Hamilton*, Frankfurter read the Free Exercise Clause narrowly to prohibit only government restrictions that directly suppressed religious practices or attempted to indoctrinate sectarian beliefs. Otherwise, religious liberty had to give way to the state's police powers, in this case the laudatory effort to promote national unity and patriotism in a time of crisis and among a diverse, multi-ethnic population in the middle of Pennsylvania. The "mere possession of religious convictions," Frankfurter wrote, "does not relieve the citizen from the discharge of political responsibilities." Jehovah's Witnesses could no more escape the patriotic ritual of the flag salute than Christian Scientists could reject smallpox vaccinations or conscientious objectors could avoid training in military science vital to the nation's defense.

Although critics sometimes called Hughes "Charles the Baptist" in reference to his father's ministerial role in that denomination, neither the chief justice nor most of his colleagues easily identified with the religious fervor that drove groups like the Witnesses. Cardozo and Frankfurter were both secular, nonobservant Jews. And Frankfurter's agnosticism had the additional overlay of patriotic zeal rooted in his immigrant's journey from Vienna to the United States.

Only Justice Stone, adhering to what he had written in *Carolene Products*, dissented. As he wrote to Frankfurter, "I cannot overcome the feeling that the Constitution tips the scales in favor of religion" (Mason 1979, 150). He wrote a short and pungent dissent: "This seems to me no less than the surrender of the constitutional protection of the liberty of small minorities to the popular will."

In Hughes's last term, the Witnesses also lost in *Cox v. New Hampshire* (1941) when a unanimous Court upheld the right of government to make reasonable regulations concerning the time, place, and manner of demonstrations, whether inspired by religious or political beliefs. A year later, however, as more Witnesses came under physical assault from patriotic vigilantes, three members of Frankfurter's majority in *Gobitis*—Black, Douglas, and Murphy—announced that they believed that decision had been wrongly decided because it placed the Free Exercise Clause in a subordinate position. (*Jones v. Opelika* [1942]). And in 1943, in one of the most stunning turnabouts in the Court's history, the justices overruled *Gobitis* in *West Virginia State Board of Education v. Barnette*, with Frankfurter now leading three dissenters.

Righting Civil Wrongs

In his *Carolene Products* footnote, Stone suggested that laws restricting access to the ballot might be "subjected to more exacting judicial scrutiny" than statutes regulating "ordinary commercial transactions." If the judicial branch displayed greater deference to legislative choice in matters touching economic affairs, Stone reasoned, the machinery for electing legislatures had to be open to competing points of view and free of arbitrary restrictions upon the right to vote. The Hughes Court had already taken important steps in this direction before 1938, especially with respect to the plague of discriminatory laws that infected the political structure of the South and left African Americans there largely disenfranchised.

Three years before Hughes arrived, the Taft Court had chipped away at the Texas "white primary" statute that sanctioned a Caucasians-only policy for those voting in the Democratic Party primary, the only election that counted in the Lone Star State. Justice Holmes, for the unanimous bench, declared the law invalid as a violation of the Fourteenth Amendment's Equal Protection Clause, although the application of that provision to voting rights had never before been entertained by the Court (*Nixon v. Herndon* [1927]). A year earlier, however, the same Court had sustained racially discriminatory real estate covenants against the challenge that they offended the Fourteenth Amendment (*Corrigan v. Buckley* [1926]). The Reconstruction amendments, Justice Sanford reaffirmed, prohibited only discrimination sanctioned by the state, not that practiced by private individuals. Seeking to exploit this doctrinal distinction between "state action" and "private choice," the Texas legislature gave party executive committees the power to set voter qualifications, which they promptly did by excluding African Americans. Five members of the Hughes Court, led by Cardozo, found sufficient state action to overturn this discriminatory arrangement, too, in *Nixon v. Condon* (1932), although the narrowness of the vote (McReynolds, Sutherland, Butler, and Van Devanter in dissent) suggested that the justices had perhaps reached the outer boundary of the distinction between public and private discrimination.

In 1935, the year that many New Deal statutes fell, the justices also emancipated the Texas Democratic Party from further constitutional restraint after the legislature had abandoned the field of determining party membership or eligibility to participate in primary elections. Despite evidence that Texas laws continued to regulate elections in a variety of ways, including the requirement that sealed ballot boxes be turned over to county clerks, Roberts and a unanimous Court declared the Democratic Party a private association beyond the reach of the Fourteenth Amendment (*Grovey v. Townsend* [1935]).

Grovey appeared to write an end to the Hughes Court's efforts to expunge white supremacy from the franchise laws of the South, although the justices did strike down Oklahoma's clumsy second effort to maintain a "grandfather clause" exception to its literacy test, a provision that penalized African Americans (*Lane v. Wilson* [1939]). In Hughes's last term, however, Stone marshaled five votes in *United States v. Classic* (1941) to sustain federal convictions of state elections officials in Louisiana who had altered and falsely counted congressional primary election ballots. The landmark prosecution had been brought by the newly created Civil Rights Division of the Department of Justice, which invoked federal statutory authority from the Reconstruction era. Stone's opinion overruled *Newberry v. United States* (1921), which had concluded that Congress lacked power under Article I, Section 4 of the Constitution to regulate party primaries. But in addition, he held that Article I, Section 2 of the Constitution guaranteed citizens the right to vote in such elections, to have their votes counted, and to exercise this right free of interference by individuals or the state. *Grovey*'s days were clearly numbered.

No opinion of the Hughes era held greater significance for the nation's racial future, however, than *Missouri ex rel. Gaines v. Canada* (1938), overshadowed at the time by *West Coast Hotel*, *Jones & Laughlin*, and the imbroglio over Roosevelt's court-packing plan. Refused admission to the University of Missouri Law School because of his race, Lloyd Gaines and lawyers for the National Association for the Advancement of Colored People (NAACP) unsuccessfully sought mandamus in the state courts to obtain entrance to the all-white institution. Missouri argued that the state planned to create a law school for African Americans and, pending its establishment, Missouri would pay Gaines's tuition to a law school in another state.

Hughes, writing for all but McReynolds and Butler, rejected that solution. Missouri, he concluded, must furnish Gaines "within its borders facilities for legal education substantially equal to those which the State there offered for persons of the white race, whether or not other Negroes sought the same opportunity." The admissibility of laws separating the races in the enjoyment of privileges by the state, Hughes continued, "rests wholly upon the equality of the privileges which the laws give to the separated groups within the State." Without confronting the "separate but equal" doctrine, the chief justice clearly doubted that Missouri's proposed new law school could meet the test of equality. Lloyd Gaines never entered law school in Missouri or, as far as anyone knows, elsewhere. But Charles H. Houston and lawyers for the NAACP had won a major victory and Hughes had signaled a new approach to "separate but equal" that would later bear fruit in *Sweatt v. Painter* (1950) and, ultimately, *Brown v. Board of Education* (1954).

Crime and Punishment

Petitioners like L. A. Nixon and Lloyd Gaines, contesting the right to vote and access to education, brought America's institutional racism to the foreground of constitutional politics during the Hughes era. So did many criminal defendants, trapped in a Southern system that from local sheriffs to appellate judges denied them equal, impartial justice under law. Chief Justice Hughes, whose dissent with Holmes in *Frank v. Mangum* (1915) had urged the justices to look beyond narrow jurisdictional issues and question the adequacy of review by state supreme courts, encouraged his Court to do just that. The result—from *Powell v. Alabama* (1932), reversing the first convictions of the Scottsboro defendants, to *Chambers v. Florida* (1940), holding that psychological coercion could produce involuntary confessions that violated the Fourteenth Amendment—constituted a due process revolution in criminal procedure that altered fundamentally American federalism and laid the foundation for the further innovations of the Warren years.

Powell, while significantly limited by *Betts v. Brady* (1942), decided a year after Hughes left the Court, became the cornerstone of the modern constitutional right to effective legal counsel, although Sutherland's opinion bounded that right initially to so-called special circumstances, including capital crimes and defendants afflicted by illiteracy and poverty.

Norris v. Alabama (1935), the second Scottsboro decision, likewise became the foundation for a fair trial, untainted by a biased, racially exclusive jury. In *Patton v. United States* (1930), decided with Hughes not participating, the Court described the essentials of trial by jury in a criminal case: a panel of twelve, no more, no less; the supervision of a judge to instruct as to law and advise as to facts; and a unanimous verdict. But until *Norris,* the mere absence of black jurors from any particular panel did not serve as a constitutional basis for challenging the jury's decision. Hughes and the majority changed the course of constitutional law when they looked behind the surface of Alabama law to reverse Clarence Norris's rape conviction, which had been secured by a jury drawn from pools that historically and systematically excluded African Americans. The Supreme Court's responsibility, the chief justice wrote, was not "merely whether it [the Equal Protection Clause] was denied in express terms but also whether it was denied in substance and effect."

Five years after *Norris,* with the nation on the brink of conflict in Europe and the Pacific, the Court placed an impartial and representative jury at the very core of American liberty. "For racial discrimination to result in the exclusion from jury service of otherwise qualified groups not only violates our Constitution and the laws enacted under it," the justices ruled, "but is at war with our basic concepts of a democratic society and a representative government" (*Smith v. Texas* [1940]).

Beginning in 1908 with *Twining v. New Jersey,* the Supreme Court spurned arguments that the due process guarantees of the Fourteenth Amendment extended the privilege against self-incrimination, protected by the Fifth Amendment, to state defendants as well. Unwilling to disturb that unfortunate precedent, Chief Justice Hughes nonetheless found a verbal formula in *Brown v. Mississippi* (1936) for reaching much the same result and placing new restrictions upon brutal state methods of law enforcement and prosecution. Mississippi had convicted three African American tenant farmers for the murder of a white planter on the basis of confessions that even the prosecution admitted at trial had been secured after police officers whipped the defendants. The state attempted to defend these convictions by citing *Twining* and arguing that in their jurisdiction defendants did not enjoy the benefits against compelled self-incrimination.

Writing for a unanimous Court, Hughes quickly dismissed that argument. The right of the state to withdraw the privilege "is not here involved," he wrote. He then proceeded to draw a distinction between the "compulsion" prohibited by the Fifth Amendment and the "compulsion" forbidden by the Fourteenth. The former, he wrote, referred to the coercion by which an accused may be forced to testify, but "compulsion by torture to extort a confession is a different matter." Rising to unusual heights of outrage, Hughes denounced the state's attempt to substitute "trial by ordeal" for trial by jury. "The rack and torture chamber may not be substituted for the witness stand. . . . It would be difficult to conceive of methods more revolting to the sense of justice than those taken to procure the confessions of these petitioners."

Hughes and his brethren displayed considerable zeal in extending the guarantees of the Bill of Rights to the states via the Fourteenth Amendment in areas touching freedom of expression and religion. But as the *Brown* decision indicated, they manifested more caution when it came to criminal justice. Hughes's unwillingness to disturb the much-criticized *Twining* precedent suggested as much. Cardozo's opinion in *Palko v. Connecticut* a year later confirmed it.

In sustaining the conviction and death sentence of Frank Palka, a result reached after the state successfully appealed errors in his first trial, Cardozo and the majority distinguished certain guarantees in the Bill of the Rights as "of the very essence of a scheme of ordered liberty, . . . principles of justice so rooted in the traditions and conscience of our people as to be ranked fundamental." These included, he conceded, freedom of speech, press, assembly, and the right to legal counsel, but not the promise of the Fifth Amendment that an individual will not be tried twice for the same crime. Due process did not, therefore, mandate its application to the states. Butler dissented, a position not vindicated until 1969, when the Warren Court overruled *Palko* and extended the double jeopardy guarantee to the states in *Benton v. Maryland.*

The major criminal justice decisions of the Hughes Court attacked some of the worst abuses flourishing under law and custom in the states, especially in those of the Old Confederacy where the twin legacies of racism and poverty dominated social and legal relations. To this extent, the Court worked hand-in-hand with the infant Civil Rights Division in the Department of Justice and with other programs of the New Deal such as the Tennessee Valley Authority, the Rural Electrification Administration, and the Farm Security Administration—all of which attempted to relieve some of the region's economic miseries and bring the South into the modern world.

Hughes and his Court confronted other significant criminal justice issues at the state and federal level, some old and one remarkably new, with important implications for the future of law enforcement and privacy. In *Lindsey v. Washington* (1937), the Court ruled that a statute making more onerous the standard of punishment violated the Ex Post Facto Clause and was void as applied to a crime committed before its enactment. And in 1937–1939 it took up the contentious problem of government-sponsored electronic eavesdropping, a technology deplored by civil libertarians since its introduction in the 1920s, but promoted by government agencies eager to prosecute crime and defend national security in a time of rising international tensions.

In *Olmstead v. United States* (1928), the Taft Court majority, over biting dissents by Holmes and Brandeis, ruled firmly that the Fourth Amendment's protection against unreasonable searches and seizures did not encompass overheard telephone conversations when there had been no physical trespass upon a home or business. In the course of his opinion, however, the chief justice made it clear that "Congress may . . . protect the secrecy of telephone messages by making them, when intercepted, inadmissible in evidence in Federal criminal trials. . . . But the courts may not adopt such a policy by attributing an enlarged and unusual meaning to the Fourth Amendment."

Taking up Taft's dicta from *Olmstead,* Congress provided in the Federal Communications Act of 1934 that "no person not being authorized by the sender shall intercept any communication and divulge or publish the existence, contents, substance, purport, effect or meaning of such intercepted communication to any person." Three years later in *Nardone v. United States* (1937), known as *Nardone I,* Justice Roberts and the majority read this provision of the statute as forbidding federal agents, as well as all other persons, from intercepting and disclosing interstate telephone messages through the use of wiretaps. Overturning Nardone's conviction, they ruled in addition that such evidence was to be excluded from federal trials, a result that prompted a dissent from Justices Sutherland and McReynolds, who complained that "the necessity of public protection against crime is being submerged by an overflow of sentimentality."

Reading the 1934 provisions broadly, Roberts and the Court also reversed a conviction two years later when federal prosecutors attempted to introduce intercepted intrastate telephone messages as evidence against one defendant when another had turned state's evidence and consented to their use (*Weiss v. United States* [1939]). And in *Nardone v. United States* (1939) that same term (known as *Nardone II*), with Frankfurter writing for all but McReynolds, the justices interpreted the law as excluding so-called indirect evidence that arose from tainted wiretap information.

The war years soon enlarged the powers of government in many areas and they produced sharp qualifications to the Hughes Court's libertarian interpretation of federal law respecting electronic surveillance. The Stone Court sanctioned the use of wiretap evidence against persons other than those whose conversations had been overheard (*Goldstein v. United States* [1942]) and it held that the use of a "bug," a more sophisticated listening device, did not violate the 1934 Communications Act, which applied only to actual interference with communication wires and telephone lines (*Goldman v. United States* [1942]).

The end of Hughes's tenure and the bombs that fell at Pearl Harbor had propelled the United States into a new constitutional era.

References and Further Reading

Badger, Anthony. 1989. *The New Deal: The Depression Years, 1933–1940.* New York: Noonday Press.

Baker, Leonard. 1984. *Brandeis and Frankfurter: A Dual Biography.* New York: Harper & Row.

Chafee, Zechariah. 1941. *Free Speech in the United States.* Cambridge, MA: Harvard University Press.

Corwin, Edward S. 1941. *Constitutional Revolution, Ltd.* Claremont, CA: Pomona College.

Cushman, Barry. 1998. *Rethinking the New Deal Court: The Structure of a Constitutional Revolution.* New York: Oxford University Press.

Danelski, David J., and Joseph S. Tulchin, eds. 1973. *The Autobiographical Notes of Charles Evans Hughes.* Cambridge, MA: Harvard University Press.

Grubb, Donald H. 1971. *Cry from the Cotton: The Southern Tenant Farmers Union and the New Deal.* Chapel Hill, NC: University of North Carolina Press.

Lash, Joseph P. 1975. *From the Diaries of Felix Frankfurter.* New York: Norton.

Mason, Alpheus T. 1979. *The Supreme Court from Taft to Burger.* Baton Rouge, LA: Louisiana State University Press.

McCloskey, Robert G. 1994. *The American Supreme Court.* 2d ed. Revised by Sanford Levinson. Chicago: University of Chicago Press.

Urofsky, Melvin I., and David W. Levy, eds. 1991. *"Half Brother, Half Son": The Letters of Louis D. Brandeis to Felix Frankfurter.* Norman: University of Oklahoma Press.

Wiecek, William M. 1998. *The Lost World of Classical Legal Thought: Law and Ideology in America, 1886–1937.* New York: Oxford University Press.

4

Legacy and Impact

In her attempt to date the origins of the modern temper, the novelist Virginia Woolf chose the postimpressionist painting exhibition in London and declared that "in or about December 1910, human character changed." Gertrude Stein selected World War I, after which, she said, "we had the twentieth century." Reading T. S. Eliot's *The Waste Land* and James Joyce's *Ulysses*, Willa Cather announced that "the world broke in two in 1922 or thereabouts." A legal historian can plausibly argue that America's constitutional world underwent a similar, fundamental transformation during the years of Hughes's tenure as chief justice, sometime between 1934 and 1938 "or thereabouts." These middle years of the Great Depression, punctuated by Roosevelt's abortive court-packing proposal, provided a series of Supreme Court rulings that simultaneously emancipated government to manage the nation's economy and enlarged greatly the scope of basic civil liberties, a result confirmed by Justice Stone's famous Footnote 4 in *United States v. Carolene Products Co.* (1938).

Whatever particular dates are chosen, there are good and substantial reasons for regarding the Hughes era as the true birthplace of modern, twentieth-century judicial constitutionalism, with its strong emphasis upon civil liberties and civil rights combined with a deferential approach to what Stone called "ordinary commercial transactions," those economic problems best left to legislatures, presidents, and administrative experts. Of course, American constitutional law has been one long, winding river of development. So, too, with Hughes and his brethren. The road to *West Coast Hotel*, *Jones & Laughlin*, or *Herndon v. Lowry* had been mapped, however faintly, by those jurists who came before them. And they, in turn, would leave a legacy that both expanded and limited the jurisprudential opportunities for those who followed after 1941.

Wholly apart from particular doctrinal areas, however, the most lasting legacy of the Hughes years flowed from the cumulative impact of its response to depression-generated programs by the states and the New Deal between 1934–1936, the court-packing fight with the Roosevelt administration, and the cluster of decisions culminating in *Steward Machine Co.* and *Helvering v. Davis* (1937). Armed with impressive erudition and strong opinions, legal scholars continue to debate whether the justices, especially Owen Roberts, made "a switch in time that saved nine" and whether these years should be regarded as a "constitutional revolution" arising from external political pressures or simply a "constitutional evolution" rooted in the internal logic of past decisions.

Scholars of the New Deal years such as Barry Cushman and Richard Friedman are right to point out that the major decisions of the Hughes Court touching upon issues of government's relationship to the economy had deep, if usually contested, roots in the doctrinal past of the Fuller, White, and Taft Courts. And the dedication of these pre-Hughes era Courts to a strict laissez-faire interpretation of the Constitution has often been grossly exaggerated. The New Dealers correctly perceived the many doctrinal openings created for their programs during the earlier progressive years and attempted to drive their innovative laws through them. But what they saw as a wide tunnel, many of the justices on the Hughes Court saw as only the eye of a needle that required careful jurisprudential threading. Revisionist scholars of the Hughes Court have reminded us, quite properly, that courts remain different from other institutions in our governmental structure, decisively so when it comes to the claims and constraints of the past. In this regard, the conventional interpretation got it right, however. The New Dealers were the radicals; Hughes and his brethren the conservatives.

But as Robert McCloskey instructed us long ago, even within the conservative constitutional tradition inherited from the Fuller-White-Taft years, room had been made for choice, opportunity for affirming the powers of government, as well as for denying those powers. A majority of the justices often opted for the doctrines that constrained rather than emancipated government's role in the economy, with their choices influenced by motives that ranged from simple political allegiance to fairly sophisticated legal philosophy. A series of external events between 1934 and 1937—rising Democratic majorities in Congress, Roosevelt's decisive reelection, mounting evidence of real class warfare—tipped the constitutional balance toward emancipation, especially when combined with the more cautious lawyering practiced by the New Dealers after 1933–1934. Did the real constitutional switch take place in 1934 with *Nebbia?* Did it come later in 1937 with *Parrish* and *Jones & Laughlin?* Did Roberts and Hughes trim their constitutional principles to fit new circumstances or did the New Dealers trim theirs?

That these issues will never be resolved to the satisfaction of every scholar appears assured, because we have no historical method for reading the minds of individual justices in 1934–1937 or weighing the veracity of interpretations made long after those years had passed. Did procedural scruples, as he claimed, dictate Roberts's votes in *Morehead* (1936) and *West Coast Hotel* (1937)? Who can say with certainty, as the available evidence can be read to both support and reject his version of events. The world beyond the closed chambers of the Supreme Court does make a difference in judicial behavior—witness how Black, Douglas, and Murphy publicly announced their rejection of *Gobitis* in response to the mounting violence directed against Jehovah's Witnesses in 1941–1942. Did the even more widespread disorders arising from the sit-down strikes weigh upon the justices who decided *Jones & Laughlin* in 1937? No doubt yes, but how decisive were those events when assessed against the inherited Commerce Clause jurisprudence, the particular facts of the NLRB cases, and the arguments advanced by government attorneys?

What we do know with a high degree of certainty is that the Supreme Court's role in the constitutional structure changed dramatically in the years after 1937–1938. The Taft and Hughes Courts combined, for example, struck down twenty-six acts of Congress between 1921 and 1941. On the other hand, the Stone and Vinson Courts that followed invalidated only two congressional statutes in the decade from 1941 to 1952 with the rate of judicial vetoes again rising under Warren and Burger.

By one simple measure, the scope of judicial power contracted significantly in the decades after Hughes, as the justices seldom overturned congressional or state statutes touching the nation's economic arrangements. When a plurality on the Stone Court, for example, reversed a long line of precedents in 1944 to hold that insurance transactions were interstate commerce and therefore subject to federal antitrust actions, Congress quickly repudiated that ruling with a new law permitting the states to continue to regulate the field (*United States v. South-Eastern Underwriters Ass'n* [1944]). Two years later, the Court bowed to Congress when it sustained the new statute (*Prudential Insurance Co. v. Benjamin* [1946]).

In 1952 the Vinson Court ruled that President Truman had exceeded his constitutional mandate as commander in chief when he seized the country's steel mills to prevent a strike during the Korean War, but that six-to-three decision did so on the grounds that only Congress could authorize such draconian measures. A year later, employing statutory construction, the Court narrowly dismissed a criminal indictment brought under a federal law prohibiting the shipment of gambling machines in interstate commerce and imposing registration requirements upon persons who did so. The indictments failed, wrote Justice Jackson, only because they did not allege that the accused dealers had bought, sold, or moved gambling devices in interstate commerce, and the Federal Bureau of Investigation had entered a country club and seized slot machines "not shown ever to have had any connection with interstate commerce in any manner whatever" (*United States v. Five Gambling Devices* [1953]).

More typical of the Court's post-1937 deference to Congress through constitutional and statutory interpretation was *United States v. Kahriger* (1953), which sustained the occupational tax provisions of the Revenue Act of 1951, specifically a levy on persons engaged in the business of accepting wagers—in other words, bookmakers. "When federal power to regulate is found," wrote Justice Reed, "its exercise is a matter for Congress. . . . It is hard to understand why the power to tax should raise more doubts because of indirect effects than other federal powers." Only Frankfurter dissented on grounds of federalism. Congress, he argued in an opinion that echoed Roberts's in *Butler*, had used the taxing power to reach a subject, the control of gambling, entrusted to the states.

After Hughes, the Supreme Court largely abandoned the field of economic policy on the wholesale level, but continued to make it on the retail level through statutory interpretation, with large consequences for the scope of regulatory power exercised by the new administrative state fostered by the New Deal and its successors. In 1944, over three dissents, the Stone Court upheld portions of the Emergency Price Control Act of 1942, which gave the federal price administrator broad discretionary authority to enforce the law, including its maximum price regulations. Rejecting the claim that Congress had unconstitutionally delegated legislative power, the majority found the standards for decision "sufficiently definite and precise."

On a case-by-case basis the justices and the lower federal courts began to flesh out the details of major New Deal laws, such as the Fair Labor Standards Act, by reviewing administrative decisions that either included or excluded certain occupations from the coverage of the federal minimum wage provisions (*United States v. Rosenwasser* [1945]). Was a fry cook on a railroad repair gang engaged in "production for commerce"? What about the elevator operators in an office building where a majority of the corporate occupants engaged in interstate commerce? Should the tips received by railway porters be counted as wages within the meaning of the statute? What exceptions were permitted with respect to the law's overtime premium pay provisions? (*Walling v. A. H. Belo Corp.* [1942]).

Outside the context of wartime emergency, the justices did not hesitate to scrutinize administrative decisions to determine whether or not they exceeded statutory authority and comported with due process. When a union of telegraphers called a strike for better terms of employment against Mackay Radio and Telegraph Company, the company replaced the strikers and continued in business until the strike was broken. On their return to work, Mackay took back all but five of the strikers, the five most active union leaders. The National Labor Relations Board (NLRB) ordered their reinstatement with back pay on the grounds that the company's refusal to take them back rested solely on their union activities. The Supreme Court sustained the board by dismissing as irrelevant the company's contention that they had ceased to be employees when they went on strike (*National Labor Relations Board v. Mackay Radio and Telegraph Company* [1938]).

On the other hand, when the National Labor Relations Board ordered the reinstatement with back pay of employees who had engaged in an unlawful sit-down strike to protest their employer's unfair labor practices, the Supreme Court held otherwise and overturned the board in *National Labor Relations Board v. Fansteel Metallurgical Corporation* (1939). Federal law protected the right of employees to engage in concerted activities to promote self-organization, Hughes wrote, but the conduct protected "is lawful conduct." In this case, the union employees "took a position outside the protection of the statute and accepted the risk of the termination of their employment."

In 1941 the justices indicated that the National Labor Relations Board had very broad powers indeed when it sustained its order requiring Phelps Dodge Corporation to "reinstate" two men, otherwise eligible applicants for work, who had been denied initial employment by the company solely on the grounds that they were active labor unionists. The Court upheld that portion of the NLRB decision requiring reimbursement for the wages lost through denial of employment, with an allowance for any income the men might have earned elsewhere in the meantime (*Phelps Dodge Corporation v. National Labor Relations Board* [1941]). In the field of labor relations, the Wage and Hours Division of the Labor Department and the NLRB proposed, but the Supreme Court still disposed.

When reviewing actions by the "fourth branch of government," the independent regulatory agencies such as the Securities and Exchange Commission (SEC) or the NLRB, the Supreme Court after 1937 continued to insist upon "due process of law," but stressed procedure over substance: Did the agency afford plaintiffs a fair hearing and did the agency's orders and findings of fact rest upon "substantial evidence"? (*Consolidated Edison Co. v. National Labor Relations Board* [1938]; and *Opp Cotton Mills v. Administrator of Wage and Hours Division* [1941]). In addition, judicial review of administrative rulings would not be afforded to plaintiffs who had failed to exhaust all of their remedies before the agency (*Myers v. Bethlehem Shipbuilding Corp.* [1938]). Congress largely codified the Court's procedural framework in 1946, when it adopted the Administrative Procedures Act (5 U.S.C. §§ 551–559).

The Hughes Court lifted the burden of substantive due process from the state's economic policies in *Nebbia* and *West Coast Hotel*, but this did not mean that the Supreme Court abandoned all scrutiny of local statutes under other constitutional rubrics. In *Mayflower Farms* (1936), it briefly invoked the Equal Protection Clause of the Fourteenth Amendment to invalidate portions of a New York milk regulation, but that constitutional barrier also fell out of use until *Morey v. Doud* (1957), when the justices struck down a provision in the Illinois Community Currency Exchanges Act that discriminated against all firms except the American Express Company. By contrast, the Vinson Court upheld a provision in New York City's traffic regulations that prohibited advertising upon all business delivery vehicles, except those advertising their own business. The ban fell heavily upon the Railway Express Agency that operated 1,900 trucks in the city and sold advertising for the most part unconnected with its own business (*Railway Express Agency v. New York* [1949]).

State statutes that impinged upon interstate commerce, either through tax provisions or more direct means, continued to receive close judicial scrutiny, although the Hughes Court and its immediate successors displayed a reluctance to invoke the preemption doctrine and accorded the states generous scope to regulate local affairs. In *Kelley v. Washington* (1937), Hughes and the Court upheld a state law requiring safety inspections of tugboats against the claim that such regulation had been barred by the federal Motor Boat Act of 1910. Three years later they likewise sustained Pennsylvania's ban on trucks carrying any other vehicle "above the cab of the carrier vehicle," although the plaintiffs had mounted a strong argument that regulations adopted by the Interstate Commerce Commission had preempted the field with respect to the safety and operation of truck equipment (*Maurer v. Hamilton* [1940]).

When it came to civil liberties, however, the Court struck a different note on preemption. In *Hines v. Davidowitz* (1941), it ruled that a federal statute barred Pennsylvania's Alien Registration Act. State laws that touched "the rights, liberties and freedoms of human beings," wrote Justice Black, were not in the same category with "state pure food laws regulating the labels on cans."

As Black's dicta in *Hines* demonstrated, the Hughes Court had begun to practice a "preferred freedoms" approach to constitutional interpretation before this concept found official expression in Supreme Court opinions by Justice Stone dissenting in *Jones v. Opelika* (1942) and by Justice Wiley Rutledge in *Thomas v. Collins* (1945). Through its commitment to civil liberties and civil rights, beginning with *Stromberg* (1931) and concluding with *United States v. Classic* (1941), Hughes's court extended federal judicial power over a range of social and political issues far beyond what could have been imagined a decade earlier.

When they heard Tom Mooney's claim in a petition for habeas corpus, for example, the justices encouraged other persons incarcerated by the states to test the constitutionality of their convictions in the federal courts. Because it denied relief to Mooney, who had not exhausted "corrective judicial process" in California, the Court's opinion stood only for the important principle that the knowing use of perjured testimony by a prosecutor constituted a denial of due process. But *Mooney v. Holohan* (1935) proved to be an important link in the chain of developing habeas corpus decisions that led later to *Fay v. Noia* (1963) and *Townsend v. Sain* (1963), which opened the federal habeas door wider when state courts had not reached the merits of a federal claim and even when they had passed upon those claims.

Withdrawing from one arena that had dominated the Court's business since the Civil War, it entered a new one that fixed the judiciary's agenda until the end of the century. Remembered usually for burying the constitutional past between 1934 and 1937, Hughes and his Court may yet be memorialized for opening the Constitution's future. Without *Stromberg* and *Herndon v. Lowry*, neither *Tinker v. Des Moines Independent Community School District* (1969) or *Brandenberg v. Ohio* (1969), which extended First Amendment protection to high school students and Klansmen, could have been decided. Without *Near v. Minnesota*, there would have been no *New York Times v. Sullivan* (1964) or *New York Times v. United States* (1971) limiting libel suits against newspapers and permitting them to print confidential and embarrassing government documents. Without *Powell v. Alabama,* there would be no *Gideon v. Wainwright* (1963), which mandated legal assistance for indigents in most criminal cases. No *Chambers v. Florida,* no *Miranda* (1966), which required legal assistance, if requested, at the time of arrest. No Lloyd Gaines, no Linda Brown, one of the plaintiffs who challenged the "separate but equal" doctrine in public schools and lent her name to the historic decision striking it down in *Brown v. Board of Education* (1954).

Until 1937, all but two members of the Hughes Court—Justices McReynolds and Brandeis—had been nominated by Republican presidents and confirmed by Republican majorities in the Senate. Roosevelt's two decisive electoral victories and mounting Democratic Party majorities in both houses of Congress between 1932 and 1936 changed fundamentally the political environment in which the Supreme Court functioned and brought forth a raft of legislative proposals in 1935–1937, climaxed by the court-packing bill, to reduce its constitutional role. FDR's assault on the court faced rough sledding in Congress even before the death of Majority Leader Joe Robinson and the *Jones & Laughlin* decision, but Hughes, Brandeis, and McReynolds took the threat seriously enough to dispute the president's claims in a public letter to the Senate Judiciary Committee, an unprecedented political intervention that drew criticism from several of their brethren, especially Justice Stone.

Seldom had the Supreme Court and the Constitution appeared more politicized, which led many contemporary observers to believe along with humorist Finley Peter Dunne's Mr. Dooley: "no matter whether th' constitution follows th' flag or not, th' supreme court follows th' iliction returns" (Dunne 1901, 145). Charles Wyzanski, among the government attorneys who argued the *Jones & Laughlin* case, believed that "the President's castor oil seemed to work" (Parrish 1982, 271). Frankfurter deplored the justices lack of "freedom from . . . the most obvious immediacies of politics," a view shared by others (Parrish 1982, 271). Recent scholarship has disputed the impact of elections and legislative attacks upon the justices by noting that following large Democratic gains in 1934, the Court struck its heaviest blows against the New Deal in 1935–1936, while in the wake of the 1938 congressional returns that reduced FDR's support in the House and Senate, the Court continued to endorse the last reforms of the New Deal. On the other hand, the electoral victories of FDR and the Democrats in 1936 and 1940 made possible the creation of a "Roosevelt Court" that codified and extended the constitutional changes wrought earlier. The widespread contemporary belief that the Hughes Court had succumbed to political pressure influenced both scholarship about the Court and the behavior of later justices for years to come.

Largely as a consequence of the controversies it helped to foment, the Court under Hughes became the burial ground for what scholars have described as legal formalism, classical legal thought, or mechanical jurisprudence. These labels referred to the idea that judges served merely as oracles of the law through whom the one true meaning of a constitutional text or the principles of the common law manifested themselves, unmediated by human will and subjectivity. This notion found its purest expression in Justice Roberts's statement in *United States v. Butler* (1936) where he explained how the majority had little choice but to declare the taxing and spending provisions of the first Agricultural Adjustment Act unconstitutional:

> There should be no misunderstanding as to the function of this court in such a case. . . . It is sometimes said that the court assumes a power to overrule or control the action of the people's representatives. This is a misconception. The Constitution is the supreme law of the land ordained and established by the people. All legislation must conform to the principles it lays down. When an act of Congress is appropriately challenged in the courts as not conforming to the constitutional mandate the judicial branch of the Government has only one duty—to lay the article of the Constitution which is invoked beside the statute that is challenged and to decide whether the latter squares with the former. . . . The only power it has, if such it may be called, is the power of judgment. This court neither approves nor condemns any legislative policy. Its delicate and difficult office is to ascertain and declare whether the legislation is in accordance with, or in contravention of, the provisions of the Constitution; and, having done that, its duty ends.

Dissenting in *Butler*, Justice Stone reminded Roberts and the majority that "any assumption that the responsibility for the preservation of our institutions is the exclusive concern of anyone of the three branches of government, or that it alone can save them from destruction is far more likely, in the long run, 'to obliterate the constituent members' of 'an indestructible union or indestructible states.'" In other words, Stone argued, courts alone are not the only guardians of the Constitution of the United States. Franklin Roosevelt held to the same view. Had the Hughes Court struck down the legislation of Congress to abrogate the "gold clauses" in federal obligations, the president had prepared an address to the nation that included Lincoln's observation in his First Inaugural Address: "If the policy of the Government upon vital questions affecting the whole people is to be irrevocably fixed by decisions of the Supreme Court, the instant they are made in ordinary litigation between parties in personal actions the people will have ceased to be their own rulers, having to that extent practically resigned their Government into the hands of that eminent tribunal" (Schlesinger 1960, 258).

Of course, jurists and presidents since the founding era had frequently challenged the Supreme Court's claim to final, definitive interpretation of the constitutional text. The 1930s, however, brought this long-running intellectual and political debate to a decisive turning point due to the rising skepticism—manifested in both constitutional and common law litigation—that judges possessed any method to ensure that their pronouncements about the law represented anything other than subjective—hence, arbitrary—interpretations of indeterminate texts and prior decisions. When deciding *United States v. Butler*, Roberts claimed, the justices simply placed the statute next to the constitutional text. The text then revealed to them the true rule of law, unmediated by the ambiguities of language or individual experience and psychology. Only the most naive observer of judicial decision making continued to believe that epistemology in the 1930s, which is why Roberts's opinion became the subject of withering ridicule.

In response to Roberts, critics asked: How did one explain why reasonably intelligent, well-educated jurists reached such different conclusions about the rule of law? Why did the Supreme Court often divide six to three or five to four about the meaning of due process of law, the scope of the commerce power, or the authority of Congress to tax and spend on behalf of the general welfare? Why did federal courts in adjoining states reach different conclusions about a gross receipts tax? Why did the rules of tort liability or contractual offer and acceptance vary from state court to state court and between state courts and federal tribunals?

The initial answer to these questions had been given as early as the turn of the century by legal scholars such as John Chipman Gray, Oliver Wendell Holmes Jr., and Roscoe Pound, who rejected the seductive idea that law was a science comparable to mathematics or physics. The attack on legal formalism and on the notion of judges as oracles who simply found the law rather than made the law reached its climax with the legal realists of the 1920s and 1930s—Karl Llewellyn, Jerome Frank, Arthur Corbin, and Felix and Morris Cohen—who delighted in demonstrating the contradictions, paradoxes, and ambiguities that plagued virtually every substantive area of legal doctrine.

Even Cardozo, a moderate realist, confessed that "the rules and principles of case law have never been treated as final truths, but as working hypotheses, continually retested in those great laboratories of the law, the courts of justice." Judges, he continued, were "tending more and more toward an appreciation of the truth that, after all, there are few rules; there are chiefly standards and degrees. . . . So also the duty of a judge becomes itself a question of degree. . . . He must balance all his ingredients, his philosophy, his logic, his analogies, his history, his customs, his sense of right, and all the rest, and adding a little here and taking out a little there, must determine, as wisely as he can, which weight shall tip the scales" (Cardozo 1947, 23, 161–62).

The belief in law as a thoroughly objective science and in the judge as an oracle through whom the Constitution spoke, unmediated by what Cardozo called "his [the judge's] history, his customs, his sense of right, and all the rest," simply could not survive the constitutional crisis of the 1930s. And compounding that particular crisis of judicial authority was the separate but reinforcing one that plagued the contributors to the American Law Institute's monumental project of "Restatements" of common law subjects, an effort intended to eliminate doctrinal uncertainty in the areas of property, tort, and contracts. But as G. Edward White has pointed out, the fierce intellectual conflicts inside the Restatement projects and the criticism leveled against the final products in the legal academy exposed the continued uncertainty and subjectivity of American law. The Restatement volumes, declared one law professor, amounted to "an authoritative suppression of the facts rather than . . . better education of the public and the bar as to the actual psychological and sociological nature of the law." Instead of reading the Restatements, he concluded, "it would be easier and more satisfactory to learn the law by random sampling of the cases with all their contradictions and complexities" (White 2001, 191).

But if law was not an objective science, if judges were not oracles who could escape the trap of subjectivity, if Sutherland's interpretation of the Due Process Clause was no better than Brandeis's, if it was all only "a question of degree," and if, finally, judges were little more than legislators, then the whole foundation of judicial authority could be questioned as never before. Some members of the Hughes Court, notably McReynolds and Butler, continued to the end to play the role of high constitutional priests, even after their fellow communicants had been driven from the temple after 1937, their orthodox faith shattered by the justices' own contradictions and the heresies of legal realism.

Newer members of the Hughes Court, notably Frankfurter and Black, who had absorbed much of the critique of the judicial role offered by the realists, sought other ways to preserve the Court's legitimacy in a post-formalist world. The Alabaman took refuge in a revived positivism that made him the champion of civil rights, "incorporation," and a literal interpretation of the Bill of Rights (*Adamson v. California* [1947]; *Dennis v. United States* [1951]). But this posture left him incapable of responding to the constitutional claim of privacy (*Griswold v. Connecticut* [1965]) or to forms of political protest outside the paradigm of pure speech (*Tinker v. Des Moines Independent Community School District* [1969]).

Frankfurter, on the other hand, adopted a posture of judicial restraint more austere than Holmes or Brandeis. As he explained to Stone in an attempt to justify his opinion in *Gobitis:* "My intention . . . was to use this opinion as a vehicle for preaching the true democratic faith of not relying on the Court for the impossible task of assuring a vigorous, mature, self-protecting and tolerant democracy by bringing the responsibility for a combination of firmness and toleration directly home where it belongs—to the people and their representatives themselves" (Mason 1979, 149). But in the next decade, "a vigorous, mature, self-protecting and tolerant democracy" eluded Frankfurter and the country. Fearful during a hot war and a cold war that followed, "the people and their representatives" demanded the relocation of Japanese

Americans, laws imposing loyalty oaths upon public officials, and the imprisonment of members of the Communist Party. Frankfurter's judicial restraint could not arrest these assaults upon individual rights and this, too, became a legacy of the Hughes era.

References and Further Reading

Cardozo, Benjamin N. 1949. *The Nature of the Judicial Process.* New Haven, CT: Yale University Press.

Dunne, Findley Peter. 1901. *Mr. Dooley's Opinions.* New York: R. H. Russell.

Mason, Alpheus T. 1979. *The Supreme Court from Taft to Burger.* Baton Rouge: Louisiana State University Press.

Parrish Michael E. 1982. *Felix Frankfurter and His Times: The Reform Years.* New York: Free Press.

Roosevelt, Elliott, ed. 1947–1950. *F.D.R.: His Personal Letters, 1928–1945.* New York: Duell, Sloan, and Pearce.

Schlesinger, Arthur M., Jr. 1960. *The Age of Roosevelt: The Politics of Upheaval.* Boston: Houghton Mifflin.

White, G. Edward. 2001. *The Constitution and the New Deal.* Cambridge, MA: Harvard University Press.

PART TWO

Reference Materials

Key People, Laws, and Events

Agricultural Adjustment Act of 1933 (Triple A)

With the exception of World War I when demand remained high, American farmers had struggled since the late nineteenth century to control the growing surplus of basic commodities such as wheat, corn, hogs, tobacco, and cotton, which depressed the market, lowered prices, and reduced farm income. Competing in world markets against producers in Argentina, Europe, and Asia, American farmers faced a grim situation after 1919 as their income fell while their fixed costs—mortgage payments, taxes, and equipment—remained high. Although farmers took millions of acres of cropland out of production after 1919, improved seed strains, the gasoline-powered tractor, and new pest control methods dramatically increased per-acre yields, boosted output, and depressed agricultural prices further. Agricultural economists such as John Black and M. L. Wilson developed the proposal of a Voluntary Domestic Allotment Plan in the late 1920s and early 1930s, whereby farmers raising basic crops would reduce their acreage in return for a government cash subsidy, the revenue to be derived from a federal tax at the processing level. Their plan won the support of Henry A. Wallace, editor of *Wallace's Farmer*, a leading agricultural publication, and Franklin Roosevelt's first secretary of agriculture, who with FDR's backing, sent the measure to Congress as part of the New Deal in March 1933. Although some farm-state members of Congress hoped the legislation would guarantee farmers the full cost of production, Roosevelt turned down that radical proposal. The president had to accept, however, an amendment offered by Senator Elmer Thomas of Oklahoma and other proponents of monetary inflation, which required the federal government to purchase substantial amounts of silver and reintroduce silver dollars into the currency supply. The recoinage of silver had a modest impact on prices, the voluntary domestic allotment plan drew support from the more prosperous farmers initially, who as landowners received a federal subsidy. On the other hand, the program took income from consumers to pay farmers with little impact upon overall economic recovery and led to the eviction of tenant farmers and sharecroppers. The Supreme Court declared the processing tax unconstitutional as a violation of the Tenth Amendment in *United States v. Butler* (1936).

Agricultural Adjustment Act of 1938 (Second Triple A)

After the Supreme Court struck down the processing tax in the first Agricultural Adjustment Act in 1936, Congress responded initially by passing the Soil Conservation and Domestic Allotment Act, which paid farmers to make improvements in soil quality by reducing acreage, the cost paid directly by congressional appropriations. When this voluntary program failed to reduce acreage significantly in cotton, wheat, corn, and tobacco, thereby continuing the problem of surpluses and depressed prices, Congress and the Roosevelt administration responded in 1938 with a second agricultural adjustment statute to be financed by a federal tax on farm commodities shipped in interstate commerce in excess of marketing quotas set by the secretary of agriculture. This second Triple A law proved a boon to large farm producers, but did not curb surpluses prior to World War II. Once two-thirds of the producers approved of acreage allotments in referendum elections, the controls went into effect. Another section of the law allowed farmers to borrow money from a new federal agency, the Commodity Credit Corporation, with surplus crops held as security. If market prices went above the value of the loan, the farmer could sell at a profit and repay his loan; if, on the other hand, prices fell below the value of the loan, the CCC absorbed the loss. A Federal Crop Insurance Corporation, authorized by the law and capitalized at $100 million, allowed wheat farmers to use their crops in payment for insurance premiums that covered losses up to 75 percent of average yields. The law also authorized the secretary of agriculture to establish a Surplus Reserve Loan Corporation to assist farmers in other emergencies. Finally, the law funded the operation of new regional research laboratories to improve soil quality and productivity, with the ironic result of again boosting output, the traditional bane of American agriculture. The Supreme Court upheld the marketing and tax features of the law in *Mulford v. Smith* (1939).

American Federation of Labor (AF of L)

Organized in the late nineteenth century as a coalition of many national unions and led until the 1920s by Samuel Gompers, the American Federation of Labor became a major force in the labor movement until challenged during the 1930s by the Committee for Industrial Organization, the forerunner of the Congress of Industrial Organizations (CIO). Headed by William Green following Gompers's death, the AF of L continued its traditional strategy of emphasizing "bread-and-butter" unionism and eschewing any radical change in capitalism by emphasizing strikes to achieve gains in wages, hours, and working conditions. By the start of the New Deal in 1933, the AF of L counted 2.3 million members in its affiliated unions, most of them in skilled trades, especially in the construction industry. Although the AF of L historically had resisted government-mandated programs such as minimum wage laws, it supported many of the initial relief, recovery, labor, and social welfare programs of the New Deal, especially Section 7a of the National Industrial Recovery Act (NIRA), which gave workers the right to join labor unions in industries covered by the new codes of fair competition. When the AF of L leadership refused to abandon its jurisdictional claims and cautious organizing efforts in mass-production industries such as automobiles and steel in the mid-1930s, however, it sparked a revolt by unions and leaders eager to do so, especially the United Mine Workers under John L. Lewis and the Amalgamated Clothing Workers led by Sidney Hillman. Lewis and Hillman formed the CIO in 1935, which mounted successful organizing drives in those industries with the eventual support of the New Deal's National Labor Relations Act. Although the CIO triumphed by forming unions in the major mass-production industries and although the two labor organizations fought many bitter jurisdictional battles after 1935, the AF of L showed renewed vitality and expansion through its affiliates such as the Teamsters.

American Liberty League

Launched in the summer of 1934 with a pledge to "defend and uphold the Constitution . . . to teach the necessity of respect for the rights of persons and property . . . [and] to preserve the ownership and lawful uses of property," the American Liberty League became the most strident and certainly the best-financed organization opposed to the New Deal and Franklin Roosevelt.

Founded by many prominent Democrats, including two former presidential candidates, John W. Davis and Alfred E. Smith, who had been accustomed to running the party, Liberty League organizers resented FDR's capture of their party, his recruitment of younger and more diverse advisers, and above all, his apparent indifference to the platitudes of states' rights and limited government. In addition to Smith, the former New York governor, and Davis, the Democrats' losing candidate in 1924, the league drew support from the former chairman of the Democratic Party, Jouett Shouse, and members of the wealthy Du Pont family, who had regarded the party as their private financial fiefdom. Although its membership never reached more than 150,000 between 1934 and its official demise in 1940, the Liberty League spent over $500,000 to defeat Roosevelt in the 1936 election and financed the distribution of hundreds of anti–New Deal pamphlets, bulletins, and radio speeches, including a 1936 broadcast by former Governor Smith that accused the New Deal of promoting communism. In addition to denouncing the New Deal's specific recovery and reform programs, especially its successful proposals to raise income taxes on the wealthy in 1935–1936, the Liberty League denounced the administration for undermining federalism and the separation of powers. League lawyers, many from prominent Wall Street firms such as Davis, also played a major role in mapping litigation strategy against New Deal measures. In an era that gave new attention to the victims of the depression, the league's list of wealthy sponsors did not resonate with ordinary Americans. FDR's victory against the League's candidate, Republican Alfred Landon, dealt a major blow to their campaign in 1936 as did the president's reelection in 1940.

Anderson, Marian

One year after the Hughes Court decided *Missouri ex rel. Gaines v. Canada* (1938), ordering the admission of an African American to the all-white law school at the University of Missouri, the world-renowned black contralto, Marian Anderson, sang a special Easter concert at the Lincoln Memorial to a crowd estimated at 75,000. Neither the *Gaines* decision nor Anderson's concert radically altered America's racial status quo of segregation during the New Deal years, but both events symbolized growing support for change by leading figures within the judicial and executive branches of the federal government. Anderson had been scheduled to give her concert at Constitution Hall in Washington, an auditorium owned by the Daughters of the American Revolution (DAR), who insisted that the event comply with their policy of segregation. Eleanor Roosevelt, a lifelong member of the DAR and an outspoken opponent of segregation, not only resigned from the organization in protest, but secured the support of Secretary of the Interior Harold Ickes to hold the event at the Lincoln Memorial. While the president often met off the record with black leaders like Walter White of the NAACP, his wife spoke out often against discrimination and Ickes broke the color barrier in his department by hiring black lawyers, engineers, and architects. Anderson's concert, with heavy sponsorship from leading figures of the New Deal, raised FDR's image among blacks at a time when many had begun to shift their allegiance to the Democratic Party, despite its continued support for segregation. Born in 1902, a native of Philadelphia, Anderson had sung with leading European orchestras in the 1930s after her debut with the New York Philharmonic in 1925. Promoted by music impresario Sol Hurok and legendary conductor Arturo Toscanini, Anderson had performed at Carnegie Hall prior to the Washington concert and became the first African American to sing with the Metropolitan Opera in New York City in 1955.

Arnold, Thurman

Born in Laramie, Wyoming, in 1891 where, following military service in World War I, he became briefly the city's mayor, Arnold had earned degrees from Princeton University and the Harvard Law School. After teaching law at the University of Wyoming and serving as the only Democrat in the state's legislature, he took the deanship at the University of West Virginia Law School in 1927 and joined the faculty at the Yale Law School three years later. Recruited to Yale by Dean Charles Clark, Arnold joined a group of young legal realists there, including William O. Douglas, Abe Fortas, and Arthur Corbin, who stressed the social consequences of legal rules and welcomed the reforms of the New Deal. While teaching at Yale, Arnold also served as counsel to the Department of Agriculture, as legal adviser to the governor general of the Philippines, and as a trial examiner for the new Securities and Exchange Commission. He achieved literary and political fame in the late 1930s with two iconoclastic books, *The Symbols of Government* (1935) and *The Folklore of Capitalism* (1937), both of which mocked many of the reigning shibboleths used to describe and validate the nation's legal and economic arrangements. In 1938, as Roosevelt launched an antitrust attack on big business and Congress created the Temporary National Economic Committee (TNEC) to investigate the monopolistic practices of corporations, Arnold took the post as assistant attorney general in charge of the Anti-Trust Division of the Department of Justice. Considerable irony attended this appointment because Arnold had dismissed the antitrust laws as largely empty, symbolic rituals in *The Folklore of Capitalism*. What followed for the next six years, however, was no joke for business and labor unions as Arnold expanded the number of lawyers and investigations in the antitrust division fivefold and filed over 200 law suits against monopolistic practices and restraints of trade. Seizing the banner of consumer protection against price gouging and what he called "bottlenecks of business," Arnold focused antitrust efforts less on corporate size and more on specific anticompetitive practices. His frequent use of consent decrees sparked criticism from more militant antitrust advocates and his suits against various labor unions, notably the International Brotherhood of Carpenters and Joiners, called down the wrath of organized labor. By 1943 Arnold's antitrust zeal placed him on the wrong ideological side of the war effort and Roosevelt elevated him to a vacancy on the United States Court of Appeals for the District of Columbia, where he served briefly before returning to private practice. After the war he joined Abe Fortas and Paul Porter to establish one of Washington's premier law firms and from that position he defended many individuals caught in the Truman-McCarthy era anticommunist crusade.

Bank Holiday and Emergency Banking Act of 1933

Two days after taking office in March 1933, President Roosevelt issued a proclamation declaring a moratorium or "holiday" on all banking operations in the United States, a decision made necessary by a financial panic that gathered momentum over several months as depositors stormed banks demanding their cash. Such a proclamation could have come earlier, in the final days of the Hoover administration, when the out-going president's advisers had drafted the document that Roosevelt eventually issued, but the president-elect agreed only to support such a proposal until his own inauguration. No action was taken, therefore, until FDR's proclamation of March

6, soon incorporated into the New Deal's Emergency Banking Act of 1933. Under the crash program following the proclamation, government officials from the Treasury, the Federal Reserve Board, and the Reconstruction Finance Corporation fanned out across the country to examine the financial health of national banks. The examiners permitted only those with unimpaired capital to reopen under federal licenses on March 15. State banking officials adopted the federal procedures to reopen institutions subject to their jurisdiction. Even before the bank holiday ended, Roosevelt's advisers and Congress, again adopting proposals generated by the Hoover administration, had framed the Emergency Banking Act of 1933. The Emergency Banking Act gave the comptroller of the currency sweeping powers over all national banks threatened with insolvency, including the authority to appoint conservators who could impose drastic reorganization plans. The law also authorized the Reconstruction Finance Corporation (RFC) to buy the preferred stock or capital notes of banks and trust companies, providing them with an infusion of capital intended to break the liquidity crisis. Finally, the statute attempted to inject more liquidity into the system by permitting the Federal Reserve Banks to accept assets from their member institutions that had been previously ineligible for discounting by the central bank. With good reason, many students of the New Deal believe that the bank holiday and the Emergency Banking Act, passed after a few hours of debate in Congress, saved the nation's commercial banks and rescued American capitalism. It clearly indicated Roosevelt's preference for preserving the essentials of the private banking system and rejecting more radical proposals such as nationalizing the banks or using the post offices as banks of deposit.

Bankhead-Jones Farm Tenancy Act of 1937

When the New Deal's first Agricultural Adjustment Act threatened the wholesale eviction of tenant farmers and sharecroppers in 1934–1935, a group of lawyers in the agency charged with enforcement, led by general counsel Jerome Frank, attempted to moderate the impact of the program by requiring landowners who received government benefit payments to retain existing tenants. Those efforts incurred the wrath of major farm organizations and the opposition of the administrative head of the agency and Secretary of Agriculture Wallace who, with Roosevelt's blessing, finally found other employment for Frank and many of his young attorneys. When the plight of farm tenants and sharecroppers continued, however, and grassroots protests erupted through organizations such as the Southern Tenant Farmers' Union, located in Arkansas and inspired by socialist Norman Thomas, the Roosevelt administration searched for a solution that would placate unrest without upsetting the racial status quo in the South or alienating powerful farm lobbies like the American Farm Bureau Federation. The result, inspired by the administration's own Special Committee on

Farm Tenancy and put into legislative form by the respective chairmen of the Senate and House committees on agriculture, John Bankhead of Alabama and Marvin Jones of Texas, became law in 1937. The statute created the Farm Security Administration, perhaps the most class-conscious of all New Deal agencies, to administer a program that eventually allocated $293 million to nearly 50,000 farmers in the ten years after 1937, with most of the funds helping tenants purchase farmland and operating equipment through low-interest government loans. Efforts to expand the modest program through government acquisition of larger tracts of land to be resold to tenants encountered strong opposition in Congress, which cut the FSA budget every year after 1941 and liquidated the agency in 1946.

Banking Acts of 1933 and 1935

In the wake of the bank holiday and the Emergency Banking Act of 1933, the Roosevelt administration and Congress adopted in 1933 and again in 1935 the most sweeping reforms of the nation's commercial banking structure since the founding of the Federal Reserve System in 1914. With bankers of every classification placed on the defensive and often blamed for the stock market crash of 1929 and the depression that followed, the president and Congress faced weakened adversaries in these legislative struggles that retained the essentials of a private banking system but moved the center of final authority over monetary policy away from Wall Street to Washington, D.C. Known as the Glass-Steagall Act in recognition of the roles played by the two chairmen of the banking committees in Congress, Senator Carter Glass of Virginia and Representative Henry Steagall of Alabama, the 1933 statute compelled commercial banks to divest themselves of all investment banking operations within one year, a separation intended to protect depositors' funds from the speculative fever that had propelled the stock market before the crash. In addition to raising the capital requirements of all national banks, the law gave the Federal Reserve Board control over all foreign operations of member institutions, and the comptroller of the currency could regulate the voting rights of any bank holding company. Over the objections of Roosevelt, who believed the provision would subsidize mismanagement and negligence, the Glass-Steagall Act also created a Federal Deposit Insurance Corporation (FDIC) to insure depositors' accounts up to a maximum of $2,500. In addition to a federal appropriation of $150 million to launch the FDIC, all national banks and state-chartered institutions that had joined the Federal Reserve System were required to pay an assessment into the insurance fund based on their capitalization, a provision deeply resented by many national banks and most state banks that regarded it as a conspiracy to destroy the nation's traditional dual banking system and force them to accept more federal regulation. In the summer of 1935, his congressional majorities swelled by the Democratic victories of a year before, Roosevelt and his advisers introduced further reform legislation designed to significantly strengthen Washington's control over the banking system. To sweeten the plan and gain the support of Senator Glass, who regarded himself as the founder of the Federal Reserve System, the proposal reduced the original assessments levied on members for the Federal Deposit Insurance Corporation and raised the government's contribution to the insurance fund. But in return, the administration won a decisive restructuring of the role and membership of the original Federal Reserve Board, renamed the Board of Governors of the Federal Reserve System. The 1935 reforms removed the secretary of the treasury and the comptroller of the currency from the new board, to be composed of seven members, all appointed by the president and confirmed by the Senate. The restructured board would also dominate a new Federal Open Market Committee with clear authority to buy and sell government securities, the critical day-to-day mechanism for setting interest rates and the volume of currency available for loans. The Board of Governors also gained new tools for regulating and supervising the affairs of the twelve regional Federal Reserve Banks. As a result of these reforms, the United States finally enjoyed a central banking system appropriate for a modern nation, one that facilitated coordinated activities between the Treasury and the private sector, and enabled the Roosevelt administration to finance its recovery efforts as well as a world war after 1941.

Berle, Adolph A.

Born in 1895, a minister's son and a child prodigy who graduated at the age of twenty-one from the Harvard Law School where he both amazed and irritated his professors, Adolph Augustus Berle became one of the original members of Roosevelt's so-called Brain Trust, a trio of advisers that included Raymond Moley and Rexford Tugwell. During the 1932 campaign and the early years of the New Deal (1933–1935), Berle, Moley, and Tugwell exercised an important influence on FDR because they believed in the necessity for national planning and the central direction of the American economy in order to overcome the depression and prevent its recurrence. Teaching at Columbia University in the late 1920s in addition to practicing law, Berle coauthored with economist Gardner Means an influential book, *The Modern Corporation and Private Property* (1932), which argued that the days of small-scale entrepreneurship had ended in the United States, replaced by the domination of 200 giant, integrated corporations run by a cadre of professional managers and owned by millions of absentee stockholders. The emergence of such a concentration of economic power required, according to Berle and Means, a national government of equivalent size and purpose to protect the public interest. During the 1932 campaign, Berle helped to write one of Roosevelt's most important speeches delivered to the Commonwealth

Club of San Francisco. In this address, FDR argued that with the passing of the frontier and the rise of big business, the economy of the United States had entered a period of maturity approaching stasis in which the management of surpluses took priority over further innovations in production. The idea that the American economy had reached the end of a growth cycle, a concept of economic stagnation advanced also by economists such as Joseph Schumpeter, influenced the direction of early New Deal programs such as the National Industry Recovery Act (NIRA) and the first Agricultural Adjustment Act, both designed to curb output and raise prices. After a brief tenure at the Reconstruction Finance Corporation in 1933, Berle retreated to New York City where he continued to bombard the president with advice through the mail and by telephone. Until he returned formally to the administration in 1938 as an assistant secretary of state, however, Berle played a significant role in the administration of New York's reform mayor, Fiorello LaGuardia, including a design for the city's financial plan to avoid bankruptcy in 1934–1935.

Biddle, Francis

Born in Paris in 1886, the son of wealthy, upper-class Philadelphians, Biddle attended FDR's alma maters, Groton and Harvard College, earned a law degree from Harvard Law School in 1911 and became secretary to Justice Oliver Wendell Holmes Jr. before entering private practice a year later. Drawn to Theodore Roosevelt's third-party campaign in 1912, Biddle considered himself a progressive Republican until the onset of the depression when he supported FDR and became a Democrat. Although his clients in private practice had included corporate giants such as the Pennsylvania Railroad, in 1934 Biddle succeeded Lloyd Garrison as chairman of the newly created National Labor Relations Board, charged with enforcing Section 7a of the National Industrial Recovery Act (NIRA), a provision intended to protect the right of employees to form labor unions and to be free of discrimination by employers if they engaged in organizing efforts. But like its predecessor, the National Labor Board, Biddle's agency had a large mandate coupled with weak enforcement powers and minimum support from the White House. Legally independent of the National Recovery Administration (NRA), then floundering in the courts and under attack for sanctioning monopoly, with authority to hold union elections and subpoena company payrolls, the board under Garrison and then Biddle hoped to impose the principle of majority rule whereby when a majority of workers chose a union, employers would be required to bargain with that union as the representative of all workers. That principle brought Biddle and his board into conflict with top NRA administrators who wanted all labor disputes settled by industry code authorities, and with Roosevelt, who undermined the majority rule framework when he permitted the important automobile industry to adopt a system of proportional union representation that seriously weakened the bargaining power of auto workers. If the board wished to enforce its rulings, moreover, it had to seek legal action from the Department of Justice. When Biddle and the National Labor Relations Board sided with the militant American Newspaper Guild, organized to represent journalists, against William Randolph Hearst's San Francisco *Call-Bulletin*, Donald Richberg, the head of the National Recovery Administration (NRA), secured from Roosevelt a decision removing all labor-management disputes from the board's jurisdiction. Although tempted to resign in the face of this rebuff, Biddle remained at the National Labor Relations Board, encouraged Senator Robert Wagner in his efforts to secure legislation creating a new labor board with broader, independent enforcement powers, and stepped down when the Supreme Court overturned the NIRA in 1935. Appointed as chief counsel to a joint congressional committee probing the Tennessee Valley Authority (TVA) in 1938–1939, he returned to the New Deal in 1940 as solicitor general and a year later, he became attorney general of the United States, serving until 1945 when he became a member of the International Military Tribunal created to try former Nazi leaders at Nuremberg.

Biggs, James C.

The very model of an affable Southern Democratic politician and lawyer, J. Crawford Biggs was born in Oxford, North Carolina, in 1872, graduated from the state university and its law school and taught there for several years before serving one term in the North Carolina state legislature and as a justice on the state's superior court between 1907 and 1911. Apart from a brief appointment in Woodrow Wilson's Department of Justice in 1917, Biggs built up a successful private practice in Raleigh, North Carolina, and became a local notable in Democratic Party politics, at one point serving as chairman of the state's board of elections from 1929 until 1932. Unable to persuade law professor Felix Frankfurter to take the position, Roosevelt named Biggs solicitor general of the United States in 1933, a post he held until 1935 in a Department of Justice led by Attorney General Homer Cummings. Frankfurter and other elite lawyers in the New Deal had only themselves to blame for what followed. Biggs and his staff of mediocrities proceeded to lose ten of the first seventeen cases they argued before the Hughes Court on behalf of the United States. Interior Secretary Harold Ickes complained that Cummings had "apparently delivered himself into the hands of the place hunters," and "hardly anyone has any respect for the standing and ability of the lawyers over there" (Parrish 1982, 223). No doubt the briefs and arguments mounted by Biggs's office played their part in the defeats of the early New Deal, but so, too, did haste and ineptness in the executive branch and Congress. Roosevelt found Biggs a less demanding job in the Department of Justice, where he remained until returning to private practice in North Carolina in 1938.

"Black Monday"

These were words of opprobrium used by many New Dealers in 1935 to describe the events of May 27, 1935, when the Hughes Court handed down three unanimous decisions striking at the New Deal. The justices invalidated the National Industrial Recovery Act (NIRA) in *Schechter Poultry Corp. v. United States*, the Frazier-Lemke Farm Mortgage Moratorium Act in *Louisville Bank v. Radford*, and declared illegal the president's removal of deceased Federal Trade Commissioner William E. Humphrey in *Humphrey's Executor v. United States*. Shocked by these rulings, Roosevelt asked, "Well, where was Ben Cardozo? And what about old Isaiah [Brandeis]?" At a follow-up news conference with reporters, he criticized the Court by comparing the *Schechter* decision to the infamous Dred Scott case and declared that the nation had been "relegated to the horse-and-buggy" definition of interstate commerce (Leuchtenburg 1963, 145).

"Brain Trust"

New York Times journalist James Kieran dubbed them the "Brain Trust" in the fall of 1932, when three professors from Columbia University–Barnard College—Raymond Moley, Rexford Tugwell, and Adolf A. Berle—met regularly with candidate Roosevelt to develop campaign themes and discuss a wide range of issues relating to the depression and economic recovery. The idea of tapping the academic world for advice arose initially from the fertile mind of FDR's legal counsel, Samuel Rosenman, who did the recruiting and often joined the meetings along with Roosevelt's law partner, Basil O'Connor. Moley, a political scientist, Tugwell, an economist with a special interest in agriculture, and Berle, an attorney and expert on corporations, shared a belief in the permanence and utility of big business, the need for broad-gauged national planning by the federal government, and a distaste for traditional policies embedded in the antitrust laws. Although the "Brain Trust" dissolved formally after FDR's election, Moley, Tugwell, and Berle continued to play important roles in the new administration that initiated programs like the National Recovery Act and the Agricultural Adjustment Act, both based loosely on their ideas. Moley served the administration briefly as an assistant secretary of state and talent recruiter in the years 1933–1935, but became disillusioned with FDR's reluctance to support international monetary stabilization. Tugwell joined the Department of Agriculture where he continued to push for greater national planning throughout the New Deal. Berle returned to private practice and remained an informal adviser and intellectual gadfly to the president.

Browder, Earl

Born on a farm in Wichita, Kansas, in 1891, one of ten children, whose formal education ended after the third grade, Earl Browder migrated from the Socialist Party, which he joined as a young man in 1906, to the general secretaryship of the American Communist Party in 1930, a post he held officially until 1945 when hard-line followers of Joseph Stalin took over the party apparatus and expelled him for deviating from Moscow's position on the Cold War. Browder's colorful life included convictions and jail time for draft evasion and conspiracy to obstruct the draft during World War I, a federal prison sentence for passport violations in 1940, efforts to organize communist trade unions in China, and several runs at the White House as the official candidate of the Communist Party of the United States. He received over 80,000 votes in 1936 and 46,000 in 1940. Browder's political and ideological problems arose fundamentally from the CPUSA's reliance upon financial support from the Soviet Union and the Communist International (Comintern), which successfully imposed their views of the world upon most national parties. He assumed leadership of the CPUSA with a platform that called for unity among all anticapitalist parties on the left, including the Socialists, opposition to fascist regimes abroad, and unremitting attacks on Roosevelt's New Deal as little more than a Wall Street conspiracy. When the Seventh Congress of the Comintern put away its revolutionary rhetoric in 1935 in favor of a People's Front or United Front of all antifascist parties, however, Browder shifted gears quickly. Suddenly, communism became "twentieth-century Americanism," and the New Deal enjoyed Browder's support as an enlightened attempt to cure the worst abuses of capitalism without fascism. In the 1936 election, although a candidate himself, he invested more effort attacking the Republican candidate, Alf Landon, than FDR. A year later, when Roosevelt denounced the aggression of Japan in China, the Italian conquest of Ethiopia, and Hitler's bloodless take over of the Rhineland with the suggestion of a "quarantine" against such behavior, Browder led the cheering section for the president. Support for Roosevelt stopped in 1939, however, when the Soviet Union and Hitler's Germany signed a nonaggression pact, an agreement that forced another flip-flop for Browder and the CPUSA. Roosevelt, he claimed, now supported an "imperialistic" war against Germany, sought to save the degenerate British Empire, and again did the bidding of Wall Street. The Soviet occupation of Poland following the Nazi invasion, he declared at one point, "had saved eleven million people from a capitalist hell . . . and . . . secured them from foreign domination" (Klehr et al. 1998, 244–245). He fought approval of the Lend Lease bill with as much zeal as any isolationist Republican and continued to oppose FDR's preparedness programs until Germany invaded the Soviet Union in the summer of 1941. That attack necessitated Browder's renewed enthusiasm for FDR, brought about a presidential pardon for his passport conviction, but inflicted further damage upon the party's sagging fortunes. While either supporting or opposing Roosevelt publicly, Browder assisted in the creation of several espionage rings that operated inside Washington during the 1930s, efforts he successfully kept independent of the Soviet spy directorate, the KGB. Browder helped the Hungarian-born agent Josef Peters organize his operation that at one time included New Dealers Harold Ware, Less Pressman, and Alger Hiss and his courier, Whittaker Chambers. He also supervised the espionage activities of Elizabeth Bentley, later called "the Red Spy Queen" and her lover, Jacob Golos, who built a network inside the Treasury Department run by Nathan Gregory Silvermaster. Humiliated by Moscow and the party's leadership after the war, Browder nonetheless received a small pension and exclusive rights in the United States to market books produced by Soviet publishers, a sinecure his former employers hoped would maintain his silence about espionage. He kept his life, remained silent, and died in 1973.

Byrnes, James F.

Probably no member of the United States Senate wielded more influence in that chamber and at the White House with Roosevelt than James F. "Jimmy" Byrnes, a native of South Carolina who served fourteen years in the House of Representatives and eleven in the Senate before FDR named him to a vacancy on the Supreme Court in 1941. During World War II he became unofficially "assistant president" by virtue of his key role in the defense effort as head of the Office of Economic Stabilization and the Office of War Mobilization. For two years after the war he served as Harry Truman's secretary of state during the tense days of the early Cold War and finally as governor of South Carolina during the school desegregation crisis of 1951–1955.

Byrnes personified the conservative, white-supremacist Southern Democrats, who because of their seniority controlled important committees in Congress and regularly delivered their states into the party's electoral column every four years. Without them, FDR would not have won the White House in 1932 or been able to achieve his legislative program during the so-called hundred days of 1933. When presidential advisers faced a problem in Congress, they were often told, "go see Jimmy." Southern leaders like Byrnes endorsed much of the early New Deal because it attempted to aid stricken agriculture and through programs like the Tennessee Valley Authority to provide the foundation for the South's economic revitalization. They drifted away from Roosevelt, however, when the administration began to promote the goals of organized labor after 1935 and to expanded the role of the federal government with respect to minimum wage legislation and other social welfare programs. During the frantic legislative session of 1933, Byrnes placed his stamp upon key New Deal measures—the Economy Act, the Securities Act, the Agricultural Adjustment Act, and the Home Owners' Refinancing Act. He promoted the Santee-Cooper public power project for South Carolina and easily won reelection in 1936 with over 87 percent of the vote. Among a handful of Southern Democrats, he supported Roosevelt's "court-packing" legislation and remained loyal to the administration throughout the battle. In 1939 he played an important role in pushing through the Senate, after heavy amendment, the White House's bill to restructure the executive branch, although by that time he believed that organized labor, Northern liberals, Mrs. Roosevelt, and minority groups exercised too much power over the president and the party. Still, he rounded up votes as FDR's floor manager at the 1940 Democratic National Convention, which assured a third term for the president, and he even swallowed Henry Wallace, darling of the liberals, as the vice presidential candidate. When Justice McReynolds finally stepped down in 1941, FDR sent this loyal soldier's name to the Senate as his replacement.

Civil Works Administration (CWA)

The Civil Works Administration, created by an executive order of the president in November 1933, represented two enduring commitments of Franklin Roosevelt: his desire to alleviate the human suffering caused by the depression and his strong dislike of any government program that resembled the dole or straight relief for the able bodied. It also advanced the New Deal career of its administrator, Harry L. Hopkins, one of FDR's most intimate advisers, and provided a trial run for the more permanent Works Progress Administration (WPA) created in 1935. Intended to reduce unemployment and curb social unrest predicted for the harsh winter of 1933, the CWA functioned under a provision of the National Industrial Recovery Act (NIRA) with a budget of $400 million taken from that program's Public Works Administration. In one of the most dramatic organizational feats of the era, Hopkins and his staff hired over 4,200,000 men and women from relief lists and the ranks of the unemployed in three months time and paid them a minimum wage, adjusted regionally, which meant forty cents an hour in the South and sixty cents in the North. "We aren't on relief any more," one woman announced. "My husband is working for the Government" (Kennedy 1999, 176). And work they did—paving roads, repairing bridges and airport runways, painting hospitals and schools, even installing 150,000 outhouses on farms. CWA workers excavated prehistoric Indian mounds and brought opera to the Ozarks. Although short-lived, the CWA pumped money into the pockets of American workers at a desperate time and, more important, gave the whole society a morale boost. The federal government managed the entire program, recruiting the workers, choosing the projects, and writing the paychecks, which made it the first direct federal jobs program in American history and one that soon inspired the strong opposition of powerful local politicians who wanted a larger slice of the patronage that came with recruitment and project choice. Those complaints, plus Roosevelt's own desire to end the program as soon as the economy displayed any spark of recovery, brought its demise in the spring of 1934. That decision proved very premature, but the CWA experience proved invaluable to those who soon ran the even larger WPA.

Civilian Conservation Corps (CCC)

Created by an act of Congress during the first hundred days of the New Deal in March 1933, the Civilian Conservation Corps (CCC), the program closest to President Roosevelt's heart, focused upon the conservation of natural resources and employed military discipline under the administrative control of the United States Army. The CCC's constituency consisted of many of those hardest hit by the depression, single men between the ages of fifteen and twenty-four, most from families already on relief, and nearly a quarter of whom were unemployed by 1933. Within two years, the corps had employed over half a million men who worked in 2,500 camps across the United States for $30 per month. Over the nine years of its existence, the CCC provided work and income for some 2.5 million men who changed the nation's landscape by fighting forest fires, building facilities in the national parks and national historic sites, constructing reservoirs, and planting trees. Members of the corps planted so many trees, over 2 billion by one count, that some referred to them as "Roosevelt's Tree Army." But in addition to strenuous labor outdoors, which appealed to FDR, the CCC sponsored education programs at the camps and taught some 35,000 men how to read and write. Like other New Deal programs, the CCC under the initial leadership of director Robert Fechner observed the status quo when it came to race relations. Over 200,000 African Americans found work with the corps, but they remained segregated in all-black camps, which meant that others could not benefit from the program until vacancies occurred. As the United States geared up for war and employment rose in the early 1940s, Congress reduced the appropriations for the CCC and finally terminated the agency in 1942.

Cohen, Benjamin V.

Born in Muncie, Indiana, in 1894, the child of Polish Jewish immigrants, Ben Cohen became a legend among New Dealers young and old because of his nonpareil skill as an attorney. If, as one scholar has claimed, the New Deal was in essence "a lawyer's deal," then Cohen represented its fullest realization. Educated as an undergraduate and law student at the University of Chicago, where he excelled above all others, Cohen went on to pursue graduate studies at the Harvard Law School, there to draw the attention of Felix Frankfurter and become one of his many prized proteges. Before Frankfurter brought him to Washington in 1933, Cohen's abilities as a lawyer served federal circuit judge Julian Mack, the United States Shipping Board during World War I, and American Zionists negotiating the future of a Jewish homeland in Palestine. He found time as well to advise corporate clients, assist the National Consumers' League, and make a small fortune in the stock market before it crashed. Cohen brought to the New Deal a corporate lawyer's understanding of the commercial world, an unsurpassed talent for crafting legislation, and a large measure of idealism that he translated into dedicated public service. Along with other Frankfurter acolytes, James M. Landis and Thomas G. "Tommy the Cork" Corcoran, Cohen rewrote the original, ineffectual version of the Securities Act in 1933 and saw the revisions become law. A year later, again teamed with Corcoran, Cohen crafted the more radical Securities and Exchange Act that gained Congress's approval after a bruising legislative battle against the legal titans of Wall Street. Although Cohen drew his paycheck officially as counsel to the National Power Policy Committee under Interior Secretary Harold Ickes while Corcoran worked at the Reconstruction Finance Corporation, they recruited and advised other lawyers working on legislation and administration across a wide range of New Deal programs. Soon labeled "the brain twins" and "Frankfurter's little hot dogs," the duo of Cohen and Corcoran gained lasting fame in their successful campaign to enact the Public Utilities Holding Company Act of 1935, a law that symbolized along with the National Labor Relations Act of that year a decisive shift in the New Deal away from its initial, cooperative relations with corporate America. Cohen soon became the chief legal strategist defending the holding company statute in the courts, a campaign that finally succeeded in *Electric Bond & Share Co. v. Securities and Exchange Commission* (1939). Cohen also had a hand in several other New Deal statutes, including creation of the Federal Housing Administration and the Tennessee Valley Authority. In addition to his well-deserved reputation as an astute legal draftsman and litigation strategist, Cohen tutored and became the role model for many younger New Deal lawyers, all of whom achieved later prominence at the bar and in academic life—Joseph L. Rauh Jr., Paul Freund, Abe Feller, Telford Taylor, Nathan Nathanson, and Willard Hurst. After assisting with the drafting of the Lend Lease bill in 1941, Cohen went to London as counselor to the American embassy there and then to James Byrnes in the Office of Economic Stabilization and the Department of State. President Truman named him to the U.S. delegation to the United Nations in 1947. Cohen died in Washington in 1983.

Congress of Industrial Organizations (CIO)

At the annual convention of the American Federation of Labor (AF of L) in 1934, nearly a third of its union membership protested the labor federation's strategy for organizing workers in the mass-production industries such as automobiles and steel. Section 7(a) of the National Industrial Recovery Act, passed a year earlier by Congress, had inspired many such workers to join labor unions and to demand recognition for their organizations. But the AF of L, consistent with its traditional craft orientation, skimmed off the skilled workers in these mass-production industries and shuttled the unskilled into second-class affiliates known as federal unions. When the dissenters, led by the chief of the United Mine Workers Union, John L. Lewis, urged the AF of L to set aside this jurisdictional machinery and organize on an industrywide basis, they received a cool reception. And a year later, the AF of L voted down their formal proposal to form industrial unions by a two-to-one margin, despite Lewis's eloquent speech that urged them to "heed this cry from Macedonia that comes from the hearts of men. Organize the unorganized and in doing this make the American Federation of Labor the greatest instrument that has ever been forged in the history of modern civilization to befriend the cause of humanity." Upon that decision, he concluded, "Methinks . . . may rest the future of the American Federation of Labor" (Schlesinger 1958, 412). It did. Rebuffed by the rank-and-file, Lewis and his followers, who included other dynamic labor leaders such as Sidney Hillman (Amalgamated Clothing Workers), David Dubinsky (International Ladies Garment Workers), and Thomas McMahon (Textile Workers), formed the Committee for Industrial Organization inside the AF of L to do what the federation refused to do: organize industrial unions. A year later, the AF of L expelled the dissidents and launched a jurisdictional war against their organization, now named the Congress of Industrial Organizations (CIO). In 1936 the CIO worked tirelessly for Roosevelt's reelection and began its assault on key sectors of the industrial economy through the Steel Workers Organizing Committee, headed by Lewis's top aide, Philip Murray, and similar organizations that targeted textiles and automobiles. The most dramatic confrontations took place in Detroit, where the United Automobile Workers, led by Walter, Victor, and Roy Reuther, launched sit-down strikes that shut down the industry. Within a year, the UAW counted nearly half a million members. In February 1937 General Motors agreed to recognize the union and accepted its demands with respect to wages and hours. A month later, before the Supreme Court upheld the National Labor Relations Act, the biggest steel producer, United States Steel, recognized the Steel Workers Organizing Committee and bowed to the inevitable. Supported after 1937 by a sympathetic National Labor Relations Board, the CIO's organizing drives bore handsome returns among workers in textiles, rubber, food processing, and electrical manufacturing. By 1940 the CIO numbered over 2.5 million members, organized in forty-one affiliated unions. And it had become the single most potent force in the Democratic Party, providing campaign funds and precinct workers that provided Roosevelt's margins of victory in both 1940 and 1944.

Corcoran, Thomas G.

When President Roosevelt floated the idea of naming Thomas "Tommy the Cork" Corcoran to the post of director of the budget in 1934, FDR's close friend and Secretary of the Treasury Henry Morgenthau Jr. confided to his diary: "This seemed to me absolutely out of the question. Tom Corcoran was a first-class lawyer, a first-class political operator, a first-class accordion player. But I felt sure he knew very little about finance and could not be relied upon to keep a tight rein over the spending policies" (Blum 1959, 231). A more telling portrait of Corcoran does not exist, although Morgenthau might have noted that Corcoran possessed a fine tenor voice and a large inventory of Irish Sea Chanties with which he often entertained the president. Born into the working-class Irish Catholic world of Pawtucket, Rhode Island, at the turn of the century, Corcoran's charm, ebullience, and brains carried him through Brown University—complete with Phi Beta Kappa key—and then to the Harvard Law School where, under Frankfurter's direction, he took a doctorate in 1926 and joined that large cadre of law students known as "Felix's boys." Frankfurter sent him on to serve as Justice Holmes's secretary, a job whose main tasks included reading Dante and Montaigne to the aging justice in the evenings. The justice found Corcoran to be "quite noisy, quite satisfactory, and quite noisy" (Leuchtenburg 1963, 149). After practicing law in New York with the firm of Cotton, Franklin, Wright and Gordon, he signed on as a lawyer in Hoover's Reconstruction Finance Corporation (RFC), where he maintained an office throughout the early New Deal while also working ad hoc for the Department of the Treasury and the attorney general. Beginning with the Securities Act in 1933, Corcoran, only in his early thirties, joined Ben Cohen to become one of the most effective legislative-drafting teams in the history of the federal government. Their triumphs included the Securities Act, the Securities and Exchange Act, the Public Utilities Holding Company Act, various extensions of RFC authority, and the founding statutes for the Tennessee Valley Authority and the Federal Housing Administration. While Cohen fine tuned the legislative language and plotted litigation strategy, Corcoran worked the corridors of the House and Senate and made the administration's arguments before congressional committees. They soon earned the title of the "gold dust twins," after a popular radio commercial that invited housewives to "let the gold dust twins do your work." By 1935 Tommy the Cork had earned such a reputation for political manipulation and cutting legislative deals that Senator Wagner once warned his assistant: "Don't have anything to do with that fellow Corcoran. I don't want to see him around the office" (Morgan 1985, 425). That year he got himself and the administration into very hot water when Senator R. Owen Brewster of Maine alleged that Corcoran had attempted to coerce his vote on the so-called death sentence in the Public Utilities Holding Company Act by threatening to block funds for a dam project in his state. After surviving a hearing in the House over the Brewster incident, Corcoran went on to serve FDR loyally during the court-packing fight of 1937 and spoke out vigorously for larger doses of government spending in 1937–1938. Disappointed that he lacked support to become solicitor general of the United States, even from his former patron Frankfurter, Corcoran left the government in 1941 and opened a private practice in Washington that specialized in navigating clients through many of the government agencies he had helped to create during the New Deal.

Coughlin, Charles E.

Known to millions of listeners in the 1930s as the "radio priest," Charles E. "Father" Coughlin was born in 1891 and raised in Hamilton, Ontario. After studying theology at the University of Toronto he entered the Roman Catholic priesthood, taught for a decade at Assumption College in Ontario, and became a parish priest in Royal Oak, Michigan, in 1926. From his church—The Shrine of the Little Flower—Coughlin launched what became one of the most popular weekly radio programs in the United States, which catapulted him to a position of influence rivaled only by FDR. On "The Golden Hour of the Little Flower," carried nationwide by CBS, Coughlin's mellifluous sermons combined religious themes and political analysis, usually peppered with large doses of anticommunism. In 1932 he urged his audience, then estimated at between 30 and 40 million, to vote for FDR, because, he said, the United States faced the choice between "Roosevelt and ruin." In a country rife with fear and insecurity by 1933, the Little Flower offered a simple analysis of the causes of the depression and a panacea for his cure. The crisis had been orchestrated, he said, by international bankers, Jews, and communists, who had fastened upon the country a monetary system based upon the "pagan god of gold." Salvation, according to Coughlin, lay in restoring "the people's money," remonetizing silver, and thereby inflating the currency. When the administration severed the link between gold and the dollar, devaluated the currency, and agreed to purchase silver for monetary purposes, Coughlin told his listeners that "the New Deal is Christ's deal." However, he changed his message very soon when the Treasury Department released a list of prominent persons who had speculated in silver futures—a list that include Father Coughlin. As his praise for Adolf Hitler, Benito Mussolini, and other fascist leaders rose, so by 1934–1935 did his attacks on Roosevelt and the New Deal as the "Jew Deal" and "anti-God." Appealing to those, he said, left behind by the New Deal—the small shopkeepers, marginal professionals, and blue-collar workers—Coughlin organized the National Union for Social Justice in 1934 on a platform that called for greater monetary inflation, redistribution of wealth, and expanded government welfare programs. Soon presiding over local chapters with a total membership estimated at 500,000, Coughlin aligned his Union for Social Justice with the other anti–New Deal and antibusiness spokesmen who hoped to form a third party—Louisiana senator Huey P. Long and Francis Townsend, a retired California dentist who advocated government pensions for the elderly. Had Long not been assassinated in 1935, he might have become the Union Party's presidential candidate in 1936, a role that then fell to another paladin of inflation, North Dakota congressman William Lemke. When this third-party challenge attracted less than a million votes against Roosevelt and Landon in 1936, Coughlin retired from the radio for several weeks, but returned with an even more vitriolic repertoire of anti-Semitic, anti-Roosevelt, and pro-Hitler messages.

Beginning in 1937, his own archbishop and some church leaders in Rome condemned the Little Flower's continuing attacked upon the administration, but he picked up the cause of isolationism along with the America First Committee before Pearl Harbor. As late as 1942, when the church finally pulled the plug on his broadcasts, Coughlin described World War II as a "Roosevelt-British-Jewish" plot. Although his National Union for Social Justice disbanded in 1944, Coughlin enjoyed a brief renaissance after the war, when his fierce brand of anticommunism again found a favorable response in the church and among cold warriors in the government.

Cummings, Homer Stille

A native Chicagoan, born in 1870, Cummings graduated from Yale College and Yale Law School before entering private practice in Stamford, Connecticut, in the 1890s. There he built a solid career in Democratic Party politics, first as the three-time mayor of Stamford and later as state attorney for Fairfield County between 1914 and 1924. Although he failed in his one attempt to win the United States Senate seat in Connecticut in 1916, Cummings became a major power in the Democratic National Committee, where he served as vice chairman in 1913 and as chairman in 1919–1920. Party loyalty and fealty to candidate Roosevelt in 1932 brought him the coveted post of attorney general of the United States in 1933 after FDR's first choice, Senator Thomas Walsh of Montana, died before he could be confirmed. Cummings held the position until January 1939. Blamed by many elite lawyers for staffing the Department of Justice, especially the solicitor general's office, with second-rate lawyers and political hacks, Cummings endured a series of spectacular defeats in the Supreme Court in 1935–1936, but with the addition of fresh legal talent he survived to witness the New Deal's litigation triumphs in 1937 and after. Neither a brilliant brief writer nor eloquent advocate before the courts, Cummings invested most of his efforts in shepherding legislation through Congress that either expanded the criminal jurisdiction of the federal government or permitted the federal courts to adopt new rules of criminal and civil procedure. In 1934 he successfully urged Congress to pass legislation granting the Supreme Court authority to prescribe rule of procedure in civil cases, a measure that passed with little opposition and led to the final adoption of such rules four years later. After the Supreme Court with Congress's authorization promulgated the limited Criminal Appeals Rules in 1934, Cummings recommended further changes that produced ultimately the Federal Rules of Criminal Procedure, effective in March 1946. As attorney general, Cummings rendered an important constitutional interpretation in 1937 after the Supreme Court upheld Washington's minimum wage law in *West Coast Hotel v. Parrish.* At issue was the status of the minimum wage law for the District of Columbia, which the Court had invalidated in 1923 in *Adkins v. Children's Hospital.* Was the earlier statute now valid? Cummings advised that the 1923 decision had only "suspended" enforcement until 1937. He cited Supreme Court opinions to the effect that "the courts have no power to repeal or abolish a statute, and that notwithstanding a decision holding it unconstitutional a statute continues to remain on the statute books" (39 *Ops. Atty. Gen. 22*, 1937).

Dewson, Mary Williams

Born in 1874 in Quincy, Massachusetts, Dewson's wide-ranging, effective social and political activism became an inspiration to many women reformers in the first four decades of the twentieth century. A graduate of Wellesley College, she served as superintendent of the Massachusetts Girls' Parole Department from 1900 to 1912 and managed the immigrant refugee program for the American Red Cross in Europe during World War I. After the war, she joined that National Consumers' League as a research secretary, where she played an important role in the organization's efforts to pass wage and hours legislation. From 1925 to 1931 she served as president of the Consumers' League of New York and developed close, personal ties with the Roosevelts and the Democratic Party. FDR's political operative and postmaster general, James Farley, tapped Dewson to head the Women's Division of the Democratic National Committee in 1933 and she became a member of the President's Committee on Economic Security that framed the Social Security Act of 1935. After Roosevelt signed the legislation, he named Dewson to the first Social Security Board, a post she held until poor health forced her to resign in 1938.

Dies, Martin, Jr.

Born in Colorado, Texas, in 1900, Martin Dies Jr. received his education at Wesley College, the University of Texas, and National University in Washington, D.C., from which he received his law degree before returning to his native state. There he practiced law in the 1920s, first in Marshall and later in Orange, Texas. In 1931 he won a seat in the House of Representatives and retained it until 1945, accumulating seniority in the lower house of Congress and becoming the prominent chairman in the late 1930s of the special House Un-American Activities Committee (HUAC). Like many other Southerners, especially Texans, Dies supported much of the early New Deal with its emphasis upon agricultural relief, banking reform, and cheap, government-financed electric power projects and reclamation. But following the 1936 election, as Roosevelt moved into a closer alliance with Northern liberals and organized labor, Die became one of the administration's major opponents in Congress. Hostile to the CIO and the urban political machines that delivered the votes of hyphenated Americans to the president, Dies began to use his chairmanship of HUAC to attack the administration for harboring communists and other subversives in government positions. New Deal liberals like Harry Hopkins and Harold Ickes suffered his abuse, but Dies reserved his harshest criticism for anyone belonging to the Communist Party or associated with it. At a minimum, he wanted such individuals eliminated from the government and loyalty oaths required of all federal employees. At the extreme, he advocated a legal ban on the party itself and the exclusion of any labor union under its influence from the protections of the National Labor Relations Act, a goal finally realized in the post-war Taft-Hartley Act. At the time, most observers regarded Dies as a cranky, fear-mongering reactionary, the scourge of civil liberties. In his 1940 book, *The Trojan Horse in America*, Dies devoted the bulk of his attack to the threat of communism and his committee compiled an extensive list of labor unions, magazines, newspapers, and other organizations it labeled as communist dominated or communist fronts. His inventory of subversive groups included the American Civil Liberties Union and even the Boy Scouts of America. In retrospect, given the evidence of Soviet espionage activities inside the Roosevelt administration, Dies's accusations appear less paranoid, although his methods often failed to distinguish between subversion and legitimate dissent. Roosevelt never directly challenged Dies, fearful of his popular support in the country and not unpleased when the HUAC chairman also turned his fire on fascist and neo-Nazi groups before and after Pearl Harbor.

"Dust Bowl"

In one of the great ecological disasters in twentieth-century America, southwesterly storms in summer and northerly blizzards in winter generated a series of violent dust storms that devastated that area of the Great Plains comprising the panhandles of Texas and Oklahoma, parts of northeastern New Mexico, eastern Colorado, and western Kansas. This blighted region became known in the 1930s as the "dust bowl," where residents endured long hours of half light and even total darkness as clouds of wind-born dirt scoured the earth, burned the lungs, and left buildings buried under mounds of dust that resembled the snow drifts of Minnesota. Although the severe drought years of 1932–1939 provided the environmental foundation for the tragedy, so did human ignorance and cupidity. Following World War I farmers on the Great Plains transformed grasslands into extensive cropland devoted to winter wheat, with many of the larger units owned by absentee landlords whose managers employed dry farming and heavily mechanized techniques that left them prey to the drought. The severe dust storms of 1935–1937 brought bankruptcy to farmers in the region and economic suffering to all the merchants and service providers who depended upon them. New Deal programs such as the Agricultural Adjustment Administration and the Resettlement Administration offered some relief for the Great Plains. The latter agency relocated some farmers from the dust bowl to more hospitable conditions, acquired their old lands, and reseeded them to grass. But only the return of adequate rainfall in the late 1930s and the adoption of new methods of tillage encouraged by the Soil Erosion Service that retained enough crop residue to hold the soil provided a long-term solutions capable of restoring the region's economic viability.

Eccles, Marriner S.

A month before Roosevelt took the oath of office and launched the first hundred days of his first administration, Marriner Eccles, a wealthy banker from Utah whose institutions in that state had all weathered the still-mounting liquidity crisis, testified before the Finance Committee of the United States Senate. For a representative from a stricken industry known for its conservatism, Eccles put on a memorable performance. While many other witnesses urged retrenchment by the federal government and a balanced budget as a confidence builder to cure the depression, Eccles proposed just the opposite. The depression, he told the Senators, arose from underconsumption and a dearth of private investment. Instead of balancing the federal budget, Washington should spend more on relief to the unemployed, public works projects, refinancing farm and home mortgages, and canceling the debts European nations still owed to the United States from World War I. Three years before the distinguished British economists John Maynard Keynes published his devastating critique of classical economics in *The General Theory of Employment, Interest, and Money* (1936), which argued that government investment and spending would have to temporarily compensate for the decline in private investment, income, and spending, Eccles had reached the same conclusion without the benefit of a college-level course in economics. Born in Logan, Utah, in 1890, Eccles had only graduated from the high school attached to Brigham Young University. Then, following three years service propagating the Mormon faith through missionary work in Scotland, he returned to Utah to take over the family's extensive business holdings, which included banks, cattle ranching, mining, and assorted construction projects. Beginning in the fall of 1933, Eccles met informally with many of the New Dealers who shared his commitment to compensatory spending by Washington and hoped to persuade the president to follow that course of action. They had little immediate success with Roosevelt. Except for emergency relief purposes and the limited public works funded under the National Industrial Recovery Act, FDR remained devoted to the fiscal orthodoxy of a balanced budget, a commitment he would not abandon until the major recession of 1937–1938. When Eccles returned to Washington, it came at the request of acting Treasury Secretary Henry Morgenthau Jr., who never shared Eccles's views on fiscal policy, but valued his expertise in monetary matters. Morgenthau also urged Roosevelt to name Eccles to a vacancy on the Federal Reserve Board, a post he agreed to fill upon the condition that the president would support legislation increasing the board's authority over the twelve district Federal Reserve Banks, especially the one in New York

City. Eccles soon became the driving force behind the legislative struggle that produced the Banking Act of 1935 and he would preside as chairman over the Federal Reserve Board until 1948. In addition to his important role in restructuring the Federal Reserve System, Eccles led the effort in 1937 to persuade Roosevelt to boost government expenditures in the face of a major recession generated in large measure by the president's earlier decision to cut federal relief and public works spending. Teaming up with the fiscal expansionists—Hopkins, Leon Henderson, Tommy Corcoran, and others—the Eccles faction finally prevailed over Morgenthau and his allies. In the spring of 1938 Roosevelt asked Congress for an additional $3 billion for the Works Progress Administration, the Public Works Administration, the United States Housing Authority, and the Farm Security Administration. By necessity, not conviction, Roosevelt had become a Keynesian or, more accurately, a convert to the ideas of compensatory fiscal stimulus espoused by Marriner Eccles.

Election of 1936

Even more dramatically than the 1932 contest between Herbert Hoover and Roosevelt, the 1936 election changed the landscape of American politics for nearly a generation. Roosevelt's victory over the Republican candidate, Kansas governor Alf Landon, was decisive and historic, a popular vote margin of 27,752,869 to 16,674,665, and a sweep in the electoral college of 523 to 8. The so-called Roosevelt coalition took shape in this election, as blue-collar ethnic voters, African Americans, liberal professionals, struggling Southern farmers, and a large number of progressive businessmen flocked to the president's banner. This coalition, constituted of many men and women who had been regarded as "outsiders" in American life—Roman Catholics, Jews, Eastern Europeans, labor organizers, academics, upstart businessmen from the South and West—would dominate American presidential elections until 1952, when the Republicans first returned to the White House. The 1936 election also saw the Democrats gain whopping majorities in the House (331 to 89) and Senate (76 to 16), a position of dominance they continued to enjoy until 1946 when the Republicans briefly recaptured Congress, only to lose it again for most of the 1950s, 1960s, and 1970s. The election became a referendum on FDR and the New Deal, with the president and his supporters painting the contest as one between the masses, who had benefited from programs such as the Civil Works Administration and the WPA, and the classes, selfish businessmen and bankers, who had been driven from the temples of power and hoped to restore the status quo. The Republican Party, although led by Governor Landon, one of the most liberal candidates in a generation, accused the New Dealers of destroying the free enterprise system, saddling the public with budget deficits and tax increases, coddling radicals, and undermining sacred constitutional principles. When the ballots were tallied, the American voter overwhelmingly endorsed the New Deal and FDR. Asked why he supported FDR despite the fact that the depression lingered on, a textile worker in North Carolina replied: "Mr. Roosevelt is the only man we ever had in the White House who would understand that my boss is a son-of-a-bitch" (Leuchtenburg 1963, 189). Seldom if ever had class lines been so sharply drawn in an American election. The businessmen who vehemently opposed the New Deal in 1936 ran companies with large blue-collar labor forces eager to join unions under the protective wing of the new National Labor Relations Act. On the other hand, FDR drew support from business leaders in areas of banking, finance, insurance, oil refining, and entertainment, where employees wore more white collars and where the threat of unionization remained considerably lower. The stunning Democratic victory produced two notable results; one that ultimately reversed Roosevelt's fortunes, the other that helped to transform the Republican Party. Flush with success at the polls, Roosevelt moved forward with his attack on the Supreme Court, a decision that alienated him from many of his own supporters in Congress. And the defeat of his "court-packing" proposal gave new life to his political enemies in 1937–1938, especially when the economy faltered and produced the "Roosevelt recession." Instead of riding the 1936 returns to further legislative triumphs, the New Deal sputtered and, except for the Fair Labor Standards Act, lost the initiative in Congress to a coalition of conservative Southern Democrats and Republicans. When Roosevelt threw his influence into the 1938 congressional elections against several right-wing Democrats, the voters rebuffed him decisively by reelecting them. Teaming up with Southern Democrats in the House and Senate, congressional Republicans frustrated Roosevelt until Pearl Harbor, but the Republican's presidential party became more progressive as a consequence of the voters' validation of the New Deal in 1936. Every Republican presidential candidate from Landon forward—Wendell Willkie (1940), Thomas E. Dewey (1944–1948), and Dwight Eisenhower (1952–1956)—endorsed, however cautiously, major portions of the New Deal and proved more liberal than Republican candidates prior to the depression. To that extent, FDR had as profound an impact on the Republicans as on his own party.

Fair Employment Practices Committee

In late June 1941, one month before Hughes stepped down as chief justice, President Roosevelt issued Executive Order 8802, which created the Fair Employment Practices Committee charged with eliminating racial and ethnic discrimination in defense industries holding federal contracts. Late in the decade the Roosevelt administration manifested a growing concern for racial justice when key figures like the president's wife and Harold Ickes organized Marian Anderson's concert at the Lincoln Memorial and when Attorney General Frank Murphy established a civil rights division in the Department of Justice. The president, however, ever sensitive to his support among white Southerners in Congress, continued to oppose efforts to pass a federal antilynching law. Executive Order 8802 flowed less from FDR's commitment to racial equality than from the astute organizational efforts of Asa Philip Randolph, the dynamic leader of the Brotherhood of Sleeping Car Porters, who threatened a massive protest march in Washington unless the administration took steps to end the "whites-only" hiring practices at companies filling orders from the War Department. Fearful that such a display of unrest would tarnish the country's image abroad, FDR assigned his wife, Eleanor, and New York's mayor, Fiorello LaGuardia, to negotiate a settlement with Randolph and his supporters. The result was Executive Order 8802, written largely by a young lawyer in the Lend Lease Administration, Joseph L. Rauh Jr., destined to become a leading advocate for civil rights and civil liberties in the postwar era. When instructed by one of the president's aides to "include something for the Poles," who had protested the lack of jobs in defense industries around Buffalo, Rauh framed the order to prohibit discrimination on the grounds of "race, color, creed or national origins," the first time nationality received protection under federal law. Pleased with the order, Randolph called off the march on Washington. For black leaders, however, the results proved very disappointing. Armed only with authority to hold hearings on complaints and issue recommendations, the FEPC lacked teeth. With a tiny staff and a small budget, the FEPC had to rely on the War and Navy Departments to enforce its recommendations, but those agencies, preoccupied with maintaining production for the military, refused to pressure contractors into compliance with FEPC complaints. As the nation's economy boomed with war orders by 1942, the FEPC suffered another blow when Roosevelt transferred it to the War Manpower Commission where conflicts with that agency's chief, Paul McNutt, further weakened its effectiveness. Prior to his death, Roosevelt again reorganized FEPC activities, renamed it the Committee on Fair Employment Practices, broadened its jurisdiction to include all federal contracting, and kept it running with temporary funds. A permanent, strengthened FEPC awaited the postwar revolution in civil rights.

Fair Labor Standards Act of 1938

The last significant reform of the New Deal, the Fair Labor Standards Act, climaxed decades of legislative effort to adopt a comprehensive federal minimum wage law. In 1923 the Supreme Court struck down the attempt to adopt a wage law covering women and children working in the District of Columbia (*Adkins v. Children's Hospital* [1923]). As part of the compromise that produced the National Industrial Recovery Act (NIRA) in 1933, Sections 7 and 7(a) prohibited the use of antiunion "yellow-dog" contracts by employers, gave workers the right to join unions and bargain collectively, and the right to minimum wages. When the Hughes Court overturned the NIRA in *Schechter Poultry Corp.* (1935), the decision wiped out the law's labor provisions in addition to the codes of fair competition. The administration returned to the battle in 1936 on the eve of the Democratic National Convention, with the Walsh-Healey Public Contracts Act that required all persons contracting with the federal government to adopt wage and hours standards fixed by the Department of Labor. Finally, in 1937, with the strong backing of both the AF of L and the CIO, armed with large majorities in Congress, and with a recession looming, Roosevelt launched a new drive for a broad federal law. Opposition from Southern congressmen, fearful that a federal law would eliminate their favorable wage differential in industries such as textiles, delayed passage until the summer of 1938. As signed into law, the law affected all workers engaged in interstate commerce or who produced goods for interstate commerce and banned the employment of people under the age of sixteen. With enforcement powers given to a new Wage and Hours Division in the Department of Labor, the FLSA fixed the initial minimum wage at twenty-five cents per hour with an increase to forty cents per hour mandated by 1940. The hours provision fixed a forty-four-hour work week in the first year with a reduction to forty hours within seven years. Nearly 13 million people received initial coverage, although as a concession to the South and other employers, the law exempted most agricultural workers, domestics, fishermen, street railway employees, and local retail clerks.

Federal Antilynching Bill

During the 1930s the Hughes Court on a case-by-case basis confronted the entrenched legacy of American racism and in many instances struck blows against the structure of segregation, prejudice, and disfranchisement that mocked the nation's claim to equal justice under law. The justices challenged the constitutionality of all-white juries and all-white primaries and attempted to force the states to truly implement the "separate but equal" doctrine. The Roosevelt administration, dependent upon white Southern votes in Congress, moved with far less determination on this moral issue. Above all, it failed to vigorously support a statute making lynching a federal crime, a measure high on the agenda of civil rights groups since World War I. Although over sixty African Americans became victims of vigilante summary executions, either shot to death or hanged by mobs between 1930 and 1934, Roosevelt would not endorse a model law drafted by lawyers for the National Association of Colored People (NAACP) and introduced in Congress by Senators Edward Costigan and Robert Wagner. In 1935, with the New Deal at high tide, the antilynching bill received a favorable endorsement from the Judiciary Committee, but supporters encountered a filibuster under Senate Rule 22, whereby two-thirds of the members had to vote to shut off debate. A united front by Southern senators, including two future Supreme Court Justices, Hugo Black and James F. Byrnes, kept the filibuster alive for days with the result that FDR feared for the fate of his other economic legislation. Without the president's intervention and unable to break the filibuster, the Senate finally adjourned without taking up the bill, and even Senator Wagner and his supporters did not renew the fight.

Federal One

In 1935 the Works Progress Administration (WPA), funded by Congress at $4.8 billion, became the largest work relief program of the New Deal. "Federal One" was the shorthand label used to describe the WPA's Federal Project No. 1, which under director Holger Cahill provided artistic and professional work for artists, writers, actors, musicians, and historians through programs such as the Federal Arts Project, the Federal Music Project, the Historical Records Survey, the Federal Writers' Project, and the Federal Theatre Project. Federal funding of the arts and professions not only saved individuals from economic privation, it brought the arts to millions of Americans who had never before seen a live play or symphony, preserved the records and artifacts of the past, and enriched the cultural life of thousands of local communities. By 1936, for example, the Federal Arts Project employed more than 6,000 persons, over half engaged directly in creating art with the remainder employed in educational activities or research and preservation. Two years later, artists in the program had created over 40,000 paintings and more than 1,000 murals on public buildings from Maine to San Francisco. Among its artists were Jackson Pollock, William Gropper, and Willem de Kooning. The Index of American Design eventually produced photographic reproductions of American art that ranged from sculptures to handicrafts and toys. Funds from the Arts Project supported local community art centers that taught painting, sculpture, and art history classes. The Federal Theatre Project, headed by Hallie Flanagan, became the most controversial of all Federal One undertakings as a result of the productions it launched that probed the nation's social and economic woes. Tapping the thousands of unemployed actors, stagehands, technicians, and playwrights in the New York City area alone, Flanagan quickly organized a variety of dramatic units, including the Negro Theatre under Rose McClendon and John Houseman; an Experimental Theatre for new productions; the Living Newspaper, sponsored by the American Newspaper Guild; a one-act play group; a Yiddish vaudeville troupe; and even a Tryout Theatre for complete novices. In its first two years, 1935–1936, the Federal Theatre Project brought to audiences not only T. S. Eliot's *Murder in the Cathedral* and the avant-garde production of *Macbeth* by Houseman and Orson Welles, but plays that explored the class and racial oppressions that crippled the New South (*Altars of Steel* by Thomas Hall-Rogers) and an inside look at struggles surrounding the Tennessee Valley Authority (in a "living newspaper" entitled *Power*). In 1936 alone, the plays performed by the FTP drew 350,000 people a week in twenty-eight cities across the United States. Conservatives in Congress denounced the theatre project as a propaganda machine for the New Deal and a hotbed of radicalism, especially when it financed new plays such as Marc Blitzstein's openly Marxist *The Cradle Will Rock* or an adaptation of Sinclair Lewis's antifascist novel, *It Can't Happen Here.* Budget cuts and political pressure prevented *The Cradle Will Rock* from opening in 1937. Congress terminated the program two years later. The Federal Music Project supported free dances and performances by jazz banks, choral groups, and thirty orchestras, including an ensemble of blind musicians. Nearly 10,000 writers found work with the Federal Writers Project, including Nelson Algren, Saul Bellow, and Richard Wright. These writers produced a magnificent series of state guidebooks and compiled a rich collection of oral histories with former slaves, white hillbillies, and various European immigrant groups, all of which began to document the history of what Roosevelt once called "the forgotten Americans."

Federal Rules of Civil Procedure

Until 1884 the Supreme Court of the United States had never adopted rules governing its own practice, although a year before, the American Bar Association (ABA) had created a committee on Judicial Administration and Remedial Procedure with the goal of encouraging Congress to adopt a bill to prepare a federal code of procedure to regulate both civil and criminal matters. By 1912, virtually every state bar association had endorsed the program of the ABA to make the practice in the federal courts uniform and the association's committee, chaired by William W. Shelton with William Howard Taft as a member, drafted a bill that granted the Supreme Court appropriate authority to write such rules. The ABA measure, however, encountered the vigorous opposition of Senator Thomas J. Walsh of Montana, who argued that the Supreme Court did not have the time to undertake the project, that separate federal rules would force practitioners to learn two systems of procedure and finally, that to give this authority to the Supreme Court would violate the Constitution. Given Walsh's long-standing opposition, the ABA disbanded its Committee on Uniform Judicial Procedure in 1933 and gave up any hope of reform. That same year, Roosevelt tapped Walsh to be his attorney general, but the senator died before assuming office and the new appointee, Homer Cummings, looked with greater favor upon the old ABA proposals. He recommended to Congress that law and equity rules be combined into one form of action in the federal courts and that the Supreme Court have the authority to prescribe the rules. The ABA-Cummings bill passed Congress with little fanfare or debate in 1934. A year later, the Hughes Court appointed a committee chaired by William D. Mitchell, a prominent New York attorney, to prepare a draft of the proposed rules. Over the next three years, Mitchell's committee wrote three drafts, each scrutinized by the federal judiciary and bar as well as by the justices themselves before the final version went to Congress for approval in September 1938. At last the federal courts had a uniform system of pleading and practice that made for greater simplicity and efficiency. The rules introduced notice pleading, which restricted the pleadings to notice of general claims and left to the discovery process the development of the dispute. In addition to merging law and equity, which gave the courts a range of remedies from monetary damages to injunctions, efforts were made to make the rules of procedure uniform in other areas such as copyright, admiralty, and patents. The rules also introduced some new procedures such as discovery, pretrial conferences, and summary judgments. The statutes of the New Deal and the decisions of the Hughes Court brought further standardization and centralization to the legal and economic structure of American life and the new Federal Rules of Civil Procedure became another important manifestation of that process.

"Fireside Chats"

Beginning on the evening of March 12, 1933, eight days after he took the oath of office and seeking to reassure the American people that their banks remained sound, President Roosevelt delivered his first radio address from the basement of the White House. By one estimate, 17 million American households tuned in to hear FDR that evening. By the time of his second radio talk in late June, the event had been labeled a "fireside chat" by Harry C. Butcher, chief of CBS's Washington office. Roosevelt had first experimented with the radio medium as governor of New York, when occasionally he made appeals over the airwaves to his constituents. During the New Deal, these "fireside chats" became his unique method for communicating to the American people in a time of economic insecurity and pending war. Over the next twelve years of his presidency, Roosevelt would deliver twenty-eight "fireside chats," which made him a dramatic, living presence in the living rooms of at least one-quarter of the American population who listened regularly to the president's discourse on recovery, relief, reform, and foreign relations. Critics accused the president of using the radio as an instrument of political propaganda, one intended to gain votes for his programs and reelections. Indeed they were, but unlike some other masters of the medium in the 1930s, notably Adolf Hitler in Germany, Roosevelt conveyed not a message of hate and violence, but one of hope and compassion.

Frank, Jerome

Born in New York City in 1889, the son of German Jewish immigrants, Frank made important contributions to the literature of legal realism in the 1930s and played several key roles in the programs of the New Deal before Roosevelt nominated him in 1941 to serve on the United States Court of Appeals for the Second Circuit, where he sat until his death in 1957. Following a brilliant academic career at the University of Chicago, where he earned both his undergraduate and law degrees, Frank practiced law with firms in Chicago and New York, most notably with Chadbourne, Stanchfield and Levy, whose clients included some of the nation's largest corporations. In 1930 he published one of the seminal works of the realist movement, *Law and the Modern Mind,* a book replete with his knowledge of both the law and psychoanalytic theory. Traditional voices in the legal academy and on the bench rose up in outrage when Frank suggested that lawyers and jurists had to become more self-conscious about what he called "the non-rational and non-idealistic elements at play" in the legal system. Frank, some critics suggested, had reduced judicial decision making to an investigation of what judges had eaten for breakfast, a vast simplification of his arguments. His reputation for stirring the pot of academic controversy continued, however, when he published several articles suggesting that the legal system could never reach uncontested conclusions even concerning questions of fact, what he labeled "fact-skepticism." In 1933, bored with practice on Wall Street, Frank landed a job with the New Deal through Felix Frankfurter and became general counsel for the new Agricultural Adjustment Administration (AAA). He recruited an able staff of young, idealistic, and left-leaning lawyers, including Abe Fortas, Adlai Stevenson, and Alger Hiss, who soon antagonized the chief Triple A administrators, George Peek and Chester Davis, who wanted to raise farm prices without engaging in structural reform of agriculture. When Frank's lawyers attempted to rewrite subsidy contracts to protect existing tenants and sharecroppers, they set the stage for a showdown with Davis, Agriculture Secretary Henry Wallace, and, finally, Roosevelt, who gave Wallace his approval for finding other employment for the general counsel and his men. Frank went back to brief practice in New York, but worked as a private litigator for Harold Ickes's Public Works Administration. He returned to Washington full time in 1937 to fill a vacancy on the new Securities and Exchange Commission under Chairman William O. Douglas. When Douglas went on the Supreme Court in 1939, Frank succeeded him as head of the agency. Still fired with the reformer's zeal, Frank allied himself with the commission brokers on Wall Street to carry through a major reorganization of the New York Stock Exchange that provided for a salaried, nonmember president, a professional staff, and a reduced role for specialists and floor traders. In no small measure, Frank helped transform the stock exchange from a private club into a public utility. And when the SEC began the serious business of reorganizing the largest public utility holding companies, Frank took the lead in demanding financial plans that protected the interests of rate payers as well as stockholders. Other members of the commission feared that their chairman promoted "an unwarranted reaching out for control of managerial functions" (Parrish 1972, 222). Over strong objections from business leaders who viewed him as a dangerous radical, Roosevelt named Frank to the federal appeals court, where he displayed a keen regard for the Bill of Rights and, like Brandeis, peppered his long opinions with citations drawn from many nonlegal sources.

Garner, John Nance

Twice Roosevelt's running mate and twice elected vice president of the United States, Texan Garner will remain forever famous for his aphorism that the second highest office in the land "was not worth a pitcher of warm spit." Born in 1868 in Red River County, Texas, Garner had little formal education, read for the law, and joined the Texas bar in 1890. In 1902, after serving several terms in the Texas House of Representatives, he won a seat in Congress and held it for the next thirty years. In 1931 as the depression deepened and the Democrats took control of the House of Representatives, they elected Garner Speaker. As a leader of the Democrats' Congressional party, anchored by moderate and conservative Southerners, Garner attempted to steer a middle-of-the-road course between support for President Hoover's antidepression measures and support for his party's alternatives. He backed creation of the Reconstruction Finance Corporation (RFC) designed to bail out ailing businesses and fund self-liquidating public works projects in 1932, but he also rounded up the votes to push through a substantial federal tax increase that year that many economists condemned as the wrong medicine for a stricken economy. As a favorite son candidate for the presidency in 1932, Garner had little hope of winning the nomination, but with Roosevelt unable to command the required two-thirds vote at the Chicago convention, Garner played the role of kingmaker when he released his delegates on the fourth ballot and indicated a preference for the New Yorker. His reward was the vice presidency. Few policy differences emerged between FDR and Garner during the first four years of the New Deal, although the Texan expressed greater enthusiasm than Roosevelt for insuring bank deposits through the Federal Deposit Insurance Corporation and muted opposition to the president's decision to reopen trade and financial relations with the Soviet Union. Although renominated by acclamation by the national convention in 1936, the Garner-Roosevelt relationship crumbled during their second term as FDR began to rely more heavily on his more liberal advisers. Like many other Southerners, Garner had little enthusiasm for the growing strength of organized labor, the president's attacks upon the Supreme Court, and the New Deal's continued commitment to spending programs for unemployment relief. When Roosevelt entered the 1938 Senate primary contests against several leading Southern conservatives, Garner broke openly with the administration, criticized FDR's decision to seek a third term, and finally entered primaries against the president in 1940. Soundly beaten in those races, Garner was dumped from the ticket at the national convention in favor of Henry Wallace, whose nomination confirmed the rising influence of the liberal-labor wing of the Democratic Party. Garner went back to his home in Texas where until his death at age ninety-nine in 1967 he continued to offer salty observations on politics and health, including the advice that several cigars and a shot of bourbon each day contributed to his own longevity.

Guffey-Snyder Bituminous Coal Stabilization Act (1935) and Guffey-Vinson Bituminous Coal Act (1937)

Like agriculture, the American coal industry had long suffered from overcapacity and falling prices that brought economic misery to miners and operators alike. In addition, the industry was plagued by fierce competition between unionized sectors in Northern states like Pennsylvania and nonunion mines in the South and West. The depression exacerbated all of these conditions and made coal mining the prototypical "sick" industry of falling prices, low wages, high unemployment, and epidemic violence between miners and operators. John L. Lewis, the charismatic leader of the United Mine Workers Union (UMW), and many of the larger Northern operators sought a legislative panacea for the industry that took shape initially in a code of fair competition under the National Industrial Recovery Act (NIRA). Even before the Supreme Court struck down that law in 1935, Lewis and his allies sought stronger federal controls that would curb production, especially from the nonunion mines in the South and West. Senator Joseph Guffey of Pennsylvania, close to both the union and the Northern coal barons, carried the legislation through Congress in 1935 with backing from the Roosevelt administration. The bill that FDR signed into law created a National Bituminous Coal Commission, which, working in cooperation with labor and management representatives, could fix coal prices on a district basis. A 15 percent federal tax on all coal produced would be rebated to companies that adhered to the commission's proposals respecting prices, wages, and hours. The Guffey-Snyder Act soon came under a flurry of law suits as operators in the South and West bitterly resisted the commission's efforts as did major railroads with substantial coal properties in the North. The Supreme Court invalidated the law in *Carter v. Carter Coal* (1936) on the grounds that Congress had sought to regulate an economic activity (coal mining) reserved to the states by virtue of the Tenth Amendment. Finding the pricing regulations inseparable from the condemned labor provisions, despite a congressional declaration to the contrary, a majority of the justices also voided the former. Emboldened by Roosevelt's overwhelming reelection, Lewis, Guffey, and Representative Fred Vinson of Kentucky proposed a new coal stabilization bill that Congress passed and the president signed in 1937. Dropping the controversial labor provisions, the Guffey-Vinson Act took aim exclusively at the problem of production and prices. Twenty-three district boards, dominated by leading operators, would propose minimum prices to be adopted by another National Bituminous Coal Commission. The law levied a modest federal tax of one cent per ton on all coal shipped in interstate commerce, compounded by a nineteen-and-one-half-cent per ton levy on all coal that did not adhere to the board's pricing system. Because the prices set remained high, critics condemned the measure as a futile effort to stabilize the soft coal industry by keeping the unionized, high-cost mines in operation, while doing little to reduce excess capacity generated by the nonunion operators in the South and West.

Henderson, Leon

Henderson joined the New Deal as director of the Research and Planning Division of the National Recovery Administration (NRA) in 1934 after a distinguished academic career teaching economics. From that year forward, he became one of the most influential economists in the federal government with his service extending through World War II. Born in Millville, New Jersey, in 1895, Henderson received his education at Swarthmore College and the University of Pennsylvania before joining the faculty at the Wharton School shortly after World War I. Following another teaching post at the Carnegie Institute of Technology, he joined the Russell Sage Foundation as its director of consumer credit in 1925 and from there went to the New Deal. Even before the Supreme Court struck down the National Industrial Recovery Act (NIRA) in 1935, Henderson had become disillusioned with its strategy of economic recovery through suspension of the antitrust laws and the enforcement of codes of fair competition. Too often, he believed, the NIRA served to legitimate oligopoly as the leading firms in each industry raised prices before consumers had sufficient income. The road to recovery in his view would come through a restoration of competition and major fiscal stimulus by the federal government through expanded public works, views he articulated after the demise of the NIRA when he served as an economic adviser to the Senate Committee on Manufacturers and to the National Democratic Party. By 1936 he had also signed on as the economic adviser to Harry Hopkins at the Works Progress Administration (WPA), where he became a leading apostle of the ideas of John Maynard Keynes and compensatory fiscal policy. Teamed with Hopkins, Marriner Eccles, and others, Henderson led the battle inside the administration for more government spending in 1937–1938, a view that finally triumphed over the deficit hawks like Treasury Secretary Henry Morgenthau Jr. In 1938 Henderson carried his strong antitrust views into the position as executive secretary of the Temporary National Economic Committee, which investigated and reported on monopolistic conditions throughout the American economy. After a three-year term as a commissioner on the Securities and Exchange Commission, he became chief administrator of the Office of Price Administration from 1941 to 1942 and then head of the Civilian Supply Division of the War Production Board. After the war, Henderson continued to preach Keynesian ideas as chairman of the liberal Americans for Democratic Action and as chief economist for the Research Institute of America.

Hillman, Sidney

Born in Zagare, Lithuania, in 1887 and educated at the Slobodka Rabbinical Seminary there, Hillman's earliest experiences as a labor leader landed him in a Lithuanian jail for participating in demonstrations to secure a ten-hour working day. In 1907 he arrived in Chicago and took a job as an apprentice suit cutter at the Hart, Schaffner and Marx clothing factory. By 1914, after participating in a series of strikes and rising to become an officer of the Chicago local of the United Garment Workers of America, Hillman became the first president of the Amalgamated Clothing Workers of America. In that post, he led Amalgamated to important organizing victories in Chicago, New York, and Philadelphia and became close friends with a number of leading progressives, including Louis Brandeis and Felix Frankfurter. During the 1920s, Hillman built the ACWA into one of the most successful and progressive labor organizations in the United States, a union that emphasized not only bread-and-butter issues of wages and hours, but sponsored unemployment insurance, a union-run bank, and housing cooperatives. When the New Dealers sought the support of labor for the National Recovery Act (NRA) in 1933, they called upon Hillman for help in drafting its provisions for protecting labor and promoting public works. And until the Supreme Court killed the agency in 1935, Hillman sat on its board along with key representatives from industry. By then, disillusioned with the halting efforts of the American Federation of Labor to organize workers in the mass-production industries, Hillman joined John L. Lewis and David Dubinsky in founding the Committee for Industrial Organization (CIO) to carry the union movement into the auto and steel industries. When the AF of L expelled Hillman and his union, he served as vice president of the CIO from 1935 to 1940. He became a major force in the national Democratic Party beginning in 1936 when he helped to found the Labor's Non Partisan League, which raised money and provided precinct workers for the party, efforts that proved essential to Roosevelt's two wartime victories in 1940 and 1944. During the war, he became codirector of the Office of Production Management, sharing the post with William Knudsen, the head of the General Motors Corporation. Hillman died in 1946.

Hoover, Herbert Clark

Had Americans known in 1928 that the nation would soon be plunged into the worst economic depression in its history, they would have chosen Hoover to lead them through the disaster. No person ever entered the White House with a more impressive resume as a brilliant organizer, managerial wizard, and compassionate humanitarian. Born in West Branch, Iowa, in 1874, orphaned as a child and raised by relatives, Hoover embodied the enduring American myth of the self-made man, someone who had literally advanced from rags to riches. After graduating from the then youthful Stanford University in 1895, Hoover launched a career as a mining engineer that would carry him to four continents and make him a millionaire by the age of forty. Plucked from private life to head the Commission for Relief in Belgium during the years before American involvement in the First World War, Hoover helped to save thousands from hunger and death in Western Europe. President Wilson turned to him to run the United States Food and Drug Administration after 1917. Able to manipulate prices, but without authority to ration basic commodities, Hoover presided over another organizational miracle that kept the supply of beef, pork, and wheat flowing to the nation's consumers while also feeding the allied and American troops abroad. Following the armistice, Wilson made Hoover part of his official delegation to the Paris Peace Conference, where he opposed the imposition of reparations upon Germany and earned the admiration of John Maynard Keynes, who called him the ablest of all the American officials attending. So luminous was Hoover's reputation by 1920, that leading Democrats like Franklin Roosevelt and Louis Brandeis considered him a desirable candidate on their ticket for the presidency, but Hoover announced as a Republican and joined Warren Harding's cabinet as secretary of commerce, where he served until 1928. Harding once referred to his secretary of commerce as "the smartest gink I know," but Hoover's lack of party credentials and political experience made him suspect to Republican regulars. He deepened these suspicions during the postwar recession of 1920–1921, when he urged expanded federal public works to soak up unemployment and stimulate the economy. As commerce secretary, Hoover preached what he called "cooperative individualism" as an alternative to strict laissez-faire and took the lead in promoting the organization of new, emerging industries such as radio and aviation. Had the party bosses prevailed, Hoover would not have won the nomination in 1928, but he had developed a superb public relations campaign, including the use of motion pictures, that gave him enough primary victories to overcome their opposition and go on to defeat New York governor Al Smith in the general election. In the wake of the stock market collapse, the liquidity crisis, and the onset of the depression, Hoover took unprecedented actions for an American president faced with similar economic downturns. He eschewed the advice of several advisers, notably Treasury Secretary Andrew Mellon, who recommended that the federal government do little to stop the slide of prices, wages, and production. Instead, invoking the ideal of "voluntary cooperation," Hoover used his office to promote recovery through the combined efforts of key interest groups, each responsible for combating the effects of the depression, but without the coercive uses of the law. The Agricultural Marketing Act, for example, encouraged farmers to form marketing cooperatives. The law authorized a new federal Farm Board to make limited purchases of surplus crops to shore up prices, but no controls on production were mandated. Bankers were urged to join the National Credit Corporation with the goal of assisting those banks on the brink of collapse. The unemployed, whose numbers continued to rise, were to receive assistance from voluntary charitable and benevolent organizations such as the Red Cross and the YMCA. When "voluntary cooperation" failed to reverse the farm crisis, the banking debacle, and the flood of unemployment, Hoover turned finally in 1932 to a government program, the Reconstruction Finance

Corporation (RFC), which began to make loans to ailing corporations and, finally, to states and cities for public works. The RFC, which grew larger with an expanded mandate under the New Deal, proved to be the limit of Hoover's willingness to deploy the powers of the federal government. While supporting indirect aid to the unemployed through public works, he flatly opposed direct relief on the grounds that it would sap the self-reliance and initiative of the American people. Other decisions by Hoover proved less helpful in the crisis. Over the protests of distinguished economists who predicted a further shrinkage in world trade, he signed the Hawley-Smoot tariff in 1930 that raised ever higher the wall of protection around the American market and made it even more difficult for Europeans to earn dollars to pay back their war debts. Then, faced with mounting deficits from falling revenues and growing outlays, he urged Congress to raise taxes, an invitation eagerly pursued by the legislators who feared an unbalanced budget as much as the chief executive, but with consequences that further eroded consumer spending. With limited experience dealing with politicians and accustomed to giving orders as an administrator, Hoover's relations with Congress and the public deteriorated in 1932–1933. Before leaving office, soundly defeated by Roosevelt, he could take credit for liberalizing the Supreme Court with the appointments of Hughes, Roberts, and Cardozo. He could also claim, with some justification, that his failed experiments with "voluntary cooperation" left no alternative for the new president but greater government intervention. Until 1935, the former president played a modest role as a critic of the New Deal, although he continued to reaffirm his opposition to government regulation in *The Challenge to Liberty*, published in 1934. With quiet determination, he sought to recapture the Republican nomination in both 1936 and 1940, but lost on those occasions to Alf Landon and Wendell Willkie. A skilled manager, always with an eye for waste and inefficiency, Hoover served Presidents Truman and Eisenhower on commissions that bore his name to improve the performance of the federal government. He died in 1964.

Hopkins, Harry L.

Probably the most intimate and influential of all of Franklin Roosevelt's advisers, Hopkins was an Iowa native born in 1890, the son of a harness maker. He attended Grinnell College and made the journey to New York City shortly before World War I, where he entered social work at Christadora House and the Association for Improving the Condition of the Poor. This firsthand experience with the plight of the indigent made him an obvious choice to become deputy director of New York's Temporary Emergency Relief Administration under Governor Roosevelt in 1931. Combining compassion with a hard-boiled approach to administration, Hopkins naturally followed FDR to Washington where he headed the Federal Emergency Relief Administration, the Civil Works Administration (1933–1934), the gigantic Works

Progress Administration (1935–1938), and served as commerce secretary from 1938–1940. Devoted to social reform, to Roosevelt, and to betting on the horses at Pimlico or Bowie, Hopkins's usually disheveled appearance and weary, haggard face belied a keen intellect that impressed no less a judge than Winston Churchill, who once referred to him as "Lord Root of the Matter" (Kennedy 1999, 161). When it came to aiding the unemployed, Hopkins shared with Roosevelt a devotion to the work ethic and a disdain for direct cash assistance, which, he believed, undermined self-respect and self-reliance. In the fierce winter of 1933–1934, Hopkins and his assistants executed one of the greatest organizational feats of the depression through the Civil Works Administration, when in the space of a few months they employed over 4 million individuals, sparing many from hunger and destitution. His lasting contribution came after 1935, however, with the Works Progress Administration that employed on average 2,122,000 each month over the next six years. Hopkins's WPA built or improved 122,000 bridges; 1,000 tunnels; 36,900 schools; 1,000 libraries; 4,000 airport buildings; 19,400 state, county, and local government buildings; and 572,000 miles of rural roads; in addition to enriching the nation's cultural life through music, theater, and historic preservation. When he gave instructions to Lorena Hickok, a former newspaper reporter, who had joined the New Deal to gather firsthand knowledge of conditions across the country, Hopkins told her to avoid statistics. "Go talk with the unemployed," he said, "those who are on relief and those who aren't. And when you talk with them don't ever forget that but for the grace of God you, I, or any of our friends might be in their shoes. Tell me what you see and hear. All of it. Don't ever pull your punches" (Kennedy 1999, 160). Hopkins's critics on the right accused him of pumping up the WPA rolls on the eve of the 1936 elections to promote Democratic gains at the polls, charges he turned aside with a wave of his cigarette. His critics on the left complained that Hopkins too readily bowed to the influence of local party bosses and did not do enough to combat racial segregation in the work relief programs, especially in the South. But that he cared deeply about the unemployed and the poor there can be no doubt. "Hunger is not debatable," he told those who attacked the New Deal's efforts (Schlesinger 1958, 353). In the heated debate over responding to the economic downturn in 1937–1938, Hopkins led the group that successfully pushed FDR for a more aggressive spending program. But at that time, suffering from severe ulcers, Hopkins gave up his WPA post and moved for a short time into the Commerce Department during the final two years of FDR's second term. He returned to the White House during World War II, however, and became Roosevelt's personal ambassador to British prime minister Winston Churchill and Soviet premier Joseph Stalin. As FDR's most trusted aide, he joined the president and Churchill at their meeting that produced the Atlantic Charter, the Arcadia Conference that set the foundation for the United Nations, and the big three meeting at Yalta shortly before Roosevelt's death in 1945. Hopkins himself died early in 1946.

Ickes, Harold L.

The most liberal member of Roosevelt's cabinet as secretary of the interior, a post he held until 1946 despite threatening to resign on numerous occasions, Ickes was born in Frankstown, Pennsylvania, in 1874 and graduated from the University of Chicago in 1897. By profession a journalist and a lawyer, but by disposition a moral crusader who usually saw the world divided between the forces of good and evil, Ickes relished a good fight, whether against the corrupt alliance of business and city government in Chicago, the evils of racism, the conservative wing of the Republican Party, or the ambitions of Samuel Insull to dominate the distribution of electricity in the Midwest. Nominally a member of Lincoln's party, Ickes joined Teddy Roosevelt's third-party crusade in 1912, backed Charles Evans Hughes for the White House in 1916 against Wilson, but abandoned the GOP when it chose Harding and Coolidge in the 1920s. He had, as one historian has noted, the virtues of his defects, which were considerable: self-righteousness and intolerance of those less intelligent and less incorruptible than himself. These were qualities that made him a superb guardian of the public interest in the Department of the Interior, an agency too long dominated by those bent on rapid exploitation of the nation's resources, and as head of the National Power Policy Committee where he pushed vigorously for the expansion of government-funded energy sources. On the other hand, his hatred of corruption and dread of scandal made him a too cautious administrator of the $3.3 billion appropriated for the Public Works Administration under the National Recovery Act. Unlike Harry Hopkins, who stressed the rapid employment of many workers on myriad smaller projects in relief programs such as the Civil Works Administration and the Works Progress Administration, Ickes emphasized only large undertakings that employed the highly skilled and he doled out the funds very slowly by insisting on signing every contract personally. What the WPA finally built over the course of the depression—huge dams, bridges, tunnels, lighthouses, sewer and water systems—made lasting contributions to the nation's infrastructure. Ickes's agency escaped the charges of waste and influence peddling that plagued other New Deal efforts, but its impact upon recovery remained smaller than WPA. A former president of the Chicago chapter of the National Association for the Advancement of Colored People (NAACP), Ickes shared with Eleanor Roosevelt a deep commitment to the fight against segregation. No member of the administration did more to attack the color barriers in government and American life. He hired African Americans in his department, integrated its cafeteria, pushed to give them a share of jobs on agency construction contracts, and supported Marian Anderson's concert at the Lincoln Memorial. He supported John Collier's reforms at the Bureau of Indian Affairs, which ended the practice of individual land allotments, expanded the base of reservations, gave Native American tribes a larger voice in the management of their own affairs, and promoted their culture. A bureaucratic infighter with few peers in the administration, Ickes protected his own turf aggressively and sought unsuccessfully to expand it by insisting that the Forest Service, transferred to the Department of Agriculture prior to World War I, be returned to his jurisdiction. He lost that battle to Henry Wallace and never realized his grand dream of bringing all conservation programs of the federal government within the Interior Department. During World War II he ran the government's Solid Fuels Conservation program with the same diligence and stream of complaints to Roosevelt that characterized his other endeavors. To his everlasting credit, he opposed the relocation and detention of Japanese American citizens in the wake of Pearl Harbor.

Jackson, Robert H.

Although he remains more celebrated for his role as an associate justice of the United States Supreme Court, nominated by Roosevelt in the summer of 1941 to fill the vacancy created by Harlan Stone's elevation to the chief justiceship, Jackson exercised an important influence over the New Deal before mounting the bench. Born in Pennsylvania in 1892 and raised in upstate New York, Jackson completed high school, but never graduated from college before reading law with Frank Mott, a prominent local Democrat, and spending one year at the Albany Law School at Union University. Felix Frankfurter once kidded Jackson for not attending the Harvard Law School, but Jackson did quite well without the Harvard imprimatur. He was admitted to the New York bar in 1913 and practiced commercial law regularly in Jamestown. He first met Franklin Roosevelt during the First World War when he advised the then secretary of the navy on matters of federal patronage. And he again caught the attention of Governor Roosevelt in the 1920s when he successfully defended local railway and telephone companies from consolidation under giant monopolies. Coming to Washington with the New Deal in 1933, his talents as a litigator were utilized in a variety of ways: general counsel for the Bureau of Internal Revenue, special counsel to the Securities and Exchange Commission, and assistant attorney general in charge of the department's antitrust division. After an unsuccessful bid to become governor in New York, Jackson returned to Washington in 1938 to become solicitor general, a task he relished and performed with flare before the Hughes Court until 1940, when Roosevelt tapped him to become attorney general. As attorney general, Jackson published one of the most scathing attacks on the Hughes Court, *The Struggle for Judicial Supremacy* (1941), which singled out the *Butler* decision and *Carter Coal* for special condemnation. In both, Jackson wrote, the majority expressed attachment to an interpretation of federalism largely irrelevant to the conditions of a modern, integrated economic system. He dismissed the notion that American agriculture remained purely a "local" problem or that the wages and hours prevailing in the coal industry had only an "indirect" affect upon interstate commerce. Once on the Supreme Court, Jackson advanced a much broader conception of Congress's authority to regulate interstate commerce, most notably in *Wickard v. Filburn* (1942).

Johnson, Hugh S.

Born in Ft. Scott, Kansas, in 1882 and graduated from West Point in 1901, it took Johnson fifteen years to rise to the rank of brigadier general, a title he kept throughout his later civilian career. His influence continued to grow during World War I as chief of the army's Bureau of Purchase and Supply, which gave him a seat on the influential War Industries Board chaired by the legendary financier-politician, Bernard Baruch. Johnson left the military in 1919 with a law degree he had earned prior to the war at the University of California and took the position as vice president and general counsel to the Moline Plow Company, a leading manufacturer of farm machinery. By 1925 he ran the company as chairman of the board and lobbied hard for federal assistance to the economically depressed farmers of the Midwest and South. Because of his experience on the War Industries Board and the patronage of Baruch, Johnson played a major role in guiding the National Industrial Recovery Act (NIRA) through Congress and then became Roosevelt's choice to head the centerpiece of the New Deal's initial antidepression effort, the National Recovery Administration (NRA), charged with administering the new law of business cooperation. The NRA and Johnson's management of it proved to be a fatal combination. "It will be red fire at first and dead cats afterwards," he told the press soon after his appointment. "This is just like mounting the guillotine on the infinitesimal gamble that the ax won't work" (Leuchtenburg 1963, 65). The general's boundless energy and enthusiasm for rescuing the nation's economy through the NIRA was exceeded only by his consumption of cigarettes and alcohol, both in enormous quantities. With the antitrust laws suspended, Johnson set out on a whirlwind tour across the country to encourage businessmen to abandon their traditional ways and organize themselves into code authorities dedicated to fair competition. Those who signed up and agreed to adhere to the wage, hours, and pricing standards in their code received the NRA's "blue eagle" symbol, designed by the general with the motto, "We Do Our Part." Traveling by army plane, speaking nonstop, cajoling, and twisting arms, Johnson secured cooperation from the cotton textile industry, shipbuilders, electrical manufacturers, and even the automobile industry, minus Henry Ford, all of whom earned the blue eagle. His campaign climaxed with a giant NRA parade down New York's Fifth Avenue, the largest outpouring of national unity displayed since the armistice of 1918. By this time, however, Johnson had become physically drained and his agency swamped by a flood of industry codes he had encouraged, most of them signed by the president with little scrutiny. Instead of focusing on major industries,

NIRA codes reached into the smallest crevices of the American economy, with codes of fair competition established for barbers, newspaper vendors, and even burlesque queens, who agreed to only so many stripteases each day. Within the year, Johnson and the NRA came under scathing criticism. Although every code authority included representatives from the industry as well as consumer groups and labor, businessmen ran the show. And the businessmen who managed to get to Washington first had the largest influence in writing the code and enforcing it. Labor representatives complained that the administration's waffling undermined Section 7(a), the guarantee of a worker's right to join a union. A report by the NRA's Review Board, chaired by the flamboyant Clarence Darrow, administered the coup de grace to the program and Johnson by documenting charges of monopoly, price gouging, and exploitation of consumers and workers. Johnson responded by drinking more heavily and warring with associates. He stepped down under pressure from Roosevelt in October 1934, having briefly lit up the New Deal sky before both he and the NRA fell to earth. Soon writing newspaper columns, the general remained loyal to Roosevelt until the recession of 1937–1938, the court-packing fight, and the president's plan to reorganize the executive branch, all of which he blamed on Roosevelt's attempts to take the United States down the road to dictatorship and a planned economy.

Jones, Jesse H.

Although he never achieved the public acclaim of other members of Roosevelt's administration, Jones became one of the most powerful figures in the New Deal by virtue of his position as head of the federal government's major lending agencies, above all the Reconstruction Finance Corporation, which he chaired until 1945. Born in Robertson County, Tennessee, in 1874, Jones became by the time of the stock market crash in 1929 the prototype of the successful Southern entrepreneur, whose private efforts, combined with government largess, remade the economy of the Old Confederacy. What Cleveland had been to Rockefeller and what New York had been to J. P. Morgan, Houston, Texas, became for Jones: the environment where one made lots of money and exercised political influence and visa versa. Beginning in his uncle's lumber company at the turn of the century, by 1933 Jones had built one of the largest economic empires in Houston, which combined real estate development and leasing, construction, the Texas Commerce Bank, ownership of the Houston *Chronicle,* and a local radio station. The Humble Oil and Refining Company, soon renamed Exxon, enjoyed Jones's initial sponsorship as well. Beginning with a local political base as chairman of Houston's Harbor Board, which built and ran the city's seaport, Jones swiftly moved up the ladder in national Democratic Party politics during World War I as head of military relief in the American Red Cross and a principal organizer of the League of Red Cross Societies of the World. In both positions he enjoyed the support and patronage of President Wilson, who became a special object of Jones's worship and philanthropy. After leaving the government in 1944, he became president of the Woodrow Wilson Foundation and funded the Wilson School of Foreign Affairs at the University of Virginia. In order to lure the 1928 Democratic National Convention to Houston, the assembly that nominated Al Smith for president, Jones's construction firm built a new 25,000-seat convention facility for the occasion. And when Houston's banks weathered the financial storm better than most in the early 1930s, President Hoover tapped Jones to become one of the original directors of the Reconstruction Finance Corporation. From that post, Jones played a critical role in implementing New Deal efforts to rescue the commercial banking system in 1933–1934 by pumping new capital into these institutions through RFC purchases of preferred stock. Within a few years, Jones's RFC had become the single largest stockholder (usually without voting rights) in many American banks. In addition to these investments, the Reconstruction Finance Corporation became the largest source of federal credit across a range of activities from agriculture to housing, extending over $50 billion during Jones's tenure. Roosevelt expanded Jones's lending empire in 1939 by making him head of the new Federal Loan Agency and then naming him secretary of commerce a year later. This latter position required a special act of Congress that permitted Jones to serve both in the cabinet and as the head of two administrative agencies simultaneously. After leaving the administration in 1945, Jones returned to Texas where he managed his Houston Endowment, Inc., then the richest foundation in the Lone Star state. He died in 1956.

Judicial Procedures Reform Act of 1937

Also known as Roosevelt's "court-packing" bill, the administration sent this proposal to Congress on February 5, 1937, with the hope that its key provision—intended to enlarge the size of the Supreme Court—would be accepted by Congress in addition to other, less controversial features designed to strengthen the government's hand in the federal courts. Although the Supreme Court had struck down key measures of the New Deal in 1935–1936 and although the president had publicly criticized the justices for what he called "a horse-and-buggy definition" of interstate commerce following the *Schechter* decision, neither he nor the Democratic Party made the Court a major issue in the 1936 election. Behind the scenes, however, FDR and his advisers, led by Attorney General Cummings, weighed various plans intended to curb the Supreme Court's influence over legislation with the realization that the justices would soon have under review other New Deal measures, including the National Labor Relations Act and the Social Security Act. Roosevelt rejected suggestions of a constitutional amendment as too time consuming and difficult. And most statutory changes, including a requirement for a unanimous vote to invalidate acts of Congress, would still face judicial interpretation. The president finally chose the plan that raised the fewest formal constitutional objections—enlarging the size of the Court—something Congress had done often since 1789, once raising the membership to ten during the Civil War. It also appealed to Roosevelt's sense of irony, since a similar proposal, limited to the lower federal courts, had been urged by Attorney General James McReynolds on three occasions between 1914 and 1916. The heart of the plan the administration sent to Congress proposed that for every federal judge over the age of seventy who had served for at least ten years and who did not resign or retire within six months of his seventieth birthday, the president could nominate one additional judge to that tribunal. Six members of the Hughes Court fell into that category, including the chief justice, Brandeis, Butler, Sutherland, Van Devanter, and McReynolds. In his message to Congress defending the plan, Roosevelt stressed "the effective functioning of the Federal judiciary," handicapped, he claimed, "by insufficient personnel with which to meet a growing more complex business," with the Supreme Court especially "laboring under a heavy burden." He also noted, what he described as "the question of aged or infirm judges—a subject of great delicacy," and the need for "a constant infusion of new blood in the courts" (Cushman 1998, 11). Constitutional objections proved to be the least of Roosevelt's difficulties. A lack of candor by the president, the patent deviousness of his plan, and its naked political thrust, proved fatal from the start. Normally the maestro of political orchestration, Roosevelt did not help his cause with a radio address on March 9 in which he declared it time "to save the Constitution from the Court and the Court from itself." The justices had refused to read the Constitution as written. They had amended the document by "the arbitrary exercise of judicial power—amendment by judicial say-so." His plan had two purposes: increased efficiency in the federal courts, but, above all, "to bring to the decision of social and economic problems younger men. . . . This plan will save our National Constitution from hardening of the judicial arteries" (Gunther and Dowling 1970, 287–288). Words more calculated to inflame even his supporters on the Court, notably Brandeis, are difficult to imagine. Two weeks later, the chief justice, writing for himself, Brandeis, and Van Devanter, responded in a letter to the chairman of the Senate Judiciary Committee, Burton K. Wheeler. The Supreme Court, Hughes affirmed "is fully abreast of its work." Increasing its size would not promote efficiency, quite the opposite. "There would be more judges to hear, more judges to confer, more judges to discuss, more judges to convince and to decide" (Gunther and Dowling 1970, 287). Even before the thunderbolt of the Hughes letter, many of the president's congressional allies had abandoned ship over his plan. Speaker of the House William Bankhead and Majority Leader Sam Rayburn, kept in the dark until the plan went to Congress, seethed with resentment. The chairman of the House Judiciary Committee told his colleagues, "Boys, here's where I cash in my chips" (Cushman 1998, 14). Wheeler's committee, with all six Democrats in the majority, voted against the plan ten to eight and issued a scathing report that condemned the measure as "needless, futile, an utterly dangerous abandonment of constitutional principle." The president's measure "would not banish age from the bench nor abolish divided decisions," but it would "destroy the independence of the judiciary, the only certain shield of individual rights" (Gunther and Dowling 1970, 288). Because Justice Van Devanter had already announced his retirement before the judiciary committee reported and the justices had sustained three New Deal measures in May, Roosevelt might have sought a face-saving compromise. Instead he fought on through the early summer of 1937 by insisting on a vote in the full Senate and promising the open seat on the Court to Majority Leader Joe Robinson of Arkansas, who many considered as conservative as McReynolds. When Robinson, worn down by the battle, collapsed and died of a heart attack on July 14, even the faintest hope of victory disappeared. The Senate ended Roosevelt's misery by sending the bill back to committee on a seventy-to-twenty vote. What finally emerged in the new version, the final Judiciary Act of 1937, minus FDR's plan for expansion, contained important reforms often ignored in assessments of the legislation. As signed by FDR, the act required notice to and authorized intervention by the attorney general in any case involving the constitutionality of an act of Congress; provided for direct appeal to the Supreme Court from a decision of a district court holding an act of Congress unconstitutional; and required a three-judge district court to be convened when an injunction was sought against the enforcement of an act of Congress on grounds of its unconstitutionality. And, finally, the new law extended retirement privileges to Supreme Court justices, a provision quickly used by Justice Van Devanter. Defeat of the court-packing measure inflicted serious wounds on Roosevelt and the New Deal. His coalition had been ruptured in Congress. FDR now appeared more vulnerable and soon suffered a second major defeat when Congress cut the heart out of his plan to reorganize the executive branch. His attempt to defeat conservative foes in Congress fizzled in the 1938 Democratic primaries. And until foreign crises gripped the country, he failed to push through Congress another significant reform, apart from the Fair Labor Standards Act.

Kennedy, Joseph P.

Born in 1888, Kennedy graduated from Boston Latin School and Harvard College. In 1914 he married Rose Fitzgerald, the daughter of the former mayor of Boston, John F. "Honey Fitz" Fitzgerald. A shrewd businessman, virtually everything Kennedy touched seemed to swell his fortune—banking, movie production, real estate investments, even the stock market of the 1920s, which crashed after he had sold out a substantial portion of his portfolio. Among the aspiring Irish Catholic politicians and businessmen who sought influence in the Democratic Party, Kennedy early put his money behind Governor Roosevelt in 1932. The president rewarded that loyalty in 1934, when he named Kennedy to the chairmanship of the newly created Securities and Exchange Commission. Although several New Deal liberals expressed shock at the appointment of a former Wall Street speculator known for his technique of selling short (i.e., selling stock one does not own with the hope the price will fall before accounts are settled), Roosevelt calculated that Kennedy's knowledge of the market would gain the confidence of the industry and equip him to crack down on the most serious abuses. Set a thief to catch a thief, Roosevelt quipped. He chose wisely. Teamed with James Landis, a future SEC chairman, Kennedy proved to be a hard-working, skilled administrator, who in addition to curbing the worse excesses of short selling, encouraged the New York Stock Exchange to see the advantages of reform through self-regulation, a policy that later bore fruit during the tenures of William O. Douglas and Jerome Frank. Kennedy money and influence flowed to Roosevelt's reelection campaign in 1936 after his service at the SEC ended, and he urged businessmen likewise to support the president in a book entitled, *I'm for Roosevelt,* which argued that the New Deal had saved American capitalism. Roosevelt put Kennedy back to work in 1937 as head of the United States Maritime Commission with the task of revitalizing the shipbuilding industry, an area Kennedy also knew well from his days building vessels at Fore River during World War I. He stayed only a year before garnering one of the biggest plums available—the American ambassadorship to Great Britain, a year before war broke out in Europe. The first Irish Catholic to hold the coveted position, it was not Kennedy's ethnic background or religion that soon antagonized the British and Roosevelt as well. Persuaded that Hitler's Germany held the upper hand, Kennedy told an audience in London that the democracies and dictators should cooperate for the common good, a far cry even from Roosevelt's call to "quarantine the aggressors." Later, he predicted democracy's death in Britain and feared that America's entrance into the war would lead to economic regimentation and socialism. One British official branded Kennedy "a very foul specimen of double-crosser and defeatist" (Kennedy 1999, 443). The day after Roosevelt won a third term, Kennedy submitted his resignation as ambassador. A week later in an interview with reporters in Boston, he launched into an attack on Eleanor Roosevelt, who, he claimed, "bothered us more on our jobs in Washington to take care of the poor little nobodies who haven't any influence." In London, he added, the president's wife was always "sending me notes to have some Susie Glotz to tea at the embassy" (Parmet 1980, 82). Although he gave lukewarm testimony in favor of the Lend Lease legislation to aid England and offered his services to Roosevelt during the war, the president never responded. Following the war, Kennedy invested his efforts in the political careers of his three surviving sons, John F. Kennedy, Robert F. Kennedy, and Edward M. Kennedy.

Keynes, John Maynard

Few non-Americans have ever exercised more influence over the nation's public policy than Keynes, regarded by many as the most influential economist since Adam Smith and surely the most distinguished of the twentieth century. Born in Cambridge, England, in 1888, educated at Eton and King's College, Cambridge, Keynes joined the British civil service after graduation and served in the India Office, the occasion soon for his first book, *Indian Currency and Finance* (1913). For the next few years he edited England's most important economics publication, the *Economic Journal* and advised the chancellor of the exchequer. It was in this capacity that he went to the Versailles Peace Conference in 1918, where he became a strong critic of the allied plan to impose substantial financial reparations on Germany. From this protest arose his much-acclaimed book, *The Economic Consequences of the Peace* (1919), which warned that reparations would become a drag on European economic recovery and produce disastrous consequences for democratic institutions. While teaching at Cambridge and displaying a knack for making money in stock trading during the 1920s and early 1930s, Keynes began his assault on conventional economic dogma with two books that questioned the utility of the gold standard as the basis of international and domestic monetary systems, *Tract on Monetary Reform* (1923) and the *Treatise on Money* (1930). Six years later with the publication of *The General Theory of Employment, Interest, and Money* (1936), he lay siege to the entire edifice of classical economic thought whose foundation was the belief that everything produced by a society created sufficient income to consume it and that in the long run the economy would always achieve equilibrium. Keynes demonstrated the fallaciousness of these propositions. Instead of equilibrium, modern economies, characterized by large units of production and complex networks of savings and investment, could decline indefinitely. A significant drop in production, employment, and consumption might become mutually reinforcing, trigger a liquidity crisis, wipe out savings, and send the economy into a prolonged depression. Instead of waiting for equilibrium while production fell, prices collapsed, companies went bankrupt, and people suffered, Keynes urged a bold program of government investment, income supplements, and spending to compensate for the decline in private investment, income, and spending. As the economy faltered, the government should be willing to unbalance its budget, either through direct spending, reductions in the level of taxation, or a combination of both. By contrast, if the economy began to experience rising price levels, the government could cool it down with less spending, higher taxes, or both. Keynes saw this strategy of fiscal intervention by the central government as the salvation of capitalism and the antidote to the twin evils of fascism and communism. Keynes hailed FDR's decision to take the United States off the gold standard in 1933 and in a celebrated letter to the new president hailed him as "the trustee for those in every country who seek to mend the evils of our condition by reasoned experiment within the framework of the existing social system. If you fail, rational change will be gravely prejudiced throughout the world, leaving orthodoxy and revolution to fight it out" (Schlesinger 1960, 656). In 1937 he urged the president to launch an expanded program of government spending, especially public housing, combined with public ownership of the utilities and nationalization of the railroads. A number of New Dealers, notably Eccles and Frankfurter, both shared and promoted Keynes's ideas, but Roosevelt, reared on classical theory, devoted to a balanced budget, and always calculating the political consequences, remained skeptical. When Keynes urged more spending on public works in 1933, the president told Frankfurter: "You can tell the professor that in regard to public works we shall spend in the next fiscal year nearly twice the amount we are spending in this fiscal year, but there is a practical limit to what the Government can borrow—especially because the banks are offering passive resistance." And when the president met Keynes personally, he complained to Frances Perkins, his secretary of labor, "He [Keynes] left a whole rigmarole of figures. He must be a mathematician rather than a political economist" (Kennedy 1999, 197). Roosevelt it seems apparent was no Keynesian in the sense of accepting deficit spending and an unbalanced budget as a matter of conscious, deliberate policy. When he endorsed fiscal expansion in 1938–1939 in response to the recession he did so more out of compassion for the unemployed and to relieve economic suffering than from dedication to Keynesian theory. Like Hoover, he never abandoned his commitment to securing a balanced federal budget and his strategies of taxation, including income tax reform and Social Security, curbed consumer spending instead of expanding it. Only defense expenditures beginning in 1940 proved the efficacy of Keynes's ideas, later embodied in the Employment Act of 1946, which for the first time formally committed the federal government to the use of fiscal and monetary policy for the purposes of maintaining a high level of employment without inflation. By the early 1970s, even Republican president Richard Nixon could proclaim, "We are all Keynesians now" (Hamby 1992, 323).

LaGuardia, Fiorello H.

Energetic, savvy, and incorruptible, LaGuardia remains one of the most famous and popular mayors in the history of New York City and the only one whose life became the basis for a Broadway musical. Born in New York City in 1882, but raised in Arizona and Missouri, where he earned a living for several years as a reporter, LaGuardia returned East to work as an interpreter at Ellis Island for incoming immigrants and earned a law degree at New York University in 1910. By that time it was said he had become fluent in seven languages, a perfect qualification for entering New York City politics, which he did as a progressive Republican and enemy of the dominant Tammany Hall, Democratic Party machine. Elected to Congress in 1914, he served two terms before enlisting in the army air corps for service in World War I. Returning to the city after the war, he twice won election as president of the Board of Aldermen (1920 and 1921) and was returned to Congress a year later, where he remained until 1933. As a member of Congress during the era of conservative Republican hegemony, LaGuardia battled often for the rights of working men and women and became the coauthor with Senator George Norris of the landmark anti-injunction law that bears his name. Prior to the National Labor Relations Act, the Norris-LaGuardia Act was the single most important piece of labor legislation adopted by Congress in the twentieth century, because it sharply limited the jurisdiction of federal courts to issue injunctions in labor-management disputes. Elected New York's mayor in 1933 on a fusion ticket that joined many liberal Republicans and dissident Democrats, LaGuardia won the affection of the city's residents over the decade by his creative political dramatics that included reading the comics to children on Sunday over the radio, leading the New York Philharmonic Orchestra, and turning up at major fires, crime scenes, and other public disasters. No mayor in the United States became more astute at plugging his city into the many new federal programs that flowed from Washington under the New Deal. Respected by Interior Secretary Ickes and relief czar Harry Hopkins, LaGuardia made certain that New York City received its full share of public works jobs and relief expenditures. New York's present infrastructure of tunnels, bridges, and highways owes much to the foundation built by LaGuardia with the assistance of federal dollars in the decade of the 1930s. Prior to his death in 1947, LaGuardia served appropriately as director general of the new United Nations Relief and Rehabilitation Agency.

Landon, Alfred M.

Soundly defeated by Roosevelt in the 1936 election when he carried only two states in the electoral college, Landon nonetheless represented the emergence of a more progressive brand of Republicanism that reached fruition with the later candidacies of Wendell Willkie (1940), Thomas E. Dewey (1944 and 1948), and Dwight Eisenhower (1952). This became a Republicanism that accepted the foundational reforms of the New Deal, especially Social Security, but advocated greater efficiency and parsimony with respect to the government's role in managing the nation's economy. Born in Pennsylvania in 1887, Landon grew up in Ohio and Kansas, attended the University of Kansas, and won admission to the state's bar in 1908. But oil, not politics, became the basis for his rise in Kansas politics as Landon's independent oil drilling firm by the late 1920s had sunk wells and earned a substantial income in the petroleum-rich fields of Kansas and Oklahoma. Entering Republican politics on the progressive side of the ledger, Landon supported Governor Henry Allen, ran the gubernatorial campaign of Clyde Reed, and became the party's state chairman in 1928. After losing that post two years later in an intraparty struggle, Landon turned his attention to defending the interests of the independent oil men from the ravages of the depression and the efforts by major producers to dominate government programs intended to protect the industry from further price wars. While FDR swept to victory over Hoover in 1932, Landon won the governorship of Kansas by defeating incumbent Democrat Harry Woodring, the future secretary of war in Roosevelt's cabinet. Two years later, in the face of surging Democratic victories, he became the only Republican governor to win reelection. He offered Kansas voters a judicious blend of moderate reform, cooperation with Washington, and fiscal probity. Prior to the national bank holiday, Landon limited cash withdrawals from the state's commercial banks. In a state dominated by agriculture, he pushed through a moratorium on farm foreclosures and fought for the state's interests in the shaping of the Agricultural Adjustment Act and other farm programs. He contributed his voice and experience to the federal government's efforts to adopt a code of competition for the oil industry and made certain that Kansas received its share of federal dollars flowing from work and relief programs such as the Civilian Conservation Corps and the Civil Works Administration. As the Republican's choice to face FDR in 1936, Landon had to walk a tightrope between his own progressive instincts and the hard-core rank-and-file party conservatives who urged an all-out war against the New Deal. Landon's efforts to find a rhetorical middle ground often failed. He pledged, for example, to maintain federal relief programs, but castigated New Deal deficits and promised to drive the big spenders out of Washington. He predicted a future of American economic abundance and denounced the New Deal for promoting planned scarcity, but could propose only less government as the solution. Above all, he took refuge in attacking FDR for seeking dictatorial powers and upsetting the constitutional balance, although he ignored the fact that Congress had abdicated much authority to the executive branch. Roosevelt's organization had an easy time linking Landon with the discredited policies of Hoover and with the more strident voices on the far right such as the American Liberty League. And when the economy, pumped up by New Deal relief efforts, showed some signs of life, eight electoral votes were all Landon could claim in November. He never again exercised national influence in the Republican Party comparable to Hoover's, but remained active in the oil business and commercial broadcasting in his home state.

Lewis, John L.

As Roosevelt dominated America's political landscape in the 1930s, Lewis towered over the American labor movement as the leader of the venerable United Mine Workers and founder of the Committee for Industrial Organization (CIO) that successfully organized the mass-production industries. Born in Cleveland, Iowa, in 1880, the son of a Welsh miner, Lewis attended high school and following a number of odd jobs entered the bituminous coal mines of southern Iowa around the turn of the century. Moving to the coal fields of Illinois in 1908, he launched his career in the United Mine Workers by becoming president of the local in Panama, Illinois, and eventually a lobbyist for the UMW throughout the state. Samuel Gompers, head of the AF of L, recognized Lewis's talent for oratory and organization in 1911 when he made him a field agent for the labor federation. Utilizing these AF of L contacts, Lewis rose to the vice presidency of the miners' union in 1917 and to the presidency three years later. Lewis would remain at the helm of the union until the year John F. Kennedy was elected president. During that time, he ruled the union with an iron fist, made alliances with socialists and communists when it suited his purposes and drove them out of the organization when it did not. He worked to establish close ties with certain operators who shared his desire for stable coal prices and labor peace while resisting the spread of nonunion competition in the South. A lifelong Republican, Lewis believed that Secretary of Commerce Herbert Hoover might bring stability to the coal industry with his emphasis upon voluntary cooperation, a partnership between the union and the operators. But Hoover meant what he said with the word "voluntary" and refused to support stronger sanctions by government with respect to output, prices, and wages. Nonetheless, Lewis endorsed Hoover for president in both 1928 and again in 1932, although he signaled a willingness to work closely with Roosevelt in the event of his election. The New Deal delivered more to Lewis and the UMW than any previous administration. Section 7(a) of the National Industrial Recovery Act (NIRA) invited workers to join unions in the expectation of collective bargaining, and they signed up with the UMW as well as with other unions even though the promise proved empty until the National Labor Relations Act of 1935. And both the Guffey-Snyder Act, invalidated by the Supreme Court, as well as the Guffey-Vinson Act of 1937 realized Lewis's long-standing objective of tripartite regulation through the unions, the major operators, and the federal government, although neither law curbed entirely the anarchic conditions in the industry produced by low entry costs and nonunion labor. Along with Sidney Hillman, David Dubinsky, and other labor leaders, Lewis perceived that the depression, the euphoria unleashed by the NIRA, and the cautious tactics of the American Federation of Labor created circumstances ripe for organizing the millions of industrial workers who did not fit easily into the AF of L's craft structure. Lewis realized, too, that the fate of his own UMW rested in part upon a successful unionization campaign in allied industries such as steel and automobiles, where major companies also owned and operated coal mines. When the AF of L refused to set aside its narrow jurisdictional claims in steel and automobiles in 1935, Lewis and his allies created the Committee for Industrial Organization (CIO) within the AF of L to facilitate their organizational efforts. A year later, branding Lewis and the CIO dissidents as saboteurs who promoted "dual unionism," the AF of L expelled them all. By 1938, following successful strikes that led to union recognition in the auto and steel industries, the CIO formally declared its independence from the AF of L and elected Lewis as its first president. By that year, too, the CIO had grown to include 3.7 million members, outstripping the AF of L. With that rising membership came greater political clout as Lewis and Hillman helped to create in 1936 Labor's Non-Partisan League, which proved to be anything but nonpartisan. It contributed countless precinct workers for the Democratic Party and poured nearly $1 million into FDR's reelection campaign, with Lewis's UMW alone contributing $500,000. When Roosevelt displayed less than uncritical sympathy for steel workers shot down by Chicago police during the little steel strike of 1937, his honeymoon with Lewis came to an abrupt end. "It ill behooves one who has supped at labor's table," Lewis declared, "to curse with equal fervor and fine impartiality both labor and its adversaries when they become locked in deadly embrace" (Leuchtenburg 1963, 243). The CIO-UMW chief blamed FDR for the economic downturn in 1937–1938 that left many miners unemployed; gave limited support to enactment of the Fair Labor Standards Act, intended to help low-wage workers outside of union organizations; and broke with the White House in 1940 when Roosevelt condemned German and Japanese aggression. In 1940 Lewis returned to his Republican roots by endorsing Wendell Willkie and he vowed to resign as president of the CIO if FDR won a third term, a promise Roosevelt forced him to keep in November. Lewis kept a tight hold on the UMW, however, boosting wages and benefits for the miners while negotiating what critics called sweetheart contracts with many operators and using the UMW's treasury to invest in banks and even nonunion mines. The man who had helped to give birth to industrial unions and the CIO in the 1930s led his union into three disastrous strikes between 1941 and 1946 that antagonized the public, inflamed politicians, and produced antiunion legislation in the form of the Smith-Connally Anti-Strike Law (1943) and the Taft-Hartley Act of 1947 that rolled back many of the gains contained in the National Labor Relations Act.

Long, Huey P.

His political cronies gave him the nickname "Kingfish" after the character George "Kingfish" Stevens, who led the Mystic Knights of the Sea fraternal lodge in *Amos 'n' Andy*, the popular 1930s radio program. New Deal scholar Arthur M. Schlesinger Jr. described him as "the Messiah of the Rednecks" (Schlesinger 1960, 42). Whatever the particular sobriquet, Huey Pierce Long, born in Winn Parish, Louisiana, in 1893, became the dominant figure in that state's turbulent politics from 1928 until his assassination in September 1935 and presented President Roosevelt with one of his most serious challenges from the left side of the ideological spectrum with his battle cry of "Share Our Wealth." With a high school education and little more than fourteen months of legal studies at the University of Oklahoma and Tulane University, Long passed a special bar examination in 1915 and returned home to open his law practice. Dating back to the Populist movement of the 1890s, Winn Parish had a long-standing reputation in Louisiana for political insurgency and dissent against the rich planters of the Delta and the dominant business classes in Baton Rouge. Long carried on that tradition and added to it his own blend of humor, florid oratory, political calculation, and ruthlessness. He launched his statewide political career in 1918 by winning a seat on the railroad commission (soon renamed the public service commission) and occupied the position as chairman following his reelection in 1924. There he earned the initial hostility of the state's powerful oil and gas industry, especially Standard Oil, when he proposed an additional "occupational license tax" on each barrel of oil refined in the state. Defeated in his first run at the governor's office in 1924, although he ran ahead of the opposition in most rural areas of the state, Long finally triumphed in 1928 on a platform whose slogan declared "Every Man a King, but No One Wears a Crown." A year later, he survived an impeachment attempt in the House of Representatives led by those who feared his reform agenda and appetite for power. He emerged stronger than ever after the failed impeachment when even the bosses of the venerable New Orleans political machine accepted his leadership and allowed him over the next five years to consolidate his power across the state. Now able to impose his will on the state legislature, Governor Long pushed through reorganization bills that gave him the authority to appoint his allies to every important state board and agency from the highway commission to vermin eradication. Told by a legislator that the state constitution did not permit the governor to do a certain action, Long retorted, "I'm the constitution around here now." He once told a reporter, "I used to try to get things done by saying 'please.' That didn't work and now I'm a dynamiter. I dynamite 'em out of my path" (Parrish 1992, 164). But Long also built things—highways, bridges, a new capitol building, and state hospitals, and increased state expenditures on education from the primary level to the university, including free textbooks. And unlike other Southern politicians of his generation, Long did not play the race card at election time, at least not overtly. Often dressing up his programs in the garb of class conflict, Long eschewed the racial demagoguery that characterized Democratic politicians in states like Mississippi, Alabama, and Georgia. Even African Americans benefited from his increased spending on education and health care. The Kingfish entered a larger pond in 1930, when he won election to the United States Senate and immediately began to attack both the Hoover administration and the conservative Democratic leadership in the upper chamber of Congress. The depression, he declared, had been produced by the maldistribution of wealth in the United States and could be corrected only through a redistribution of income from the very rich to the middle classes and the poor. In 1932 he campaigned vigorously for FDR, but soon became disillusioned with the New Deal when Roosevelt's proposals for banking reform proved too conservative. He voted for but denounced the National Recovery

Act. "Every fault of socialism is to be found in this bill," he said, "without one of its virtues. Every crime of monarchy is in here, without one of the things that would give it credit" (Parrish 1992, 323). In February 1934 Long announced his alternative to the New Deal—his Share Our Wealth Society—with a platform that guaranteed every family a "homestead allowance" of $5,000 and a minimum annual income of $2,500, all financed by heavy income and inheritances taxes. No one, Long said, should have a personal fortune above $5 million or an annual income above $1.8 million. Critics denounced Long as a communist, socialist, or fascist, but he was none of these because he rejected national planning and state ownership of basic industries. His economic utopia consisted of independent proprietors who would use their new found capital stake to open a grocery store, a gas station, a bowling alley, or a barber shop. By 1935 his organization boasted over 8 million members in more than 25,000 local chapters. One national public opinion poll gave him about 12 percent of the popular vote, not enough to win the presidency, but enough to carry eight or nine states. His attacks on Roosevelt, ridiculed as "Prince Franklin," became more pungent and he bragged to a friend that he could defeat the FDR in 1936: "I can take him [Roosevelt]. . . . I can out-promise him, and he knows it. People will believe me and they won't believe him" (Parrish 1992, 325). Roosevelt and his advisers hit back by exposing Long's dictatorial methods in Louisiana, his own accumulation of substantial wealth, and by scouring his income tax records for evidence of fraud. Long's threatened challenge to FDR as a possible third-party candidate ended in the halls of the new Louisiana capitol building on September 8, 1935, when a young doctor, Carl Weiss, who blamed the Kingfish for his father-in-law's failed political career, opened fire with a pistol. Long's bodyguard shot Weiss to death, but not before his bullets struck home. Two days later, after a botched surgery, Long died with the result that his Share Our Wealth movement passed into the hands of an unstable neofascist, Gerald L. K. Smith. Teamed with Father Coughlin and Francis Townsend, the proponent of a national pension program for the elderly, Smith organized the National Union Party, whose presidential candidate, William "Liberty Bell" Lemke, received a dismal 882,479 votes running against Roosevelt in 1936.

Miller-Tydings Act of 1937

In the wake of the Supreme Court's decision in 1935 striking down the National Industrial Recovery Act (NIRA) (*Schechter Poultry Corp. v. United States*), the Roosevelt administration and Congress responded with a series of individual laws aimed at addressing particular economic problems spawned by the depression, notably the Guffey-Snyder Act and the Guffey-Vinson Act for the coal industry. Among these so-called Little NIRA statutes was the Miller-Tydings Act of 1937 that significantly amended the venerable Sherman Anti-Trust Act of 1890 to permit fair-trade laws. A key provision of the law permitted manufacturers and producers to establish a minimum resale price for their products in an effort to prevent destructive, cutthroat competition. Such minimum resale prices would not be subject to prosecution as restraints of trade or commerce among the states. But in addition, the law provided that any conspiracy or collusion among competing firms to establish such minimum resale prices would remain subject to the Sherman Act. Many states had already adopted similar resale minimum price laws, known as fair-trade statutes, when Congress passed Miller-Tydings, and in 1936 the Hughes Court sustained these laws in *Old Dearborn Distributing Co. v. Seagram Distillers Corp.* The intention of the statutes, the Court held, was not to sanction unlawful restraints of trade, but to protect the property right of the manufacturer in goodwill. Miller-Tydings exemplified the widespread belief at the time that the American economy had reached a point of maturity and stagnation where overproduction and destructive competition constituted the most significant barriers to improved profits and increased employment.

Moley, Raymond

The unofficial leader of FDR's "Brain Trust" in the 1932 campaign, Moley was born in Berea, Ohio, in 1886 and earned degrees from Baldwin-Wallace College, Oberlin College, and Columbia University, where he received his doctorate in 1918. He brought to the New Deal his varied experiences as a high school teacher, superintendent of public education, university professor, prolific author, and director of the famous Cleveland Foundation that investigated the American criminal justice system between 1919 and 1923. While teaching government at Columbia, he became director of research for the New York State Crime Commission in 1926–1927 and the New York State Commission on the Administration of Criminal Justice (1931–1933), where his articulateness drew the attention of Governor Roosevelt's chief legal adviser, Samuel I. Rosenman, who recruited him to head the small group of Columbia academics, including Adolf Berle and Rexford Tugwell, who supplied candidate FDR with ideas for major speeches and varied advice on economic policy. In the first year of the New Deal, Moley took an official post as an assistant secretary of state, but his unofficial role as talent recruiter (often working with Felix Frankfurter) and legislative adviser proved equally important to the administration's success. Although he believed in the benefits of national economic planning as embodied in the National Recovery Act, Moley voiced skepticism about a large public works program and the Tennessee Valley Authority. And his commitment to national planning did not extend to FDR's desire to uncouple the dollar from the international gold standard in order to lower the debt burden of Americans and inflate the currency. Sent to the London Economic Conference in the summer of 1933 as one of the president's key negotiators, Moley had no sooner announced his support for currency stabilization when

FDR declared that he would veto any such scheme. Not long after suffering that humiliation, Moley resigned from the government to become editor of the magazine *Today*, where he continued to support many key reforms of the New Deal, including the Securities and Exchange Act, the Banking Act of 1935, and the National Labor Relations Act. Roosevelt's commitment to tax reform between 1935–1937 drew mild criticism from Moley, who finally became openly critical when FDR launched his effort to "pack" the Supreme Court in 1937 and expanded federal spending as an antidote to the recession of 1937–1938. Roosevelt's bid for the third term sealed Moley's abandonment of both the president and the Democratic Party as he worked for Republican candidate Wendell Willkie in 1940. Both during the 1930s and later he became an important early interpreter of the New Deal with books such as *After Seven Years* (1939) and *The First New Deal* (1966), both of which argued that the administration had made a fatal mistake in forsaking cooperation with business after 1934 and engaging in appeals to class warfare. He died in 1975, the author of more than a dozen books and monographs.

Morgenthau, Henry, Jr.

Born to wealth and comfort on New York City's Upper West Side in 1891, Morgenthau became one of Franklin Roosevelt's oldest and most intimate friends by virtue of their common love of farming in Dutchess County and endless games of Parcheesi played while FDR recovered from poliomyelitis in the 1920s. The son of a wealthy lawyer and investor who served as President Wilson's ambassador to Turkey, Morgenthau attended Phillips Exeter Academy and then entered Cornell University in 1909 with the intention of pursuing a career in architecture. He abandoned that goal after three semesters, spent time in Texas, and took up farming on several hundred acres near FDR's Hyde Park estate where they became friends prior to Roosevelt's near-fatal illness. Beginning in 1922 he also published the farm journal, *American Agriculturalist*, and when FDR began his political comeback in the late 1920s, Morgenthau served as one of his key advisers along with Louis Howe and Eleanor Roosevelt. In FDR's New York administration he served both as chairman of the state's Agricultural Advisory Commission and commissioner of conservation where he played a major role in New York's ambitious reforestation program. Naturally enough, Morgenthau hoped for the post of secretary of agriculture in the first New Deal, but the job went to Iowa's Henry Wallace instead, and Morgenthau settled for the chairmanship of the new Federal Farm Board with the mandate to consolidate the various federal programs extending financial assistance to the nation's stricken farmers. Within a year as head of the Farm Credit Administration, the gentleman farmer from Dutchess County had refinanced thousands of farm mortgages and saved countless agricultural producers from bankruptcy. When illness forced the retirement of William Woodin,

FDR's first secretary of the treasury, Morgenthau stepped in as acting secretary in late 1933 and was confirmed by the Senate as the permanent secretary a month later. He would hold that post until three months after Roosevelt's death in 1945. When he took office in 1934, the federal government was spending a little over $5 billion a year, even in the depths of the depression. When he left office a decade later, Washington pumped almost $100 billion a year into the American economy as a result of New Deal programs and the massive expenditures required by World War II. Although lacking a deep background in financial matters, Morgenthau recruited very able administrators and lawyers to staff the sprawling bureaucracy of the Treasury Department that managed everything from the Secret Service and the Public Health Service to the Coast Guard and Bureau of Internal Revenue. Once Roosevelt took the nation off the international gold standard in 1933 and endorsed a limited remonetization of silver in the Agricultural Adjustment Act, Morgenthau spent the next five years attempting to maintain the value of the dollar against the devaluation efforts of other countries eager to undercut American exports. He endorsed the major banking, financial, and tax reforms of the New Deal and by maintaining monetary stability and low interest rates permitted the expansion of federal spending at modest cost to Washington. Less gifted with a talent for oratory and invective than other New Dealers such as Wallace or Harold Ickes (FDR referred to him in jest as "Henry the Morgue"), the sober and efficient Morgenthau was nonetheless a skilled political and bureaucratic infighter. He did not hesitate to unleash the Bureau of Internal Revenue against the administration's critics, including Father Coughlin and Huey Long. He argued tirelessly and passionately against increases in federal spending for relief and public works, even in the face of the sharp economic downturn in 1937–1938, but lost such policy debates to those like Hopkins who pushed for bigger countercyclical expenditures. Roosevelt shared his friend's fiscal conservatism, but ranked it second to the need to minister to the unemployed and the hungry.

National Industrial Recovery Act of 1933

Known as the NIRA in the alphabet soup of the early New Deal and as the birthplace of the "Blue Eagle" that symbolized its commitment to a new American economic regime of fair competition and economic recovery, the National Industrial Recovery Act embodied the hopes and aspirations of a diverse number of interest groups, congressional leaders, and administration spokesmen, including Roosevelt himself. And its eclectic birth promised a turbulent future, one fully realized until the Supreme Court declared it unconstitutional in 1935, a death that many, but not FDR, regarded as merciful. At the heart of the National Industrial Recovery Act lay a theory of the Great Depression that stressed the maturity of the nation's economic system, often analogized as an elderly patient, now exhausted, who had run out of energy and innovation and whose best days had vanished along with the closing of the frontier, the end of railroad construction, and the stimulus provided by the automobile. The stock market crash of 1929 had exposed the inherent structural flaws in a capitalist system that had reached a point of stagnation, where overproduction had become a curse, competition an unmitigated evil, and vast income disparities a fact of life. For some of FDR's formal and informal advisers, notably Justice Brandeis, the solution could be found in policies designed to redress the imbalance in incomes by taxing the wealthy, reforming the financial structure, and engaging in substantial public works projects. Others advocated the nostrum of monetary inflation through devaluation and the recoinage of silver. Berle, Tugwell, Moley, leaders of the initial "Brain Trust," urged a larger measure of economic planning directed by the federal government. They found allies among key business leaders such as Gerard Swope of General Electric; Henry I. Harriman of the United States Chamber of Commerce; and Bernard Baruch, the former head of the War Industries Board during World War I—all of whom advocated a relaxation of the antitrust laws, formal acceptance of cartel agreements, and closer cooperation with government to curb price cutting and overproduction. Into this policy mixture was also thrown leading congressional figures such as Senator Robert Wagner of New York, a longtime ally of organized labor, and potent union leaders John L. Lewis and Sidney Hillman, who insisted that any legislation provide protection for union membership and collective bargaining. These disparate forces came together under Senator Wagner's leadership in the spring of 1933 in an effort to sidetrack a bill advanced by Senator Hugo Black and Representative William Connery, the so-called thirty-hour workweek proposal, that would have barred from interstate commerce all goods produced in factories that employed people for more than thirty hours each week. With the support of the White House, key industrialists, and labor leaders, Wagner's omnibus bill passed Congress and Roosevelt signed it into law on June 16, 1933. Title I of the National Industrial Recovery Act, intended as its preamble declared to eliminate unfair competition, raise purchasing power, reduce unemployment, and protect national resources, gave many business groups, especially those with well-developed trade associations, the benefit of suspending the antitrust laws and drafting codes of fair competition that the president might endorse or modify. Section 7 required such codes to contain basic labor standards, including a minimum wage. Section 7(a) banned the use by employers of yellow-dog contracts and protected the right of workers to join unions and bargain collectively. Section 9, the so-called hot oil provisions, gave the president authority to regulate the shipment of petroleum across state lines. The advocates of public works won Title II, which created a Public Works Administration, soon headed by Harold Ickes, funded at $3.3 billion to finance the construction of naval vessels, highways, dams, and federal buildings. Title III authorized an excess-profits tax to defray the expenses of Titles I and II, although even normal profits appeared fleeting in the summer of 1933. With prudence and abundant attention to detail, Ickes ran a program that survived the constitutional demise of Title I, although the pace of his expenditures remained too slow for most New Dealers. Despite initial euphoria and hoopla, Title I soon encountered formidable difficulties. Although the law required representatives from business, government, labor, and consumer groups to participate in code writing and enforcement, the major voice heard by the government representatives usually came from businessmen eager to raise prices and limit production, but largely uninterested in the impact of such policies upon labor and consumers. Those businessmen excluded from the code writing and enforcement machinery soon screamed "monopoly" and "unfair competition," words that found many sympathetic ears in Congress and the press. When employers refused to accept a single union as a bargaining agent for their employees, Roosevelt enraged most labor leaders by supporting the employers and advocating multiple bargaining units, a solution that guaranteed strikes, jurisdictional battles, and general labor chaos. The National Recovery Administration (NRA), newly created and lacking organizational experience except for the businessmen recruited by General Johnson, groaned under the burden of attempting to police too many codes in too many marginal economic areas. Even the energetic and seemingly tireless Johnson finally broke down physically and emotionally under the strain. By the summer of 1935 when Hughes and his brethren finally administered the final coup de grace, the Blue Eagle had been mortally wounded by business defections, labor violence, congressional attacks, and a report by its own review board. Those in the administration who supported antitrust enforcement, restored competition, and fiscal expansion cheered its demise, even as FDR attacked the Court's decision, lamented the death of the Blue Eagle, and continued to hope that it might rise again, phoenixlike, to save the country.

National Labor Relations Act of 1935

Roosevelt and his party reaped huge political dividends from the emergence of powerful industrial labor unions in the 1930s, many of which became the backbone of the Democratic Party for years to come. It is therefore ironic that the central legal concept that guaranteed labor's new strength—collective bargaining through majority rule—had little initial appeal to FDR and encountered active hostility from many of his initial advisers. A patrician, taught from childhood to aid the downtrodden, Roosevelt had to confront the fact in 1933 that millions of working-class Americans intended to change their economic circumstances, not through the benevolence of their social betters, but through their own collective efforts. For those Americans who went out on strike and walked picket lines to secure union recognition between 1933 and 1940, the question of who would represent them became of the highest importance. FDR did not grasp its significance in 1934 when he told a reporter with some irritation in his voice that workers could choose anyone they wished to represent them—a union, the Ahkoond of Swat, or the Royal Geographic Society (Leuchtenburg 1963, 108). In order to build a broad coalition behind the National Industrial Recovery Act (NIRA) of 1933 that included both business and labor, however, the president and congressional leaders accepted Section 7(a) of that law, which protected the right of employees to join labor unions and to bargain collectively over wages and other benefits. Armed with that provision, union organizers swarmed into the nation's factories, mines, and mills in search of new members, and when the organizers did not arrive quickly, employees did their own organizing. Employers, fearful of autonomous organizations, created their own company unions in order to head off these efforts and to comply with the law's formalities. Strikes erupted across the United States in 1934, the most violent in places like Minneapolis and San Francisco. In an effort to bring peace, the National Labor Board, chaired by Senator Robert Wagner and charged initially with implementing Section 7(a), proposed secret ballot elections and the principle of majority rule to resolve the question of employee representation. This so-called Reading Formula enjoyed the support of one of the Labor Board's key business representatives, Gerard Swope of General Electric, who told one protesting employer: "This is America and that's the way we do things here" (Schlesinger 1960, 147). But other major employers resisted the Reading Formula. The Labor Board had no independent enforcement powers, and Roosevelt sabotaged the principle by sanctioning a scheme of proportional representation for the automobile industry. The administrative chiefs of the National Recovery Administration (NRA), General Hugh Johnson and later Donald Richberg, regarded strikes for union recognition as a devastating blow to economic recovery. Johnson at one point equated them with strikes against the government itself. When Senator Wagner introduced legislation in 1934 that would have given a new National Labor Relations Board clear statutory authority to hold representation elections, along with a provision for majority rule, and prohibitions on coercive behavior by employers, Roosevelt encouraged the Senate majority to sidetrack the bill in favor of a mild resolution that contained few teeth. One angry supporter of Wagner declared that "the New Deal is being strangled in the house of its friends" (Schlesinger 1960, 151). A year later, several weeks after the Supreme Court invalidated the floundering NIRA, Roosevelt signed into law a version of Wagner's proposal nearly identical to the one he had cast aside earlier. What had changed his mind? The off-year election of 1934 had swelled the ranks of prolabor supporters in Congress. Wagner had the votes to win. Strikes over union representation continued to plague any recovery efforts. The existing National Labor Relations Board, now headed by Francis Biddle, had referred thirty-three cases of noncompliance by employers with Section 7(a) to the Department of Justice, but that agency had acted on none of them. Wagner's law changed all that by institutionalizing the right of labor to organize the employees to bargain effectively with employers through the principle of majority rule. The measure specifically adopted the Reading Formula—the union elected by a majority of workers in a free election would be the sole bargaining agent for all the workers in a company. Employers were required to bargain "in good faith" with the employees' representatives and prohibited from engaging in "unfair labor practices," which included antiunion espionage, discrimination against union members, strikebreaking, the use of yellow-dog contracts, or promoting company-sponsored unions. And finally, the statute created a new National Labor Relations Board as an independent agency with the power to investigate complaints, subpoena witnesses, and seek remedial action in the courts, all the powers that had been lacking under Section 7(a). William Green, head of the American Federation of Labor, without much exaggeration called the National Labor Relations Act, labor's Magna Carta. When a fresh wave of strikes rolled over the nation after 1935, spearheaded by the new CIO and the old AF of L, the National Labor Relations Board, supported by the Supreme Court decision in *Jones & Laughlin* (1937) stood ready when necessary to resolve them. Leading employer organizations such as the National Association of Manufacturers had vehemently opposed the Wagner Act as the demise of free enterprise and the dawn of class despotism, but their more enlightened counterparts in the corporate world soon realized that the law and the National Labor Relations Board that enforced it offered a more stable union environment capable of ensuring labor peace and one that seldom threatened managerial prerogatives or seriously endangered profits.

Norris, George W.

The dean of Senate progressives who cosponsored landmark legislation during the Great Depression, including the Norris-LaGuardia Act and the Tennessee Valley Authority Act, Norris was born in Sandusky County, Ohio, in 1861. Educated at Baldwin-Wallace College and Valparaiso University, he was admitted to the Indiana bar in 1883 and, after briefly teaching in the public schools of Ohio and Washington, he moved to Nebraska and began the practice of law in 1885. His experience with economic hard times began with the depression of the 1890s, which ruined the agricultural producers of the Great Plains as well as his own fortunes in the mortgage business and flour milling. After a decade holding local political office as a prosecuting attorney and state judge, Norris ran on the Republican ticket for Congress in 1902 and won. In the House of Representatives, where he would serve until 1913, Norris quickly gave expression to his political independence by joining with other progressive Republicans from the Midwest who supported more effective federal regulation of the railroads, expanded government aid to farmers, and structural reforms of the lower chamber itself. Although he supported Theodore Roosevelt's legislative agenda when TR occupied the White House, Norris refused to join the

Rough Rider's third-party crusade in 1912, remained loyal to the Taft wing of the party, and won election to the United States Senate that year, the first of his five consecutive terms. While supporting Woodrow Wilson's domestic reforms, he balked at the president's saber rattling against Mexico, opposed arming American merchant ships against German U-boat attacks, and was among a handful of senators who voted against the declaration of war in the spring of 1917. And like other Midwestern political leaders with substantial constituencies among German Americans, Norris also broke with Wilson over the postwar settlement fashioned at Versailles, which blamed Germany for the conflict and imposed stiff reparations upon the defeated nation. During the era of Harding, Coolidge, and Hoover, Norris displayed growing disaffection from the Republican Party when he denounced the successful efforts of Treasury Secretary Andrew Mellon to reduce the federal tax burdens (including his own) of the very wealthy. He also alienated party leaders when it came to the facilities built by the United States at Muscle Shoals, Alabama, during the war. Had Norris not blocked their plans, the Harding-Coolidge regime intended to sell off the government-built dams, steam plants, and nitrate facilities to Henry Ford, the Alabama Power Company, American Cyanamid, or Union Carbide. When Norris trumped the administration by pushing his own bill through Congress in 1928 that authorized the federal government to operate a fertilizer plant at Muscle Shoals and sell surplus power to municipal utilities, Coolidge gave it a pocket veto and told congressmen that the Nebraskan attempted "the opening wedge for socialism" (Parrish 1992, 55). When President Hoover also vetoed Norris's Muscle Shoals bill with the remark that it constituted "the negation of the ideals upon which our civilization has been based" (Schlesinger 1958, 322), that negative response became one of the reasons Norris deserted the president in 1932 and endorsed Franklin Roosevelt. Prior to FDR's inauguration, Norris achieved two other notable victories, however, when the Norris-LaGuardia Act that bore his imprint curbed the jurisdiction of federal courts to issue injunctions in labor-management disputes, and the states finally ratified the Twentieth Amendment to the Constitution, which eliminated the long lame-duck period between the election and inauguration of a new president. Roosevelt's New Deal realized Norris's dream for Muscle Shoals as he became the principal sponsor of the historic legislation creating the massive Tennessee Valley Authority in 1933. The initial dam built by the new agency and its model community would bear his name. Ever the advocate of public power, Norris also guided through Congress in 1936 the Rural Electrification Act that finally brought cheap power to the American countryside. By 1936 Norris had severed virtually all ideological and political ties with the Republican Party and won his fifth term in the Senate as an independent. And as war clouds gathered in Europe and Asia, the aging Nebraskan modified his foreign policy views to support FDR's proposed revisions of the neutrality laws that allowed England to buy war materials on a "cash and carry" basis and also the president's Lend-Lease bill that offered more direct aid to those fighting Hitler's Germany. Defeated for reelection in 1942, he died two years later.

Perkins, Frances

Confirmed as President Roosevelt's secretary of labor in March 1933, Perkins became the first woman to serve in a cabinet post. Born in Boston in 1880, Perkins brought to the New Deal an incomparable background in social work at the local and state levels and a tireless devotion to improving the lot of working men and women through support for organized labor and progressive legislation. In New York state during the 1920s she entered the decades-long battle to curb sweatshops and to put a ceiling on the hours of work from women and children. In these efforts she first met and gained the support of the state's leading progressives, including Senator Robert Wagner, Governor Alfred E. Smith, Congressman Fiorello LaGuardia, and Franklin and Eleanor Roosevelt. Smith appointed Perkins his commissioner for industrial affairs in 1928, a post she continued to hold under Roosevelt from which she pushed for expanded state relief for the jobless and unemployment insurance. She campaigned vigorously for Roosevelt's election against Hoover and became the most logical candidate for the labor department, a fiefdom long dominated by balding middle-aged men with some vague connection to the American Federation of Labor. Over the next twelve years, until her retirement soon after FDR's death, Perkins built the Department of Labor into an effective bureaucratic voice for the union movement, the unemployed, and the poor while also playing a major role in the shaping of important New Deal legislation. In 1933, for example, during the so-called Hundred Days of the first Roosevelt administration, her influence was felt in the creation of the Civilian Conservation Corps, the labor provisions of the National Recovery Act, especially Section 7(a), which sought to guarantee collective bargaining, and the Federal Emergency Relief Act. During this fertile period, too, she chaired the special Committee on Economic Security, which along with congressional allies wrote the landmark Social Security Act of 1935 providing old-age pensions, unemployment compensation, and direct federal aid to the blind, the disabled, and dependent children. The second burst of New Deal reforms between 1935 and 1938 found Perkins again at the negotiating table where Senator Wagner and others put together the National Labor Relations Act. A year later she realized one of her oldest dreams with passage of the Walsh-Healey Public Contracts Act of 1936, which mandated federal contractors to adopt an eight-hour day, a forty-hour work week, and a minimum wage. The Fair Labor Standards Act of 1938, another long-standing Perkins project, extended these wage and hours provisions across all of interstate commerce.

While lobbying tirelessly for FDR's legislative agenda, Perkins brought new scope and vitality to her own department by enlarging the activities of the Bureau of

Women and Children, beefing up the Mediation and Conciliation Service, and turning the Bureau of Labor Statistics into a more effective instrument for collecting reliable data on the state of the nation's economic health. With passage of the Fair Labor Standards Act she also assumed jurisdiction over its new enforcement wing, the Wage and Hours Division, which sought aggressively to expand coverage of the federal minimum wage provisions.

Public Works Administration (PWA)

Created by Title II of the National Recovery Act of 1933 and headed until 1939 by Secretary of the Interior Harold Ickes, the Public Works Administration founded the first federal housing program and financed some of the nation's most spectacular capital projects, including Grand Coulee Dam on the Columbia River and the Queens Midtown Tunnel in New York City. But compared to other New Deal programs aimed at spurring economic recovery by employing the millions who remained out of work, the PWA's role remained modest. It spent nearly $6 billion over the course of the decade, but that can be compared to the $4.8 billion appropriated in a single year for the larger Works Progress Administration in 1935. On average, PWA projects employed only 140,000 workers each year, most of them in skilled trades. It completed a little more than 34,000 projects in total. On the other hand, by one accounting over half of all the school buildings and virtually all of the municipal water and sewer systems built in the United States during the depression years owed 30 percent of their capital cost to Ickes's agency, which, in addition, funded municipal electric plants, assorted public buildings, roads, hydroelectric dams, and bridges. Although federal public works had long had their advocates in the Bureau of Reclamation, the Army Corps of Engineers, and the Bureau of Roads, it required the catastrophe of the depression to put a large-scale program on the nation's agenda as a method for relieving unemployment and stimulating recovery. By 1930 congressional leaders such as Senators Robert M. LaFollette Jr. and Robert Wagner attempted to secure passage of a major public works bill, but the Hoover administration resisted such efforts until 1932 when the president finally agreed to the Emergency Relief and Construction Act as an amendment to the original Reconstruction Finance Corporation law. That law authorized $2 billion to be loans for what were called self-liquidating projects, which meant that the funds could be spent only for projects generating revenues sufficient for repayment of the loans. The New Deal's PWA built upon this Hoover-era foundation, but changed the funding formula in a significant way. The $3.3 billion initially authorized for the PWA in Title II was to be divided between direct federal grants (30 percent), with the balance allocated as federal loans. Ickes absorbed most of the key staff members from the Hoover program, especially the engineers, who had already developed many feasibility studies. Aside from making certain that prominent state and local Democrats gained a voice in PWA projects, Ickes ran a program notable for scrupulous planning down to the smallest contractual detail, rigorous accounting and repayment standards, and the absence of major scandals. Roosevelt and other New Dealers became so impatient with the pace of Ickes's efforts that the president relieved him of $400 million in the winter of 1933–1934 and gave the money to Harry Hopkins's Civil Works Administration, which hired the jobless at a much faster clip. When it became clear that the agency would spend only $2.8 billion of its initial appropriation, FDR and Congress shifted the majority of relief spending to the new Works Progress Administration. Ickes received only $300 million in 1935 from the Emergency Relief Appropriation Act of that year and did not receive another significant increase in funding until the recession of 1937–1938. A year later, he allowed the PWA to be folded into the Federal Works Agency as part of the Reorganization Act passed by Congress.

Railroad Retirement Acts of 1934, 1935, and 1937

Few legislative efforts of the New Deal era encountered more constitutional hurdles than the long struggle to adopt a federally mandated pension system for railroad employees. In order to bring greater uniformity to the patchwork of private railroad pension schemes that had evolved over the decades, Congress passed a Railroad Retirement Act in the summer of 1934, a measure sponsored by Senators Robert Wagner of New York and Henry Hatfield of West Virginia. This law, administered by a Railroad Retirement Board, levied a 2 percent payroll tax on all railway employees to be matched by a 4 percent contribution from the carriers. Denounced by management and challenged in the courts as an unconstitutional exercise of the commerce power and an arbitrary taking of property, the Hughes Court invalidated the measure a year later in *Railroad Retirement Board v. Alton Railroad Co.* (1935), where the majority, over four dissents, accepted the employers' constitutional arguments. In response to the *Alton* decision, Senator Wagner and Representative Robert Crosser of Ohio secured a revised pension law from Congress that exempted railroad employees from the old-age pension system of the new Social Security Act, imposed a 3.5 percent payroll tax on them, and levied a similar amount on the carriers in the form of an income tax. The Association of Railway Executives found this statute no more palatable and sued to stop enforcement. A federal district court overturned the taxing provisions a year later. Faced with this second judicial veto, Roosevelt invited the carriers and the railway unions to agree to a new pension formula that would not foment more litigation. This became the Railroad Retirement Act of 1937, administered by a three-person board, with funds derived from the Carrier Taxing Act that taxed the income of both the roads and the employees.

Randolph, Asa Philip

One of the most creative and dynamic labor leaders of the century, Randolph was born in Florida in 1889 and educated at Cookman Institute in Jacksonville and the City College of New York. On the eve of America's entrance into World War I, he had his first successful experience as a labor organizer when he spearheaded the successful effort to form a union of New York's elevator operators. That year, too, he founded along with Chandler Owen a militant weekly journal called *The Messenger*, a publication aimed at mobilizing the nation's African Americans on behalf of economic justice and an end to racial segregation. Although never successful as a political candidate on the Socialist ticket in New York City, Randolph achieved his greatest victory in the 1920s when he formed the Brotherhood of Sleeping Car Porters with the goal of winning a collective bargaining agreement with the historically antiunion Pullman Company, the principal railroad passenger service corporation. Soon called "The Chief" by his devoted union members, Randolph took advantage of greater legal security provided by the New Deal to win union recognition and a contract for the porters with the Pullman Company in 1937. He fought for another decade to win membership in the all-white Federation of Railway Brotherhoods. As the United States geared up for war in 1940, with federal defense contracts soaking up the unemployed, Randolph proposed to dramatize the discrimination faced by blacks with a march on Washington. Fearful that Randolph's march would become a public relations disaster for the nation poised to resist Hitler and other authoritarian regimes, Roosevelt called upon his wife, Eleanor, and New York mayor Fiorello LaGuardia to negotiate a truce with the head of the Sleeping Car Porters. In exchange for FDR issuing Executive Order 8802, which created the Fair Employment Practices Committee and banned discrimination on grounds of race, color, creed, or national origins in defense contracting, Randolph called off the demonstration. In the postwar era, Randolph's zeal for racial justice and superb organizational skills led him to campaign against discrimination in the armed forces and the AFL-CIO. And in 1963 he became one of the principal organizers of a second march on Washington at which Dr. Martin Luther King Jr. delivered his stirring "I Have a Dream" speech.

Rayburn, Samuel

One of the most astute and powerful legislators in the history of the United States House of Representatives, Rayburn was born on a farm in Tennessee in 1882, but remained forever identified with Texas, where his family took up the cultivation of cotton five years later. In addition to raising cotton, Rayburn's Texas nourished the political movement of populism and radical democracy during the 1890s with its accumulated grievances against high railroad rates, high interest rates, and low prices for the farmers' crops, all of which left portions of the South and the Great Plains in a perpetual state of economic bondage to the bankers and corporations of the Northeast. After graduating from East Texas Normal College and teaching school for a few years, Rayburn won a seat in the state legislature in 1906. Six years later as the Democratic Party and President Wilson swept into Washington, he took his seat in Congress for the first time. He would not leave Washington for the next forty-nine years and slowly accumulated seniority in the House as a result of the one-party domination enjoyed by Texas Democrats until the 1970s. When Roosevelt launched the New Deal in 1933, Rayburn became a more-than-willing ally as chairman of the important House Committee on Interstate and Foreign Commerce where since the Wilson era he had advocated federal regulation of the railroads and the securities industry centered on Wall Street. Sensing the limitations of his own committee staff, Rayburn secured the assistance of Raymond Moley and Felix Frankfurter in drafting what became the Securities Act of 1933. They, in turn, put Rayburn in touch with three able lawyers—Harvard law professor James Landis, Benjamin V. Cohen, and Thomas G. Corcoran, who not only wrote the final version of the new statute, but provided Rayburn with the rhetorical weapons to defend it in the House. According to Cohen, "Rayburn did not know whether the bill passed so readily because it was so damned good or so damned incomprehensible" (Parrish 1970, 70). A year later, again teamed with Cohen and Corcoran, Rayburn guided the far more radical Securities and Exchange Act through his committee, the whole House, and to passage by Congress. The law created an independent Securities and Exchange Commission to administer both laws, segregated the functions of brokers and dealers in securities, prohibited a range of market manipulations used by inside traders in the past, and gave the Federal Reserve Board broad powers to set margin rates for those purchasing securities on credit. In addition to bringing the securities industry under a measure of public accountability, Rayburn actively supported other early programs of the New Deal, especially those aimed at relief for Southern farmers and those designed to bring electric power to rural areas such as the Tennessee Valley Authority and the Rural Electrification Administration. A longtime critic of the private power industry, which he blamed for failing to deliver cheap electricity to the sparsely developed countryside, Rayburn won his toughest legislative battle in 1935 when Congress passed the Public Utilities Holding Company Act, written largely by Cohen and Corcoran, intended to restructure and consolidate the sprawling holding companies that had gobbled up local operating utilities during the 1920s with little attention to efficient operation or geographic integration. Although the final legislation, a compromise between House and Senate, did not contain the strict language of a mandatory "death sentence" for the largest companies, it did bring them under regulation and eventual restructuring by the Securities and Exchange Commission. In 1940, when Speaker of the House and fellow Texan Henry T. Rainey died, Rayburn realized his life's ambition by succeeding him, a post he would hold when Democrats controlled the House until the presidency of John F. Kennedy.

Reconstruction Finance Corporation (RFC)

Three years after the stock market crash triggered a devastating liquidity crisis, hundreds of banks, insurance companies, savings and loan associations, railroads, and utilities faced bankruptcy with the prospect of generating more unemployment throughout the nation's economic system. In order to shore up this tottering financial and corporate structure, President Hoover urged Congress to create the Reconstruction Finance Corporation, modeled after the War Finance Corporation of World War I, which had made loans to critical defense industries. In 1932 Congress gave the RFC $2 billion and authorized it to make low-interest loans to endangered banks, insurance companies, other financial institutions, and railroads, although some critics pointed out that to saddle these entities with larger debts, even at low rates of interest, did not make a whole lot of economic sense. From the perspective of Hoover and his advisers, however, the key to economic recovery lay in restoring confidence in the soundness of financial markets and business institutions. Other critics condemned the program for aiding corporations while other people went hungry. In response to that criticism, Hoover agreed finally to permit the RFC to make low-interest loans to fund self-liquidating public works programs on the state and local levels, but only when these governments had exhausted their own legal borrowing powers. Under Hoover, therefore, the RFC represented a bold but largely ineffectual remedy to the banking crisis and the mounting unemployment problem. With the Emergency Banking Act of 1933, the New Deal fundamentally changed RFC policy by permitting the agency to invest directly in the preferred (nonvoting) stock of commercial banks. By 1935 the RFC had become a principal stock holder to the tune of $1.3 billion in over 6,000 commercial banks, an infusion of capital that did not reverse the credit crunch, but that did prevent further contraction and saved the industry. By 1939, headed by the shrewd Texas entrepreneur Jesse Jones, the RFC had been transformed by congressional legislation and administrative edict into America's lending agency of last resort, pumping money into more than a dozen other New Deal programs, including the Farm Credit Corporation, the Federal Housing Administration, the Home Owners' Loan Corporation, and the Rural Electrification Administration. The agency's Electric Home and Farm Authority, working in tandem with the Tennessee Valley Authority, extended low-interest loans to consumers for the purchase of electric fans, vacuum cleaners, irons, and heaters, thereby extending the market for TVA as well as for the small appliance from General Electric and Westinghouse. The RFC's Commodity Credit Corporation became the chief source of farm subsidies under the New Deal's various agricultural adjustment plans. Another RFC subsidiary, the Export-Import

Bank, extended credit to American producers who hoped with the aid of government subsidies to penetrate the markets of Europe, Asia, and Latin America. In order to bring this sprawling credit network under a greater measure of control, Roosevelt finally created the Federal Loan Agency under the Reorganization Act of 1939 and placed Jones in charge, although the RFC continued its independent existence throughout the war years and played a major role in the procurement of domestic and foreign war materials.

Reorganization Act of 1939

Apart from President Roosevelt's proposal to expand the size of the Supreme Court in 1937, no plan from the White House stirred greater anxiety and opposition in Congress than the *Report of the President's Committee on Administrative Management*, sent to the House and Senate in January 1937. Since the turn of the century during the administration of Theodore Roosevelt, American presidents, their gubernatorial counterparts on the state level, and experts in public administration had all urged reforms designed to strengthen the executive arm of government with the goal of improved efficiency and accountability. Until the 1920s, however, the United States government did not have a Bureau of the Budget and most state governors lacked constitutional authority to present an executive budget to the legislature. In 1932 and 1933, largely in response to falling federal revenues and the budget deficits that followed, Congress passed two Economy Acts that gave Presidents Hoover and Roosevelt the authority to regroup agencies of the executive branch, subject to a legislative veto within sixty days. Roosevelt invoked the measure to slash the federal payroll, but did not otherwise pursue systematic reorganization until after 1935. Instead, the New Deal spawned an incredible array of new, so-called emergency agencies such as the National Recovery Administration or the Agricultural Adjustment Administration that usually bypassed the existing organizational chart of the executive branch. By 1936, with the New Deal coming under attack by conservatives for condoning waste and mismanagement, FDR created a Committee on Administrative Management to provide a blueprint for executive branch reorganization. He named three distinguished academics from the world of public administration—Louis Brownlow, Charles E. Merriman, and Luther Gulick as members of the committee, with Brownlow serving as chairman. Their recommendations, soon known as the Brownlow Report and sent to Congress as the president's, represented at the time the most sweeping reorganization of the executive branch and enhancement of the president's managerial capacity in the nation's history. In addition to giving the president an enlarged White House staff of six administrative assistants, the report called for the creation of a National Resources Planning Board, the consolidation of administrative controls over the federal civil service in a single director, two new cabinet positions, the regrouping of all independent regulatory commissions and executive branch agencies into twelve super departments, and White House control over accounts and all budget planning. The Brownlow proposals could not have been floated at a more politically inexpedient moment, a month before Roosevelt submitted his plan to reorganize the federal courts. Immediately, both became linked in the fevered imaginations of the president's opponents inside and outside of Congress. Roosevelt, so the argument went, sought to destroy the independence of the courts and to erect an executive despotism through the Brownlow plan. Behind the scenes, but no less effective, powerful bureaucrats in the executive branch whose independent fiefdoms appeared threatened by the reorganization proposals, lobbied against the bill. Especially energetic in this regard were the heads of the Forest Service, the Public Health Service, and the Veterans' Administration. It required all of FDR's political wizardry to get the measure passed by the Senate and then by a margin of only eight votes. The House, however, even with Democrats in the majority, killed the bill, a defeat that, when combined with the almost simultaneous death of the judicial reorganization plan, destroyed the myth of FDR's political invincibility. A chastened Roosevelt submitted a watered-down reorganization proposal to Congress in 1939, which passed Congress with little opposition. Congress gave the president his six administrative assistants, but all reorganization plans became subject to a joint legislative veto. Gone were the proposals for new cabinet posts and super departments as well as executive control over accounts. And many agencies were exempted entirely from any presidential reorganization scheme. Roosevelt availed himself of these tokens by creating a Federal Security Agency, a Federal Loan Agency, and an Executive Office of the President, which was to include the Bureau of the Budget, transferred from the Treasury Department, and a National Resources Planning Board (without real power) relocated from the Interior Department.

Roosevelt, Ana Eleanor

Born in 1884 into a New York society family whose ancestors traced their roots back to the European conquest of North America, Eleanor Roosevelt experienced rejection and abandonment from a very early age, circumstances that in later life made her the champion of those in the United States who suffered other forms of discrimination. Her mother, who died when her daughter was barely eight, called her "Granny" (Morgan 1985, 92). Her father, moving usually in an alcoholic haze, left her unattended in hotels. Within a few years, both her father and younger brother had also died, leaving Eleanor and her older brother in the care of their maternal grandmother. Sent to the Allenswood School outside of London, her intellectual and emotional life received its first real nourishment from the institution's headmistress, Marie Souvestre. She worked briefly at a settlement house after returning to New York in 1901, the year her uncle, Theodore Roosevelt, became president of the United States. Her correspondence from those years reveals a young woman still afflicted with class snobbery and anti-Semitism. Eleanor Roosevelt's world narrowed again after 1905, when she married her dashing distant cousin Franklin and very shortly became responsible for the care of five children, while forced to live under the ever-watchful eye of a mother-in-law who could never be pleased. Franklin's appointment as assistant secretary of the navy in 1913, their move to Washington, and America's entrance into World War I changed her life forever. She plunged into wartime social work with the Red Cross and other organizations ministering to the needs of soldiers. Then she experienced another devastating abandonment when she learned of her husband's love affair with Lucy Mercer, her former social secretary. From that moment on, Eleanor knew that she could count only on herself and she began to shape a life largely independent of Franklin's, although she utilized his name and influence for her own purposes. Following FDR's defeat in 1920 as the Democratic Party's vice presidential candidate, Eleanor turned her attention almost full time to social reform and politics in New York state, where she became a leading member of a formidable if informal network of women activists, including Rose Schneiderman of the Women's Trade Union League, Ester Lape of the League of Women Voters, and Marion Dickerson, head of the women's division of the Democratic Party. When polio felled her husband in 1921, she alone kept the Roosevelt name alive in party affairs through the women's platform committee and speaking engagements across the state where she advocated a ban on child labor, wage and hours legislation, and protection for union organizing. A social feminist, she opposed the Equal Rights Amendment to the Constitution advocated by the National Women's Party in 1923 because she feared the strict prohibition on sex discrimination would lead to the abandonment of laws that protected working-class women from the worst forms of economic exploitation. As the nation's first lady beginning in 1933, she now had a larger arena in which to promote her twin goals of domestic social reform and expanding the influence of women inside government. Along with Mary Dewson, head of the Women's Division of the Democratic Party, and Labor Secretary Frances Perkins, Eleanor helped to recruit more women into the administration and worked with them to defend the interests of women in the various programs of the New Deal. Both behind the scenes and in a newspaper column, "My Day," she spoke out against wage discrimination in most NRA codes and against the policies of public and private employers who fired married women in order to give their jobs to men. Due largely to her influence, the New Deal created a modest network of camps for unemployed single women, similar to those run by the Civilian Conservation Corps. And she lobbied Harry Hopkins with some success to provide work relief for women through the Civil Works Administration and the Works Progress Administration. Each night before retiring to her own bedroom in the White House, she left a stack of memos by her husband's bed recommending new appointments and new program initiatives. The pile became so large that FDR finally insisted she leave only one or two memos each night, an edict Eleanor followed, although the length of the memos doubled. By the end of the 1930s she had become the liberal conscience of the New Deal, often advocating positions that her husband failed to pursue either because of his ingrained conservatism or political expediency. This was especially true with respect to the issues of racial discrimination and segregation. She and Harold Ickes made certain that Marian Anderson could sing before an integrated audience at the Lincoln Memorial. She endorsed a federal antilynching law, pushed the appointment of Mary McLeod Bethune to the board of the National Youth Administration, and participated in the negotiations that both forestalled Asa Philip Randolph's threatened march on Washington and led to the president's executive order banning discrimination in federal defense contracts. Touring the country each year on her own behalf and in support of New Deal programs, she could be found in the shacks of Mississippi tenant farmers and in the fetid coal mines of West Virginia. Finding common cause with FDR's more liberal advisers and supporters in the union movement, she endorsed Henry Wallace's nomination as the party's vice presidential nominee in 1940, a position that put her at even greater odds with the party's white Southerners. Following her husband's death, she became the grande dame of the party, ever espousing the most advanced programs of social welfare and the candidates who believed as she did in the necessity for a strong and compassionate government.

Roosevelt, Franklin D.

When FDR died on April 12, 1945, a young army journalist, writing in the publication *Yank*, observed that people of his age had known only one president—Franklin D. Roosevelt—who had become, he concluded, "the Commander-in-Chief of our generation," the man who had guided them through both depression and war. On buses and trains, in office buildings and in parks, anywhere people learned of the news, men and women broke down in tears. When a man riding in a New York City elevator responded to the event by declaring, "Isn't it about time," a well-tailored society matron standing near slapped him across the face with her glove (Asbell 1961, 146). As president, Franklin Roosevelt evoked strong, often violent emotions from both supporters and opponents. Franklin Roosevelt stimulated such passionate feelings because his New Deal transformed the relationship between the American people and their national government as no series of events had since the Revolution, the founding era of the Constitution, and the Civil War of 1861–1865. Those moments had established national independence, nationhood, and the survival of the union. The New Deal brought that union and federal government into closer relationship with individual Americans than ever before by ministering to their most basic necessity—

economic security. Prior to the New Deal when Americans talked seriously about their rights, they talked the language of civil and political entitlements—the right to vote, to hold office, to speak and think and worship as one pleased, even though these rights were often poorly distributed, distorted by class, race, and gender. To this traditional bundle of rights, the New Deal added economic ones, what Roosevelt called in his annual message to Congress in January 1941, "freedom from want and from fear"—the right, for example, to have one's life savings insured in a bank account; to invest in securities untainted by deliberate fraud; to earn a decent return on one's wheat crop; to receive a minimum wage; to join a labor union; and to receive a pension when one's working days ended. Government, he told the New York legislature in 1931, was the machinery "through which . . . mutual aid and protection is achieved" (Kennedy 1999, 99). He kept that promise. For all of its contradictions, false starts, and compromises, the New Deal remade the United States for the remainder of the twentieth century. No one expected Franklin Roosevelt to preside over such changes in 1933, despite his experience as an assistant secretary of the navy under Wilson, his failed candidacy for the vice presidency in 1920, and his solid achievements as governor of New York between 1928 and 1933. He was perceived as a charming fellow who possessed all of the social graces befitting his patrician upbringing and someone educated at Groton and Harvard, but he was said to lack what a later generation would call "gravitas." Justice Holmes, no mean judge of mental acuity, said he had "a second-rate intellect, but a first-rate temperament" (Kennedy 1999, 100). Even more cutting, journalist Walter Lippmann dismissed him in 1932 as "an amiable Boy Scout" and "a pleasant man, who, without any important qualifications for the office, would very much like to be President" (Kennedy 1999, 101). But what some critics mistook for weaknesses proved to be FDR's greatest assets as a leader in crisis times: unbounded optimism, a rhetorical talent for communicating that optimism to the American people, and a willingness to experiment boldly. Many of the New Deal programs proved to be abject failures such as the National Industrial Recovery Act, or to produce results that simply took income from one group and redistributed it to another without sparking a general recovery, a criticism rightly lodged against the Agricultural Adjustment Act. But despite the long unemployment lines that lingered into 1939 and an economy that appeared stuck somewhere in neutral, FDR never doubted that his programs would work eventually to provide freedom from want and fear. As for the millions of Americans who gathered around their radios in the evenings to hear him, they believed, too. A reporter once quizzed the president about his political philosophy. How would FDR describe himself—a socialist? A fascist? A communist? Throwing back his head and puffing on his ever-present cigarette, Roosevelt retorted, "Philosophy? Philosophy? I am a Christian and a Democrat" (Kennedy 1999, 131). Simple, naive, but it captured the essences of his beliefs. In an age when rigid ideologies often trumped practical common sense, Roosevelt's very lack of political philosophy and intellectual coherence freed him to act pragmatically. In European nations governed by socialist and labor parties during the depression, leaders often sacrificed economic relief to ideological rigor. Unable to adopt a total socialist program of nationalization, they insisted on following strict capitalist theory, including pursuit of a balanced budget, even in the face of massive unemployment. Hoover likewise believed that even the smallest compromise with free enterprise, such as the Tennessee Valley Authority, would lead the nation inevitably down hill toward a socialist hell. Roosevelt rejected such philosophical straight jackets. If one program did not work, he tried another, and another, and another. As one journalist observed in 1945, "in a six-month crisis, he always had a six-month solution" (Asbell 1961, 132). This meant, of course, that the New Deal lacked a consistent, integrated theory capable of mastering the depression such as the one put forth by Keynes. But even had Roosevelt and the New Deal possessed such a theory, the very structure of American government, federal, state, and local, would have proved to be a major obstacle to its implementation. In addition to his optimism and pragmatism, Roosevelt had a superb knack for identifying and recruiting men and women of genuine talent, who raised the level of public service to new heights—Hopkins, Ickes, Wallace, Perkins, Moley, Frankfurter, Berle, Cohen, Corcoran, Landis, and Frank. Secure in his own social status as an aristocratic, Anglo-Saxon Protestant, he opened the doors of opportunity and the corridors of power to those who had been excluded in the past—Irish Catholics, Jews, Eastern Europeans, Negroes, and young men and women from the South and West like Lyndon Johnson and William O. Douglas. Spurned by the old establishment as "a traitor to his class," FDR simply created a new one. Like many popular presidents who win a decisive second term, Roosevelt's hubris led him to disaster in 1937, when he challenged the Supreme Court and proposed a major restructuring of the executive branch as well. Both efforts exposed him to charges of despotism, divided his own party, and gave new life to his enemies. And only the dogs of war, unleashed in Europe and Asia, allowed him to regain the initiative by 1940 and to become once again the commander in chief of a generation.

Securities Act of 1933 and Securities and Exchange Act of 1934

Prior to Roosevelt's inauguration, the stock market crash, the ensuing liquidity crisis, and the near collapse of the nation's commercial banking system gave rise to demands for increased government regulation of the securities industry and the stock exchanges. Beginning in 1932 a sweeping Senate investigation, headed by Ferdinand Pecora, a former New York district attorney, exposed to the public the many varieties of fraud and corruption involving brokers' loans to customers, fictitious securities, margin buying, and outright misrepresentation of corporate earnings that plagued the nation's financial markets. In one of his first messages to Congress in March 1933,

Roosevelt demanded legislation providing for full disclosure of all new securities, with the burden placed on sellers to "tell the truth" to the investing public. The original legislation, written by former Federal Trade Commissioner Huston Thompson, called for the FTC to review and either authorize or oppose the marketing of new issues. Representative Sam Rayburn of Texas introduced the bill in the House, which immediately came under heavy fire from Wall Street as too punitive and from others as implying government endorsement of the soundness of securities. Rayburn's cry for help to revise the Thompson bill launched the New Deal careers of three proteges of Felix Frankfurter—Benjamin V. Cohen, James Landis, and Thomas G. Corcoran. Their revisions, sponsored by Rayburn and Senator Duncan Fletcher of Florida, became law with Roosevelt's signature on May 27, 1933. It required companies issuing securities to file detailed information with the Federal Trade Commission, including ownership of 10 percent or more of prior securities, a detailed description of the purposes of the financing and the financial conditions of the company, plus the salaries of its officers. Evidence of fraud or misrepresentation in the disclosure statement could lead to both civil and criminal penalties, including five years in prison and a fine of $5,000. Furthermore, the commission could issue so-called stop orders to suspend the effectiveness of disclosure statements, and any sales following such an order became illegal. The Securities Act had the modest objective of preventing egregious exploitation of investors through the sale of fraudulent or worthless securities by placing the burden of proof upon those who sold to the public. Many Wall Street bankers and their attorneys denounced the law as an unwarranted intrusion of government into their private affairs and predicted a "drying up" of the nation's capital markets because of the liability and financial burdens imposed by the disclosure process. But supporters of the law, including many brokerages that dealt directly with the public, approved of the new regulations because they predicted restored confidence in their industry once the disreputable "fly-by-night" operators were banned. A year after the Securities Act became law, Roosevelt sent a second proposal to Congress written by Cohen, Landis, and Corcoran that gave the FTC sweeping power over the individual stock exchanges, prohibited the buying and selling of securities by many exchange members for their own personal accounts, banned short sales, and allowed the commission to fix all margin requirements for the purchase of stock on credit. That version encountered withering criticism from Wall Street and forced revisions in the House and Senate before Roosevelt finally signed the measure into law. The most significant changes wrought in Congress created a new, independent regulatory agency, the Securities and Exchange Commission, to enforce both the Securities Act and the Securities Exchange Act; gave the SEC broad discretion to regulate many exchange activities instead of prohibiting them outright; and gave the Federal Reserve Board rather than the commission authority to set margin requirements. To the chagrin of many New Dealers, Roosevelt named Joseph P. Kennedy, a legendary stock market operator, to the first chairmanship of the SEC, but balanced that appointment with Landis, who in addition to helping to draft both statutes had pioneered the development of administrative law as a field of study at the Harvard Law School. Under Kennedy's brief leadership, the SEC stressed the necessity for self-regulation by the exchanges, the securities industry, and the accounting profession—a strategy that helped to revive private capital investment by demonstrating that government regulation did not threaten legitimate profits on Wall Street. The SEC became one of the shining examples of administrative competence under the New Deal both in its enforcement of the two statutes and in implementing the later Public Utilities Holding Company Act of 1935, which compelled the reorganization of dubious financial structures that had distorted that industry in the 1920s. The SEC experienced a fresh burst of regulatory zeal at the end of the depression under the chairmanships of William O. Douglas and Jerome Frank, both of whom became skeptical of excessive self-regulation by the industry. When the New York Stock Exchange refused to adopt new trading rules and bylaws to give brokers a larger voice in the institution's affairs, Douglas forced the changes by threatening direct SEC intervention. The Douglas-Frank regime also brought a degree of order to the volatile over-the-counter markets by encouraging the creation of a powerful, but self-governing, trade association of brokers who specialized in this area.

Sinclair, Upton B.

Born in Baltimore, Maryland, in 1878, Sinclair became one of America's most prolific if not profound novelists, whose passion for social justice and commitment to socialism brought him a devoted following and equally venomous opposition from the economic establishment when he ran for the governorship of California in 1934. A writing machine, usually linked with Frank Norris, Jack London, Stephen Crane, and Theodore Dreiser as a founder of American realism, Sinclair produced ninety works of fiction and nonfiction in his ninety years. The most famous appeared in 1906, *The Jungle*, a hair-raising expose of the conditions under which immigrant workers labored in the nation's meatpacking industry. Sinclair hoped the book would ignite the conscience of his readers to seek legislation to improve the wages, hours, and conditions in the industry. As background for this message, however, Sinclair included graphic descriptions of the appalling conditions under which the workers processed meat, including scenes of employees urinating on the floor, large rodents enjoying a tasty meal of hamburger, even the death of one worker who fell into a steaming vat and turned up in a tub of lard. These accounts, many of them fictional, outraged consumer groups and hastened the passage of the first federal meat inspection statute under Theodore Roosevelt. The wages, hours, and union efforts of the packinghouse workers, however, changed little until the New Deal. "I aimed at the public's heart," Sinclair lamented, "and by accident I hit it in the stomach" (Cooper 1990, 86). In addition to *The Jungle*, Sinclair devoted his pen and his social conscience to explorations of other social injustices. *King Coal* (1917) chronicled the misery of miners in the Colorado fields. *Boston* (1928) argued that Sacco and Vanzetti, Italian anarchists executed for murder and robbery, had been railroaded into the electric chair. In 1934, much to the consternation of the state's regular Democratic organization and President Roosevelt, Sinclair captured the party's nomination for governor. He ran on a platform with the slogan "End Poverty in California," or EPIC for short. He proposed that idle factories and farmlands not already in crop be turned over to the unemployed to encourage self-sufficiency, that the state nurture cooperative stores to provide food and clothing, and that California raise taxes on the wealthy to pay for such programs. The state's economic elites, spearheaded by the oil and gas industry and the motion picture industry, mobilized behind his Republican opponent, Frank Merriam, who benefited from an extensive propaganda campaign that accused Sinclair of endorsing every economic heresy known to man as well as free love and nudism. Despite pleas from some progressive Democrats, FDR distanced himself from Sinclair's crusade, which ended in his decisive defeat. Beginning in 1940, he authored an eleven-volume series known as the "Lanny Budd" novels that chronicled the history of the world during the first four decades of the century by pitting its hero against the forces of tyranny and economic exploitation. In 1943 his antifascist novel, *Dragon's Teeth*, won the Pulitzer Prize.

Social Security Act of 1935

In the summer of 1935, Roosevelt signed into law the Social Security Act, which, apart from the National Labor Relations statute of that same year, became the single most important piece of legislation adopted by Congress during the depression. The law created a Social Security Board charged with administering the act's substantive provisions, including unemployment compensation, old-age insurance, and financial assistance to the blind, the disabled, and dependent and delinquent children. The law remained virtually unchanged, except for benefit increases, until President Clinton and Congress eliminated the entitlement provisions for mothers with dependent children in the 1990s. Roosevelt's measure established a cooperative federal-state system of unemployment compensation, initially financed by a federal tax on employer payrolls equal to 1 percent in 1936 and rising gradually thereafter. The program was administered locally by each state that participated under federal guidelines and received a credit up to 90 percent of the federal tax. The old-age and survivor's retirement program, managed exclusively by the federal government, was financed initially by an equal tax of 1 percent on employers and employees, with an increase to 3 percent taking effect in 1949. Beginning in 1942, the government began to pay pensions to eligible people over the age of sixty-five, with benefits ranging from $10 to $85 a month. Finally, the law gave direct grants to the states to aid them in defraying the cost of state-run pension systems and in making payments to the blind and dependent children. A number of New Dealers and members of Congress had hoped to finance the programs out of general income tax revenues because of their generally progressive nature, but Roosevelt and other members of Congress insisted on the more regressive system of payroll levies that placed a larger burden on the working poor and the middle class. The president feared that reliance on general revenues would permit a later Congress to reduce or destroy the entire structure, whereas the payroll levies gave each worker a long-term vested interest in the survival of the retirement system. Compared to other advanced, industrialized nations, the United States lagged far behind in the provisioning of unemployment insurance, old-age pensions, and other economic safety nets. Leading trade union organizations such as the AF of L did not endorse unemployment insurance until 1932 in the belief that such benefits should flow from collective bargaining agreements. As late as 1935 only one state, Wisconsin, had adopted a mandatory program with employers shouldering most of the costs. By the 1930s old-age retirement programs had not spread beyond a limited number of public service occupations such as police, firefighters, and teachers. Only the richest and most progressive corporations such as General Electric had initiated private pension programs. The depression undermined many of these private pension programs and revealed the complete inadequacy of unemployment insurance coverage. The initiative for a federal law came from the President's Committee on Economic Security, chaired by Labor Secretary Perkins, which put old-age pensions at the top of its legislative agenda. And those efforts received an enormous political boost from Senator Long's Share-Our-Wealth crusade and from a grassroots movement arising in California under the leadership of a Long Beach dentist, Francis Townsend. His plan, embodied in legislation proposed by Representative John McCroarty, proposed giving every American over the age of sixty-five a federal cash payment of $200 each month, financed by a heavy tax on incomes, with the only condition being that the recipient had to spend the money within thirty days. Townsend's movement attracted thousands of eager supporters, who argued that his Revolving Old-Age Pension Plan would provide for the elderly while simultaneously stimulating recovery. The administration's bill, sponsored by Senator Wagner and Congressman David Lewis of Maryland, adopted the Perkins committee's recommendations for federalizing the old-age pension provisions, but it compromised on unemployment compensation by providing for joint federal-state administration. New Deal critics on the right condemned the law as one step on the road to communism and the end of self-reliant individualism in the United States. Opponents on the left denounced the financing methods as regressive and bemoaned the stingy benefits such as the maximum grant for each destitute blind person that reached only $20 per month beginning in 1940.

Temporary National Economic Committee (TNEC)

Franklin Roosevelt launched the New Deal in 1933 by calling on Congress to suspend the antitrust laws and encourage cooperation between business and government through the National Industrial Recovery Act (NIRA). He concluded the New Deal five years later with a message to Congress calling for an investigation of antitrust enforcement and supporting the efforts of Thurman Arnold, his new attorney general, to prosecute violators. Congress responded by creating the Temporary National Economic Committee, which held hearings and conducted investigations over the next three years in the most wide-ranging government inquiry into the competitive practices of American business ever conducted. When it concluded in 1941, the TNEC hearings filled a small bookshelf with thirty-seven volumes that covered every topic from cartels to life insurance and probed industries that ranged from petroleum to poultry. The committee's expert staff of economists, accountants, and statisticians produced forty-three monographs that likewise explored the structure and strategy of various sectors of the economy, but among the many recommendations made by the committee to Congress, only one, a revision of patent law, received any legislative attention as the country entered World War II. In short, the TNEC produced a treasure trove of information about the nation's economy, but its policy implications were nil. Roosevelt's message to Congress in 1938 urging an antitrust inquiry arose from his own frustrations about economic policy in the midst of a sharp economic recession that his critics had dubbed "Roosevelt's recession." Still intellectually wedded to the concepts embedded in the NIRA, FDR also knew that a revival of that approach stood little chance of gaining support in Congress. He has also become persuaded by advisers such as Harry Hopkins, Lauchlin Currie, Benjamin Cohen, and Leon Keyserling that compensatory government spending combined with vigorous enforcement of the antitrust laws would break the economic stalemate. In addition, popular hostility to monopoly had deep roots in American political culture that the president could exploit and deflect criticism from the administration's less-than-successful policies. Led by Senator Joseph O'Mahoney of Wyoming, Congress made certain that it shared the spotlight with the executive branch when it came to membership on the TNEC. Three senators and three congressmen served along with representatives from the Securities and Exchange Commission, the Federal Trade Commission, and the Departments of Justice, Treasury, Commerce, and Labor. Professionally, the committee included lawyers (nine in all), economists, an engineer, and five university professors. Events at home and abroad quickly rendered the TNEC hearings less and less relevant to the nation's economic destiny. While rhetorically attacking big business for anticompetitive behavior, FDR began to lay the foundation for closer ties between business and government that reached fruition during the war. By 1940 he had courted them through the formation of a Business Advisory

Council and with appointments to various war agencies. And as federal defense contracts began to fatten paychecks and corporate profits as early as the winter of 1939–1940, an antitrust crusade did not appear to be an effective instrument for promoting full production and employment.

Tennessee Valley Authority (TVA)

Beginning in the administration of Theodore Roosevelt, who created an Inland Waterways Commission that put forth proposals for the comprehensive development of the nation's major rivers through multipurpose projects that included flood control, improved navigation, and the development of hydro-electric projects, progressive voices at the federal level had never abandoned the dream of such a grand national program. During World War I, the federal government began the construction of two dams and nitrate plants at Muscle Shoals, Alabama, a strategic spot on the Tennessee River where the river drops over 140 feet in a thirty-mile stretch. But the sudden end to the war left the facilities unfinished and Republican administrations in the 1920s attempted to sell the property to various private developers, including Henry Ford. Those efforts were blocked by Senator George Norris of Nebraska, who envisioned the development of cheap electric power at Muscle Shoals and government-operated fertilizer plants that could aid American farmers. But Presidents Coolidge and Hoover also exercised the veto power over Norris's attempt to put federal dollars again into a Muscle Shoals project. That changed when Norris gained the backing of Roosevelt, a longtime supporter of public power in New York state, who backed his legislation in Congress and signed legislation creating the Tennessee Valley Authority in April 1933. The TVA statute authorized a three-person board who would run the independent agency with a mandate to improve the navigability of the river, provide flood control, operate hydro-electric facilities, engage in reforestation, and encourage the industrial and agricultural development of the entire region. The strongest and most sustained opposition to TVA came, of course, from private utilities that feared competition from a federal agency, although they had done little before 1933 to bring power to areas outside the region's largest cities. Southern businessmen and farmers, on the other hand, saw the agency as a potential engine of economic growth, one capable of spurring its industrial development and overcoming the region's grinding poverty. Roosevelt's initial appointments to the TVA board, however, ensured a divided strategy and bitter conflict among the three men chosen to lead this experiment in regional development—Arthur Morgan, the former president of Antioch College, who foresaw the potential for a harmonious relationship between the agency and private business, including the utilities; Harcourt Morgan, who wished to focus TVA's energies upon aid to commercial agriculture; and David Lilienthal, a protege of Felix Frankfurter and Justice Brandeis, who advocated a bold expansion of TVA's electric power production even at the risk of a prolonged legal war with the industry. By 1938, as Harcourt Morgan and Lilienthal formed an alliance against what they regarded as Arthur Morgan's utopianism, the bureaucratic infighting had become so brutal and so public that FDR fired Arthur Morgan. By default the president gave a green light to the imperial plans of Harcourt Morgan and Lilienthal, plans that by that date fit the New Deal's need for enlarged public spending in the face of recession and impending war abroad. Backed by skillful lawyering and federal funds flowing from Harold Ickes's PWA to many municipal power companies, Lilienthal won major battles against the private utilities led by Wendell Willkie and his Commonwealth and Southern Company. By 1938, operating nine main river dams and others along tributaries, the TVA had become the largest producer of electric power in the United States. In addition, the agency built model cities, constructed extensive flood control projects along the Tennessee River and its tributaries, manufactured chemicals for fertilizer, and ran experimental farms to bring the benefits of soil and seed science to the region's farmers. More than any other single New Deal program, the Tennessee Valley Authority brought a rising standard of living to the more than 3 million Southerners touched by its myriad projects. Within fifty years, as the industrial appetite of the Tennessee Valley steadily grew, the agency produced 120 billion kilowatt-hours per year and had a gross income from power sales in excess of $3 billion. And to meet this growing demand, the agency began to operate coal-fired and nuclear-powered plants that raised the ire of environmental activists who singled out the TVA as the region's chief source of air and water pollution.

Twenty-First Amendment

The Democratic Party had long been bitterly divided between opponents of national prohibition, many of them representing immigrant constituencies, and dedicated foes of alcohol, most of whom resided in rural areas of the South and Midwest. That division between the so-called wets, symbolized by New York governor Al Smith, and the drys, led by the spiritual heirs of Williams Jennings Bryan, had helped to paralyze the party at its 1924 national convention where it required 103 ballots to choose a presidential candidate under the party's two-thirds rule. By 1931, however, the social and political tides turned against the Eighteenth Amendment and the Volstead Act that enforced it. A distinguished panel of legal experts, chaired by former Attorney General George Wickersham, found that the costs of prohibition outweighed its benefits. The Volstead Act, they argued, encouraged disrespect for law because so many citizens flouted it. It promoted lawlessness by the police who often used illegal methods to track down and arrest violators, and it had placed an intolerable burden on federal courts, swamped with prohibition cases that crowded out important civil litigation. The Wickersham Committee could not gain a majority for a single solution, but the

Democratic Party's 1932 platform advocated repeal of the Eighteenth Amendment. After the party won the 1932 election, the lame-duck Congress submitted the proposed amendment to the states. It repealed the prohibition amendment but made it illegal to transport or import into any state, territory, or possession of the United States any intoxicating liquor in violation of local laws. This became the first amendment to the Constitution submitted by Congress for ratification by conventions in the states rather than by state legislatures. That procedure enhanced the votes of the "wets," ratification came quickly and the Twenty-first Amendment became a part of the Constitution on December 5, 1933.

Wagner, Robert F.

No member of Congress during the depression era surpassed Wagner's grasp of unemployment, economic security, and labor issues and none brought forth more fertile legislative proposals for confronting them. Born in Germany in 1877, Wagner and his family came to New York City when he was eight. Like Franklin Roosevelt and Alfred E. Smith, his political fortunes flourished with the rise of immigrant and labor constituencies in the Empire State following his first election to the state legislature in 1904. Elevated to leadership in the state senate by 1911, Wagner teamed up with Smith, then speaker of the assembly, to create the New York Factory Investigating Committee that successfully pushed labor reforms through the legislature on the eve of World War I. Elected to the United States Senate in 1926, he became the most effective spokesman for greater federal aid to the unemployed as the depression deepened after 1930. In the winter of 1931, for example, he put forward a plan for a $2 billion emergency public works program, which Congress reduced to $1.5 billion and restricted to self-liquidating projects, but the measure formed the basis for Hoover's Emergency Relief and Construction Act a year later. As private charities, cites, and states ran out of money to provide relief, Wagner sponsored the Federal Emergency Relief Act of 1933 that provided grants, not loans, to the states for relief purposes. Wagner's fingerprints could be found on various sections of the New Deal's National Recovery Act in 1933, especially the $3.3 billion provided for public works and Section 7(a) designed to protect union membership and collective bargaining. Roosevelt turned to Wagner to chair the National Labor Board created to enforce Section 7(a), where he forcefully advocated the principle of majority rule to govern union representation decisions. However, Wagner found himself undermined by the NRA's top administrators and Roosevelt, who sought to pacify employers with a commitment to proportional representation. Lacking support from the White House, Wagner nonetheless pushed ahead with legislation to create an independent labor board with greater enforcement powers and when the Supreme Court struck down the National Recovery Act, even FDR finally endorsed what became the National Labor Relations

Act of 1935, also known as the Wagner Act. As early as 1932, Wagner had begun to sponsor an unemployment compensation plan and led congressional efforts to provide a pension system for railway workers, a statute initially invalidated by the Supreme Court in the *Alton* decision of 1935. Based on this experience, he became—along with Congressman David Lewis of Maryland—a major contributor to the Social Security Act of 1935. The Wagner-Lewis bill, first introduced in 1934, became the basis for the unemployment compensation provisions of the Social Security Act that Wagner introduced on behalf of the administration.

Riding the crest of his 1935 legislative achievements, Wagner next turned all of his energies to gaining support for a federal housing program, a goal he had sought as early as the National Industrial Recovery Act. By 1937, working with Congressmen Henry Ellenbogen and Henry Steagall, he guided through Congress the legislation creating the United States Housing Authority.

Wallace, Henry Agard

Farmer, journalist, plant geneticist, politician, Wallace became by 1940—when Roosevelt tapped him to be his vice presidential running mate—the hope of many New Dealers for the continued growth and expansion of liberalism into the American future. While Henry Luce, publisher of *Time* magazine, predicted "an American century" on the eve of Pearl Harbor, Wallace called for "the century of the common man." Agricultural politics and the plight of America's farmers colored Wallace's life virtually from his birth in Adair County, Iowa, in 1888 as the son of Henry Cantwell Wallace, editor of the influential farm journal, *Wallace's Farmer*, and a future secretary of agriculture in the Republican administrations of Harding and Coolidge. After graduating from Iowa State College in 1910, the younger Wallace joined his father's publication and became senior editor of the journal by 1924, later changing its name to *Iowa Homestead and Wallace's Farmer*. At this same time, pursuing a boyhood enthusiasm for the scientific study of plants, he also produced the first successful hybrid seed corn for commercial use and founded the Hi-Bred Seed Company over which he presided as president until joining the New Deal in 1933. By then, his fame as a plant geneticist equaled his influence as a spokesman for commercial farmers. The genetic revolution in agriculture that Wallace helped to foster contributed ironically to the economic crisis afflicting American farmers in the 1920s—farm productivity exceeded consumer demand, which contributed to falling prices for basic commodities on the world market and left American producers trapped between high fixed costs and declining revenues. Millions of acres of marginal farm land were taken out of production between 1919 and 1930, but the per acre yield of crops such as corn and wheat, due to plant genetics and soil science, tripled and quadrupled output. Abundance on the farm put the economic squeeze on farmers. Wallace became one of the principle advocates of increased government intervention to boost farm prices, a policy that challenged the prevailing ideology of free enterprise even among many agricultural producers. He lobbied hard during the Coolidge-Hoover era for legislation embodied in the McNary-Haugen bill, a measure backed by the Farm Bureau Federation, which called upon the federal government to raise the domestic price of basic commodities, dump the surplus abroad, and levy a small tax on farmers to finance the anticipated government deficit. Coolidge and Hoover vehemently opposed the legislation, and even those friendly to it noted that it contained a fatal defect: no incentives were offered for farmers to curb production. Republican opposition to McNary-Haugen prompted Wallace's conversion to the Democratic Party and he supported Al Smith against Hoover in 1928 and backed Roosevelt in 1932. He became the logical choice to head the Department of Agriculture in the New Deal and assumed leadership of the administration's initial farm programs, especially the Agricultural Adjustment Act, which put him almost immediately at the center of intense bureaucratic infighting and constant political controversy. With the 1933 crops already planted and the fear of more surpluses on the horizon, Wallace ordered the destruction of 10 million acres of cotton and the slaughter of 6 million baby pigs, decisions, he said, that exposed the moral bankruptcy of an economic system that simultaneously permitted farmers to go broke and other people to go hungry. When young, idealistic lawyers in the general counsel's office of the Triple A attempted to aid tenant farmers and sharecroppers threatened with eviction due to the acreage reduction plan central to the new policy, Wallace sided with those, including Roosevelt, who did not wish to rock the agricultural boat and removed the offending lawyers. He also found himself locked in a battle with the first administrative chief of the AAA, George Peek, a devoted supporter of the discredited McNary-Haugen plan, who loathed production controls and did everything possible to subvert the program he had been appointed to run. Wallace won that battle, too, when FDR found another assignment for Peek, soon a bitter critic of Wallace and the New Deal, which he accused of bringing communism to the countryside. Wallace could not defeat the United States Supreme Court, however, which struck down the Triple A in the *Butler* decision (1936) and forced the administration to find another constitutional route to managing the nation's agriculture. Under Wallace's guidance, Congress quickly passed the Soil Conservation and Domestic Allotment Act of 1936, which dressed up acreage controls in the garb of conservation and offered government payments to farmers who agreed to plant crops like soybeans rather than corn, cotton, or tobacco. Even that statute could not bring the productive bounty of American farmers under control, which spurred Wallace to push for the passage of the second Agricultural Adjustment Act in 1938. This law, the basis of American farm policy for a generation, revived many features of the original AAA statute: extending conservation payments, adopting mandatory marketing quotas enforced by means of taxation, and offering farmers more crop loans and crop insurance. Wallace sought to gain broad public support for the program by attaching the label to it of “the every-normal granary,” which, he argued, would store up surpluses and raise farm prices at government expense when crops were bountiful and assure consumers a plentiful supply of food at times of agricultural distress. But even Wallace failed to grasp the enormity of the surplus problem, which grew larger and larger on the eve of World War II. That curse became a blessing, however, as the bulging American warehouses and grain elevators subsidized by the Commodity Credit Corporation became as vital to the nation’s victory over Germany and Japan as the tanks and ships rolling off the assembly lines in Detroit and Seattle. In 1940, with the support of the most liberal New Dealers, including the president’s wife, Wallace became Roosevelt’s vice presidential candidate, a boon to the ticket that had to win against two other Midwesterners, Wendell Willkie and Charles McNary. During the war, he served effectively as chairman of the Board of Economic Warfare. Dropped from the national ticket in 1944 when Southerners and party regulars forced the president to go with a more conservative candidate, Senator Harry Truman of Missouri, Wallace was shuffled off to the obscurity of the Department of Commerce in 1945. From that post he launched public criticism of President Truman’s negotiations with the Soviet Union and was forced to resign in 1946. Two years later, running on the Progressive Party ticket, an organization dominated by the American Communist Party, he challenged Truman, but ran a disappointing third behind the incumbent and Republican Thomas E. Dewey.

Willkie, Wendell L.

Born in Elwood, Indiana, in 1892, Willkie earned his undergraduate and law degrees from Indiana University in 1913 and 1916 and soon joined the legal department of the Firestone Tire and Rubber Company in Akron, Ohio. A Wilson Democrat in those days, Willkie supported the president’s plan for American membership in the League of Nations, spoke out against the influence of the Ku Klux Klan in the party’s affairs, and supported New York governor Al Smith for the presidency in both 1924 and 1928. Beginning in 1929 when he moved to New York, Willkie became identified with the economic and political interests of the electric utilities industry as a partner in the firm of Weadock and Willkie. He handled legal affairs for the Commonwealth and Southern Corporation, one of the largest holding companies in the United States with extensive properties throughout the South Atlantic and Deep South region. In the year that FDR entered the White House, Willkie became president of the company and soon found himself locked in legal combat with the administration over the activities of the Tennessee Valley Authority, the Public Works Administration, and enforcement of the Public Utilities Holding Company Act—all of which threatened his company’s domination of urban and rural markets in the South. Willkie could delay but not stop the eventual triumph of public power and gained national recognition with his criticism of the New Deal, which he blamed for throttling business initiative and running up the public debt. Switching his party allegiance to the Republicans, he backed Governor Landon's candidacy in 1936 and made himself available for the party's nod four years later. Energetic, handsome, and a decent orator, Willkie became the darling of Henry Luce, influential publisher of *Time* magazine, and other Republicans who sought an attractive candidate to oppose Roosevelt's bid for a third term. Mobilizing a group of youthful and enthusiastic supporters, Willkie and his managers took the national convention by storm and defeated New York governor Thomas E. Dewey on the sixth ballot. Unfairly labeled as a Wall Street reactionary by Roosevelt's campaign entourage, Willkie showed strength in early polls against the president, but events in Europe, especially the Nazi conquest of France in the summer of 1940, combined with rising employment figures, doomed his chances. When Americans cast their ballots in November, FDR defeated Willkie by over 5 million popular votes and crushed him in the electoral college, 449 to 82. Willkie died of heart failure four years later, but not before demonstrating his Wilsonian roots by supporting Roosevelt's policy of aiding Great Britain's struggle against Hitler, notably the Lend-Lease legislation of 1941.

References and Further Reading

Asbell, Bernard. 1961. *When F. D. R. Died.* New York: Holt, Rinehart and Winston.

Blum, John M. 1959. *From the Morgenthau Diaries: Years of Crisis 1928–1938.* Boston: Houghton Mifflin.

Cooper, John M., Jr. 1990. *Pivotal Decades: The United States 1900–1920.* New York: Norton.

Cushman, Barry. 1998. *Rethinking the New Deal Court: The Structure of a Constitutional Revolution.* New York: Oxford University Press.

Gunther, Gerald, and Noel T. Dowling. 1970. *Cases and Materials on Constitutional Law.* 8th ed. Mineola, NY: Foundation Press.

Hamby, Alonzo. 1992. *Liberalism and Its Challengers: From FDR to Bush.* New York: Oxford University Press.

Kennedy, David M. 1999. *Freedom from Fear: The American People in Depression and War.* New York: Oxford University Press.

Klehr, Harvey, John Earl Haynes, and Kyrill M. Anderson, eds. 1998. *The Soviet World of American Communism.* New Haven, CT: Yale University Press.

Leuchtenburg, William E. 1963. *Franklin D. Roosevelt and the New Deal, 1932–1940.* New York: Harper & Row.

Morgan, Ted. 1985. *FDR: A Biography.* New York: Simon and Schuster.

Parmet, Herbert S. 1980. *Jack: The Struggles of John F. Kennedy.* New York: The Dial Press.

Parrish, Michael. 1970. *Securities Regulation and the New Deal.* New Haven, CT: Yale University Press.

———. 1982. *Felix Frankfurter and His Times: The Reform Years.* New York: Free Press.

———. 1992. *Anxious Decades: America in Prosperity and Depression, 1920–1941.* New York: Norton.

Schlesinger, Arthur M., Jr. 1958. *The Age of Roosevelt: The Coming of the New Deal.* Boston: Houghton Mifflin.

———. 1960. *The Age of Roosevelt: The Politics of Upheaval.* Boston: Houghton Mifflin.

Chronology

1930 Chief Justice William Howard Taft retires.

Charles Evans Hughes is nominated by President Hoover to be chief justice and confirmed by the Senate.

Associate Justice Edward Terry Sanford dies.

Federal Judge John J. Parker is nominated by President Hoover to fill Sanford's seat on the Court, but his confirmation is defeated in the Senate, thirty-nine to forty-one.

Owen J. Roberts is nominated by President Hoover and confirmed by the Senate.

Democrats win control of Congress for the first time since 1916.
More than 1,300 banks close by the end of the year, including all sixty branches of the United States Bank.

1931 *Stromberg v. California* is decided, holding that a state violates the First Amendment guarantee of free speech when it prosecutes persons who raise a red flag as a symbol of opposition to organized government.

Near v. Minnesota holds that a state law permitting an injunction against a newspaper that prints malicious or defamatory articles is a prior restraint of the press in violation of the First Amendment.

The Wickersham Commission, appointed by President Hoover, finds national prohibition ineffective.

Nine negro youths in Scottsboro, Alabama, are convicted of rape and sentenced to death.

Japan invades Manchuria.

President Hoover vetoes legislation to create a government-funded power plant at Muscle Shoals, Alabama.

1932 Associate Justice Oliver Wendell Holmes Jr. retires.

Benjamin N. Cardozo is nominated by President Hoover to fill Holmes's vacancy and is confirmed by the Senate.

Powell v. Alabama holds that under the particular circumstances of this case, including the age and education of the defendants and the capital charge of rape, the failure of the trial court to provide those charged with effective legal counsel constitutes a denial of due process.

Nixon v. Condon holds that the exclusion of African Americans from primary elections, a result arising from the actions of Texas's Democratic Party, denies them equal protection of the laws when the party functions as the agent of the state.

Wood v. Broom holds that absent statutory authority, federal courts cannot act to correct malapportionment in state districts. When Congress omitted from the Apportionment Act of 1929 the requirement that electoral districts for congressional elections be contiguous, compact, and equal, it repealed similar provisions in earlier laws.

Franklin D. Roosevelt is elected president of the United States.

The Norris-LaGuardia Act restricts the jurisdiction of federal courts in labor-management disputes.

World War I veterans, known as Bonus Marchers, are driven from Washington, D.C., by federal troops under General Douglas MacArthur. They sought early payment from Congress of their promised service bonus.

Adolf Hitler receives 32 percent of the vote for the presidency of Germany.

1933 In *Liggett Co. v. Lee* the Supreme Court holds that a portion of a state's taxation statute that imposes a higher levy upon stores conducting business in more than one county violates the Fourteenth Amendment's guarantee of equal protection of the laws.

Congress passes and President Roosevelt signs the Civilian Conservation Act, Federal Emergency Relief Act, Tennessee Valley Authority Act, Securities Act, National Industrial Recovery Act, and Agricultural Adjustment Act.

The Twenty-first Amendment to the U.S. Constitution is ratified, advancing inauguration day of the president from March 4 to January 20, thereby reducing the lame-duck period from election to inauguration.

Presidential Proclamation No. 2065 officially repeals the Eighteenth Amendment to the Constitution, which had prohibited the sale of alcohol throughout the nation.

Adolf Hitler becomes German Chancellor.

Germany and Japan withdraw from the League of Nations.

The United States resumes diplomatic and economic relations with the Soviet Union.

1934 In *Home Building & Loan Ass'n v. Blaisdell* the Supreme Court upholds the constitutionality of a state mortgage moratorium law against the challenge that it violates the ban on state actions impairing the obligations of contracts.

Nebbia v. New York rejects the concept of "business affected with a public interest" as the litmus test for determining what economic activities are subject to a state's police powers. The Court upholds a New York law that sets minimum prices for the sale of milk at retail.

Congress passes and President Roosevelt signs into law the Gold Reserve Act, the Home Owner's Loan Act, the Municipal Bankruptcy Act, the Railroad Retirement Act, the Federal Farm Bankruptcy Act, the Taylor Grazing Act, the Securities Exchange Act, and the Federal Communications Act.

Dust storms devastate large portions of the Great Plains and Midwest.

The first general strike in the United States paralyzes San Francisco.

Agents of the Federal Bureau of Investigation kill John Dillinger outside a Chicago theatre.

1935 In *Railroad Retirement Board v. Alton Railway Co.* the Supreme Court holds unconstitutional on Due Process and Commerce Clause grounds the Railroad Retirement Act of 1934, which created a mandatory pension program for railway employees. The plan, according to the majority, was not related to interstate commerce and the mandatory contributions required of employers deprived them of property without due process.

Schechter Poultry Corp. v. United States holds that Congress exceeded its powers to regulate commerce among the states when it enacted the National Industrial Recovery Act of 1933. Provisions allowing the president to approve or impose codes of fair competition under certain conditions delegated undefined legislative powers to the executive. Further, the law attempted to regulate activities, notably hours and wages, that affected interstate commerce only indirectly.

The Supreme Court's decision in the *Gold Clause Cases* sustains the power of Congress to regulate the value of currency, including the power to abrogate clauses in private contracts requiring payment in gold. But it also holds that the federal power to borrow money on the credit of the United States prohibits Congress from abrogating such clauses contained in government securities or other federal contracts, although the amount of damages recoverable against the government may be small.

In *Norris v. Alabama* the Supreme Court holds that the systematic exclusion of African Americans from both grand and trial juries denies to the accused equal protection of the laws and requires a new trial.

Panama Refining Co. v. Ryan is decided, holding invalid a provision of the National Industrial Recovery Act that authorizes the president to prohibit the interstate shipment of oil produced in violation of state quotas. This congressional delegation of authority to the president is too broad and leaves too much discretion to the chief executive.

In *Humphrey's Executor v. United States* the Supreme Court qualifies the broad removal power granted to the president in *Myers v. United States*

(1926). The Court denies the president the power to remove members of independent regulatory agencies without the consent of Congress.

In *Louisville Bank v. Radford* the Supreme Court holds unconstitutional the Frazier-Lemke Emergency Farm Mortgage Act of 1933 on the grounds that the law gave the debtor rights in property that had belonged to the creditor prior the statute's enactment, a violation of the just compensation provision of the Fifth Amendment.

Grovey v. Townsend holds that the Texas Democratic Party did not violate the Fourteenth Amendment when it barred African Americans from membership, thereby excluding them from voting in the party's primary elections. The Supreme Court says that a political party is a private association and the Fourteenth Amendment prohibits only discrimination mandated by the state.

Congress passes and Roosevelt signs into law the Soil Conservation Act, the Public Utilities Holding Company Act, the Guffey-Snyder Bituminous Coal Stabilization Act, the Emergency Relief Appropriation Act, the Social Security Act, and the National Labor Relations Act.

The Federal Arts, Music, Theatre, and Writers' Projects are established under the Works Progress Administration.

Senator Huey Long is assassinated in Louisiana.

Italy invades Ethiopia.

John L. Lewis and other labor dissidents organize the Committee for Industrial Organization (CIO).

Hitler denounces the Versailles Treaty and disarmament.

1936 In *United States v. Butler* the Supreme Court holds unconstitutional the Agricultural Adjustment Act of 1933 on the grounds that its taxing provisions sought to regulate a matter, agricultural production, outside the scope of federal authority.

Ashwander v. Tennessee Valley Authority upholds the statute authorizing the establishment of the Tennessee Valley Authority by sustaining the agency's right to enter into a contract for the sale of surplus electricity generated at one of its dams. Construction of the dam was within the Article I powers of Congress and the federal government had broad authority to dispose of its own property.

In *Jones v. Securities and Exchange Commission* the Supreme Court overturns an order of the SEC that imposed sanctions upon a registrant who attempted to withdraw his application to market securities once the agency questioned its truthfulness.

Carter v. Carter Coal Co. strikes down the Bituminous Coal Conservation Act of 1935 on the grounds that Congress had unconstitutionally delegated legislative power to private parties when it allowed a majority of coal mine operators to impose mandatory wage and hours standards for the entire industry. The majority of the Supreme Court also strikes down the labor provisions of the statute on the grounds that they had only an "indirect" effect upon interstate commerce.

In *Morehead v. New York ex rel. Tipaldo* the Supreme Court invalidates New York's minimum wage law for women and children workers on the grounds that such a regulation constitutes an unwarranted interference with freedom of contract.

Brown v. Mississippi holds that states may not use coerced confessions, obtained by means of torture, in the trial of an accused. Such involuntary statements employed for purposes of conviction violate due process.

In *Grosjean v. American Press Co.* a state law that imposes a gross receipts tax on certain newspapers but exempts others is found to be a prior restraint of publication prohibited by the First and Fourteenth Amendments.

In *United States v. Curtiss-Wright Export Corp.*, which describes the powers of the president in the conduct of foreign affairs as "plenary and exclusive," the Supreme Court sustains an act of Congress authorizing the president to embargo arms shipments to foreign belligerents. The plenary nature of the federal government's power over foreign affairs permits Congress greater latitude in delegating power to the president in international relations than in domestic affairs.

Congress passes and Roosevelt signs into law the Soil Conservation and Domestic Allotment Act, the Rural Electrification Act, the Walsh-Healey Public Contracts Act, and the Federal Anti-Price Discrimination Act (Robinson-Patman Act).

Franklin Roosevelt is reelected president.

German troops occupy the Rhineland.

Civil war begins in Spain.

"Sit-down" strikes begin at General Motors.

1937 President Roosevelt sends Judicial Procedures Reform bill to Congress. Critics call it FDR's "court-packing" plan and immediate opposition swells in Congress.

West Coast Hotel v. Parrish, sustaining a minimum wage law from the state of Washington, is decided by the Supreme Court. The Court overrules *Adkins v. Children's Hospital* (1923), which had held such regulations to be a violation of freedom of contract protected by the Due Process Clause.

In *National Labor Relations Board v. Jones & Laughlin Steel Corp.* the Supreme Court upholds the National Labor Relations Act of 1935 on the grounds that the federal power to regulate commerce among the states permits Congress to regulate intrastate matters that directly burden or obstruct that commerce. Here the Court finds that a labor dispute between management and employees that threatened to shut down the company's large Pennsylvania plant thereby disrupted interstate commerce.

The Supreme Court decides *Steward Machine Co. v. Davis*, holding that a system to induce employers to join a federal unemployment compensation program by taxing them and then giving those who participate a tax credit is a valid exercise of the taxing and spending powers given to Congress in Article I of the Constitution.

The Supreme Court's ruling in *Helvering v. Davis* sustains the old-age retirement portion of the Social Security Act of 1935. A statute that places a tax on employers and employees with the revenue going to pay benefits to retired persons is a constitutional exercise of the power to tax and spend for the general welfare.

Palko v. Connecticut rules that the Due Process Clause of the Fourteenth Amendment does not require the states to observe the double jeopardy guarantee of the Fifth Amendment. The Due Process Clause protects only those rights deemed "fundamental" such as freedom of speech and press, and the promise that one will not be tried twice for the same offense is "not of the very essence of a scheme of ordered liberty."

In *DeJonge v. Oregon* the Court holds that the First and Fourteenth Amendments prohibit a state from making it a crime to organize and participate in a meeting at which no illegal action is discussed, even when the meeting is held under the auspices of an organization with the professed goal of overthrowing the government. For the first time the Court recognizes that the right of assembly is protected by the Fourteenth as well as the First Amendment.

Breedlove v. Suttles upholds a Georgia law that requires all inhabitants of the state between the ages of twenty-one and sixty to pay an annual poll tax of one dollar. Such a levy does not violate the Fourteenth Amendment or constitute racial discrimination in voting prohibited by the Fifteenth Amendment, according to the Supreme Court.

Congress passes and Roosevelt signs into law the Guffey-Vinson Bituminous Coal Act, a new Railroad Retirement Act, the Bankhead-Jones Farm Tenancy Act, the Wagner-Steagall Housing Act, and the Judicial Procedures Reform Act. The latter, branded the "court-packing" plan, is a watered-down version of Roosevelt's initial proposal.

"Sit-down" strikes close fifteen General Motors plants.

Associate Justice Willis Van Devanter retires.

Hugo L. Black is nominated by President Roosevelt to fill the vacancy left by Van Devanter and is confirmed by the Senate.

The United States Steel Corporation and United Steel Workers Union sign a labor agreement.

Amelia Earhart, attempting to fly around the world, vanishes over the Pacific.

1938 Associate Justice George Sutherland retires.

Stanley F. Reed is nominated by President Roosevelt to fill Sutherland's position. He is confirmed by the Senate.

The Supreme Court decides *Missouri ex rel. Gaines v. Canada*, which holds that a state denies equal protection of the laws to an African American student when it refuses him admission to its all-white law school, even though the state offers to pay his tuition to any institution in a nearby state.

In *Lovell v. City of Griffin*, a city ordinance that prohibits the circulation on public streets of handbills or literature of any kind without written permission from the city manager is found to be an unconstitutional prior restraint on freedom of the press.

The Supreme Court decides *Johnson v. Zerbst*, holding that the Sixth Amendment guarantee of a right to counsel means that the federal courts may not deprive anyone of life or liberty unless he or she has been provided with an attorney at trial or has explicitly waived that right to aid.

Congress passes and President Roosevelt signs into law the second Agricultural Adjustment Act, the Fair Labor Standards Act, and amendments to the federal Food and Drug laws.

Congress establishes the Temporary National Economic Committee to investigate the effectiveness of the antitrust laws.

Congress creates the House Committee on Un-American Activities (HUAC).

Germany invades Austria.

The Munich Pact cedes part of Czechoslovakia to Germany.

1939 An ailing Justice Benjamin Cardozo dies.

Felix Frankfurter is nominated by President Roosevelt to fill Cardozo's spot and is confirmed by the Senate.

Justice Brandeis retires.

William O. Douglas is nominated by President Roosevelt for Brandeis's place and is confirmed by the Senate.

The Court decides *Mulford v. Smith*, sustaining the second Agricultural Adjustment Act against the challenge that the marketing quotas limited production, an activity over which Congress has no authority. The Court rules that Congress has the authority to limit the amount of any commodity shipped in interstate commerce and may impose taxes to accomplish that objective.

Coleman v. Miller rules that it is the responsibility of Congress, not the Supreme Court, to resolve "political questions" such as the "reasonable" time period for the ratification by the states of a proposed constitutional amendment and whether a state that has rejected an amendment may later change its mind and ratify.

In *Hague v. Congress of Industrial Organizations* the Supreme Court rules that the right to speak and assemble in public may not be arbitrarily prohibited by federal, state, or local governments, whether this right derives from the privileges and immunities of national citizenship or from the guarantees of the First and Fourteenth Amendments.

Graves v. New York ex rel. O'Keefe overrules two venerable decisions from the nineteenth century that held the income of state and federal government employees immune to taxation by the nonemploying government body.

In *Lane v. Wilson* the Court invalidates a second attempt by Oklahoma to maintain a racially discriminatory system of voter registration. In 1915 the Court had invalidated that state's "grandfather clause" that exempted from registration requirements all those registered prior to the enfranchisement of African Americans. The state legislature then adopted a new registration law that continued to exempt all those registered while the "grandfather clause" remained in effect in 1914. This, too, the Court rules violated the Fifteenth Amendment ban on racial discrimination.

Congress passes and President Roosevelt signs the Hatch Act and the Reorganization Act creating the Federal Loan Agency, the Federal Security Agency, the Federal Works Agency, and the National Resources Planning Board.

Fascists under General Franco win the civil war in Spain.

Germany invades Poland.

Great Britain declares war on Germany and sends 150,000 troops to France.

Germany and the Soviet Union sign a nonaggression pact.

Congress amends neutrality laws permitting Britain and France to buy arms in the United States on a "cash and carry" basis.

1940 Associate Justice Pierce Butler dies.

Frank Murphy is nominated by President Roosevelt to fill Butler's seat. He is confirmed by the Senate.

Cantwell v. Connecticut holds that the states may limit the free exercise of religion only when the statutes are narrowly drawn and applied in a nondiscriminatory manner. A state may not convict a sidewalk preacher for "breach of the peace" under a general statute that sweeps "a great variety of conduct under a general and indefinite characterization."

In *Minersville School District v. Gobitis* the Supreme Court sustains a mandatory flag salute required of all school children against the challenge that it violates the free exercise of religion. Religious liberty, writes the majority, must give way to political authority so long as the latter is not used to propagate or restrict religion.

Sunshine Anthracite Coal Co. v. Adkins holds that the use of the taxing power as a penalty is an appropriate means for Congress to use in regulating interstate commerce. The justices sustain the second Coal Conservation Act, which places a high tax on coal shipped interstate, but exempts from payment those producers who agree to industrywide price and competition regulations.

In *Thornhill v. Alabama* the Court invalidates a state law that prohibits all manners of picketing. The Court for the first time gives picketing First Amendment protection. The law at issue did not regulate specific aspects of labor demonstrations, such as the number of pickets, but banned every practicable method whereby the facts of a labor dispute might be publicized.

Congress passes and President Roosevelt signs a second Hatch Act restricting the political activities of federal employees.

Roosevelt asks Congress for a record $1.8 billion for national defense.

Winston Churchill becomes prime minister of Great Britain.

Germany conquers France and begins daily aerial bombardment of England.

Roosevelt wins a third term by defeating Wendell Willkie.

The United States gives Great Britain fifty destroyers in exchange for naval bases.

Germany, Japan, and Italy sign a ten-year Axis Pact.

1941 Charles Evans Hughes retires as chief justice of the United States Supreme Court.

President Roosevelt nominates Harlan Fiske Stone as chief justice. He is confirmed by the Senate.

Roosevelt nominates Robert H. Jackson to replace Stone, and he is confirmed by the Senate.

Justice James C. McReynolds retires.

James F. Byrnes is nominated by President Roosevelt to the vacancy left by McReynolds. He is confirmed by the Senate.

In *United States v. Darby Lumber Co.* the Supreme Court upholds the Fair Labor Standards Act of 1938, ruling that Congress has the authority to prohibit the shipment in interstate commerce of any goods manufactured in violation of federally mandated minimum wage and maximum hours standards. The Court overrules *Hammer v. Dagenhart* (1918).

Cox v. New Hampshire holds that the First Amendment guarantee of freedom of speech does not bar states from setting the time, place, and manner of parades or other demonstrations on public streets in order to maintain public safety. But such regulations must be narrowly drawn and applied in a nondiscriminatory fashion.

President Roosevelt issues Executive Order 8802 to establish a Fair Employment Practices Committee and to prohibit discrimination on the grounds of race, color, creed, or national origin in federal contracts.

Congress passes the Lend-Lease Act, providing military aid to Great Britain.

Germany invades the Soviet Union.

President Roosevelt embargoes oil and scrap metal to Japan.

One hundred crew members die as the United States destroyer *Reuben James* is sunk off the coast of Iceland.

Japan attacks Pearl Harbor.

Table of Cases

Adair v. United States, 208 U.S. 161 (1908)
Adams v. Tanner, 244 U.S. 590 (1917)
Adams Manufacturing Co. v. Storen, 304 U.S. 307 (1938)
Adamson v. California, 332 U.X. 784 (1947)
Adkins v. Children's Hospital, 261 U.S. 525 (1923)
Aetna Life Insurance Co. v. Haworth, 300 U.S. 277 (1937)
Alabama Power Co. v. Ickes, 302 U.S. 464 (1938)
Allgeyer v. Louisiana, 165 U.S. 578 (1897)
Arizona v. California, 283 U.S. 423 (1931)
Arizona Publishing Co. v. O'Neil, 304 U.S. 543 (1938)
Ashton v. Cameron County Water District, 298 U.S. 513 (1936)
Ashwander v. Tennessee Valley Authority, 297 U.S. 288 (1936)
Associated Press v. National Labor Relations Board, 301 U.S. 103 (1937)
Bailey v. Alabama, 219 U.S. 219 (1911)
Bailey v. Drexel Furniture Co., 259 U.S. 20 (1922)
Baldwin v. G.A.F. Seelig, Inc., 294 U.S. 511 (1935)
Baldwin v. Missouri, 281 U.S. 586 (1930)
Barber v. Minnesota, 136 U.S. 313 (1890)
Bartles v. Iowa, 263 U.S. 412 (1923)
Belmont v. United States, 301 U.S. 324 (1937)
Benton v. Maryland, 395 U.S. 784 (1969)
Betts v. Brady, 316 U.S. 455 (1942)
Black and White Taxicab Co. v. Brown and Yellow Taxicab Co., 276 U.S. 518 (1928)
Block v. Hirsh, 256 U.S. 135 (1921)
Booth v. United States, 291 U.S. 339 (1934)
Borden's Farm Products v. Ten Eyck, 297 U.S. 251 (1936)
Bradley v. Public Utilities Commission, 289 U.S. 92 (1933)
Brandenberg v. Ohio, 395 U.S. 444 (1969)
Breedlove v. Suttles, 302 U.S. 277 (1937)
Bridges v. California, 314 U.S. 252 (1941)

Brig Aurora, The v. United States, 7 Cranch 382 (1813)
Brown v. Board of Education, 347 U.S. 483 (1954)
Brown v. Mississippi, 297 U.S. 278 (1936)
Buck v. Bell, 274 U.S. 200 (1927)
Buttfield v. Stranahan, 192 U.S. 470 (1904)
Cantwell v. Connecticut, 310 U.S. 296 (1940)
Carroll v. United States, 267 U.S. 132 (1925)
Carter v. Carter Coal Co., 298 U.S. 238 (1936)
Chambers v. Florida, 309 U.S. 227 (1940)
Champion v. Ames, 188 U.S. 321 (1903)
Chaplinsky v. New Hampshire, 315 U.S. 568 (1942)
Chicago Board of Trade v. Olson, 262 U.S. 1 (1923)
Chicago, Burlington & Quincy Railroad Co. v. City of Chicago, 166 U.S. 226 (1897)
Chicago, Burlington & Quincy Railroad Co. v. McGuire, 219 U.S. 549 (1911)
Chicago Sanitary District v. United States, 266 U.S. 405 (1925)
Clark Distilling Co. v. West Maryland Railway Co., 242 U.S. 311 (1917)
Coleman v. Miller, 307 U.S. 433 (1939)
Colgate v. Harvey, 296 U.S. 404 (1935)
Collector v. Day, 11 Wall 113 (1871)
Connecticut General Life Insurance Co. v. Johnson, 303 U.S. 77 (1938)
Consolidated Edison Co. v. National Labor Relations Board, 305 U.S. 197 (1938)
Coppage v. Kansas, 236 U.S. 1 (1915)
Coronado Coal Co. v. United Mine Workers, 268 U.S. 295 (1925)
Corrigan v. Buckley, 271 U.S. 323 (1926)
Cox v. New Hampshire, 312 U.S. 659 (1941)
Crowell v. Benson, 285 U.S. 22 (1932)
Currin v. Wallace, 306 U.S. 1 (1939)
Dartmouth College v. Woodward, 4 Wheaton 519 (1819)
Davis v. Beason, 133 U.S. 333 (1890)
Debs, In re, 158 U.S. 564 (1895)
DeJonge v. Oregon, 229 U.S. 353 (1937)
Dennis v. United States, 341 U.S. 494 (1951)
DiSanto v. Pennsylvania, 273 U.S. 34 (1927)
Dobbins v. Erie County, 16 Pet. 232 (1842)
Donham v. West-Nelson Manufacturing Co., 273 U.S. 657 (1927)
[Dred] Scott v. Sandford, 19 Howard 393 (1857)
Dunn v. United States, 284 U.S. 390 (1932)
Electric Bond & Share Co. v. Securities and Exchange Commission, 303 U.S. 419 (1939)

Employers' Liability Cases (I), 207. U.S. 463 (1908)
Employers' Liability Cases (II), 223 U.S. 1 (1912)
Erie Railroad Co. v. Tompkins, 304 U.S. 64 (1938)
Euclid v. Ambler Realty Co., 272 U.S. 365 (1926)
Falbo v. United States, 320 U.S. 209 (1943)
Fay v. Noia, 372 U.S. 391 (1963)
Federal Communications Commission v. Sanders Bros. Radio Station, 309 U.S. 470 (1940)
Federal Power Commission v. Hope Natural Gas, 320 U.S. 551 (1944)
Federal Power Commission v. Natural Gas Pipleline, 315 U.S. 575 (1942)
Ferguson v. Skrupa, 372 U.S. 726 (1963)
Field v. Clark, 143 U.S. 649 (1892)
First National Bank v. Fellows, 244 U.S. 416 (1917)
Fiske v. Kansas, 274 U.S. 380 (1927)
Fletcher v. Peck, 6 Cranch 87 (1810)
Frank v. Mangum, 237 U.S. 309 (1915)
Freeman v. Hewit, 329 U.S. 249 (1946)
Frost v. Corporation Commission, 278 U.S. 515 (1929)
Frothingham v. Mellon, 262 U.S. 447 (1923)
Gelfert v. National City Bank, 313 U.S. 221 (1941)
Gideon v. Wainwright, 372 U.S. 335 (1963)
Gilbert v. Minnesota, 254 U.S. 325 (1920)
Giragi v. Moore, 301 U.S. 670 (1937)
Girouard v. United States, 328 U.S. 61 (1946)
Gitlow v. New York, 268 U.S. 652 (1925)
Gold Clause Cases: (Norman v. Baltimore & Ohio Railroad Co.; Nortz v. United States; Perry v. United States), 294 U.S. 240 (1935)
Goldman v. United States, 316 U.S. 129 (1942)
Goldstein v. United States, 316 U.S. 114 (1942)
Graves v. New York ex rel. O'Keefe, 306 U.S. 466 (1939)
Griswold v. Connecticut, 381 U.S. 479 (1965)
Grosjean v. American Press Co., 297 U.S. 233 (1936)
Grovey v. Townsend, 295 U.S. 45 (1935)
Gwin, White & Prince v. Henneford, 305 U.S. 434 (1939)
Hague v. Congress of Industrial Organizations, 307 U.S. 496 (1939)
Hale v. Bimco Trading, Inc., 306 U.S. 375 (1939)
Hamilton v. Regents of the University of California, 293 U.S. 245 (1934)
Hammer v. Dagenhart, 247 U.S. 251 (1918)
Henneford v. Silas Mason Co., 300 U.S. 577 (1937)
Herndon v. Lowry, 301 U.S. 242 (1937)

Hill v. Wallace, 259 U.S. 44 (1922)
Hines v. Davidowitz, 312 U.S. 52 (1941)
Hipolite Egg Co. v. United States, 220 U.S. 45 (1911)
Hirabayashi v. United States, 320 U.S. 81 (1943)
Hitchman Coal & Coke Co. v. Mitchell, 245 U.S. 229 (1917)
Holden v. Hardy, 169 U.S. 366 (1898)
Holyoke Water Power Co. v. American Writing Paper Co., 300 U.S. 324 (1937)
Home Building & Loan Ass'n v. Blaisdell, 290 U.S. 398 (1934)
Humphrey's Executor v. United States, 295 U.S. 602 (1935)
Hygrade Provision Co. v. Sherman, 266 U.S. 497 (1925)
Interstate Commerce Commission v. Brimson, 154 U.S. 447 (1894)
J. W. Hampton Jr. & Co. v. United States, 276 U.S. 394 (1928)
Jacobson v. Massachusetts, 197 U.S. 11 (1905)
Johnson v. Zerbst, 304 U.S. 458 (1938)
Jones v. Opelika, 316 U.S. 584 (1942)
Jones v. Securities and Exchange Commission, 298 U.S. 1 (1936)
Kelley v. Washington, 302 U.S. 1 (1937)
Kentucky Whip & Collar Co. v. Illinois Central Railroad Co., 299 U.S. 334 (1937)
Kidd v. Pearson, 128 U.S. 1 (1888)
Knickerbocker Ice Co. v. Stewart, 253 U.S. 149 (1920)
Korematsu v. United States, 323 U.S. 214 (1944)
Lane v. Wilson, 307 U.S. 268 (1939)
Lanzetta v. New Jersey, 306 U.S. 451 (1939)
Lauf v. E.G. Skinner & Co., 303 U.S. 315 (1938)
Liggett Co. v. Lee, 288 U.S. 517 (1933)
Lindsey v. Washington, 301 U.S. 397 (1937)
Lochner v. New York, 198 U.S. 45 (1905)
Louisville Bank v. Radford, 295 U.S. 555 (1935)
Louisville Bridge Co. v. United States, 242 U.S. 409 (1917)
Lovell v. City of Griffin, 303 U.S. 444 (1938)
Lynch v. United States, 292 U.S. 571 (1934)
Madden v. Kentucky, 309 U.S. 83 (1940)
Marbury v. Madison, 1 Cranch 137 (1803)
Massachusetts v. Mellon, 262 U.S. 447 (1923)
Maurer v. Hamilton, 309 U.S. 598 (1940)
Mayflower Farms v. Ten Eyck, 297 U.S. 266 (1936)
McCardle, Ex parte, 7 Wall 506 (1869)
McCarroll v. Dixie Greyhound Lines, 309 U.S. 176 (1940)
McCray v. United States, 195 U.S. 27 (1904)
McCulloch v. Maryland, 4 Wheat. 316 (1819)

McGoldrick v. Berwind-White Coal Mining Co., 309 U.S. 33 (1940)
Meyer v. Nebraska, 262 U.S. 390 (1923)
Milk Control Board v. Eisenburg Farm Products, 306 U.S. 346 (1939)
Milwaukee Social Democratic Publishing Co. v. Burleson, 255 U.S. 407 (1921)
Minersville School District v. Gobitis, 310 U.S. 586 (1940)
Minnesota v. Blasius, 290 U.S. 1 (1933)
Minnesota Rate Cases, 230 U.S. 252 (1913)
Miranda v. Arizona, 377 U.S. 201 (1966)
Missouri ex rel. Gaines v. Canada, 305 U.S. 337 (1938)
Mooney v. Holohan, 294 U.S. 103 (1935)
Moore v. Dempsey, 261 U.S. 86 (1923)
Morehead v. New York ex rel. Tipaldo, 298 U.S. 587 (1936)
Morey v. Doud, 354 U.S. 457 (1957)
Morgan v. United States, 298 U.S. 468 (1936)
Mortensen v. Security Insurance Co., 289 U.S. 702 (1933)
Mulford v. Smith, 307 U.S. 38 (1939)
Muller v. Oregon, 208 U.S. 412 (1908)
Munn v. Illinois, 94 U.S. 113 (1877)
Murphy v. Sardell, 269 U.S. 530 (1925)
Muskrat v. United States, 219 U.S. 346 (1911)
Myers v. Bethlehem Shipbuilding Corp., 303 U.S. 41 (1938)
Myers v. United States, 272 U.S. 52 (1926)
Nardone v. United States (I), 302 U.S. 379 (1937)
Nardone v. United States (II), 308 U.S. 338 (1939)
Nashville, Chattanooga & St. Louis Railway Co. v. Wallace, 288 U.S. 249 (1933)
National Labor Relations Board v. Fansteel Metallurgical Corporation, 306 U.S. 240 (1939)
National Labor Relations Board v. Friedman-Harry Marks Clothing Co., 301 U.S. 58 (1937)
National Labor Relations Board v. Fruehauf Trailer Co., 301 U.S. 49 (1937)
National Labor Relations Board v. Jones & Laughlin Steel Corp., 301 U.S. 1 (1937)
National Labor Relations Board v. Mackay Radio and Telegraph Company, 304 U.S. 333 (1938)
Near v. Minnesota, 283 U.S. 697 (1931)
Nebbia v. New York, 291 U.S. 502 (1934)
Nelson v. Sears Roebuck & Co., 312 U.S. 359 (1941)
New State Ice Co. v. Liebmann, 285 U.S. 262 (1932)
New York ex rel. Bryant v. Zimmerman, 278 U.S. 63 (1928)
New York Times v. Sullivan, 376 U.S. 254 (1964)
New York Times v. United States, 403 U.S. 713 (1971)

Newberry v. United States, 256 U.S. 232 (1921)
Nixon v. Condon, 286 U.S. 73 (1932)
Nixon v. Herndon, 273 U.S. 536 (1927)
Norris v. Alabama, 294 U.S. 587 (1935)
Norwegian Nitrogen Products Co. v. United States, 288 U.S. 294 (1933)
O'Gorman & Young v. Hartford Fire Insurance Co., 282 U.S. 251 (1931)
Oklahoma v. Atkinson Co., 313 U.S. 508 (1941)
Old Dearborn Distributing Co. v. Seagram Distillers Corp., 299 U.S. 183 (1936)
Olmstead v. United States, 277 U.S. 438 (1928)
Opp Cotton Mills v. Administrator of Wage and Hours Division, 312 U.S. 126 (1941)
Osborn v. Ozlin, 310 U.S. 53 (1940)
Palko v. Connecticut, 302 U.S. 319 (1937)
Panama Refining Co. v. Ryan, 293 U.S. 388 (1935)
Patton v. United States, 281 U.S. 276 (1930)
Pennsylvania Coal Co. v. Mahon, 260 U.S. 393 (1922)
Pensacola Telegraph Co. v. Western Union, 96 U.S. 1 (1878)
Phelps Dodge Corporation v. National Labor Relations Board, 313 U.S. 177 (1941)
Philadelphia, Baltimore & Washington Railway v. Smith, 250 U.S. 101 (1919)
Pierce v. Society of Sisters, 268 U.S. 510 (1925)
Plessy v. Ferguson, 163 U.S. 537 (1896)
Pollock v. Williams, 322 U.S. 4 (1944)
Powell v. Alabama, 287 U.S. 45 (1932)
Prudential Insurance Co. v. Benjamin, 328 U.S. 408 (1946)
Radio Commission v. Nelson Brothers Co., 289 U.S. 266 (1933)
Railroad Commission v. Pullman, 312 U.S. 496 (1941)
Railroad Commission v. Rowan and Nichols Oil Co., 310 U.S. 573 (1940)
Railroad Retirement Board v. Alton Railroad Co., 295 U.S. 330 (1935)
Railway Express Agency v. New York, 336 U.S. 106 (1949)
Reynolds v. United States, 98 U.S. 145 (1879)
Ribnick v. McBride, 277 U.S. 350 (1928)
Roe v. Wade, 410 U.S. 113 (1973)
Santa Clara County v. Southern Pacific Railroad, 118 U.S. 394 (1886)
Schechter Poultry Corp. v. United States, 295 U.S. 495 (1935)
Schenck v. United States, 249 U.S. 47 (1919)
Screws v. United States, 325 U.S. 91 (1945)
Second Employers' Liability Cases, 223 U.S. 1 (1912)
Shreveport Rate Case (Houston East & West Texas Rail Co. v. United States), 234 U.S. 342 (1914)
Skinner v. Oklahoma, 316 U.S. 535 (1942)
Slaughterhouse Cases, 16 Wallace 36 (1873)

Smith v. Allwright, 321 U.S. 649 (1944)
Smith v. Texas, 311 U.S. 128 (1940)
Smyth v. Ames, 169 U.S. 466 (1898)
Snyder v. Massachusetts, 291 U.S. 97 (1934)
Social Security Cases (*Steward Machine Co. v. Davis*, 301 U.S. 548 [1937]; *Helvering v. Davis*, 301 U.S. 619 [1938])
Sonzinsky v. United States, 300 U.S. 506 (1937)
South Carolina State Highway Dept. v. Barnwell Bros., 303 U.S. 177 (1938)
Southern Railway Co. v. United States, 222 U.S. 20 (1911)
Stafford v. Wallace, 258 U.S. 495 (1922)
Standard Oil Co. v. United States, 221 U.S. 1 (1911)
Stettler v. O'Hara, 243 U.S. 629 (1917)
Stromberg v. California, 283 U.S. 359 (1931)
Stuart v. Laird, 1 Cranch 299 (1803)
Summers, In re, 325 U.S. 561 (1945)
Sunshine Anthracite Coal Co. v. Adkins, 310 U.S. 381 (1940)
Sweatt v. Painter, 339 U.S. 629 (1950)
Swift v. Tyson, 16 Pet. 1 (1842)
Swift & Co. v. United States, 196 U.S. 375 (1905)
Tagg Bros. & Moorhead v. United States, 280 U.S. 420 (1930)
Tennessee Electric Power Co. v. Tennessee Valley Authority, 306 U.S. 118 (1939)
Texas & New Orleans Railroad Co. v. Brotherhood of Railway and Steamship Clerks, 281 U.S. 548 (1930)
Thomas v. Collins, 323 U.S. 516 (1945)
Thornhill v. Alabama, 310 U.S. 88 (1940)
Times-Mirror Co. v. Superior Court, 314 U.S. 252 (1941)
Tinker v. Des Moines Independent Community School District, 393 U.S. 503 (1969)
Toledo Newspaper Co. v. United States, 247 U.S. 402 (1918)
Townsend v. Sain, 372 U.S. 293 (1963)
Twining v. New Jersey, 211 U.S. 78 (1908)
United Mine Workers v. Coronado Coal Co., 259 U.S. 344 (1922)
United States v. Appalachian Electric Power Co., 311 U.S. 377 (1940)
United States v. Belmont, 310 U.S. 324 (1937)
United States v. Bland, 283 U.S. 636 (1931)
United States v. Butler, 297 U.S. 1 (1936)
United States v. California, 297 U.S. 175 (1936)
United States v. Carolene Products Co., 304 U.S. 144 (1938)
United States v. Classic, 313 U.S. 299 (1941)
United States v. Constantine, 296 U.S. 287 (1935)
United States v. Curtiss-Wright Export Corp., 299 U.S. 304 (1936)

United States v. Darby Lumber Co., 312 U.S. 100 (1941)
United States v. E. C. Knight Co., 156 U.S. 1 (1895)
United States v. Five Gambling Devices, 346 U.S. 441 (1953)
United States v. Kahriger, 345 U.S. 22 (1953)
United States v. Lefkowitz, 285 U.S. 452 (1932)
United States v. Macintosh, 283 U.S. 605 (1931)
United States v. Rock Royal Cooperative, 307 U.S. 533 (1939)
United States v. Rosenwasser, 323 U.S. 360 (1945)
United States v. South-Eastern Underwriters Ass'n, 322 U.S. 533 (1944)
United States v. Sprague, 282 U.S. 716 (1931)
Virginia Railway Co. v. System Federation No. 40, 300 U.S. 515 (1937)
Voehl v. Indemnity Insurance Co., 288 U.S. 162 (1933)
W. B. Worthen Co. v. Kavanaugh, 295 U.S. 56 (1935)
W. B. Worthen Co. v. Thomas, 292 U.S. 426 (1934)
Wabash, St. Louis & Pacific Railway Co. v. Illinois, 118 U.S. 557 (1886)
Walling v. A. H. Belo Corp., 316 U.S. 624 (1942)
Washington, Virginia & Maryland Coach Co. v. National Labor Relations Board, 301 U.S. 142 (1937)
Wayman v. Southard, 10 Wheat. 1 (1825)
Weaver v. Palmer Bros. Co., 270 U.S. 402 (1926)
Weiss v. United States, 308 U.S. 321 (1939)
West Coast Hotel v. Parrish, 300 U.S. 379 (1937)
West Virginia State Board of Education v. Barnette, 319 U.S. 628 (1943)
Western Live Stock v. Bureau of Revenue, 303 U.S. 250 (1938)
Whitney v. California, 274 U.S. 357 (1927)
Wickard v. Filburn, 317 U.S. 111 (1942)
Willing v. Chicago Auditorium Ass'n, 277 U.S. 274 (1928)
Wilson v. New, 243 U.S. 332 (1917)
Wolff Packing Co. v. Court of Industrial Relations, 262 U.S. 522 (1923)
Wright v. Mountain Trust Bank, 300 U.S. 440 (1937)
Yamashita, In re, 327 U.S. 1 (1946)
Younger v. Harris, 401 U.S. 37 (1971)

Glossary

absolutism, First Amendment The view, articulated by Justice Hugo Black but never endorsed by a majority on the Supreme Court, that the Speech and Press Clauses of the First Amendment forbid all government regulation of these forms of communication. Black did not extend protection to certain forms of "symbolic" speech such as the wearing of armbands by students to protest the Vietnam War.

amicus curiae (lit., "friend of the court") An individual or group given permission by a court to file a brief or participate in other ways in litigation on behalf of one of the parties in a case.

bad tendency test A restrictive standard often used by the Supreme Court, especially during World War I and the 1920s, to place certain spoken or printed words outside the protection of the First Amendment if the majority believed their use tended to encourage immoral or unlawful behavior.

"business affected with a public interest" The doctrine employed by the Supreme Court until *Nebbia v. New York* (1934) to determine which economic activities could be constitutionally regulated by government. The standard permitted the regulation of most public utilities, such as railroads, but barred regulation of most private enterprises.

certiorari, writ of (lit., "to be informed of") Since the 1920's, the most important discretionary writ issued by the Supreme Court through which it orders the record of a decision by a lower court sent to it for further review and consideration.

chilling effect The concept invoked by a court to invalidate laws that inhibit or restrict free expression because they are unduly vague or so broad in their scope that persons may overcompensate and restrict their speech excessively so as not to cross the line into illegal expression.

clear and present danger test The First Amendment test, first developed by Justices Holmes and Brandeis in dissent, under which the government may not punish speech unless the words are likely to incite immediate unlawful conduct.

comity The willingness of one court to grant a privilege or respect the decision of another legal jurisdiction, not as a matter of law, but out of deference, respect, and good will.

common law The collection of judge-made legal rules and principles developed first in the royal courts of England beginning in the twelfth century and incorporated into the law of American jurisdictions beginning in the colonial period.

"court-packing" plan The pejorative label attached to President Roosevelt's proposed legislation in 1937 to expand the number of federal judges, including those on the Supreme Court, when sitting members who had served at least ten years did not retire within six months of their seventieth birthdays.

current of commerce Sometimes defined as "stream of commerce," the doctrine developed first by Justice Holmes in *Swift & Co. v. United States* (1905) that permits the federal government to regulate many local economic activities that are not isolated but part of a continuous process of production and trade in interstate commerce.

de facto segregation Racial separation or discrimination that arises in areas such as education or housing not from direct government decrees, but from nongovernmental influences such as the distribution of income or other resources.

de jure segregation Racial separation that arises in public or private institutions as a result of deliberate governmental decisions.

declaratory judgment A judicial decision that simply declares the rights of the parties or expresses the opinion of the court on a question of law, without ordering anything to be done by the parties.

direct/indirect test The standard usually invoked by the Supreme Court during the 1920s and 1930s to determine whether a particular local economic activity had a palpable impact or a negligible effect upon interstate commerce and was therefore subject to regulation by the federal government or beyond its jurisdiction.

discrete and insular minorities The term used by Justice Stone in his Footnote 4 in *Carolene Products* (1938) to describe those individuals and groups, especially racial or religious minorities, who deserved special protection by the courts because they lack sufficient political power to protect themselves from oppressive legislation.

disenfranchisement The denial of voting rights to a person based on various legal grounds of disqualification, usually a felony conviction, but historically including devices such as poll taxes and literacy tests that barred the poor and racial minorities.

dual federalism The doctrine that held otherwise valid laws of Congress unconstitutional on the grounds that they violated the Tenth Amendment, which reserved certain powers to the states.

due process, procedural The principle that the Fifth and Fourteenth Amendments to the Constitution prohibit wholly arbitrary decisions by government with respect to issues of life, liberty, and property, and that the government must adhere to fair procedures (such as a hearing) before interfering with these rights.

due process, substantive The concept, often invoked by the Supreme Court prior to 1937, that federal or state laws must be evaluated on the basis of a "reasonableness" standard by the courts and that statutes failing the test are constitutionally invalid under either the Fifth or Fourteenth Amendment.

Equal Protection Clause The provision in the Fourteenth Amendment that forbids state governments from adopting laws that impose invidious distinctions or deny privileges to persons or groups based on characteristics such as race.

ex post facto law A retroactively applied criminal statute that punishes an individual. Such laws are prohibited by Article I, Sections 9 and 10, of the Constitution.

federal preemption The principle that Congress, by virtue of a statute, may preclude the states from similar legislation on a matter that the Constitution has entrusted to the national legislature under Article I, Section 8 of the Constitution.

federalism The division of authority, usually explicit, between the national government and the states, stated in the Tenth Amendment, but expressed in other constitutional provisions that either delegate authority to the federal government or deny it to the states.

fighting words The concept that certain words do not enjoy constitutional protection under the First Amendment because their tendency is to provoke immediate violence or social disorder.

"grandfather clause" A legislative device employed by several Southern legislatures designed to exclude African Americans from the franchise while permitting whites to vote by allowing the latter to register without a literacy test if they were descendants of Confederate veterans or persons who voted in 1865.

habeas corpus, writ of (lit., "you have the body") A court order that requires the release of persons from unconstitutional or otherwise illegal imprisonment.

Hughes Court The Supreme Court during the tenure of Charles Evans Hughes (1930–1941).

incorporation, selective The doctrine, forcefully articulated by Justice Cardozo in *Palko v. Connecticut* (1937), that the Due Process Clause of the Fourteenth Amendment requires the states to enforce only selected provisions of the Bill of

Rights, principally those the Court deems "fundamental . . . to the concept of ordered liberty," such as freedom of speech and press, but excluding others, such as the freedom from double jeopardy and self-incrimination.

incorporation, total The argument, advanced initially by Justice John Marshall Harlan and later Hugo Black and others in the 1940s, that the framers of the Fourteenth Amendment intended its provisions to apply (i.e., incorporate) the specific guarantees of the Bill of Rights and make them binding upon the states.

incorporation-plus The contention, advanced by Justices Frank Murphy, William O. Douglas, and others, that the Fourteenth Amendment incorporates all of the specific guarantees of the Bill of Rights as well as other unenumerated fundamental rights, such as privacy, and makes them binding upon the states.

judicial activism The belief that courts are the sole guardians of the Constitution and empowered to strike down acts of the political branches that violate it, known as negative activism. Also the belief that the courts may discover and enforce even unenumerated rights, known as positive activism.

judicial review The power of a court, in an appropriate case, to strike down any law or other official action found to be in conflict with provisions in the Constitution.

judicial self-restraint The belief, often associated with justices such as Holmes, Brandeis, and Frankfurter, that courts are not the sole guardians of the Constitution and must display deference to the policy choices of the political branches (legislatures especially) in all but the clearest instances of constitutional violation.

laissez-faire jurisprudence The judicial posture, often articulated by judges in the late nineteenth and early twentieth centuries, that the Constitution was fundamentally a contract of limitations rather than a charter of powers, thereby restricting in many cases the extent of government interference with the economic marketplace.

mootness doctrine The doctrine that holds that courts should not decide cases that have already been resolved by other circumstances, such as a private settlement or the expiration of a particular government policy.

multiple burdens test The principle espoused by some justices during the Hughes era, notably Justice Stone, that the Constitution did not forbid state taxation of interstate economic activities, except in cases in which the law would impose multiple burdens on particular enterprises due to the failure of states to carefully apportion their share of the business.

opinion, concurring A separate opinion by a justice who usually agrees with the result set forth by the majority, but not necessarily with its reasoning.

opinion, dissenting An opinion filed by a justice who disagrees with the ruling of the majority.

opinion of the court The opinion, written by a justice in the majority, announcing the decision of the court and its rationale.

opinion per curiam An unsigned opinion of the court, often issued when the justices decide a case without a lengthy statement of reasons and when the result, based upon precedent, is open to little doubt.

overbreadth test The doctrine that reasonable government restrictions on freedom of expression (for example, regulating the time, manner, and place of speech) must be narrowly tailored so that they do not penalize constitutionally protected forms of expression.

police power The broad category of government regulations intended to protect the health, welfare, and morals of the community, including, for example, criminal laws, but also zoning ordinances, statutes restricting the hours of labor, licensing occupations, and mandating certain safety requirements.

political question doctrine The doctrine that courts may decide only cases capable of judicial resolution, not those entrusted to another branch of the government or for which standards do not exist for a judicial determination, such as the conduct of foreign relations or the impeachment power.

precedent (also *stare decisis,* lit., "stand by the decision") The principle that courts should decide the case before them on the basis of the rule established in an earlier, similar case.

preferred freedoms The argument, suggested initially by Justice Stone in *Carolene Products* (1938), that the Constitution contains a hierarchy of rights to be enforced by the judicial branch, and that those at the "top"—specifically the right to vote and those guaranteed by the Bill of Rights—require that particularly careful scrutiny be given to laws that abridge them.

prior restraint Any effort by the government to impose censorship before publication or to prohibit publication will encounter strong judicial objections as a violation of the First Amendment.

privileges and immunities clauses Both the original Constitution and the Fourteenth Amendment contain provisions that prohibit the states from discriminating against citizens of other states or impairing rights attached to national citizenship, although the Supreme Court has seldom applied these provisions.

rational basis test The lowest constitutional standard invoked by the Supreme Court to determine whether a legislative action is constitutional, requiring only that the law at issue have a "rational" relationship to a valid governmental purpose. After 1937 the Supreme Court used it often to review New Deal legislation with the result that it gave legislatures broad latitude to adopt laws regulating economic affairs.

Roosevelt Court The Supreme Court during the chief justiceship of Harlan Fiske Stone (1941–1946), so named because President Roosevelt's nominees, eight in all, came to dominate it.

separation of powers The doctrine under which the powers of the federal government are allocated among legislative, executive, and judicial branches, with each branch maintaining its separate, but at times cooperative, functions and powers.

solicitor general The government attorney, the second ranking member of the Department of Justice, who officially represents the United States in litigation affecting its interests.

special circumstances The doctrine, rooted in the first Scottsboro case, *Powell v. Alabama* (1932), that due process requires the states to provide criminal defendants in capital cases who are impoverished and lacking in education the assistance of legal counsel.

standing doctrine The judicial rule that requires those who challenge a law or who seek relief from other government action to allege a direct and substantial injury to a legal right or interest for which the court can provide a remedy.

Stone Court The Supreme Court during the tenure of Chief Justice Harlan Fiske Stone (1941–1946), also known as the Roosevelt Court.

symbolic speech Nonverbal conduct, such as the labor picketing at issue in *Thornhill v. Alabama* (1940), intended to communicate ideas, which is protected under the First Amendment. Like other types of speech, it is subject to governmental regulations as to the time, place, and manner of the expression, so long as the regulations are narrowly tailored and are not intended to restrict the expression entirely.

takings clause The Fifth Amendment provision that forbids the government from taking private property for a public use (through the power of eminent domain) without paying just compensation.

white primary The devise employed in states such as Texas to restrict membership in a political party and hence voting privileges in its primary elections to Caucasians only, thereby excluding African Americans from the franchise.

yellow-dog contract A contract of employment in which the employee agrees, as a condition of employment, that he or she will not join a labor union or participate in efforts to organize one.

Annotated Bibliography

Books

Abraham, Henry J. *Justices and Presidents: A Political History of Appointments to the Supreme Court.* 4th ed. Lanham, MD: Rowman and Littlefield, 1999.

An engagingly written account of presidential nominations to the Supreme Court and the conflicts that often followed, plus cogent portraits of the presidents and their nominees, including Hoover, Roosevelt, and the justices they chose.

Ackerman, Bruce. *We the People: Transformations.* Cambridge, MA: Harvard University Press, 1998.

A grand synthesis of American constitutional history that stresses the importance of constitutional change arising from moments of great social and political crisis such as Reconstruction and the Great Depression.

Arkes, Hadley. *The Return of George Sutherland: Restoring a Jurisprudence of Natural Rights.* Princeton, NJ: Princeton University Press, 1994.

A passionate effort to restore the reputation of one of the Four Horseman of the Hughes Court by demonstrating that he supported numerous progressive causes before joining the Supreme Court, respected civil liberties in many cases, and did not always vote in favor of a laissez-faire Constitution.

Asbell, Bernard. *When F.D.R. Died.* New York: Holt, Rinehart and Winston, 1961.

A touching account of the public response by the powerful and the not-so-powerful to the death of President Roosevelt in April 1945.

Badger, Anthony J. *The New Deal: The Depression Years, 1933–1940.* New York: Noonday Press, 1989.

A crisply written account of the major New Deal programs that demonstrates both their successes and their dramatic failures.

Baker, Leonard. *Brandeis and Frankfurter: A Dual Biography.* New York: Harper & Row, 1984.

A very sympathetic dual biography of two men whose lawyering and later judicial careers helped to shape the progressive movement and the New Deal through their support for social legislation and judicial self-restraint.

Blum, John M. *From the Morgenthau Diaries: Years of Crisis 1929-1938.* Boston: Houghton Mifflin, 1959.

A superbly edited and annotated volume based on the intimate diaries of one of Roosevelt's most trusted advisers, with especially revealing sections on New Deal monetary and fiscal policy.

Chafee, Zechariah. *Free Speech in the United States.* Cambridge, MA: Harvard University Press, 1941.

A classic statement by a celebrated Harvard Law School professor on the evolution of First Amendment law, with special attention to the World War I era and the origins of the "clear and present danger" test by Holmes and Brandeis.

Cooper, John M., Jr. *Pivotal Decades: The United States 1900–1920.* New York, Norton, 1990.

A lively narrative on the political, economic, and social changes that shaped the progressive era, especially thorough with respect to business-government relations and the conduct of American foreign relations.

Corwin, Edward S. *Court over Constitution: A Study of Judicial Review as an Instrument of Popular Government.* Princeton, NJ: Princeton University Press, 1938.

A pro–New Deal account of the uses of judicial review by the Supreme Court to invalidate legislation designed to cope with the depression.

———. *Constitutional Revolution, Ltd.* Claremont, CA: Pomona College, 1941.

A series of lectures that sets forth in brief compass the changes wrought in constitutional doctrine by the Hughes Court majority, with special attention to the year 1937 and emphasis upon the political pressures that drove the Court's decisions.

Cushman, Barry. *Rethinking the New Deal Court: The Structure of a Constitutional Revolution.* New York: Oxford University Press, 1998.

One of the most innovative pieces of legal history produced in the last quarter century, it contains a strongly revisionist interpretation of the Hughes Court and the constitutional conflicts of the depression years by arguing that adherence to key doctrinal developments, not political pressure, shaped the Court's response to the New Deal.

Danelski, David J., and Joseph S. Tulchin, eds. *The Autobiographical Notes of Charles Evans Hughes.* Cambridge, MA: Harvard University Press, 1973.

A largely unrevealing and self-justifying account of Hughes's public career that places much emphasis upon the period before 1930 and far less upon the controversial encounters with the New Deal and the other justices on his Court.

Degler, Carl. *Out of Our Past: The Forces That Shaped Modern America.* New York: Harper & Row, 1959.

Provocative interpretations of seminal events in American history since the founding, with a classic essay on the New Deal as "The Third American Revolution."

Dunne, Findley Peter. *Mr. Dooley's Opinions.* New York: R. H. Russell, 1901.

Humorous and pungent commentary on the foibles of American politicians, institutions, and policy at the turn of the century, featuring Dunne's fictional Mr. Dooley, an Irish rogue who skewers the mighty and the pompous.

Friedman, Leon, and Fred L. Israel, eds. *The Justices of the United States Supreme Court, 1789–1978.* New York: Chelsea House, 1978.

A multivolume collection of profiles of Supreme Court justices, some more insightful than others, but including all of those who served under Hughes.

Gordon, Colin. *New Deals: Business, Labor and Politics in America, 1920–1935.* New York: Cambridge University Press, 1994.

A revisionist telling of the early New Deal that stresses the mutual interests of key business and labor leaders who saw in government intervention the road to industrial peace and capitalist stability.

Grubb, Donald H. *Cry from the Cotton: The Southern Tenant Farmers Union and the New Deal.* Chapel Hill: University of North Carolina Press, 1971.

A harrowing and tragic account of the disasters visited upon sharecroppers and tenant farmers by the New Deal's initial agricultural programs.

Gunther, Gerald. *Learned Hand: The Man and the Judge.* New York: Alfred A. Knopf, 1994.

One of the most distinguished judicial biographies of this century about the most celebrated federal jurist who never sat on the Supreme Court, with copious insight into Hand's relationship with Felix Frankfurter and his appraisal of the Hughes Court.

Gunther, Gerald, and Noel Dowling, eds. *Cases and Materials on Constitutional Law.* 8th ed. Mineola, NY: The Foundation Press, 1970.

A classic law-school casebook packed with historical documents other than Supreme Court opinions and including insightful comments on the Court's history.

Hall, Kermin, ed. *The Oxford Companion to the Supreme Court.* New York: Oxford University Press, 1992.

A superb one-volume collection of major decisions, doctrines, and profiles of Supreme Court justices from 1789 to the present.

Hamby, Alonzo. *Liberalism and Its Challengers: From FDR to Bush.* New York: Oxford University Press, 1992.

An account of why the programs and ideas of the New Deal flourished and why they lost support in the 1960s and 1970s.

Holmes, Oliver Wendell, Jr. *The Common Law.* Boston: Little, Brown, 1923.

Published originally in 1880. Although not an entirely reliable guide to the history of the common law, nonetheless a revealing document of Holmes's evolving philosophy of law, which influenced subsequent generations of legal reformers, especially the progressives and the legal realists.

Jackson, Robert H. *The Struggle for Judicial Supremacy: A Study of a Crisis in American Power Politics.* New York: Alfred A. Knopf, 1941.

As the title suggests, an insider's account by the former solicitor general and future Supreme Court justice of the conflict between the Hughes Court and the Roosevelt administration that focuses more upon its political dimensions rather than close doctrinal analysis with the result that it becomes a brief for the reasonableness of the New Deal and the reactionary posture of most of the justices.

Kaufman, Andrew L. *Cardozo.* Cambridge, MA: Harvard University Press, 1998.

The most comprehensive biography of Cardozo in print that focuses special attention upon his private legal practice and long tenure on the New York Court of Appeals. Somewhat less revealing about his brief career on the Supreme Court of the United States.

Kennedy, David M. *Freedom from Fear: The American People in Depression and War, 1929–1945.* New York: Oxford University Press, 1999.

A sweeping and powerful narrative of the Roosevelt era based on both exhaustive archival research and mastery of the relevant secondary literature, unsurpassed with respect to the New Deal's impact on American life and the prosecution of the Second World War.

Klehr, Harvey, John Earl Haynes, and Kyrill M. Anderson, eds. *The Soviet World of American Communism.* New Haven, CT: Yale University Press, 1998.

Based largely on documents from the archives of the former Soviet Union, the volume testifies to the high degree of financial and ideological influence flowing from Moscow to the American party, both its open and its secret branches.

Lash, Joseph P. *From the Diaries of Felix Frankfurter.* New York: Norton, 1975.

The vivid biographical essay that begins this volume remains a superb introduction to the thought and behavior of professor, later Justice Felix Frankfurter, although the diary itself focuses more attention on the period after 1939 than before.

Leuchtenburg, William E. *Franklin D. Roosevelt and the New Deal, 1932–1940.* New York: Harper & Row, 1963.

Still the most judicious, balanced, and concise account of the New Deal in print today.

———. *The Supreme Court Reborn: The Constitutional Revolution in the Age of Roosevelt.* New York: Oxford University Press, 1995.

In the interpretative tradition of Robert Jackson and Edward Corwin, an account of the constitutional struggle between the Court and the New Deal that places most of the blame upon the conservative ideologues on the bench and far less on the president and his advisers.

Levy, Leonard W., ed. *Encyclopedia of the American Constitution.* New York: Macmillan, 1986.

A multivolume collection of essays on major constitutional topics and periods in the history of the Supreme Court.

Mason, Alpheus T. *Brandeis: A Free Man's Life.* New York: Viking Press, 1956a.

An exhaustive account of the life and values of one of the twentieth century's most fascinating reformers and jurists, with a thorough accounting of his critical opinions on the Supreme Court.

———. *Harlan Fiske Stone: Pillar of the Law.* New York: Viking Press, 1956b.

A long, detailed account of Stone's public career that stirred high anxiety among members of judiciary when published because Mason quoted copiously from the justice's private conference notes and correspondence with other members of the Taft, Hughes, and Stone Courts. A gold mine of information about judicial affairs—grand as well as petty.

———. *The Supreme Court from Taft to Burger.* Baton Rouge: Louisiana State University Press, 1979.

One of the best short introductions to the history of the Supreme Court from the 1920s to the 1970s, written from a decisively progressive perspective.

McCloskey, Robert G. *The American Supreme Court.* 2d revised ed. Edited by Sanford Levinson. Chicago: University of Chicago Press, 1994.

Perhaps the best short introduction to the history of the Supreme Court from John Jay to William Rhenquist, with a superb section on the rise of the welfare state and the constitutional crisis of the Great Depression that stresses the open texture of doctrines and the choices facing the justices.

McElvaine, Robert S. *The Great Depression: America 1929–1941.* New York: Times Books, 1984.

An excellent narrative history of the era, especially strong on the causes of the depression and popular responses to the crisis.

Morgan, Ted. *FDR: A Biography.* New York: Simon and Schuster, 1985.

Not among the most historically sophisticated biographies of Roosevelt, but a lively read nonetheless.

Murphy, Paul. *The Constitution in Crisis Times 1918–1969.* New York: Harper & Row, 1972.

The author's magnum opus and a standard-setting account of the Supreme Court and constitutional change from Edward White to Earl Warren.

Novick, Sheldon. *Honorable Justice: The Life of Oliver Wendell Holmes.* Boston: Little, Brown, 1989.

An engaging and sympathetic biography of the justice whose passion for judicial restraint often led progressives to mistake him for one of their own.

Parmet, Herbert S. *Jack: The Struggles of John F. Kennedy.* New York: Dial Press, 1980.

Although heavily focused on the rise of JFK, the volume contains useful information about his father's career, especially as ambassador to England.

Parrish, Michael E. *Securities Regulation and the New Deal.* New Haven, CT: Yale University Press, 1970.

Based on extensive archival research, the volume traces the evolution of federal policy with regard to the marketing of securities and the regulation of the stock exchanges, with special emphasis upon the early administrative history of the Securities and Exchange Commission.

———. *Felix Frankfurter and His Times: The Reform Years.* New York: Free Press, 1982.

A thorough account of Frankfurter's pre-Court careers as a lawyer, spirited reformer, and adviser to numerous presidents, especially Franklin Roosevelt.

———. *Anxious Decades: America in Prosperity and Depression, 1920–1941.* New York: Norton, 1992.

A highly readable synthesis of the United States between the wars, with special attention to the rise of "consumer culture" and its impact upon politics and government.

Polenberg, Richard. *The World of Benjamin Cardozo: Personal Values and the Judicial Process.* Cambridge, MA: Harvard University Press, 1997.

A stimulating, often highly critical, account of the relationship between Cardozo's personal values and private life and his role as a jurist. Far and away the best short introduction to his life.

Purcell, Edward A. *Brandeis and the Progressive Constitution: Erie, the Judicial Power, and the Politics of the Federal Courts in Twentieth Century America.* New Haven, CT: Yale University Press, 2000.

An intellectually sophisticated account of Brandeis's long war to cabin the power of the federal courts, especially the doctrine of *Swift v. Tyson* (1842), which he held responsible for the aggrandizement of judicial authority and for sanctioning the domination of large corporations in American life.

Pusey, Merlo. *Charles Evans Hughes.* 2 vols. New York: Columbia University Press, 1963.

A highly sympathetic biography of the chief justice, secretary of state, presidential candidate, and Wall Street lawyer that argues the case for the Court rather than the New Deal when it examines the constitutional deadlock of the 1930s.

Roosevelt, Elliott, ed. *FDR: His Personal Letters.* New York: Duell, Sloan and Pearce, 1947–1950.

The most extensive published collection of the president's correspondence.

Schlesinger, Arthur M., Jr. *The Age of Roosevelt: The Coming of the New Deal.* Boston: Houghton Mifflin, 1958.

A narrative in the grand style of the conflicts and compromises that formed the early years of the Roosevelt administration, with striking vignettes of the administration's major actors and policies.

———. *The Age of Roosevelt: The Politics of Upheaval.* Boston: Houghton Mifflin, 1960.

The second volume of a trilogy on the New Deal that examines the shift from the "first" New Deal of the NRA to the "second" New Deal of 1935 with its emphasis upon major reforms such as relief, tax revisions, and the National Labor Relations Act.

Strum, Philippa. *Louis D. Brandeis: Justice for the People.* Cambridge, MA: Harvard University Press, 1984.

A compact and insightful study of Brandeis's many-sided public life as "the people's lawyer," social reformer, and Supreme Court justice who remained forever opposed to "the curse of bigness," whether manifested in giant corporations or the federal government under Roosevelt.

Swindler, William F. *Court and Constitution in the 20th Century: The New Legality, 1932–1968.* Indianapolis and New York: Bobbs-Merill, 1970.

A survey of the Court and its major decisions from Hughes to Warren, long on details but somewhat short on analysis and interpretation.

Urofsky, Melvin I., ed. *The Supreme Court Justices: A Biographical Dictionary.* New York: Garland, 1994.

Brief but usually illuminating portraits of the justices written by leading legal scholars.

Urofsky, Melvin I., and David W. Levy, eds. *"Half Brother, Half Son": The Letters of Louis D. Brandeis to Felix Frankfurter.* Norman: University of Oklahoma Press, 1991.

A fascinating and superbly annotated series of letters between two men whose joint careers in law and politics helped to shape the agenda of progressive reform from the turn of the century to World War II, with especially rich material on the personalities and conflicts of the Taft and Hughes years.

Watkins, T. H. *The Hungry Years: A Narrative History of the Great Depression in America.* New York: Henry Holt, 1999.

A compelling account of the decade from the perspective of ordinary men and women who endured the worst of the economic crisis.

White, G. Edward. *The American Judicial Tradition: Profiles of Leading American Judges.* New York: Oxford University Press, 1976.

In a collection of sparkling individual vignettes, White captures the core values of leading American jurists, with notable portraits of Holmes, Brandeis, and the Four Horsemen of the Hughes Court.

———. *The Constitution and the New Deal.* Cambridge, MA: Harvard University Press, 2001.

Endorsing the views of those revisionist scholars who see a constitutional evolution rather than a revolution in the 1930s, the book calls attention to many neglected legal issues, including the Constitution and foreign relations, the rise of administrative law, and the general crisis over judicial objectivity.

Wiecek, William. *The Lost World of Classical Legal Thought: Law and Ideology in America, 1886–1937.* New York: Oxford University Press, 1998.

A complex, sophisticated account of the rise and fall of classical legalism (often called legal formalism or mechanical jurisprudence), which ran aground sometime between 1900 and 1937 when the structures of social and economic life no longer fit the dominant framework of constitutional doctrines.

Articles

Cushman, Barry. "Lost Fidelities." *William and Mary Law Review* 41 (1999): 95.

A strongly revisionist interpretation of the jurisprudence of Justice Owen Roberts and his role in the constitutional issues of the Hughes and Stone Courts.

Friedman, Richard. "Switching Time and Other Thought Experiments: The Hughes Court and the Constitutional Transformation." *University of Pennsylvania Law Review* 142 (1994): 1891.

A major revisionist attempt to reassess the "constitutional revolution" of the 1930s, which stresses the importance of decisions before 1937 and challenges the conventional view that elections influenced judicial behavior.

Parrish, Michael E. "The Hughes Court, the Great Depression, and the Historians." *The Historian* 40 (1978): 286.

An assessment of how historians from the 1930s through the 1970s interpreted the Hughes Court and its struggles with the New Deal.

———. "The Great Depression, the New Deal, and the American Legal Order." *Washington Law Review* 59 (1984): 723.

The impact of the New Deal upon American legal and political culture, with emphasis upon how government reforms expanded opportunities for ordinary Americans.

Pepper, David. "Against Legalism: Rebutting an Anachronistic Account of 1937." *Marquette Law Review* 82 (1998): 63.

A counterrevisionist argument that stresses the continuing conservatism of the Hughes majority even after *Nebbia* (1934) and the disinclination of lower federal courts to perceive fundamental changes in the doctrines of the high court.

Rauh, Joseph L., Jr. "A Personal View of Justice Benjamin N. Cardozo: Recollections of Four Cardozo Law Clerks." *Cardozo Law Review* 1 (1979): 10.

A moving tribute to the justice and his impact on American law by his last law clerk.

Thayer, James B. "The Origin and Scope of the American Doctrine of Constitutional Law." *Harvard Law Review* 7 (1893): 129.
The classic articulation of the necessity for judicial restraint by a law professor who influenced Holmes, Frankfurter, and others.

Internet Sources

Emory University School of Law
http://www.law.emory.edu/LAW/refdesk/toc.html
This site offers useful categories of information regarding federal and state laws and selected laws from other nations. It contains as well sections organized by subject, legal periodical, and legal institutions.

Federal Judicial Center
http://www.fjc.gov/
The web page for the Federal Judicial Center, which contains links to the federal system and other courts. It contains a link to the History of the Federal Judiciary, a site featuring a database of biographical information on all federal judges who served since 1789.

Findlaw
http://www.findlaw.com/
One of the most important sites on the web for legal historians. It contains federal and state cases and codes, and links to bar associations, law firms, and lawyers, as well as all of the decisions of the U.S. Supreme Court beginning in 1893.

Lexis-Nexis Academic Universe
http://www.web.lexis-nexis.com/universe/
This subscription-based service covers a wide range of news, business, and reference information. Most educational institutions provide access to its database that includes federal and state cases and codes and citations to major legal periodicals.

Supreme Court
http://www.supremecourtus.gov/
A site that provides a complete overview of the Supreme Court, its history, procedures, calendar, and docket. The site also contains biographical information on past and present justices.

Index

Michael E. Parrish is professor of history at the University of California at San Diego. His previous books include *Securities Regulation and the New Deal* and *Felix Frankfurter and His Times*.